P9-ASK-066

Gramley Library
Salem Academy and College
Winston-Salem, N.C. 27108

SECOND LANGUAGE WRITERS' TEXT

Linguistic and Rhetorical Features

ESL AND APPLIED LINGUISTICS PROFESSIONAL SERIES

Eli Hinkel, Series Editor

Hinkel/Fotos (Eds.) • New Perspectives on Grammar Teaching in Second Language Classrooms

Hinkel • Second Language Writers' Text: Linguistic and Rhetorical Features

Birch • English L2 Reading: Getting to the Bottom

SECOND LANGUAGE WRITERS' TEXT

Linguistic and Rhetorical Features

Eli Hinkel
Seattle University

LAWRENCE ERLBAUM ASSOCIATES, PUBLISHERS
2002   Mahwah, New Jersey   London

Gramley Library
Salem Academy and College
Winston-Salem, N.C. 27108

Copyright © 2002 by Lawrence Erlbaum Associates, Inc.
   All rights reserved. No part of the book may be reproduced in
any form, by photostat, microform, retrieval system, or any other
means, without the prior written permission of the publisher.

Lawrence Erlbaum Associates, Inc., Publishers
10 Industrial Avenue
Mahwah, New Jersey 07430

Cover design by Kathryn Houghtaling Lacey.

Library of Congress Cataloging-in-Publication Data

Hinkel, Eli
   Second language writer's text : linguistic and rhetorical features / Eli Hinkel.
      p.   cm.
   Includes bibliographical references and index.
   ISBN 0-8058-3888-0 (cloth : alk. paper)—ISBN 0-8058-4033-8 (pbk. : alk. paper)
      1. English language and—Study and teaching—Foreign speakers. 2. English
language—Rhetoric—Study an teaching. 3. Report writing—Study and teaching
(Higher)
      4. Second language acquisition. 5. College prose—Evaluation. I. Title.
PE1128.A2.H534 2002
428′.0071—dc21   2001023175

Books published by Lawrence Erlbaum Associates are printed on acid-free paper,
and their bindings are chosen for strength and durability.

Printed in the United States of America
10 9 8 7 6 5 4 3 2 1

Contents

Foreword

THE WALL: TEACHING HEURISTICS OF ENGLISH WRITING AMONG LANGUAGE LEARNERS

Robert B. Kaplan
Emeritus Professor of Applied Linguistics
University of Southern California

> *Histories make men wise; poets, witty; the mathematics, subtle; natural philosophy, deep; moral [philosophy], grave; logic and rhetoric, able to contend.*
> *(Sir Francis Bacon, 1561–1626, Of Studies)*

Some fifty years ago, when I was an undergraduate at a small liberal arts college, I was asked one day by the then Dean of Students whether I would mind rooming with the institution's first three foreign students—a Czech, a Frenchman, and a German. All had the equivalent of high school diploma. All were worldly and courageous; or they would not have attempted what has come to be called *International Educational Exchange.* The reason for the Dean's invitation grew from the fact that I was a bit older than most of my classmates, had traveled a bit, and spoke French and Russian reasonably well; I was delighted with the opportunity. (There was as yet to be an ESL course at the institution; indeed, there were few such courses besides the English Language Institute at the University of Michigan. Of course, I had no knowledge of the Michigan ELI.) The Dean had specifically charged me with helping these foreign students learn English, especially with the writing of academic English, about which my knowledge was comparable to that of any other undergraduate—my writing was, as my English professor remarked, very good and very original, but where it was good it was not original, and where it was original it was not good.

Once ensconced together in our dorm room, our conversations were astonishing *tours de force.* The Czech student spoke Russian and German, so he could translate for the German student; I spoke Russian, so I could converse with the Czech student; and I spoke French, so I could converse with the French student and could relay information from the French student to the Czech student who in turn, could relay it to the German student, and vice versa. Thus, at all times there were five languages in the environment. And although I spoke reasonable French and Russian, my vocabulary control was frequently entirely insufficient for our needs. After any conversation of more than 15 minutes duration, I had a terrible headache; I cannot speak for my roommates but I suspect that they were also struggling with this strange, inefficient polyglot environment.

The French student (a Humanities major) thought everyone should speak French (since all truly intellectual people did) so he had no great interest in learning English. The German student (an Engineering major) knew for certain that all important scientific information was available in German, so he had no need to learn English. Only the Czech student had a powerful urge to become fluent in English; after all, how many people outside Czechoslovakia actually spoke Czech or used it for international academic communication? The Czech student did me the honor to invite me to teach him. (He was unaware of the Dean's imperative). I undertook to do so, and within an academic year, the Czech had made astonishing progress—I honestly believed that I had been instrumental in teaching him. Only years later did I come to understand that he was highly motivated (and would have learned just as quickly without me), that he was very intelligent, that he already spoke two languages, that he was getting comprehensible input all over, and that he was both extroverted and highly social. Indeed, after a time, we managed to graduate together, and he went on to become a professor of his academic discipline (a social science) at a major U.S. university. It was this misunderstood experience that led me into applied linguistics and ESL teaching, a career decision I do not regret, although I entered under a misconception; it was not nearly so easy to teach ESL at the tertiary level as that first experience had suggested.

What does this anecdote have to do with the volume that follows this Foreword? The anecdote is a positive demonstration of what is involved in language learning and a badly flawed example of what is involved in language teaching. Although I was, at the time, by no means a trained ESL teacher, I was vaguely aware of the dominant paradigms in the field. I taught all my roommates grammar rules and vocabulary. I was absolutely unaware of the issues involved in the interference in the L2 from the L1, unaware of what has come to be called *second language acquisition theory*, unaware of the frustration of trying to write academic texts in a second (actually, a third or fourth) language. My three students' (obviously varying) struggles to use English productively led to any number of awkward situations—awkward for them, but amusing for me and for the other denizens of the dormitory we inhabited—all essentially English monolinguals. Looking back, I can only marvel at the motivation of the Czech student and at his tolerance of the sophomoric behavior of his teachers and his classmates, including me.

Although I had learned a couple of languages, I had not done so under the intense pressure of an academic situation and peer pressure.

It was not only the Czech student who learned; I did too. And what I learned has influenced my subsequent professional development. Early on, I realized that one does not learn (or understand) what one does not notice. I also realized equally early on that a fantastic grasp of grammar rules does not facilitate speaking and/or writing in an unfamiliar language. It was obvious that the classmates and teachers of this group of non-native speakers could tolerate grammatical mistakes in the several interlanguages circulating in the environment, but that those classmates and teachers were less tolerant of pragmatic errors, as were our coresidents in the dorm. Although I had a dim realization of these issues, I did not have the slightest awareness of their importance.

Much later—perhaps 35 or 40 years later—researchers in applied linguistics demonstrated the validity of some of my early realizations. For example, L2 speakers and writers select and arrange evidence in terms of their ". . . abilities to convey just those analyses . . . of event[s] that are most compatible with the linguistic means provided by their languages . . ." (Berman & Slobin, 1994, p. 12). In their study, Berman and Slobin present several versions of the same phenomenological event interpreted in different languages to illustrate the point that the resources available to speakers of different languages can prompt somewhat different presentations of events. Berman and Slobin (1994) claimed that the difference between these excerpts is to some extent determined by the linguistic possibilities inherent in each of the languages examined. They asked children to describe in their L1s what they saw in pictures from the Frog stories. Two examples, in English and German, describe the complexity of an event (a fall) via a series of adverbial particles and prepositional phrases (*tips off, over a cliff, into the water; schmiß, den Abhang hinunter, ins Wasser*). The verbs *tip* and *schmeißen* (to hurl) signify the manner in which a deer causes the fall. The Spanish and Hebrew versions, while they resembled each other, differed from the English and German versions. In this pair, the event is recounted as a series of episodes. First, there is a description of location (cliff with river below, place with swamp underneath); then the deer acts, and as a result the boy and the dog fall. Berman and Slobin point out that the verbs chosen (*throw, fall, stop*) are "bare descriptions of change of state, with no elaboration of manner" (Berman & Slobin, 1994, p. 12). The differences they describe are illustrative of the effect of ". . . the linguistic means provided by their [the children's] languages. . . ."

These are not random differences between the narrative styles of these . . . children, but rather show their abilities to convey just those analyses of the event that are most compatible with the linguistic means provided by their

languages. English and German provide large sets of locative particles that
can be combined with verbs of manner, thereby predisposing speakers
toward a dense style of encoding motion events. . . . A different style arises in
[Spanish and Hebrew], which rely more on simple change-of-state and
change-of-location verbs, . . . predisposing speakers towards more extended
analyses of motion events (Berman & Slobin, 1994, p. 2).

In sum, the order of presentation appears to be culture specific, condi-
tioned by the linguistic resources available in the L1, but also by customary
modes of perception. Note that these differences are expressed largely
through verbs.

There have been enormous changes in the understanding of language
learning. One model, relatively recently introduced into the field—the
Universal Grammar (UG) model—assumes an equation between linguistic
theory and grammatical theory and does not recognize that language is
only one "tool set" for construing experience; as Halliday wrote: "language
is the essential condition of knowing, the process by which experience
becomes knowledge" (1993, p. 94). Thus, language is supplemented by the
resources of other semiotic systems, some combination of which have been
developed over cultural history, shaping, and shaped by, the various activities in which they are used. Language is not—cannot be—an isolated system, and grammar cannot be equated with language.

This distinction has come to be central in defining the difference
between *Applied Linguistics* and *Linguistics Applied*. (For extensive discussion
of this distinction, see Davies, 1999.) As Enkvist put it:

> The important point is to realize that the text is the father of the sentence,
> and that text strategies come before the syntactic formation of individual sen-
> tences. Giving a sentence its textual fit, its conformity with the text strategy, is
> not a cosmetic surface operation polishing the sentence after it is already
> there. Textual fit is a far more basic requirement, determining the choice of
> words as well as the syntactic structure of a sentence. To modern text and dis-
> course linguists this is so obvious that it seems curious that grammarians and
> teachers of composition have, through the centuries, spent so much time and
> effort on syntactic phenomena within individual sentences, while overlook-
> ing the fundamental questions of text strategy and information flow (1997,
> p. 199).

The strong inclination to restrict analysis to morphosyntactic phenomena has made the analysis of text structure virtually impossible because
text is never simply the sum of its subsumed syntactic structures. To focus
only on morphosyntactic structure means that pragmatic functions are
irrelevant, but all text is heavily dependent on pragmatic functions
(again, a major distinction between Applied Linguistics and Linguistics

Applied). The analysis of text involves not merely the recognition of correct syntactic structures but the recognition of the appropriate usage of various correct (or incorrect) syntactic structures. Additionally, any UG view overlooks the role of culture, situation, and a variety of other important variables. Speakers of any two different languages organize the same perceived reality in somewhat different ways. (Consider, for example, a description of an open landscape by a military strategist, farmer, or a hydrological engineer, even when all three speak the same L1.) That they should do so seems obvious, because different languages will provide different, readily available means for organizing text. However, the filtering of text logic through language is largely unconscious; that is, students of any given L2 will not be consciously aware of how their L1 influences the way they organize text logic, nor will they be aware that there is a difference in text organization between their L1 and the L2 they are studying, because they will not be aware of the way in which an L2 organizes text logic—they will not have "noticed" it.

> Most of what falls under "thinking for speaking [or writing in an L2]" is usually inaccessible to meta-awareness . . . We probably do not "notice" the way the L2 does its filtering, . . . and we probably have no awareness of the language-specific nature of our own options. . . . Such knowledge may be very largely "unanalyzed. . . ." In the absence of such awareness, the L2 does not provide loci for (mis)generalization of L1 material. . . . The blueprint established for the verbal expression of experience continues to function regardless. . . . Coping with new ways of "thinking for speaking [or writing] . . ." means attending to features of context that are either not relevant or are defined differently in the native language . . . (Kellerman, 1995, p. 141).

Mauranen (1993) expresses a similar perception but expresses it in a less theoretical manner:

> . . . [writers] differ in some of their culturally determined rhetorical practices, and these differences manifest themselves in typical textual features. *The writers seem not to be aware of these textual features, or the underlying rhetorical practices.* This lack of awareness is, in part, due to the fact that textlinguistic features have not been the concern of traditional language teaching in schools. Sometimes text strategies are taught for the mother tongue, but rarely if ever for foreign languages separately. Such phenomena have therefore not been brought to the attention of [writers] struggling with writing. . . . Nevertheless, these sometimes subtle differences between writing cultures, often precisely because they are subtle and not commonly observable to the nonlinguist, tend to put . . . [various] native language [writers] at a rhetorical disadvantage in the eyes of [L2] readers. . . . This disadvantage is more than a difference in cultural tastes, since it may not only strike

readers as lack of rhetorical elegance, but as lack of coherent writing or even [coherent] thinking, which can seriously affect the credibility of non-native writers (1993, pp. 1–2; emphasis added).

All this argues for a model that places emphasis on "noticing," as Schmidt (1990, 1993) has argued. It is not necessarily the case that teachers ought to eschew the teaching of grammar; on the contrary, without some awareness of the grammar of the L2, the learner will be unable to generate intelligible text. Some of the grammar that is necessary—the grammar that concerns the basic structure of sentences and the rules that permit transformations from declarative to interrogative, from clause to sentence or sentence to clause—is really prerequisite to writing. But once writing instruction has begun, the learner needs to become aware of—to notice—" . . . that text strategies come before the syntactic formation of individual sentences. . . ."

That's all very well, but how does one achieve that objective? This question leads directly into the product–process debate. Much has been written on the each side of the debate (see, e.g., Grabe & Kaplan 1996, pp. 237–265 for an extended discussion); some claim that encouraging students to write extensively (any text) helps in the development of the writing process, while others claim that:

> Expository tasks force students to clarify meanings, discover implications, establish connections, formulate problems for intended goals, and evaluate decisions. An approach which relies predominantly on expressive writing and on narrative recounting [knowledge telling] does not typically make as great a set of demands or provide as many opportunities for knowledge transforming (Grabe & Kaplan, 1996, p. 245–246).

In reality, obviously, any process leads to some product, and any product is the outcome of some process. The fact is that in academic writing, the product counts—no amount of knowledge telling can bring learners to products that demonstrate knowledge transforming. In the disciplines, students do not need to know about the intricacies of the writing process and of self examination. Students have a job to do (i.e., to study and to demonstrate their learning through writing academic text). To accomplish their goals, students need a tool to work with (i.e., language). Motivated students will, no doubt, learn on their own. (Despite my amateurish flailing about, the Czech student learned largely on his own. However, life is made considerably easier if someone can call attention to what should be noticed. Teachers have a responsibility; i.e., to teach learners what to look for and what to notice. If, however, teachers themselves do not know what to look for, then students are left with the option of learning by themselves. (For evidence, see Villanueva, 1995.) Of course, they also have the option of simply not learning—of achieving some level of functional fossilization and then quitting.

It is an awareness of these issues that has led Hinkel to try to describe the difference between the writing of English native speakers and six groups of speakers of other languages learning English as a second language by looking at approximately 60 text features across six different prompts among speakers of seven different languages (including English). What she has found, through careful and painstaking analysis, sheds a great deal of light on the differences, with specific reference to such matters as the uses of verbs, of modals, of genres, of text organizing strategies and of a large number of other features.

This is an important work, providing researchers and teachers with a great deal of information on the subtle differences in performance between English L1 writers and English L2 writers—differences that cannot be dismissed as simply some manifestation of less than perfect grammatical proficiency on the part of the L2 learners. What Hinkel's work shows, among other things, is precisely these learners' ". . . abilities to convey just those analyses . . . of event[s] that are most compatible with the linguistic means provided by their languages . . ." (Berman & Slobin, 1994, p. 12). For the first time in recent history, Hinkel has provided the empirical evidence for this contention. By the time the students in this research have completed the course (for which the essays analyzed constituted the entry measure), they will have learned to notice not only that there are differences but, consequently, to understand the nature of the differences. They will have learned to cope ". . . with new ways of 'thinking for speaking [or writing] . . .' [and to attend] . . . to features of context that are either not relevant or are defined differently in the native language . . ." (Kellerman, 1995, p. 141). They will be able to generate text—product—that will not ". . . strike readers as [demonstrating a] lack of rhetorical elegance, [or a] lack of coherent writing or even [coherent] thinking, which can seriously affect the credibility of non-native writers . . ." (Mauranen 1993, pp. 1–2). Hopefully, this book will help teachers to move beyond trial and error guessing of what to teach in writing classes (as opposed to grammar classes), and will take them a step closer to knowing on what to focus. Ultimately, however, teachers have a responsibility to their students to know more about writing than their students do.

Would that I had had this information fifty years ago; had I had it (and had I been prepared to understand it), the young Czech student who struggled to learn academic (and social) English with me would have progressed faster, and would have learned to write in ways that he learned subsequently, years after he escaped my well-intentioned but ignorant tutoring.

REFERENCES

Berman, R, & D. Slobin (Eds.). (1994). *Relating events in narrative: A crosslinguistic developmental study.* Hillsdale, NJ: Lawrence Erlbaum Associates.

Davies, A. (1999). *An introduction to applied linguistics: From practice to theory.* Edinburgh: Edinburgh University Press.

Enkvist, N. E. (1997). Why we need contrastive rhetoric. *Alternation,* 4(1), 188–206.

Grabe, W., & Kaplan, R. B. (1996). *Theory and Practice of writing: An applied linguistic perspective.* London: Longman.

Halliday, M. A. K. (1993). Towards a language-based theory of learning. *Linguistics and Education, 5,* 93–116.

Kellerman, E. (1995). Crosslinguistic influence: Transfer to nowhere. In W. Grabe (Ed.), *Annual review of applied linguistics (Vol. 15): A broad survey of the entire field of applied linguistics* (pp. 125–150). New York: Cambridge University Press.

Mauranen, A. (1993). *Cultural differences in academic rhetoric.* Scandinavian University Studies in the Humanities and Social Sciences (Vol. 4). Frankfurt am Main: Peter Lang.

Schmidt, R. (1990). The role of consciousness in second language fluency. *Applied Linguistics, 11,* 129–156.

Schmidt, R. (1993). Awareness and second language acquisition. In W. Grabe (Ed.), *Annual review of applied linguistics, 13: Issues in second language teaching and learning* (pp. 206–226). New York: Cambridge University Press.

Villanueva, V. (1995). *Bootstraps: From an American academic of color.* Urbana, IL: National Council of Teachers of English.

Preface

With the number of non-native students increasing in most colleges and universities in the United States and other English-speaking countries, the quality of their writing skills and the characteristics of *second language* (L2) text have been gaining increasing attention in the academy. Although much attention, time, effort, and resources are devoted to teaching L2 academic writing and its conventions, it appears that *non-native speaker* (NNS) text differs substantially from that of *native speakers* (NSs) of similar academic standing. The teaching of L2 text features, discourse, and writing has become an important focus (and challenge) in many U.S. colleges and universities. This study was designed to help identify the specific areas of L2 teaching and learning that require close attention.

This volume presents the results of a large-scale study of university-level L2 text with the purpose of determining the specific syntactic, lexical, and rhetorical features that differ from those in comparable NS text. The ultimate goal of this book is to provide insight for L2 pedagogical applications of the study findings. Although a substantial number of texts have been published on the teaching of L2 writing, there appears to be no volume that analyzes L2 text and addresses the implications of its analysis for teaching. This volume is oriented for ESL and EFL teachers and researchers, teacher-trainers, curriculum designers, and material developers who often lack a basis for their decisions, applied linguists, graduate students in applied linguistics, and experienced instructors who need to update their familiarity with current research. Because of its detailed examination of L2 texts and compositions, this volume can serve as a comprehensive source of up-to-date information to focus the teaching of L2 grammar, lexis, and writing.

The volume consists of three major parts: an overview of the research on the role of text in discourse construction, the text features, and the findings. Part I surveys research on text and discourse in Anglo-American academic prose and other rhetorical traditions as they apply to the analysis of ESL student text, and presents the study methodology. In Part II, descriptions of text features and their functions in discourse in seven languages are summarized to provide the background for the discussion of the findings. The results of the data analysis, their significance, and practical uses are also detailed in Part II. As a side note, it may be interesting to mention that the number of words included in the corpus of student essays in this analysis equals that contained in a 900 to 1,000-page book.

ORGANIZATION OF THE VOLUME

The overarching goal of this book is to provide a detailed examination of ESL texts and compositions that can serve as a detailed source of up-to-date information to focus the teaching of L2 grammar, lexis, and writing.

In Part I, the first four chapters are an overview of earlier work on discourse and text, linguistic features of academic text in English, student and ESL writing and text, written discourse and text in the rhetorical traditions of students whose L2 writing is examined, and prevalent approaches to teaching L2 writing. Chapter 5 explains the types of essays in the corpus, describes the L2 proficiency and academic standing of the writers, and the analysis methodology adopted in the research. Specifically, the chapter clarifies how frequency counts of linguistic and rhetorical features of text were obtained and discusses the statistical tests employed in the computations.

Study findings and the results of comparative analyses are presented in Part II. This analysis deals with phrase-level syntactic and lexical features of student text and presents bird's eye view comparisons of NS and NNS text by pooling the data obtained from the essays on different topics by NSs, and speakers of Chinese, Japanese, Korean, Indonesian, Vietnamese, and Arabic. The purpose of this analysis is to identify the differences in L1 and ESL text regardless of prompts.

The chapters in Part II also provide grounding for the inclusion of phrase-level structures and lexis in frequency counts, based on their syntactic and functional prominence in English and the other six languages represented by the essay writers. Chapter 6 examines the textual functions of nouns, pronouns, and nominals in English, and whenever possible, discusses proximate structures in the rhetorical traditions and texts in students' L1s. The examination of the textual functions of these features is followed by the uses of these features in student texts. Similarly, chapter 7 examines the functions of verb phrase elements such as tenses and aspects, lexical classes of verbs, modals verbs, the passive voice, and infinitives, accompanied by the analyses of this usage in L2 essays. The functions and uses of adjectives and adverbs are discussed in chapter 8. Chapter 9 establishes the background for the functions and uses of three types of dependent clauses in English (i.e., noun, adjective, and adverb). Chapter 10 focuses on the textual functions of several rhetorical and cohesive features of English text to identify the use of these features in NNS texts.

Because the essays were written in response to six different prompts, the presentation of study findings and results of textual comparisons in Part III examine the uses of textual and rhetorical features in essays in prompt-by-prompt comparisons. However, the results of analysis of student texts written toward particular prompts indicate that the six prompts fall into two groups, where the first group of three prompts elicited somewhat different types of L2 text than did the second group. Thus, the presentation of the findings is organized according to the prompt clustering in the two groups. Chapter 11 discusses the findings associated with the Parents, Grades, and Wealth prompts. Findings dealing with Manner, Opinion, and Major topics follow in chapter 12. This discussion centers around the phrasal, clausal, and rhetorical features discussed in Part II, and highlight the findings associated with the text and rhetorical markers in the essays of L2 writers.

To examine the effects of the prompts on the feature use in NS and NNS texts, chapter 13 focuses on significant differences in feature use by students in various L1 groups across prompts and concentrates on the impact of various prompts on student essay text. Chapter 13 also investigates rank-orders of median frequency rates of features examined in the study of NS and NNS texts to determine priorities in the practical applications of the study results. The outcomes of the study for methodological approaches to L2 composition instruction, as well as teacher training and curricula for teaching L2 writing are discussed in chapter 14, which is also the concluding statement for the volume.

Appendix A includes a table that contains ranked median frequency rates of all features, relative to those in NS essays. Tables B1 through B7 in Appendix B present comparisons of feature frequencies in the essays written by each L1 group and show that different essays prompts led to significant differences in the writing of students within every group.

ACKNOWLEDGMENTS

The volume owes its existence to many people. Christopher Hadley and Bethany Plett, affiliated with Seattle University at the time as research assistants during the various phases of corpus analysis, spent many months counting the occurrences of features in student texts, and their help was instrumental in compiling the data. Their pain and suffering remain untold, and their patience and perseverance are highly laudable. Robert and Audrey Kaplan continue to be my very dear friends, despite the fact that the counting of text features and their analysis took place during two long years. Bob's guidance and encouragement salvaged the gathering and analyses of data from recurrent opportunities for ruin and disaster. Rodney Hill, a documentation manager at Microsoft Corporation, created the many types of software and large-scale data processing tools needed to make sense of the data. His down-to-earth approach to the benefits of applied linguistics and the practical applications of its methods and findings shaped the research presented here. Jim Brown of Charleston Southern University, Jim Kenkel of Eastern Kentucky University, John Bean, Sharon Cumberland, and Mary Cheadley, all of Seattle University, Leslie Jarmon of the University of Texas at Austin, and Lawrence Bouton of the University of Illinois at Urbana–Champaign, helped to gather a good sample of student diagnostic essays. Sandra Fotos of Senshu University, Tokyo, assisted with essay gathering during the exploratory stages of this study. James Lantolf of Pennsylvania State University provided crucial advice when it was needed to save my sanity. In the final stages of the book's development, two reviewers provided helpful comments and suggestions for the style and content: John Hedgcock of Monterey Institute of International Studies, and Barbara Birch of California State University, Fresno. Naomi Silverman, Senior Editor at Lawrence Erlbaum Associates, also deserves special gratitude for her support, insight, and open-mindedness.

—*Eli Hinkel*

Background:
Research in Written Text and Discourse

Because written discourse and text occupy a prominent place in the academy in the United States and other English-speaking countries, much research has been devoted to formal discourse genres, their characteristics, and common linguistic features encountered in academic text. In addition, because the teaching of writing represents an instructional area that spans all students in colleges and universities, a great deal of work has been published dealing with writing pedagogy and its outcomes for the academy. When students who were non-native speakers of English (NNSs) entered the academic arena in English-medium institutions of higher learning, the pedagogical tasks associated with improving students' writing skills became far more complicated than they had been in writing instruction to native speakers (NSs) of English.

An examination of linguistic features in second language (L2) texts cannot begin without first taking a look at many various domains of research that are closely connected to academic discourse and text and conventions, as well as instructional methodologies for teaching writing to NSs and NNSs, the trends in writing pedagogy, and methods of L2 text analysis.

Part I brings together the many background issues that directly and indirectly affect the research presented in this book. Chapter 1 leads off with the findings of contrastive rhetoric, text linguistics, corpus analyses of published texts, and critical examinations of discourse conventions and writing pedagogy. Research into conventions of academic discourse and text in English is reviewed in chapter 2. The chapter also looks at studies on features of L2 writing in English and trends in the assessment of L2 writing.

A large body of earlier work has established that L2 written discourse and text are invariably affected by NNSs' first language (L1) discourse norms and paradigms. Therefore, chapter 3 presents an overview of findings dealing with properties of discourse and text in rhetorical traditions other than Anglo-American, specifically, Confucian, Indonesian, and

Koranic, as well as NNS students' learning to write in English. Popular methodologies for teaching L1 and L2 writing are examined in some detail in chapter 4, which questions the applicability of writing instruction developed for NSs to teaching NNS students. Part I concludes with a detailed description of the methodological considerations that underlie the study presented in this book, including demographic facts of student writers, their essays and prompts, the linguistic features of text that are discussed in later chapters, and the statistical analyses.

Writing as Text

This volume presents the results of a large-scale study of university-level L2 text. The study compares the uses of 68 linguistic and rhetorical features in L2 texts written by advanced NNSs of English to those in the essays of NSs enrolled in required first-year university composition courses (corpus size approximately 434,768 words). The selection of features for inclusion in the analysis is based on their textual functions and meanings, as identified in earlier research on English language grammar and lexis. The findings of corpus analyses pertinent to the uses, meanings, and functions of these features in published academic genre in English are also included. Corpus analysis of L2 text can inform the teaching of L2 grammar and lexis, as well as discourse, and serve as a basis for L2 curriculum and course design.

The study also compares the uses of syntactic, lexical, and rhetorical features by speakers of the same L1s across the six essay prompts to determine the feature variations elicited by different prompts. Thus, the findings of the study can be employed in the development of topics and tasks for the purposes of testing and assessing L2 writing. This volume presents a comprehensive and detailed analysis of L2 text and writing. The research detailed in this book is based on the analysis of approximately 1,457 NS and NNS essays written in response to six prompts, administered in routine placement and diagnostic tests in comprehensive universities. Of this number, 242 essays were written by NSs of American English and 1,215 by advanced NNSs, who were speakers of six languages: Chinese, Japanese, Korean, Vietnamese, Indonesian, and Arabic.

Whenever possible, the uses of proximate syntactic, lexical, and rhetorical features in NNSs' L1s are also discussed in the study. Based on earlier research in contrastive rhetoric, as well as in the available descriptions of discourse in Chinese, Japanese, Korean, Vietnamese, Indonesian, and Arabic, it has been established that NNSs often employ linguistic and rhetorical features of their L1s in producing texts in English. For this reason, research on contrastive rhetoric and textual features of L2 writing is also surveyed and discussed. In general terms, the research methodology adopted in this study relies on the theoretical underpinnings and empirical approaches developed in contrastive rhetoric to compare the uses of linguistic and rhetorical features of language in text, and corpus analysis to obtain and statistically analyze the frequencies of their occurrences. The analytical approach adopted in this study is derived from that developed in text analysis to identify important syntactic, lexical, and rhetorical features of text and employs quantitative and statistical techniques adopted in corpus analysis, as well as contrastive rhetoric to compare the data obtained from a cross-cultural sample of written text.

THEORETICAL UNDERPINNINGS AND RESEARCH TRENDS

Since the emergence of applied linguistics as a discipline in the 1950s and 1960s, three large domains of research have focused on the analysis of written text and discourse. Contrastive rhetoric initiated and continues to promote examination of L2 text and discourse paradigms in the genre of ESL (English as a second language) student writing and academic texts. Text linguistics occupied a prominent place in studies of linguistic features and cohesion in the 1960s, 1970s, and 1980s, and continues to yield information about the way discourse is organized and text is constructed. With the development of technology and accessibility of computerized text analysis, studies of large written and spoken corpora of language have changed how applied linguistics looks at text and the ways in which its regularities can be analyzed. In a parallel development, studies in the critical discourse analysis have begun to focus on the connections between the spread of the teaching of English around the world and the social, cultural, and economic contexts in which English is used. This introduction looks at each of these briefly to establish the research background for the comparative study of text and its linguistic features in the L1 and L2 student essays discussed in the rest of the book.

CONTRASTIVE RHETORIC

Over the past several decades, studies in applied linguistics, most prominently in the area of contrastive rhetoric, have examined discourse frameworks and paradigms as they are manifested in rhetorical traditions other
than Anglo-American and as they affect L2 writing and text in English. R.
B. Kaplan's seminal work in the 1960s introduced the proposition that English text written by NNSs followed discourse patterns specific to the rhetorical traditions prevalent in NNSs' L1s and were distinct from those in text
written by NSs. In that work, Kaplan proposed that discourse moves in written text are culturally determined within the paradigms of various rhetorical traditions. Although Kaplan's initial publication met with some criticism (primarily about the applicability of some of the observations to some
discourse traditions), the ideas prompted a genuine advancement in
understanding how L2 written discourse is constructed and its message
communicated. Subsequent work in contrastive rhetoric gave rise to a large
body of work that shed light on L2 writing, discourse, and text. The study of
contrastive rhetoric that originated with Kaplan's (1966) publication
undertakes to investigate the organization of discourse paradigms and
rhetorical structure of text in languages other than English. By extension,
contrastive rhetoric further studies the effects of NNSs' L1 rhetorical construction of textual frameworks on the text that NNSs produce in ESL.

In many investigations, discourse construction in L2 writing has been
compared to that found in texts in writers' L1s or comparable L2 genre.
Research that sets out to establish similarities between written discourse
paradigms in the writers' L1s and L2s proliferated in the area of contrastive
rhetoric, which became a flourishing domain of applied linguistics. Many
studies compare specific discourse frameworks in the L2 writing of speakers of Arabic to rhetorical paradigms in classical Arabic (Ostler, 1987;
Sa'adeddin, 1989), essays written by Thai students of English to those in
Buddhist and foundational Thai texts (Bickner & Peyasantiwong, 1988;
Indrasuta, 1988), and the L2 writing of Chinese (Mohan & Lo, 1984; G.
Taylor & Chen, 1993) and Korean speakers (Y.-M. Park, 1988) to similar
writing of NSs of English. Others reviewed discourse moves in introductions to essays (Scarcella, 1984) and textual divergences in various types of
rhetorical modes and writing (Grabe & Kaplan, 1987; Kaplan, 1988; Reid,
1993).

Investigations of discourse paradigms in various rhetorical traditions,
including those in Anglo-American writing, provided much insight into
and understanding of how text is constructed and, thus, how findings in
contrastive rhetoric can inform the teaching of L2 writing. As Kaplan
(1988) pointed out, research in contrastive rhetoric pursues the goal of

descriptive accuracy that originates in pedagogical necessity. He specified that L2 students enrolled in U.S. colleges and universities are expected to produce academic texts that are congruent with Anglo-American rhetorical paradigms. However, these students bring to the larger academic arena the fundamental discourse paradigms that reflect their L1 conventions of writing, and need to be taught the textual constructs accepted in writing in English.

Another venue for L2 writing analyses includes ethnographic studies of L2 writing and NNS writers also centered around contrastive rhetoric. Such studies as Johns (1990a, 1997) and Swales (1990b) delved into writers' approaches to constructing text and developing academic essays. These investigations shed light on teaching L2 academic writing and discourse variation found in textual paradigms in certain disciplines and essays for different academic purposes.

Among the longer works, Connor and Kaplan's (1987) volume presented applications of contrastive rhetoric to L2 text analysis, pedagogy, and further development of empirical research in written discourse. The authors examined various issues in L2 writing that dealt with argumentation patterns in L2 student essays, text-type research, and the specific features of L2 text, produced by speakers of such languages as Korean and Arabic. In other volumes, for example, Purves (1987), Carson and Leki (1993), and Reid (1993), contrastive rhetoric occupied an important place and has had much to contribute to the quality of L2 pedagogy in written and oral discourse. Contrastive rhetoric has had so much influence on the evolution of L2 writing instruction and teacher training that today, it would be practically impossible to find a book on methods for teaching L2 composition that does not deal extensively with various rhetorical traditions and discourse paradigms in languages other than English.

The most thorough literature survey on contrastive rhetoric can be found in Connor (1996), which reviews the contributions of the discipline to what is known about discourse paradigms in rhetorical traditions other than Anglo-American. Furthermore, Connor addressed the foundational theory of contrastive rhetoric as a domain of applied linguistics and written text analysis. The author approached writing and discourse as an activity embedded in culture and in conjunction with the constructs of literacy, translation studies, and investigations into academic and professional writing. Connor pointed out that the benefits of contrastive rhetoric research extend beyond L2 pedagogy to expand the knowledge base about text and discourse.

In their definitive volume on the theory of writing, Grabe and Kaplan (1996) provided extensive evidence that contrastive rhetoric has its roots in the study of literacy as language socialization, as well as the social construction theory and disciplinary studies of textual genre. In their view, in the early stages of contrastive rhetoric research, its findings were not sufficiently refined to account for genre variations in texts written in the same language (e.g., it may not be particularly helpful to compare L2 student writing to published academic texts). In addition, Grabe and Kaplan pointed out that to date, a unified theoretical model of contrastive rhetoric has not been developed and, as an outcome, divergent research methodologies in empirical studies of text and discourse in various rhetorical traditions have yielded results that are not always possible to compare.

However, Grabe and Kaplan (1996) also emphasized that contrastive rhetoric has contributed to the development of knowledge in several domains important in the teaching of writing: rhetorical patterns in text and their frequency of occurrence in discourse, conventions associated with writing and text development in learners' L1s and the target language, particularly as they apply to various discourse genre, morphosyntax of the target language, textual devices for coherence, and characteristics of audience in different rhetorical traditions. The authors noted that the expansion of knowledge about rhetoric and discourse that can be obtained by means of comparative analyses in contrastive rhetoric primarily concerns the product and not the process of writing. It is important to note that contrastive rhetoric has also contributed to the development of text linguistics that has led to the popularity of corpus analyses in the 1980s and 1990s (see next section).

TEXT LINGUISTICS

When applied linguistics and text analysis in its modern form arrived on the scene in the middle of the 20th century, the analysis of written text and associated genre and cohesion patterns were not something to be taken for granted. Although traditionally the study of rhetoric and stylistics focused on how a message is conveyed and how logical structures of text and rhetorical persuasion affect the audience, few formal accounts of written text had been developed. Text analysis was a groundbreaking evolution of language study that undertook to investigate how, why, and when written and spoken texts were used to communicate a message and convey its intentions.

However, even after a cursory examination, applied linguists engaged in text analysis discovered that the task was not at all simple. It turned out that the way text is arranged and the way lexicon and syntactic structures are used differs depending on the purpose for which the text is written. In contemporary terms, the text in newspapers differs from that in fiction or academic publications, and even worse, the text in various types of newspaper articles, such as news reportage or editorials, and, for example, romance novels and travelogues, is not used in the same way. Even at the first glance, an average reader can tell that the purpose of the text determines how discourse organization, the lexicon, and types of grammatical structures are used. To further complicate the task of text analysis, the types of text that commonly exist in practically any modern society may be as numerous as the communicative goals of their writers (Olson, 1994). Thus, at the outset, it became apparent that to analyze how and why particular features of text are employed, applied linguists needed to address the features of similar texts, that is, texts written with similar purposes, separately from other types of texts.

Nonetheless, despite the divergent purposes with which texts are written and their varied features that are intended to attain their communicative goals, it is possible to identify characteristics shared by all texts. These features of text stem from their purposes to communicate information in a way that a reader can understand the writer's communicative purpose. In their seminal study of text linguistics, de Beaugrande and Dressler (1972/1981) identified seven characteristics of text that they called "standards" (p. 11): cohesion, coherence, intentionality, acceptability, informativity, situationality, and intertextuality. The authors further noted that these standards are "constitutive principles" (p. 11) of textual communication in that they are identifiable in textual communication and that without them the text's message cannot be conveyed. In addition, however, de Beaugrande and Dressler stipulated that "[t]here must also exist regulative principles . . . that control textual communication rather than define it" (p. 11). These principles can be categorized as *efficiency,* which has the goal of minimizing participants' effort in communication, *effectiveness,* which creates favorable conditions for attaining the goal of textual communication, and *appropriateness of communication,* which ensures agreement between the setting and the socially accepted standards of textuality.

In his substantial follow-up volume, de Beaugrande (1997) examined "text as a communicative event wherein linguistic, cognitive, and social actions converge" (p. 10) through a system of connective elements and a wide variety of functions. He also proposed that text both reflects and contributes to the creation of knowledge. As an outcome of constructing knowledge rooted in text and textuality, cultural beliefs and attitudes are also created and perpetuated by means of text and its principles of acceptability (e.g., cohesion and coherence). de Beaugrade emphasized that text conventions and the social stratification of knowledge about text often mark such social phenomena as consolidation of power, ingroup solidarity, and access to information.

The work on text analysis in English continued extensively to investigate the principles of cohesion and the interaction of grammar and lexicon. Halliday and Hasan's (1976) analytical approach to text construction and linguistic and lexical means by which intertextual semantic relationships are established became instrumental in subsequent text linguistics. Their work was groundbreaking because for the first time the intuitively identified relationships between propositions in text and text flow were formalized and defined in terms of the linguistic and discoursal functions of elements. Halliday and Hasan explained that cohesion occurs "when interpretation of some element in discourse is dependent on another" (p. 4). The authors further investigated how discourse organization and logical structure contributes to overall cohesiveness of text and the role that contextuality plays in that text is understood. In general terms, Halliday and Hasan indicated that linguistic cohesion has three main functional and semantic components: the *ideational, interpersonal,* and *textual.* Ideational cohesion deals with the content (ideas) expressed in text (including the context of culture); the interpersonal component includes the social, expressive, and contextualized functions of language use, as well as the writer's attitudes, judgments, and tone; and the textual element is concerned with the linguistic means of constructing text and making it cohesive, for example, phrases and clauses used functionally within the purpose of discourse. Halliday and Hasan's work led to further advancements in text linguistics to formalize the ways in which lexical and syntactic elements combine to make text coherent and allow it to be understood.

Malcolm Coulthard's (1977/1985) pioneering work on discourse and text analysis advanced a claim that spoken and written discourse share common features that need to be examined in systematic ways. He proposed that the goals of discourse studies are to identify operational rules of discourse (the macro-level of text) and demonstrate how functions of features are related to their grammatical and lexical realizations in text (the microlevel). According to Coulthard, another priority in analyzing discourse is to determine the interpretive rules that allow texts to be understood in particular ways. One of the most important contributions of his earlier work lies in attempted standardizations of data gathering and analysis to make results useful and applicable to various contexts in which discourse is used. Coulthard's subsequent two-volume collection of articles on text analysis (1992, 1994) brought together work on spoken and written discourse and text linguistics. This collection shows how to apply consistent data gathering and analysis to lexical and syntactic signals to identify and label discourse moves and operations (e.g. topic shifts and expansions), ideational and clause relationships in the text's information structure, referential framing in narratives, as well as discourse organization in academic and scientific publications. In part, the Coulthard (1992, 1994) volumes present novel approaches to text linguistics based on computerized analysis of published corpora that allowed new insights into how text and discourse are constructed.

The role of text and discourse in communication was thoroughly described in the work of van Dijk (1985, 1997), in which principles of discourse analysis are presented as intertwined with the fundamental frameworks of society and culture. These include work on naturally occurring text and talk to include corpora of real-life language use, the constitutive local, global, social, and cultural contexts in which text and discourse occur, the social practices of cultural discourse groups, the functionality and rules of discourse in its sociocultural contexts, and discourse as a representation of knowledge, attitudes, ideologies, norms, and values. In van Dijk's view, the analysis of text and discourse is inseparable from the social and cultural fabric of social and cultural contexts, language users, and their communicational intentions and beliefs. Discourse analysis encompasses mutually dependent domains of construction, that is, macrostructures, such as logical progression and purpose of ideas, then moves down to microlevels that reflect contextual and social features of text, and then back again when microstructures affect the macrolevel of the discourse whole. Van Dijk specified that it may not be possible to separate discourse studies from studies in psychology, sociology, and social interaction, as well as social and political institutions and organizations.

CORPUS ANALYSES

Text linguistics with its goal of identifying the principles and regularities of textual communication gave rise to computer analyses of large corpora in the 1960s, 1970s, and 1980s, when the development of technology permitted investigations to determine how texts were constructed to attain their communication goals. In a subsequent development in the 1980s and 1990s, applied linguistics has experienced a rapid growth of studies based on corpus analysis of written and spoken text (Biber, 1988, 1995; Biber & Finegan, 1991; Channel, 1994; Collins, 1991; Hoye, 1997; Hyland, 1998; McCarthy & Carter, 1994; Sinclair, 1990). These investigations usually have the goal of determining how particular features of text are used in authentic texts, such as academic prose, newspaper articles on various topics (e.g., hobbies, religion, news reportage, or editorials), or conversations. Studies of language corpora include large amounts of computerized data that allow researchers to undertake a variety of investigative projects and, for example, describe regularities in the use of discoursal, syntactic, lexical, semantic, and collocational features of language. Such studies, however, largely examine published written or transcribed spoken texts because computer software has not advanced sufficiently to reliably recognize handwritten texts (Biber, Conrad, & Reppen, 1998). In part for this reason, in addition to many other complex considerations (e.g., copyright or even reimbursements), investigations of developmental and instructed L1 and L2 writing and college composition have lagged behind investigations of published and transcribed corpora.

The availability of and research into computerized discourse corpora have led to the creation of new methodologies in language analysis and recommendations for the inclusion of specific linguistic features, lexis, and collocations in learner dictionaries, textbooks, and other instructional materials. In a majority of U.S. colleges and universities, as well as in preparatory academic ESL/EFL programs, academic writing and composition occupy a prominent place in L1 and L2 foundational instruction. However, thus far, analyses of composition texts and their linguistic features have not been extended to identifying the specific differences between L1 and L2 academic and composition writing. The benefits of such investigations, as in this study, can provide insights and gains somewhat similar to those that have resulted as an outcome of corpus analyses of English language published and spoken corpora. Specifically, they can assist in developing focused L2 grammar and vocabulary curricula, as well as instructional approaches to discourse and its frameworks.

To determine regularities in the uses of syntactic and lexical features of English, other researchers have undertaken large-scale analyses of published corpora that include fiction, newspaper texts, academic publications, formal spoken texts, such as sermons and speeches, and transcribed informal conversations. The Brown Corpus and the Lund Corpus were the first of this kind, and the information about text structure by means of their analyses further advanced our knowledge about text written in English. The research on the Brown and the Lund Corpora greatly affected the course of English text linguistics and led to a formalization of a corpus analysis as a research area within applied linguistics.

Analyses of corpora also shed a great deal of light on the construction of spoken and published English texts under the auspices of the London–Lund corpus, LOB corpus, Longman–Lancaster corpus with 30 million words, Cobuild corpus of written and spoken English, and Cambridge and Nottingham corpus. These analyses have resulted in large numbers of publications that include research books and articles, dictionaries of English usage, comprehensive grammar volumes, and learner workbooks, all of which are designed to explain how English text works in real life.

The work of Michael Stubbs (1996) directly addresses theoretical and practical connections between discourse and text linguistics and analyses of language corpora. In his view, linguistics and, by extension, discourse analysis are essentially social sciences that analyze natural data and apply their findings to teaching ESL/EFL, teacher training, and dictionary making. For this reason, the data in the analysis have to consist of authentic language uses and whole texts, and not intuitive and invented textbook samples. Stubbs emphasized that in keeping with the Hallidayan tradition of discourse analysis, in linguistic examinations of texts the grammatical form

Gramley Library
Salem Academy and College
Winston-Salem, N.C. 27108

and meaning are inseparable in as much as syntax is inseparable from the lexicon. Furthermore, because language behaviors involve both novel and routinized uses of structures and lexis and because culture is transmitted by means of language, analyses of language corpora can provide access to data that may not be obtainable by other means. According to Stubbs, corpus analysis can contribute to our understanding of grammar, lexicon and collocation, the many issues in grammar teaching, and language variability across different genre.

One of the most promising examples in corpus analysis was developed by Biber (1988). In his study, based on approximately 1 million words, he included various genre of written text, such as press reportage, newspaper editorials, press reviews, articles on religion, skills, and hobbies, popular lore, biographies, official documents, academic prose, and other published works. In addition, his corpus of spoken texts included face-to-face, telephone, and public conversations that were recorded and transcribed, as well as broadcasts, and spontaneous and planned speeches. The prominence of Biber's corpus analysis lies in the fact that it established the frequencies with which specific linguistic features were used in written and spoken text and identified their co-occurrence patterns prevalent in written and spoken texts. His study also determined that in actuality, written and spoken text employed divergent linguistic features to convey their message, even though their structural and discourse organization may not be particularly different. In his follow-up book, Biber (1995) described the text analysis methodology based on a large corpus of data and provided detailed explanation of how corpuses analysis may be conducted and how statistical analyses of data can lead to insights into language regularities in various corpora.

Biber et al.'s (1999), *Longman Grammar of Spoken and Written English,* based on the analysis of the Longman–Lancaster corpus, is by far the most thorough volume on the structure and uses of English grammar, lexicon, discourse, and registers in various genres (e.g., spoken and written). In general terms, the goal of the book is to present real-life uses of grammatical and lexical features of various genre in English, such as news reports, academic prose, introductory textbooks, and fiction, as well as conversational data. Inasmuch as corpus analysis pursues to describe discourse features, the consideration of social settings and pragmatic characteristics of text are also taken into account in the presentations of feature uses that pertain to the writer's stance in discourse, idiomaticity, and cohesion. The book is comprehensive indeed, and it presents the results of large-scale quantitative analysis of frequency counts of features to include words, phrases, dependent and independent clauses, lexical classes of nouns and pronouns, verbs and features of verb phrases (tense, aspect, and voice), adjectives and adverbs, complex and compound noun phrases, and adverbials.

Among the three areas of applied linguistics mentioned earlier, that is, contrastive rhetoric, text linguistics, and corpus analysis, none undertake a detailed and thorough examination of ESL university text. Although Stubbs (1996) commented that the findings of discourse and corpus analyses are directly applicable to teaching ESL/EFL, the implied approach to teaching is rather global in nature and assumes a top-down methodology. That is, analyses of the uses of English determine, for example, how discourse moves affect the construction of text and how text features contribute to its structure, functionality, and cohesion, and then ESL/EFL teachers can help learners develop the skills necessary for understanding and producing appropriate written and spoken text in L2. Though at first glance this seems to be a reasonable approach to applying the findings of various linguistic analyses to teaching ESL/EFL, reality seems to be a bit messier than this. For instance, L2 learners usually have substantially smaller ranges of vocabulary and syntactic structures than those found in published corpora in English.

As Grabe and Kaplan (1996) pointed out, results of various empirical studies sometimes can be less than definitive, and direct applications of many studies to teaching ESL/EFL have not been clearly established. Most important, however, L2 teaching and learning are enormously complex processes the nature of which has not yet been clearly understood, and it is not even known whether direct instruction in, for instance, L2 grammar and writing actually leads to learning and acquisition of L2 grammatical and discourse features. Because in general L2 teaching and learning are confounded by a large number of factors, it may not always be possible to determine how these factors combine to affect the outcomes of L2 learning processes.

However, by analyzing naturally occurring data obtained from L2 writing samples, researchers can identify what features of text, syntax, lexicon, and discourse may require special attention in the teaching of L2 skills to enhance and focus the quality of teaching. The present volume is a step along that path and examines the uses of syntactic, lexical, and rhetorical features in L2 texts relative to comparable NS texts.

CRITICAL DISCOURSE ANALYSIS

An inevitable point of dissention arises whenever multiple discourse paradigms or perspectives on discourse construction are discussed. In the late 1980s and early 1990s, studies emerged to identify connections between language, discourse, and power in society (e.g., the reasons that in various school systems L2 and minority learners are persistently taught to produce spoken and written text according to the relatively rigid discourse frameworks specific to the Anglo-American academy). The works of such authors as Benesch (1996) Fairclough (1989, 1995), Pennycook (1994), Phillipson (1991), and Skutnabb-Kangas (1991) focus on the need to approach discourse and discourse pedagogy critically. In the view of these authors, the frameworks of English uses and the teaching of English are associated with many complex issues in power and ideology because the worldwide hegemony of English necessarily implies the inequality of languages and their discourse traditions.

One of the fundamental principles in critical discourse analysis is that language is in itself a social practice and is inseparable from society. Critical discourse analysis seeks to interpret discourse, its participants' roles, as well as social and ideological constructs in which all language is used in communication. Thus, critical language studies are distinguished from studies in linguistics proper, which describes and analyzes language systems without a great deal of regard to the organization of society and the social order.

It may be unquestionably true that there are issues of power and conflicts of ideology that complicate the teaching and learning of Anglo-American academic discourse frameworks. Placement tests such as those on which this study is based are common in college and university settings and in standardized testing, where they determine university admissions and the course of students' careers. This study, however, is not concerned with the underlying ideology of education or discourse. An underlying assumption of this research, however, and one of the demonstrable conclusions is that NNS writers produce text that differs significantly from the text that NS writers produce. A further assumption is that knowing what those differences are is of value to teachers and researchers in applied linguistics.

2

Research in Academic and ESL Written Discourse and Text

Features of Academic Discourse and Text in English

In rather self-evident terms, written academic text is produced in the academy, and in most text analyses, it has been divided into two types that are relatively easily accessible for examination. Published academic papers represent the most studied variety, and in research, investigations have been mindful of pronounced differences between various academic genre, such as those in published articles in chemistry as opposed to philosophy (Chang & Swales, 1999). The other type of academic texts comprises those generated by students in the form of written assignments and essay tests. These varieties of student writing are also somewhat distinct in their form, content, and organization. Research in academic text has included studies of both published articles and student essays.

As mentioned in the introduction, the analytical frameworks created to identify features of text established macro- and microlevels of text construction, that is, those that deal on a "macro" basis with logical, appropriate, and often expected organization of ideas and information in discourse, and syntactic and lexical features of text on a "micro" level that mark and contribute to the discourse flow and logical structure (Coulthard, 1977/1985; de Beaugrande & Dressler, 1972/1981; Halliday & Hasan, 1976). This chapter reviews the findings of discourse and text studies of published academic articles, large-scale corpus analyses, and contrastive rhetoric studies of L2 student essays because these investigations identify important characteristics of written academic discourse and text in English. In addition, the discussion briefly touches on research into rater-based impressionistic assessment and academic evaluations of L2 writing because such studies often specifically note features of academic discourse and text considered to be important.

To a great extent, the findings of research on published and student academic texts are relevant to the comparisons of feature uses in NS and NNS university essays because in many cases, the curricula for teaching L2 academic text to NNS is derived from the discourse paradigms and textual devices found in the published genre, including a wide range of works from literary memoirs and personal narratives to syntheses of relevant literature and critiques (Prior, 1998; Weese, Fox, & Greene, 1998). Furthermore, writing instruction and its assessment criteria are by and large determined by the norms and expectations of discourse and text in the greater academic arena. It goes without saying that the quality of published academic papers and the expected rigor of writing in these papers probably far exceeds those found even in most college-level writing, not even to mention the fact that published works undergo several rounds of editing and copyediting before they reach their readers.

Findings of Discourse Analyses and Text Linguistics

The discourse-level organization of ideas and content plays the role of a map in a piece of writing (de Beaugrande & Dressler, 1972/1981). The academic genre and academic publications have received much attention in the literature in part because they have been of immediate relevance and accessibility to the linguists who were engaged in the study of writing. Thus, substantial inroads were made in the study of global discourse and text features in the academic genre that later provided the springboard for corpus analyses, which mostly centered on syntactic and lexical features of text (indeed, it would be difficult to analyze discourse organization by means of computers because, e.g., logical progression of ideas or efficiency in communication may not be as easily identifiable as coordinating conjunctions).

In discourse and text analysis, the notion of genre in writing stems from the Halliday approach to determining the functions of language and its features in context, rather than from the abstract syntactic categories of language, as is done in the theory of syntax. From this perspective, language is used to express meaning, and text features are used to express it coherently, cohesively, and effectively. As an outcome, one genre of language (e.g., academic or personal) differs from another in the way in which it expresses meaning, and thus, by virtue of discourse or textual features that are necessary or desirable to convey a particular meaning. For example, most people would consider a personal letter written in an academic genre of text inappropriate and vice versa. On the other hand, a lack of familiarity with the discourse and text features appropriate in a certain genre may prove to be severe handicap, as in the case of many NNS students in English-speaking academic settings (Atkinson, 1991; Poole, 1991). Halliday (1978) commented that rhetorical strategies in constructing discourse and text reflect the patterns of language use within the social structure. In his view, the social construction of discourse creates rhetorical modes and styles and the appropriate genres to express them.

A discussion of written academic genre and discourse frequently cited in literature belongs to Swales (1990a), a work in which he coined the term "academic discourse community" to explain that academic discourse and text are rather distinct from many other types of writing. Swales defined discourse communities as "sociorhetorical networks that form in order to work towards sets of common goals" (p. 9). He explained that one important characteristic of discourse communities is that their "established members" possess "familiarity with the particular genres that are used in the communicative furtherance of those set goals" (p. 9).

According to Swales (1990a), academic discourse and text in published articles in such diverse disciplines as mathematics and rhetoric share several important characteristics. For example, average sentence length remained constant at around 25 words, and the frequency of relative clauses was less than that of noun and adverb clauses of cause and temporality. In addition, subjects of main clauses included a large number of abstract nouns and nominalized forms (such those with *-ion* and *-ness* suffixes), and concrete nouns were relatively infrequent. In terms of information organization, practically all articles included reviews of literature and earlier research, followed by discussion and conclusion sections, both of which can be somewhat lengthy and complex.

In addition, Swales (1990a) cited much earlier research to show that academic text is conventionalized in terms of syntactic and lexical features that are considered to be appropriate. For example, the uses of past and present tenses are governed by the discourse organization: The past tense is often found in literature review sections but not in the discussion and conclusion sections, where the present tense is used almost exclusively. Modal verbs represent a common form of hedging, and nominal clauses are employed more frequently than other types of subordinate structures. Similarly, citations of earlier work in the body of articles follows rigid rules, described in publication manuals of various disciplines. Within introduction, discussion, and conclusion sections, subsets of rules also apply to logical organization of discourse, as well as syntactic and lexical choices that are considered to be appropriate (e.g., introductions that include descriptions of issues are expected to be written in the present tense and followed by a shift to the past tense in literature review).

Following Swales, Bhatia (1992, 1993) undertook to investigate the specifics of genre in articles and other types of discourse in various academic disciplines, such as psychology, sociology, and law. His study identified smaller scale divisions within introductions, discussions, and conclusions. For instance, introductions typically include four discourse moves: establishing the field, summarizing previous research, preparing for present research, and introducing present research. Bhatia also noted that some amount of variability can be found in classical models of published academic papers, even though variations on the discourse structure are not particularly dramatic. In student academic papers, such as lab reports and dissertations, discourse moves also largely adhered to the paradigms of the academic discourse community, with the exception that lab reports devoted less attention to establishing the field and previous research summaries, whereas dissertations did so to a greater extent than published articles. In regard to syntactic features of academic text, Bhatia also commented that complex nominal constructions, nominalizations, and gerund phrases are typically associated with the academic genre and that students need to be explicitly taught to use appropriate nominal constructions.

Discourse analyses of the academic genre further underscored the need for detailed examinations of textual features that essentially played the role of road signs in the infrastructure of language in text. Text analyses of academic publications carried out in the 1980s and 1990s provided for substantial insights into the uses of syntactic and lexical features in text to determine how the macrostructure of discourse is marked and dealt with at the microlevel of syntax and lexis. In fact, in some schools of thought, discourse- and text-level analyses are so closely intertwined that they may not be (and probably should not be) looked at in isolation (Coulthard, 1977/1985; Halliday & Hasan, 1976; van Dijk, 1985, 1997), particularly when findings of such analyses are applied to language teaching (McCarthy, 1991; McCarthy & Carter, 1994).

However, as knowledge and understanding of the discourse organization and the lexicogrammatical features of text expanded, it became clear that a detailed and thorough study of language in academic text may be difficult, unless researchers endeavor to examine these features in some sort of manageable way. As an outcome, a series of works emerged that were devoted to investigations of textual features in the academic genre to identify the road signs that mark the discourse infrastructure.

Among the many studies of textual features in academic texts, there have been investigations of discourse markers (Schiffrin, 1987, 1994), tenses (Matthiessen, 1996; Schiffrin, 1981), modal verbs (Coates, 1983;

Hermeren, 1978), hedges (Holmes, 1984; Huebler, 1983), and vagueness. To illustrate, Channel's (1994) substantial work on the uses of vague language in academic texts points to the fact that "strategic vagueness" (p. 27) is a common device in academic texts used to avoid the writer's commitment to the truth value of propositions. She noted that hedging has many similar functions and explained that the lexical and syntactic means of being vague in written text are so numerous that they require elaborate classification. For example, in addition to approximators *(approximately, about, near, at least, at most,* and *fewer/less than),* there are also vague plurals *(tens, thousand),* plural quantifiers *(a lot of, several, many, a few),* as well as adverbs or frequency and exaggeratives.

Another example of the textual features of the academic genre is the collection of articles edited by Ventola and Mauranen (1996) that similarly includes work on strategic vagueness to demonstrate how vagueness allows writers to hedge the definitiveness of their results and articulate connections between results and implications in academic studies. In academic texts, vagueness achieved by means of coordinating expressions and conjunctions, comparisons, and compound modifiers (e.g., *working independently, that is to say)* (Myers, 1996). The volume includes Bloor's (1996) article on the uses of hypothetical constructions as strategic devices in academic texts and argumentation, when they are employed to set conditions to delimit the applicability of claims (e.g., *if this were to happen, then . . .*). One of the foci of the book is to point out that numerous cultural differences exist in the uses of syntactic and lexical features of texts written by NSs and NNSs in academic publications and that constructing academic discourse and text is a culturally defined linguistic milieu. A more recent approach to analyses of discourse and text works with variations in ideational organization and textual devices within the sociocultural frameworks of academic writing, for example, the pragmatics of interaction between the writer and reader (Myers, 1999), the role of the audience in the production of academic text, and the markers of the writer's stance in research articles (Hyland, 1999).

The analyses of discrete lexicosyntactic features of academic text and their textual and discourse functions that first appeared in the late 1960s and continued during the 1970s and 1980s readily lent themselves to computerized analysis of text because, unlike macrolevel frameworks of the academic genre, they were relatively easy to isolate. Hence, in the 1980s and 1990s, aided by the great strides in computer technology, researchers delved into several concurrent examinations of text features on a large scale. This research venue has proved so fruitful that in view of some linguists, intuitive analysis of syntactic and lexical features and their textual functions may be somewhat diminished in value and importance (Aarts, 1991).

Findings of Corpus Analyses

The analyses of syntactic and lexical features in computerized corpora of language proved to be relatively easy to carry out based on large amounts of text samples that usually included the academic genre. These studies expanded the current knowledge base in regard to the specific structures and lexical features of written academic text and included, for instance, examinations of modal verbs (Collins, 1991), prepositional phrases, stock phrases, and collocations (Kennedy, 1991; Kjellmer, 1991; Renouf & Sinclair, 1991), as well as matters of style and variation in various written discourse genre. Other studies investigated the lexicogrammatical meanings and functions of negatives and predicatives (Tadros, 1994), the cohesive functions of nouns and noun phrases, the functional role of adverbs (Hoye, 1997), the frequency and meanings of fixed expressions (Moon, 1994) and the role of demonstratives as cohesive devices (McCarthy, 1994).

In just 5 years between 1996 and 2000, several volumes were published that dealt with specific lexicogrammatical features of the written academic text, such as various types of hedges, including modals, epistemic adjectives, adverbs, and nouns, and syntactic features of hedged structures (Hyland, 1998), as well as classes of collocations, idioms, synonyms, adverb clauses, and text-referential cohesion (Partington, 1998).

For instance, based on their analysis of large corpora, Hunston and Francis (2000) developed what they called "pattern grammar" to identify combinations of words that occur relatively frequently and that may be dependent on a particular word choice to convey clear and definable meaning. In their exploration, they developed a system of frequent patterns of verb, noun, and adjective uses and variations in their meanings, depending on the syntactic and lexical contexts in which they occur. In addition, Hunston and Francis' analysis of patterns extends to cohesive features of the discourse structure, such as subordinating conjunctions, embedded clauses, and information flow.

One of the most detailed analyses of syntactic and lexical features of academic prose was carried out by Biber (1988) as a part of his larger analysis of written discourse. According to his findings, in academic texts, the use of the past tense is relatively infrequent compared to that of the present tense. Similarly, frequencies of third-person pronouns considerably exceed those of the first- and second-person pronouns. In addition, agentless passive structures are used far more often than passives with *by*-phrases, although occurrences of other types of prepositional phrases are numerous. In general terms, Biber noted that the amount of variation among several types of academic texts was high, and, for example, published articles in the sciences employed syntactic and lexical features markedly differently. Nonetheless, common characteristics of the academic genre include a high rate of occurrence of nouns, gerunds, attributive (descriptive) adjectives, and several lexical classes of verbs (e.g., private, as *think, feel, believe,* and suasive, as *allow, ask, determine),* whereas predicative adjectives and adverb clauses were far less common.

Though findings of text and corpus analyses of the written academic genre may not be directly applicable to classroom instruction and studies of student texts, they provide insight into discourse and text conventions of published academic and other types of texts. Furthermore, they often help explain how written academic prose is constructed and by implication, can inform writing instruction and pedagogy. An additional benefit of corpora studies is that they shed light on how enormously complex and frequently lexicalized the uses of language and text in the academic genre actually are.

FEATURES OF STUDENT ESSAY WRITING

Contrastive Rhetoric: Discourse and Text Analysis

Studies in contrastive rhetoric published in the 1970s, 1980s, and 1990s included detailed comparisons of discourse moves in written text, rater-based evaluations of L2 writing, frequency counts of particular features used in L1 and L2 writing, and other comparative methods of discourse and text analysis. Although contrastive rhetoric research has not dealt directly with L2 teaching or composition instruction, applications of its findings have become a staple of teacher training and L2 composition books, as well as other domains of discourse and text linguistics. As Kaplan (2000) commented, contrastive rhetoric identifies the fact that "there are differences between languages in rhetorical preference" (p. 84) of text construction and organization that can be perceived by "every" language speaker, who knows what happens in his or her language and what happens in other languages. Kaplan stated that "[t]hat fact constitutes the central idea" (p. 84) of contrastive rhetoric.

Advances in contrastive rhetoric and attendant studies in the ethnography and assessment of L2 writing gave rise to pedagogical work, rooted in the research and analysis of rhetorical paradigms and textual features identified in the published academic genre (Carson, 1993; Fathman & Whalley, 1990; Friedlander, 1990; Kroll, 1990a; Leki, 1993; Raimes, 1983). The various approaches to L2 writing pedagogy addressed L2 rhetorical and written discourse paradigms, exposure to and learning from L2 text, the teacher's role in L2 writing pedagogy, the developmental stages in learning to write in L2, background and characteristics of L2 writers, as well as syntactic and lexical features of L2 writing and academic texts in English.

In keeping with the methodologies developed for the analysis of discourse- and text-level structures, studies in contrastive rhetoric largely concentrated on comparisons of L1 texts to those written by L2 students in U.S. colleges and universities. Investigations in contrastive rhetoric delved into comparative analysis of discourse and textual features of L2 student essays and published articles whose authors were speakers of Chinese (Hinds, 1990; Matalene, 1985; Mohan & Lo, 1985; Scollon, 1991), Korean (Hinds, 1990, Hinkel, 1997a; Scarcella & C. Lee, 1989), Arabic (Ostler, 1987; Sa'addedin, 1989), Japanese (Hinds, 1984, 1990; Tsujimura, 1987), or Thai (Bickner & Peyasantiwong, 1988; Indrasuta, 1988). For example, the findings of some studies point to the fact that discourse in the classical Chinese rhetorical tradition, which also influenced the rhetorical traditions in Japan and Korea, is structured differently than that in Anglo-American formal written text. The differences in discourse structure can make the L2 essays of Chinese students appear to be indirect when the writer's position is not expressed directly but is alluded to and implied. Similarly, the rhetorical and communicative purpose of overt persuasion may not be prominent in the discourse paradigms based on the traditional Confucian approach to argumentation and support for one's thesis. Confucian argumentation is based on the harmonious exchange of ideas between the writer and the audience and does not promote the ideas of one individual.

Similarly, comparative analyses of textual features in the essays of NSs and L2 students who were speakers of Chinese, Korean, and Japanese have shown that the texts written by L2 students frequently appear more indirect than those written by NSs (Hinkel, 1995c, 1997a). The reasons lie in the fact that L2 essays are often overhedged and include too many rhetorical questions, denials and refutations, and indirect syntactic constructions, such as the passive voice, indefinite pronouns, and demonstratives.

On the other hand, Ostler's (1987) study of essays of Arabic students in a U.S. university demonstrated that the discourse structure employed by these L2 writers frequently adopted a global approach to introducing to essay topics and began by stating broad (and "indisputable") generalizations (e.g., *All families in my country have a special tradition different from the other families in the world,* p. 182). Ostler found such introductions of topics different from those in the essays of NS students and indicated that such generalizations did not occur in NS texts. Furthermore, she found that the essays of the speakers of Arabic contained a dramatically higher number of discourse divisions and moves, and she explained that L2 essays contained a large number of ideas that were not as fully developed as a smaller number of ideas covered in NS essays. Similarly, her text analysis of the syntactic and lexical features in the essays indicates that speakers of Arabic used a significantly higher number of coordinating conjunctions, whereas the frequencies of subordinate clause use were significantly lower. Ostler concluded that "the prose style of Arabic-speaking students writing in English has been shown to be quantitatively different from that of English-speaking writers" (p. 184).

Other investigations into L2 student writing also addressed such important features of discourse and text as development of narrative, and presentation of characters, and narrative structure in the writing of school-age children, who were speakers of Vietnamese and Arabic, relative to those of NSs of similar age (Soter, 1988), cultural differences in logical organization and rhetorical reasoning skills in TOEFL-type (Test of English as a Foreign Language) essays (e.g., compare/contrast, advantages/disadvantages) and their evaluations according to different rater-based schemes (Carlson, 1988), and the effects of the writing topic (e.g., farming and space exploration) on the writing of Chinese and NS students with particular majors (Y.-M. Park, 1988).

In his substantial study of the causes of difficulties in learning to write in English as an L2, Kaplan (1983) focused on the need to distinguish between "what is culture-bound and what is specifically language bound" (p. 150). He stressed that discourse phenomena that are culture-bound can be explained and illustrated, and it may not particularly complicated to demonstrate that, for instance, in English discourse, reiterating the same point several times in a parallel fashion is considered to be undesirable or that lexical repetition is strongly discouraged. In Kaplan's view, some features of discourse construction can be relatively easy to teach. On the other hand, he emphasizes that in constructing L2 text, the issues of establishing and maintaining a rhetorical topic and developing ideational cohesion in appropriate ways are far more complex because a NNS "brings with him/her the alternatives available in the L1 and applies those alternatives in the L2, thereby creating a tension between the apparent relationship of ideas to topic and the possibly inappropriate realization" (p. 150) of topic construction by syntactic and lexical means. That is, NNSs may bring with them L1-based concepts of what presuppositions about the topic development and its focus may be shared between the writer and the reader and how and which syntactic and lexical devices can be used in text to maintain and focus the topic. Kaplan's experiments, which involved hundreds of subjects, repeatedly demonstrated that NSs and NNSs have significantly different conceptualizations and strategies that they "bring to bear on the development of any given topic" (p. 153) by means of syntactic and lexical choices in their repertoire. According to Kaplan (1987), the features of text that create for clarity, cohesion, and topic maintenance can be particularly difficult to teach because these concepts reflect illocutionary values in discourse that can be as significant as those associated with discourse structure.

In all these studies, practically without exception, pronounced and significant differences were identified in the writing of NSs and NNSs that dealt with discourse and text levels of writing. In particular, contrastive rhetoric research of student essays found that NNSs do not structure, organize, and develop their pieces of writing in ways similar to those of NSs. In the majority of these studies, the results pointed to the fact that L2 writing frequently relies on the discourse structure and logical development found in the rhetorical traditions of students' L1s; for example, the essay organization in the essays of Chinese often followed the construction of discourse in the Chinese rhetorical tradition (Scollon, 1991) and the compositions of Japanese included organizational styles common in Japanese texts (Hinds, 1984).

Lexicogrammatical features of language in NNS essays also exhibited important differences compared to those of NSs. For example, the uses of complex sentences, the passive voice, pronouns, content words, and word length differed significantly in the text of students who were speakers of Arabic, Chinese, Spanish, and English (Reid, 1990). In general terms, contrastive rhetoric research into L2 student essays demonstrated definitively that the structure and language of academic essays, discourse, and text requires persistent and focused instruction, without which NNSs may have difficulty attaining writing competencies expected in the academic discourse communities (Swales, 1990a).

Studies in the Assessment and Evaluation of L2 Writing

Assessment of L2 writing takes places in various academic venues. In addition to L2 standardized tests, such as the TOEFL or Michigan English Language Assessment Battery (MELAB), the assessment and evaluation of L2 writing is also carried out by means of institutional placement tests in both ESL and English composition programs, as well as by faculty in the disciplines, after NNS students are admitted and enrolled in the universities of their choice. Thus, it is important to take a look at the criteria for assessing and evaluating L2 discourse and text to determine the criteria considered to be important in various domains of academic language testing and the larger arena of the academy. A crucial point that needs to be made is that all criteria for evaluating the quality of L2 writing discussed later are concerned exclusively with the product of writing, without regard to the writing process.

One of the most well known organizations created with the direct and overt purpose of assessing L2 language and writing proficiency of NNSs is the TOEFL arm of the Educational Testing Service (ETS), which designs, develops, and administers the test. The Test of Written English is administered as a part of the TOEFL and is rated holistically based on the criteria established by ETS for assessing L2 writing. These criteria are published and disseminated widely together with the TOEFL Bulletin and other ETS materials, such as essay prompts for writing practice and test study kits sold to students who plan to take the test. The criteria established for assessing the quality of essays on the Test of Written English include rhetorical organization and structure, correct sentence- and phrase-level syntax, syntactic variety and range of structures, detailed rhetorical support and cohesion, morphological/inflectional accuracy ("word form"), appropriate uses of vocabulary/word choice, and general "facility in the use of the language" (ETS, 2000, p. 17). The list of parameters for L2 writing assessment developed by the ETS (2000) does not explicitly state what specific levels of competence in L2 discourse and lexicogrammatical features need to be demonstrated in L2 writing to receive high evaluation. However, the criteria for evaluating L2 discourse and text seem to include many of those identified earlier in discourse, text, and corpus analysis of academic prose (Biber, 1988; Swales, 1990a).

The assessment criteria employed in standardized tests of L2 writing proficiency created by MELAB contain discourse as well as syntactic and lexical features similar to those found in ETS publications. In addition to rhetorical organization, such considerations of linguistic variety and accuracy as the use of complex sentences, coordinating conjunctions, and appropriate and broad-range vocabulary, as well as spelling and punctuation, play a crucial role (Hamp-Lyons, 1991). In fact, according to Hamp-Lyons, the MELAB scoring guide for the assessment of L2 discourse and text appears to be a great deal more rigorous than that established by the ETS for the Test of Written English. In line with the features of published academic discourse and text identified in text linguistics in the 1970s through 1990s, in addition to discourse organization and lexicogrammatical features, L2 essays are assessed in regard to topic development, text cohesion as demonstrated in the use of sentence transitions and lexical connectors, coherence and the evidence of structure and planning, the sophistication of communicated ideas, fully fluent, broad, and appropriate vocabulary, and accuracy in punctuation. In fact, the *MELAB Technical Manual* (1994) indicates that, in addition to the topic being "richly and fully developed," "flexible use of a wide range of syntactic (sentence level) structures, accurate morphological (word forms) control . . . control of connections" (p. 7) and a wide range of appropriately used vocabulary are expected among the necessary features of academic text, if it is to receive a high score. In addition, Davidson (1991) noted that inflectional and morphological accuracy, a varied range of syntactic structures, clause coordination and subordination, and the appropriate uses of formal and informal register markers in writing represent the essential assessment criteria for ESL writing developed by the American Council on the Teaching of Foreign Languages.

However, high expectations of L2 discourse and text in standardized tests do not appear to be drastically different from those of rater-based assessments. Research of L2 writing in rater-based holistic assessment and evaluation also occupies a prominent place in studies of L2 writing (Connor & Carrell, 1993; Connor & Lauer, 1988; Hamp-Lyons, 1990). These analyses determined that trained and experienced evaluators of L2 writing often had similar impressions of the writing quality found in academic essays of NNSs. The studies of how raters assess the quality of L2 writing show clearly that such factors as discourse structure and organization, syntactic and morphological accuracy, lexical range and appropriateness, as well as text cohesion and coherence, play an important role (Davidson, 1991).

The studies of rater evaluations of L2 writing further underscore that assessing the quality of writing is a complex process in which a multitude of variables come into play. In addition to the issues of syntactic and lexical accuracy, rhetorical organization, textual clarity, spelling and punctuation, even the legibility of handwriting and paragraphing affected rater evaluations of L2 text (Vaughan, 1991). It is important to remember that on standardized tests, such as the TOEFL and MELAB, the assessment of L2 essays is also based on the holistic judgment of raters who are specially trained to be consistent and selected from among university faculty and ESL teachers (Davidson, 1991; ETS, 2000; *MELAB Technical Manual*, 1994).

In the teaching of ESL and preparatory academic programs, rater-based assessment and evaluation of L2 writing is one of the prevalent means of determining whether a student should be advanced to the next level of study and/or can be considered prepared to enter degree programs in colleges and universities. Similar to standardized placement tests, institutional placement tests are expected to measure specific aspects of writing skills, such as sentence structure, use of cohesion devices (e.g., coordination and sentence transitions), and rhetorical features of essays, such as organization and textual support. Vaughan (1991) investigated the criteria used by raters in holistic essay evaluations of L2 writing. She found that although the measures for assessing writing are somewhat flexible and vary among universities, they usually include considerations of rhetorical organization, grammar (tense and verb errors), morphology and word form, sentence structure (sentence complexity and the frequency of fragments/run-ons), idiomaticity of language use, vocabulary range, and spelling and punctuation. She concluded that although rater-based assessment of L2 writing is common, it may be subjective and, thus, should not be used "to make important decisions in students' lives" (p. 121).

Reid (1993) reported that among the many properties of academic text, L2 student essays are usually evaluated based on discourse organization, the content and the ideas discussed in an essay, vocabulary, syntactic features, and punctuation, paragraphing, and even letter capitalization. Her study shows that the range of vocabulary, the idiomaticity of language in text, the uses of appropriate word form, and "word-form mastery" (p. 236) are considered to be among the most important criteria for evaluating L2 lexical repertoire. On the other hand, the syntactic features of L2 text that are evaluated include a much greater range: sentence construction, the use of complex clausal construction, correct negation, subject–verb agreement, tense uses, correct and appropriate uses of the active and the passive voice, appropriate uses of singular and plural nouns and pronouns, correct word order, articles, prepositions and prepositional phrases, fragments and run-ons, and subject, object, and morphological omissions. Reid emphasized that evaluating L2 essays based on explicit language-centered criteria allows students to assess their own writing in regard to audience expectations of writing quality and, thus, make NNS writers aware of the parameters by which their writing is evaluated.

In the larger academic arena, evaluations of L2 discourse and text take place throughout NNS student careers in university degree programs. Because faculty in the disciplines are not expected to be trained in the complexities of L2 writing, in the 1980s and 1990s, several studies undertook to find out what specific features of university-level discourse and text were deemed important and how L2 written discourse was evaluated in the academy. As an outcome of these studies, it became evident that the skills of university-bound students were not being evaluated exclusively by the ESL professionals who taught them but, rather, the faculty in the disciplines who were on the receiving end of the students' ability to perform the academic work ordinarily expected of all college students (Johns, 1997; Kroll, 1979), for example, read textbooks, take written exams, and produce analytical research papers.

To determine the expectations of the faculty in the disciplines, ESL researchers and curriculum designers undertook to investigate what specific L2 skills had to be addressed to improve their students' foundational language skills. A large body of work emerged to describe the views of the faculty on the types of reading, writing, listening, note taking, and other tasks required of NNS students. Because NNS students were enrolled in widely divergent disciplines, such as natural and social sciences, business, engineering, and urban planning and architecture, the faculty in many departments were surveyed separately, and their responses analyzed from several perspectives. For instance, the importance of various types of language skills valued by education faculty differed from those that had a top priority in natural sciences or urban studies (Kroll, 1979; Ostler, 1980). Professors in social sciences, biology, physics, and engineering were asked to evaluate the severity of various types of ESL linguistic, discourse, and lexical errors (Johns, 1981; Santos, 1984; Vann, Meyer & Lorenz, 1984;). However, it appears that the parameters employed in the evaluations of L2 writing by university faculty (Johns, 1981) and institutional raters of L2 placement essays (Vaughan, 1991) are not particularly different from other assessment criteria established for standardized and proficiency tests.

Horowitz (1986) investigated the types of writing tasks students were expected to perform in the disciplines. However, when he sent out 750 requests to faculty to provide information on the types and contents of assignments in their courses, only 38 responded, and his study findings were based on this reduced sample. Horowitz found that written assignments included substantial work on identifying connections between theory and interpretations of data, synthesizing information from published sources, and research projects. In well over half of the assignments, faculty provided detailed instructions for content organization, lexical clarity, a need for an explicit and clear thesis, coherence, and argumentation support. Horowitz concluded that in ESL programs, instruction must focus on the recognition and organization of data and "de-emphasize invention and personal discovery" because the academic writer does not create personal meaning. These concepts are "absent outside of English composition," and in the disciplines, concerns of "academic writing texts (sentence-level grammar, use of discourse markers, and so on) remain vital" (p. 455).

It is interesting to note that in many disciplines, in their evaluations of L2 writing, faculty were particularly concerned with the product of writing and were not interested in the process of its creation. Faculty expectations concentrated on the traditional features of academic writing, for example, grammar (e.g., morphology/inflections, verb tenses and voice, and pronoun use), sentence structure, vocabulary, the syntactic word order, and spelling and punctuation (Ostler, 1980; Santos, 1984; Vann, Meyer, & Lorenz; 1984,). The faculty appraisals of the types of tasks NNS students were expected to perform often included analyses of the shortfalls in NNS language preparation.

For example, Vann, Lorenz, and Meyer (1991) surveyed 490 faculty in a large state university to identify the criteria according to which NNS writing is evaluated in the disciplines. In their study, the faculty who responded to the questionnaire included professors in humanities, education, social sciences, engineering, mathematics, physics, and natural sciences, such as biology, agriculture, and medicine. The researchers reported that in academic assignments and papers, the faculty considered the appropriate and accurate use of English syntax, morphology, and lexis to be important and specifically noted L2 problems with verb forms, tenses, the passive voice, and various features of the noun phrase (e.g., singular and plural distinctions), although they were less concerned with prepositions and article uses. Other studies, such as those of Santos (1984), Horowitz (1986), and Johns (1981) also endeavored to investigate the characteristics of L2 discourse and text that were perceived to be essential in the evaluation and assessment of NNS writing among the faculty in various departments, including English. Their results indicate clearly that the expectations of faculty remain consistently focused on lexicogrammatical features of text, such as sentence structure, vocabulary, the syntactic word order, morphology/inflections, verb tenses and voice, and pronoun use, as well as spelling and punctuation.

Earlier research has established that certain linguistic features are prevalent in academic text in English, and the study discussed in this book narrowly focuses on the rates of their uses in essays composed by L1 and L2 writers. One of the benefits of this analysis is that the findings can serve as a basis for curriculum and course design in the teaching of L2 writing and composition. Although impressionistic ratings represent the most prevalent means of assessing L1 and L2 writing, several studies have demonstrated that these ratings are not always consistent, and their outcomes can be misleading (Hamp-Lyons, 1990; Hinkel, 1997a; Mohan & Lo, 1985; G. Taylor & Chen, 1991). On the other hand, comparisons of uses of linguistic and rhetorical features found in actual L1 and L2 writing can allow for specific and detailed analyses of similarities and differences, and thus, help explain the bases for such impressionistic ratings.

3

Written Discourse and Text in Different Rhetorical Traditions

Following Kaplan's (1966) publication, applied linguists, ethnographers, and L2 teachers became interested in discourse and text conventions in rhetorical traditions other than Anglo-American. In part, their interest was driven by their realization that little was known about the rhetorical frameworks outside the English-speaking world and by the need to understand the writing traditions that seem to have affected the L2 writing of NNS students in the academy. After all, whereas a great deal of knowledge was becoming available about the discourse and text construction of academic prose in English, it seemed to be difficult to propose that L2 discourse and text paradigms in NNS writing were affected by their L1 socialization into discourse and language use when little information about them was available.

The examination of rhetorical traditions and their discourse manifestations in non-Anglo-American traditions has largely been carried out by means of ethnographic studies, in which researchers provided detailed and thorough descriptions of how discourse paradigms and text are constructed. Ethnographic studies combine methodological elements of several disciplines, such as anthropology, discourse analysis, sociolinguistics, and cross-cultural communication. The discussion in this chapter first takes a look at the findings of ethnographic and communication research and follows with what has been learned about various discourse traditions in contrastive rhetoric studies. As has been mentioned, the Hallidayan approach to text analysis focuses on the function of linguistic features of discourse and text, and some examples from text analyses dealing with languages other than English are also presented. However, because the study discussed in this book is devoted to how NNS students construct discourse and text in English as L2, this overview also briefly notes research on the obstacles students face in learning to write according to the norms of the L2 academic discourse community that are often crucially different from those in the students' L1s (Swales, 1990b).

WRITTEN DISCOURSE AND TEXT IN NON-ANGLO-AMERICAN RHETORIC

Chinese, Japanese, Korean, and Vietnamese Rhetorical Traditions

Together with the emergence of a large number of studies on contrastive discourse traditions, much interest arose in how discourse and text are developed in various non-Western cultures and languages. Works on rhetorical traditions, such as Chinese, Japanese, and Korean, occupied a prominent place in ethnographic studies because the number of students who spoke these languages as their L1s was rising in U.S. colleges and universities. The ethnographic studies of John Hinds in the 1970s and 1980s are particularly notable.

In his studies, Hinds (1975, 1976, 1984, 1990) analyzed discourse organization and features in Chinese, Japanese, Korean, and Thai, although his work on Japanese and Korean rhetoric has had the greatest impact. Hinds found that rhetorical traditions in many Asian languages have several common features that actually determine the flow of information in text. For example, the purpose of a text (e.g., an essay thesis) is delayed until the end of the piece of writing, causing it to be inductive rather than deductive as is common in Anglo-American writing. The goal of such discourse organization is to convince the reader of the validity of the writer's position and lead the audience to support the writer's stance, instead of employing overt persuasion, which may be considered to be excessively direct and forceful. Hinds was one of the first researchers to point out that overall, there are few common characteristics between the Anglo-American discourse structure and that in Asian languages. He noted, for instance, that the notion of a paragraph and its purposes of ideational division of text is not proximate to the discourse apportioning in Japanese (Hinds, 1975) and that Korean text flow is often structured along the lines of ideational sequence rather than the relevance of ideas to the text's purpose (Hinds, 1976).

Given that discourse is a social activity that involves both the writer and the reader, Hinds (1987) further explained that discourse construction in

Japanese, Korean, and Chinese places the responsibility for text clarity and explication on the reader and not on the writer as is considered to be the norm in written discourse in English. That is, the writer is vested with the authority to be ambiguous, vague, and indirect, and it is the reader's task to tease out the text's meaning and purpose. An implication of discourse ambiguity and the reader's role in understanding the text is that an overt statement of purpose in an essay is actually unnecessary and that the discourse structure does not need to follow the kind of logical progression of ideas that it does in Anglo-American text. Furthermore, Hinds commented that because text clarity does not represent one of the writer's objectives, discourse unity and coherence are also not common in writing in Japanese, Korean, and Chinese: The reader is ultimately responsible for understanding how and why ideas are included in the text. In particular, his 1984 study of how Japanese students process written text in Japanese and English makes a powerful point that, in reading, many were unable to identify the discourse structure in English because they were not expecting to find the main point of the essay stated at the beginning, the ideas to be hierarchically organized, and the paragraph divisions to reflect the separation of ideas.

Because in many cases, discourse construction may not be separable from the syntactic and lexical features that serve to support the discourse purpose, Hinds' analyses also involved a detailed examination of the functions of textual features in Japanese and Korean. He indicated that these languages include large numbers of ambiguous nouns, particles, referential and indexal pronouns, and adverbs that can impart multiple interpretations to the author's meaning. In fact, Hinds explained that the eloquence of text is often judged by the degree of its textual ambiguity that allows the author to convey variable ideas with economy, while inducing the reader to ponder the writer's meanings (1976) and "to ferret out whatever meaning the author has intended" (1987, p. 152).

The indirectness in the L2 writing of Chinese students was similarly identified by Matalene (1985), who also noted that the main point of their essays is delayed until the end of the text and/or conveyed indirectly. Similar to Hinds' observations about the writing of Japanese and Koreans, she found that ESL compositions of Chinese seem to be rigidly structured and include historical allusions, overgeneralizations, direct appeals to the reader, and proverbs and sayings that are intended to state general truths applicable to practically any audience. The common characteristics of written discourse among speakers of distinctly different languages, such as Chinese, Korean, and Japanese, confirmed Kaplan's (1966) observations that Asian rhetorical traditions share many discourse and text features that NNSs employ in their L2 writing in English. However, it was not until the

1980s that the research into L2 discourse paradigms and contrastive rhetoric identified the influence of classical Chinese rhetoric and Confucian philosophy on the structure of discourse and text in various cultures (although they were alluded to in the work of Hinds in the 1970s).

Confucian rhetoric pursues several clearly established goals: to achieve harmony by recognizing and identifying interests of all members of the society and to benefit them equally, no matter what their social standing and wealth, to attain true understanding of other people, and to clearly represent the author's true nature (Oliver, 1971). To accomplish these goals, Confucius outlined about a dozen persuasive methods, most of which play an important role in Chinese rhetoric today. The purpose of speech and writing is to benefit the audience, to be persuasive by means of supporting one's contentions with the authority of tradition rather than one's own individual ideas and notions, to present the simple truth that is derived from prolonged and thoughtful study of the world and humanity, to be sincere in using persuasion, and to be conciliatory in words and manner of discourse. Other features of Confucian persuasion include not being too lengthy in speech and writing so as not to impose, understanding the prejudice of emotion that can distort the truth, choosing topics that befit the occasion and that are practical, and avoiding matters that lie outside of one's own knowledge and responsibility (Oliver, 1971).

In addition to noting the characteristics of discourse that establish the foundations of Confucian rhetoric, it is also important to note those that are not included. The Aristotelian approach to overt persuasion (*ethos, pathos, logos*) does not assume harmonious social relationships, but rather has the goal of convincing the audience (and appealing to the sentiments of the audience); logical proof and justification of one's position represent part and parcel of rational argumentation; rhetoric is a way of thinking that establishes connections between ideas and benefits the personal goals of the speaker/writer, as well as those who are to be persuaded in the veracity or applicability of the speaker's/writer's ideas. In the Aristotelian discourse still widely accepted in the Anglo-American rhetorical tradition many of these properties of persuasion are reflected in academic writing, for example, representation of the writer's personal goals and points of view, factual validation of opinions and propositions, logical arrangement of ideas in text to demonstrate their connectivity from one to another and to the text's purpose, and discussion and debate of ideas. None of these foundational constructs of rational argumentation are found in rhetorical traditions outside of those based on the Greco-Roman rhetoric and philosophy.

The importance of communication studies on the effects of cultural frameworks in Chinese, Korean, and Japanese discourse and text is that they identify the philosophical underpinnings and communication patterns in the rhetorical traditions of the three languages. The collection of articles, *Communication Theory: Eastern and Western Perspectives,* edited by D. Lawrence Kincaid (1987), made an important contribution to discourse analysis in Chinese, Korean, and Japanese. The contributions to the book examine these discourse traditions in some depth and include, for instance, discussions of Chinese narrative and political communication structures, the influence of Confucianism and Buddhism on Korean discourse and rhetorical patterns, and ambiguity, vagueness, and indirectness in Japanese discourse.

In particular, the studies in Kincaid's (1987) edited volume present an overview of Asian perspectives on discourse and text and point out that classical Chinese rhetoric continues to have a great deal of influence on the structure and organization of modern Chinese discourse. In addition, the Confucian emphasis on writing and rigid structure in discourse were derived from the political philosophy of hierarchical social order, harmony, and beneficence for all members of the society, and these postulates of the rhetorical tradition became preeminent in Korean and Japanese writing, as well. In her study of Korean discourse patterns, Yum (1987) pointed out that Confucian rhetoric has had such a great impact on the structure and text of Korean discourse that it may not be possible to examine Korean rhetorical tradition without specifying the principles of Confucian philosophy. In another chapter included in the volume, Tsujimura (1987) made similar observations regarding Japanese rhetoric and noted that, together with Buddhism, the Confucian rhetorical tradition underlies the written discourse construction, the use of language features in text, and even the very purpose of writing.

The influence of classical Chinese rhetoric and Confucian essay organization on writing and discourse in Chinese, Korean, and Japanese is researched in detail in Insuk Taylor's (1995) volume, *Writing and Literacy in Chinese, Korean, and Japanese.* According to the author, the Chinese civil service exam system was modeled in many Asian countries, including Korea, Japan, and Vietnam. The exams required familiarity with the work of Confucius and the classics and the ability to compose formal essays that strongly adhered to classical Chinese rhetorical paradigms. Usually, the study of Confucian classics began early during the schooling process and continued for several years. Taylor commented that as an outcome, in Korea and Japan, it was practically impossible to be considered educated and literate without detailed familiarity with the philosophical works of the classics and Chinese rhetoric. According to her findings, Chinese, Korean, and Japanese discourse and text rely on numerous and similar paradigmatic patterns that stem from the adoption of similar education in composing and language uses for exposition and persuasion.

In his analysis of the discourse, syntactic, and lexical features of the Vietnamese language, Nguyen (1987) also observed that the traditional Vietnamese system of civil service exams closely followed that adopted in China. The rigorous system of education necessitated years of studying the works of Confucius and other classics. For the exams, knowledge of the Confucian texts and classics, memorization of large portions of classical texts, and the ability to compose a formal essay and a poem in accordance with the classical rhetorical paradigm were requisite. Nguyen reported that according to some historical sources, the political, philosophical, religious, and educational ties between Vietnam and China were so strong that for centuries the Vietnamese considered themselves to be a part of China.

The work of Ronald Scollon (1991, 1993a, 1993b, 1995), as well as the books and articles published jointly with his wife Suzanne Wong Scollon (Scollon & Scollon, 1991, 2001) made an important contribution to the analysis of the influence of Confucian philosophy and rhetoric on Chinese written discourse. R. Scollon (1991) explained that the classical "eight-legged essay" became the standard of the civil service examinations and, hence, formed the established framework of Chinese persuasive and expository prose. The "eight-legged" construction of essays is very specific and clear-cut: The length, the idea organization (the opening, generalization, brief exposition, first, second, third, and final points, followed by a conclusion), and the appropriate topics (social good and harmony, propriety in behavior, and loyalty to tradition and family) are explicitly prescribed. Based on his examination of a large number of essays written by Chinese university students in their L1, Scollon showed that the framework "eight-legged essay" remains the principle form of the discourse in written rhetoric.

In his subsequent work, R. Scollon (1993a, 1993b) also found that text construction in classical Chinese rhetoric employs subtle and ambiguous forms of persuasion, such as inductive reasoning (also noted by Hinds, 1975, 1976, 1990) in Korean and Japanese discourse), overstatements and broad generalizations intended to reduce the writer's responsibility for the truthfulness of the proposition, rhetorical questions, and repetition. According to R. Scollon (1993a) and R. Scollon and S. W. Scollon (1991), these features of text, as well as the employment of conjunctions to establish text and discourse cohesion, direct appeals to the audience and, hence, the use of second-person pronouns reflect the traditional Confucian rhetoric that even today is commonly used in formal Chinese writing and oral discourse. R. Scollon and S. W. Scollon (1995) commented that the Confucian tradition of hierarchical social relationships also applies to the distribution of responsibilities between the writer and the reader and that the writer's authoritative stance shifts the responsibility for text clarity to the reader, also discussed in regard to the Korean and Japanese systems (Hinds, 1987).

On the other hand, Maynard (1997) noted that although some Japanese discourse paradigms represent direct borrowings from Chinese rhetoric with their allusions to history and philosophical works, vagueness, and indirectness, others do not. She commented that although in practically all Japanese discourse structures the conclusion is rarely made explicitly, in certain written genre, such as newspaper editorials, commentaries, and opinion columns, the writer's views are expressed directly. Maynard explained, though, that in her study, only 12% of all news articles included the writer's statement of opinion in the initial paragraph. She further pointed out that with the advent of technology, article syndication by international news agencies, and rapid transmission of written texts, the practice of stating the purpose of writing at the outset is likely to become more common. In regard to the L2 writing of Korean students, C. Lee and Scarcella (1992) noted similar developments: the growing number of Koreans educated in Western countries, the increases in the numbers of ESL teachers who are NSs, and the changing expectations of the English proficiency in Korean education and business, the Korean rhetorical tradition based on the Confucian "eight-legged essay" may also undergo change and become more Westernized.

A number of researchers (Ahn, 1995; Fu & Poon, 1995; Kohn, 1992; C. Lee & Scarcella, 1992; Namba, 1995; Tse, 1995) point out severe shortcomings in national and standardized curricula for the teaching of writing and writing in English in particular in such locations as China, Hong Kong, Taiwan, Japan, and Korea. These authors uniformly commented that in general, writing instruction in these countries does not accomplish instructional objectives imposed by the government, and the teaching of writing in English fares far worse than that in students' L1s. Overall, according to these researchers, the teaching of English in China, Hong Kong, Taiwan, Japan, and Korea leaves much room for improvement in practically all students' L2 skills, including writing.

One notable exception to this rather dismal picture is the teaching of writing and English in Singapore, where English is the premier language of the four official languages and is the main medium of instruction at all levels of schooling. However, even in Singapore a wide gap exists between the curricular expectations of learners' L2 writing proficiency and their actual skills, because Singaporean teaching of English is geared toward examinations and test scores rather than language competence (Pakir & Ling, 1995).

A Bit of Indonesian History

Unlike the Chinese, Korean, and Japanese rhetorical traditions, the structure of written discourse in Indonesian has not been researched in detail, and in fact, only scant information is available. The reason that Indonesian rhetoric has received little attention in the literature is that until recently, the numbers of Indonesian students in U.S. universities were rather small, and Indonesian trade ties with the United States were relatively insignificant. For example, the only text on the social aspects of speech in Indonesian available in English was published in 1967 and the most recent book on the history of the language in 1959. In the 1990s, however, the population of Indonesian students began to grow dramatically and has continued to increase following the political upheaval and the economic downturn in that country.

It is important to point out that Indonesian is not the mother tongue of the majority of the population in Indonesia, and native speakers of this language represent a rather small minority group (7%). All in all, around 300 different languages are spoken on the Indonesian archipelago, and their exact number is not known. Only several major languages, such as Javanese and Sundanese, had orthography and a developed writing system. During a large part of the country's early history, Malay was the official language of the country's government and the legal system. However, the official written language went through many changes that reflected the political and government control of Indonesia, such as the Portuguese in the 16th century, followed by the Malacca sultanate in the 17th century. The Malacca government had a great impact on the rhetorical tradition of the country and adhered to the Islamic rhetorical traditions.

More recently, at the beginning of the 19th century, Indonesia was divided into the Dutch and the British political territories (Prentice, 1987). It was the Dutch that oversaw the centralized government, the government educational system, the universities, and the production of books, newspapers, and virtually all print media. In particular, during a large part of the 19th century and the first half of the 20th century, Indonesian writers, scientists, and intellectuals were educated in Holland and, to a smaller extent, Great Britain. Until 1945, Dutch was the language used in practically all formal writing. In the 1930s, however, the government made a concerted effort to reduce the vast number of languages spoken on the archipelago by mandating the use of Indonesian in small outlying communities, where the greatest number of various languages is spoken (Walker, 1993). These efforts resulted in substantial language shifts toward Indonesian among many indigenous groups, who speak hundreds of different languages. The modern Indonesian orthography that attempts to unify many official languages adopted on the archipelago was developed in 1972 (Cribb & Brown, 1995).

It is important to note, however, that a vast majority of Indonesian students in U.S. colleges and universities are ethnic Chinese, whose families settled in Indonesia at the beginning of the 20th century and who were allowed to retain their Chinese citizenship until the 1980s (Cribb & Brown,

1995). Recently, following the political turmoil of the 1990s when the Chinese minority was persecuted and when many lost their livelihoods in the anti-Chinese riots, large numbers of ethnic Chinese students and immigrants began to enter the United States, Canada, and Australia, and this migration trend is expected to continue and increase. Because the Chinese minority in Indonesia represents the most affluent and educated section of the population, in many cases, those who can and choose to emigrate speak fluent English. A great majority of educated Indonesian Chinese studied in universities in Europe (particularly, Holland), the United States, Australia, and Singapore.

The Arabic Rhetorical Tradition

Due to the proliferation of Islam throughout the Middle East, Northern Africa, and parts of India, the Arabic language exerted a great influence on the languages of the people in these regions. The spread of Islam and the linguistic influence of Arabic resulted in the fact that today, many regional dialects are spoken in various Muslim countries (around 50 in all), and the distinction between Classical Arabic and the dialects needs to be made as it applies to the rather divergent types of spoken and written discourses (diglossa). The "high" style used in formal contexts (e.g. university texts and lectures, print media, the Koran, and sermons) is learned through formal education, and "low" colloquial styles of speaking and writing in local dialects (e.g., used in newspapers or magazines) is the native language of most speakers of Arabic (Kaye, 1987).

Despite the fact that Arabic rhetoric has an ancient tradition, to date, no in-depth study of Arabic discourse has been published in English. Thus, several articles that appeared in the 1980s and 1990s are included in this overview to provide a general idea of the discourse and text in the Arabic rhetorical tradition. The importance of the Koran for the development of the foundations of the society, morality, government and legal systems, education, and rhetoric in the Arabic culture cannot be underestimated, and it may not be possible to understand the guiding principles of Muslim sociocultural frameworks without understanding Koranic doctrines. The 114 chapters of the Koran not only serve as a model for writing, but are often considered to be the epitome of Arabic rhetoric to be emulated, memorized, and closely followed (Nydell, 1997). Koranic chapters consist of rhythmic verses that are to be recited for the purposes of education because of the beauty of its style and language and the highest social value of its content. In traditional Arabic education, reciting and analyzing the verses is inseparable from the very process of learning. A great deal of prestige and stature is accorded to writing in Classical Arabic, and other types of texts have a much reduced value and are often considered to be simplistic and trivial. The ability to write in Classical Arabic is much admired, and to become literate, students are required to attain at least some proficiency in the classical language, instead of the daily uses of Arabic and its dialects (Nydell, 1997).

The existence of two different styles in Arabic discourse has many social and political implications in the various contexts of language use. Although Modern Classical Arabic is taught at all levels of schooling, including the university, people's eloquence and erudition are frequently judged by the how well they can use the "high style." However, the quality of education among schools and even countries differs widely, and so it does among the Arab students in U.S. colleges and universities. Though many researchers in L2 writing and contrastive rhetoric believe that Arab ESL learners transfer written discourse paradigms and textual features from their L1 rhetoric, it is not always clear whether they rely on the rhetoric and style of Classical or colloquial Arabic, predominantly used in almost all dialects.

For instance, in her study of L2 writing of Arab students in a U.S. university, Ostler (1987) pointed out that the influence of the Koran on the construction of written prose in many Arabic countries is so great that until today, language study and scholarship, as well as grammar teaching in schools focuses on Classical Arabic, in which the Koran is written. She also noted that "a diglossic condition" (p. 173) has developed among native Arabic speakers who do not use the Classical Arabic taught in schools in their daily lives. Formal and semiformal oratory adheres to the high Koranic style, in which the syntactic structure of the language creates balance and rhythmic coordination, symmetrical word order, and the uses of adjectives and relative clauses. In particular, she commented on the prominence of adjectival modification of nouns, coordinated construction of sentences and phrases, and relative clauses used to attain the parallel balance of the appositive relationship between the subject and the predicate portions of the sentence. The results of Ostler's study show that compared to the discourse organization and the syntactic structures of essays written by NSs, the rhetorical style of Classical Arabic has had a great deal of influence on the writing of ESL Arab students. Ostler also commented that the writing of these students exhibits many discourse and text features not typically found in the writing of NSs, such as the parallel development of main and dependent clauses, a high frequency of coordinating conjunctions, and complex strings of adjective, verb, and prepositional phrases.

However, researchers of the Arabic rhetorical tradition make a distinction between the discourse and rhetoric of the high style and other types of writing. Sa'adeddin (1989) pointed out that "aural" and "visual" (p. 38) modes of text in Arabic represent two options in discourse construction.

The "visual" style is prevalent in formal rhetoric and scholarly writing and does not include repetition, parallel construction of coordinate phrases and clauses, and exaggerations and overassertions, such as those identified in the ESL writing of Arab students. Sa'adeddin noted that, on the other hand, the "aural" style, which has little to do with Classical Arabic, permits repetition of ideas and lexis for the purposes of persuasion, as well as the use of coordinators as sentence and phrase connectors, and the predominance of long clausal strings. In fact, the author pointed out rather sardonically that Arab ESL students probably need much further training in Arabic rhetoric and writing to be able to construct discourse and text in accordance with the norms of Classical Arabic. In his view, the ESL writing of these students demonstrates not the transfer of the discourse paradigms and textual features of the Arabic rhetorical tradition but colloquial "aural" style that is commonplace in daily language use.

Similarly, Fakhri (1995) examined 20 published Arabic texts, 20 published English texts, and 20 English essays written by Arab students to identify differences and similarities in their ideational construction of text. Specifically, his study focused on the uses of nouns to identify sentence subjects and ideational topics, syntactic means of developing text progression (i.e., coordinate parallel constructions or sequential topic development), and ideational repetition. According to Fakhri's findings, there were no significant differences in topic marking and text progression between published Arabic and English texts, both of which contained few parallelisms and coordinating structures. On the other hand, the writing of Arab ESL students showed that they employed a higher number of topics and subtopics without elaboration by merely stating generalized ideas and unsupported claims, which can lead to a construction of pseudo-sequential progression.

Although other researchers, such as Bar-Lev (1986) and Aziz (1988), agree that Arabic written discourse relies on parallelism and coordination of structures, it appears that this rhetorical style does not represent the influence of Classical Arabic and Koranic texts. Bar-Lev found that texts written in Semitic languages are characterized by fluidity, that is, nonhierarchical progression of ideas in topic development, instead of the rigidly ordered topic progression commonly found in English discourse. He also indicated that the syntactic preponderance of coordinating conjunctions, such as *and, but,* and *so,* used in Arabic and other Semitic languages contributes to the fluid style of written discourse. On the other hand, Aziz emphasized that Arabic text relies on the topic/theme and predicate phrase/rheme repetition patterns for the purposes of rhetorical persuasion. He noted that such repetition is frequently employed in parallel constructions and can create an impression that the topics in Arabic essays lack progression.

Rhetorical persuasion strategies, however, represent culturally bound notions, and their manifestations in text can have different values in various cultures. Johnstone (1989) found that the ESL writing of Arab students frequently displayed persuasion devices considered to be inappropriate in academic discourse in English. She observed that the uses of emphatics, amplifiers, and paraphrases of earlier text from the same essays were common and seem to be unlike the persuasion devices in the essays of NSs. She also made similar observations of persuasive techniques employed in formal interviews when Muslims often use analogies and poetic discourse, restatements, and repetition to make their points decisively. In her view, analogical and paraphrasal persuasion is narrative in style and is rooted in the belief that analogies and traditional allegories pivot on historical precedents instead of evidence and logic based on the rhetoric of Aristotelian argumentation. According to Johnstone, discourse construction and organization in various languages are inseparable from the culture, the history of rhetoric, and the sociocultural frameworks that determine what is and is not valued in text.

LEARNING THE NORMS OF L2 ACADEMIC DISCOURSE

Although today most L2 teachers and researchers largely assume that NNSs in U.S. colleges and universities bring with them the norms of written discourse and text, it is also widely known that attaining L1 literacy and learning to write according to the rhetorical paradigms in L1 represent language skills acquired during the socialization process. Thus, if NNSs are expected to attain advanced L2 writing proficiency to succeed in their studies, they are required to learn to construct written academic discourse and text according to the norms of the L2 discourse community (Swales, 1990a). Nonetheless, the experience of teachers and the many studies of learning to write in L2 show clearly that this is indeed a very difficult process. For instance, Johns (1997) and Prior (1998) reported that even after many years of preparation, the participation of NNS graduate students in the U.S. academy is severely restricted by the shortfalls in their writing skills and ability to produce text and discourse according to the norms of the L2 academic discourse community.

To identify the causes of difficulties in learning the appropriate norms of L2 written discourse, Strevens (1987) proposed that several complex cognitive and sociocultural impediments play an important role and often confound learning. He stated that when the notions of precision in discourse and text, rational argumentation, and logical proof and justification are absent in the NNS L1 discourse tradition, their L2 constructions do not appear to learners to be self-evident and, thus, may be rejected as unnecessary and even undesirable. Strevens further explained that the very fact of teaching L2 academic discourse is an inherently cultural activity.

In sociolinguistics, specifically among the studies on critical discourse analysis and critical pedagogy, which emerged as important schools of thought in the 1980s and 1990s, teachers and researchers alike have begun to question the value, validity, merits, and personal and social costs of teaching L2 discourse conventions to NNSs, who were socialized in language communities and social-cultural constructs dramatically different from those in Anglo-American societies. Among other specialists on the teaching of L2 writing, Johns (1997) and Prior (1998) called for a reexamination of the rigid and restrictive discourse conventions in the U.S. academy to allow NNS writers to analyze and critique the predominant text types. Similarly, Benesch (1996) pointed out that needs analysis and curriculum development in preparatory ESL programs for university-bound students rest on descriptions of the existing discourse norms and conventions in the academy. In her view, NNS students' needs may be better served by initiating a crucial change in the power relationships and challenging the requirements of conventionalized discourse norms, testing, and other characteristics of "teacher-dominated" instruction (p. 734). Nonetheless, despite these critical discourse analysis and pedagogy movements, the crucial question remains whether the powerful majority that controls the participatory mechanisms in discourse and pedagogy can undertake to shape how knowledge is transmitted, obtained, and displayed within the rigid paradigms of dominant cultures (Gee, 1990, 1994; R. Scollon & S. Scollon, 1981).

Following Swales' (1990a) definition of the academic discourse community, Baynham (1995) further proposed that a discourse community shares a register and a set of institutional practices through that register, which has a threshold level of members with a suitable degree of discoursal experience. In his view, one of the expectations of academic essay writing is that novices simply learn to be effective writers in the discourse community and adapt to the discourse conventions. Baynham explained, however, that although such a response may seem to be relatively straightforward, its costs may not be so obvious, particularly in the case of learners whose L1 discourse norms and conventions contravene those of the L2 discourse expectations. According to the author, in this case, some learners, faced with the need to attain new discourse conventions, may see this as abandoning the ways in which they were socialized to see writing, the conventions of writing, and the purpose of written text. Baynham emphasized that learning the conventions of L2 discourse is not necessarily additive but can be subtractive. In his view, the problems in learning L2 discourse seem to arise when the conventions of one sociocultural or discourse community contradict those of another, particularly when a relationship of unequal power of one language and another requires accommodation, whether conscious or unconscious. For learners, "acquiring new discourse conventions, particularly those that are socially powerful, raises important questions of identity: am I the same person that I was before I learned to speak/write like this or has the process changed me? If it has changed me, is the change some sort of betrayal of what I was?" (p. 243).

As Y. Kachru (1999) pointed out, the uses of language in discourse and text are intimately bound up with cultural identity and the social constructs of literacy, and she argued that they should not be prescribed within educational contexts. In Fairclough's (1995) example, in English-speaking academic institutions, a tense relationship emerges between the pressures on NNS students to conform to the norms of the L2 traditional academic discourse and text and their own "cautious and nervous attempts to project their own identity in their writing" (p. 229). This tension is further exacerbated by the faculty's negative evaluations of students' texts if they do not follow the expected conventions of academic discourse. Like Kachru, Fairclough questioned the "appropriacy of appropriateness" (p. 229) in academic discourse conventions and their gate-keeping role within the constructs of the sociolinguistic order, which implies a culturally homogeneous language community.

There is little doubt that in mainstream education in English-speaking countries, faculty almost universally believe that the written discourse of students is expected to follow Anglo-American (and, hence, Greco-Roman) rhetorical conventions (Silva, Leki, & Carson, 1997). Nonetheless, research has shown that successful language learning and acquisition depend on the learner's perceived social, psychological, and cultural distance from the target language community (Schumann, 1977). Thus, it is not obvious whether NNSs from cultures in which discourse is not based on rational argumentation, logical proof, and writer-centered responsibility can indeed make a successful transition to a discourse community that highly values contradictory discourse norms. Grabe and Kaplan (1989) questioned the extent of responsibility that the writer assumes for constructing discourse and text according the expectations of Anglo-American readers and the kinds of shared knowledge the writer can be assumed to have when composing in a language that is not his or her own.

Furthermore, given that NNSs are socialized into rhetorical constructs and discourse genre different from those in the Anglo-American academy, it may be reasonable to believe that they have their own assumptions of how discourse and text are to be constructed and knowledge accumulated, attained, and demonstrated in education (Hinkel, 1999a). One of the common objections heard in the academy is that if NNSs wish to obtain American (British, Canadian, Australian) education, they need to be taught the norms of the Anglo-American academic discourse community, and once trained, NNSs can be expected to adhere to those that are unquestionably requisite. Such arguments, however, seem to be in contradiction with the self-imposed and almost universally claimed mission of developing students' ability to think critically and express their views with (Aristotelian) validity and manifest identity. To this end, the question remains of what indeed is the goal of the Anglo-American academic discourse community and how it plans to educate the rising numbers of the students socialized in other rhetorical traditions.

4

The Goals and Politics of Teaching ESL Writing

It may not be possible to zero in on how NNS students use language features in written text without a brief overview of how L2 writing and composition are taught. This chapter takes a look at prevalent methodologies for teaching L2 writing in many, if not most, ESL programs and outlines the historical progression of these methodologies in the past half a century. Following the brief historical excursus, this chapter also examines some analyses of learning to compose formal prose as a part of language development.

THE IMPORTANCE OF L2 LEARNERS IN THE ACADEMY

During the 1950s, approximately 35,000 international students enrolled in U.S. colleges and universities annually. Their numbers doubled in the 1960s, and in the 1970s, their numbers doubled yet again. In 1984, about 350,000 international students attended U.S. institutions of higher learning. On the whole, a 1,200% increase in the numbers of international students took place between the 1950s and 1990s (*Open Doors*, 1997/1998). The number of immigrants enrolled in U.S. colleges and universities also grew more than tenfold from the 1960s to the 1990s. Currently, in many schools, the two types of NNS populations, international and immigrant, represent 20% to 30% of all students, and their educational and language-training needs have led to significant changes in academic curricula and instruction.

With the growing size of the NNS student population, their language skills and abilities to perform academic tasks have been given a great deal of attention in general education and specialization courses, and particularly so in business and engineering where over half of all NNSs enroll (*Open Doors*, 1997/1998). Many students enter preparatory ESL programs and institutions to improve their L2 skills before beginning their studies in the academic disciplines at universities.

The vast majority of college- and university-bound students in the United States are required to take courses in English composition as a part of their general education to provide them the writing skills essential in their studies. Students usually take these courses simultaneously with other courses in natural and social sciences, business, or engineering. On the other hand, most graduate students enter studies in the disciplines directly.

In the teaching of L2 writing, and its evaluation and assessment, several disparate trends have emerged that are contradictory in their goals and outcomes. When the methodologies for teaching L1 writing to NSs of English moved away from their traditional focus on the product of writing and shifted to teaching the writing process, the teaching of L2 writing to NNSs adopted politically and methodologically congruent trends (Johns, 1990b; Reid, 1993).

On the other hand, outside English composition courses, the evaluations of NNSs' L2 writing skills by faculty in the disciplines and general education courses, have remained focused on the product of writing, and NNS students' ability to succeed in mainstream studies is determined by their performance on traditional product-oriented language tasks, most frequently reading and writing (Leki & Carson, 1997; see also chap. 2, this volume). Furthermore, the assessment of L2 writing skills on standardized and institutional placement testing has largely remained focused on the writing product, without regard of the writing process, by means of which English writing and composition are taught (ETS, 2000; *MELAB Technical Manual*, 1994). The disparity between the teaching methods and evaluation criteria of L2 writing has produced outcomes that are damaging and costly for most ESL students enrolled in academic and language-training programs.

ENGLISH COMPOSITION FOR NATIVE SPEAKERS

In the 1950s and 1960s, the study of rhetoric and composition was predominantly concerned with analyzing literature and the students' writing style. Writing assignments consisted of discussions of literary works, and writing pedagogy mostly addressed grammar and the rhetorical structure. The standards of grammatical and stylistic correctness and rhetorical organization were rather rigid and adhered to the traditional modes of classical writing (Hairston, 1982). The quality of student assignments was evaluated according to the analysis of literature and writing style, which included such considerations as the presence of thesis and rhetorical support, coherence, cohesion, and uses of vocabulary and syntax. The teaching and evaluations of papers and assignments focused almost exclusively on the product of writing.

In reaction to rigid and somewhat restrictive views of stylistic quality and evaluations, methodologies for teaching rhetoric and composition began to move away from a focus on the product of composing. The classical rhetorical formality, the study of literature, and the standards for grammatical accuracy were overthrown in "the revolution in the teaching of writing" (Hairston, 1982, p. 77). Instead of focusing on the product, the humanistic teaching of composition began to emphasize the writing process. The new instructional methodology centered on invention and the discovery of personal meaning, and teachers were expected to help students create ideas and discover the purpose of their composing. In the teaching of the writing process, composing was seen as a means of learning and personal development. The rhetorical features of the writing process include considerations of audience and purpose, and the reason for writing, within the format of expressive and expository rhetorical modes. The process of writing is seen as a purpose-oriented activity of creating, informed by the findings in human sciences, cognitive psychology, and language studies (Reid, 1993).

Within the process-centered paradigm for teaching L2 writing, the process of creating writing is evaluated on the quality of prewriting, writing, and revision. Teachers' jobs include developing and facilitating the student's composing process and recognizing that writing involves both rational and emotional thought processes (Reid, 1993; Zamel, 1982). Because the product of writing is seen as secondary to the writing process, and even inhibitory in the early stages of writing, issues of L2 grammar and lexis are to be addressed only as needed in the context of writing, and NNSs with proficiency levels higher than beginning are exposed to text and discourse to be able to learn from them and, thus, acquire L2 grammar and lexis naturally.[1]

Free writing is greatly encouraged in teaching the writing process, with the goal of providing students an opportunity to express and explore ideas,

---

[1]To deal with shortfalls in student preparation for academic studies, the Writing Across Curriculum (WAC) movement initiated in Great Britain in the 1960s arrived in the United States in the late 1970s. The original and the primary purpose of WAC in the United States is to strengthen literacy skills of minority students in the disciplines. WAC pedagogy centers around rhetoric and academic norms of discourse in the sciences and humanities (Herrington & Moran, 1992).

discover meaning, and develop their own, authentic "voice." For example, such writing topics as "Why do I have to be perfect," "My opinion about myself/my family/my social responsibility," and "The Last Word Was Love," based on the writer's personal views and/or relevant readings (Smoke, 1999) became popular in writing and composition assignments.

Composition pedagogy with its focus on the writing process and the political trends that dominated the teaching of rhetoric and composition in many English departments in U.S. universities in the 1970s and 1980s arrived in the teaching of ESL writing and determined how L2 writing was to be taught and evaluated in composition instruction. However, although the methodologies for teaching L2 writing have changed, in the academic arena outside the composition pedagogy for NSs and L2 students, the assessment of student writing has remained focused on the end product, without regard to the invention techniques, the number of drafts, or the iterations of revision required to arrive at the end product.

L2 WRITING INSTRUCTION
FOR NON-NATIVE SPEAKERS

In the early 1980s, Vivian Zamel published two papers that have proved to be highly influential in the teaching of L2 writing to NNSs. In these papers, she largely equated the processes involved in L1 and L2 college writing and composition. Zamel (1982) advanced a hypothesis that research findings on the composing processes of L1 writers can be applicable to ESL writers because both groups of students may be "experiencing writing as a creative act of discovery" (p. 199). In particular, she observed that the writing of proficient ESL students was basically free of language-related errors and, thus, permitted them to concentrate on the composing processes. She concluded that:

> It is quite clear that ESL writers who are ready to compose and express their ideas use strategies similar to those used by native speakers of English. Their writing behaviors suggest approaches to the teaching of composition that ESL teachers may have felt were only appropriate for native speakers but, which in fact, may be effective for teaching all levels or writing, including ESL composition (p. 203).

In line with this conclusion, Zamel (1982) also recommended that in teaching writing as a process of discovery, teacher-guided revision becomes the main focus of instruction because students learn while they are creating writing. According to Zamel, many facets of the pedagogy developed for teaching L1 writing and composition were also applicable to teaching L2 writing. For example, invention, prewriting, producing multiple drafts of essays, peer review of compositions, and revising became a staple of ESL writing classes because by means of these activities, NNS students were engaged in the writing processes and given opportunities to explore and discover (Zamel, 1982).

In a follow-up article, Zamel (1983) examined the characteristics of the writing process as it was described by six NNS students, "who represented a variety of language groups (Chinese, Spanish, Portuguese, Hebrew, and Persian)" (p. 171). She emphasized that "none" of these learners viewed grammar or lexis as areas of particular concern because they "made meaning first" (p. 180). The learners edited their essays in subsequent drafts, but in some cases, their later drafts were "basically neater copies" of their originals. In Zamel's view, however, the students who were more concerned with the use of language in their writing than the expression of ideas were simply less skilled than those to whom the exploration of meaning was accessible. Despite the fact that such students "had no sense of" possible revision, Zamel's study of the six students who provided self-reports of their writing process served as further proof that the teaching of ESL writing can successfully follow the path developed for NSs in composition courses. She again emphasized that NNS students need to be taught to articulate their ideas, receive "truly effective feedback" from their teachers (p. 182), and "teach us what we need to know" (p. 183).

As a result of these and many other publications that sought to identify similarities between L1 and L2 writing processes (e.g., Johns, 1990b; Krapels, 1990, Reid, 1993), two methodological approaches with product or process objectives emerged in teaching ESL. Applying the writing and composition pedagogy for NSs to teaching L2 writing to NNSs appealed to many ESL instructors because the teaching of L1 writing relied on the research and experience of the full-fledged and mature discipline of rhetoric and composition, which continues to occupy a prominent place in the U.S. academy. Thus, in the teaching of ESL writing, it was possible to find a few shortcuts that, theoretically, could allow ESL teachers and curriculum designers to accomplish their instructional goals based on solid research findings and pedagogical frameworks (Leki, 1995), which were developed, however, for a different type of learner. In addition, because many ESL practitioners were trained based on methodologies for teaching the writing process, employing these approaches, techniques, and classroom activities entailed working with known and familiar ways of teaching. The fact that teaching ESL writing focused on the writing process and revising through multiple drafts also permitted many ESL practitioners to hope that over time, when L2 writers develop and mature, their L2 errors and concerns about grammar and vocabulary use would decrease (Zamel, 1983). In many cases, the quality of writing did get better after teachers corrected students' grammar and lexical errors in multiple drafts (Leki, 1990).

PROCESS-CENTERED TEACHING CENTER STAGE

The popularity and the impact of applying the methods for teaching writing to NSs in ESL pedagogy cannot be overestimated. Many textbooks for ESL writing, solidly rooted in the instruction for teaching NSs have gone through re-editions, and some have become best-sellers (Leki, 1999; Raimes, 1992; Reid, 2000a, 2000b; Scarcella, 1994; Smoke, 1999). Most important, however, the methods for teaching L2 writing and teacher-training materials are almost exclusively devoted to the writing process, similar to the teaching of composition to NSs. In L2 teacher training, little attention is given to the writing product, and as in teaching L1 composition, product-oriented teaching is devalued. As Reid (1993) commented, "the field of ESL writing research has expanded significantly, in many cases paralleling studies of [native English speaker] writers" (p. 33). She noted that within the methodology for teaching L2 writing as process, it is expected that NNS writers would be able to edit their language errors through revision, as their writing skills mature and their proficiency improves. An implication of teaching the writing process is that L2 grammar and lexis are not addressed in the curriculum.

However, in the 1980s, several important points emerged from studies of the views of university faculty on the language needs and skills of NNS students, discussed in some detail in chapter 2. For one thing, because faculty represent a wide variety of disciplines, their opinions on the types of academic tasks in their courses vary a great deal. Although reading skills are seen as essential by faculty in practically all domains of academics, writing essay exams is not (Horowitz, 1986; Ostler, 1980; Santos, 1984). Another outcome of these surveys was a realization among researchers and ESL professionals that in general, little was known about the genre of academic reading and writing tasks and the genre of speaking and writing in various disciplines. It also became apparent that academic ESL programs could not adequately prepare their students for the tasks that were not clearly understood and/or were extraordinarily diverse (Leki & Carson, 1997).

CONTENT-BASED INSTRUCTION FOR WRITING IN THE DISCIPLINES

The studies of faculty assessments of the needed L2 skills gave rise to an ESL teaching methodology centering on content-based instruction. Brinton, Snow, and Wesche (1989) argued in their book *Content-Based Second Language Instruction* that "for successful language learning to occur, the language syllabus must take into account the eventual uses the learner will make of the target language" (p. 3). Thus, the authors proposed that the

51

informational content perceived to be relevant by the learner is bound to increase motivation for learning. Most important, however, they emphasized that in line with the communicative methodology for ESL teaching (following Krashen's comprehensible input hypothesis), appropriate language input creates a necessary condition for successful language acquisition. In content-based instruction, given the presence of comprehensible input, the learner will develop the associations of form and meaning required for successful "comprehension [that] feed into a developing stock of formal, functional and semantic relationships" (p. 3) and acquire new elements of language. The authors further proposed that comprehended input in the target language "is a sufficient condition for acquiring productive skills in the second language" (p. 3).

Content-based methodology advocated an instructional method of language use and exposure to relevant domains of language based on the evidence of "soldiers, traders, immigrants, inhabitants of border areas, prisoners of war, . . . and even tourists" (Brinton et al., 1989, p. 4). The authors observed that these types of learners acquired L2 skills through contact with speakers of the language, when the contact is extensive enough and motivation sufficient. Thus, for university-bound learners, the content-based model of language teaching incorporates theme or topic-based sets of materials for reading and writing in academic-like domains, such as "heart disease, noise pollution, solar energy . . . " (p. 15).

Although the content-based methodology for ESL teaching did not discuss the development of academic L2 writing skills specifically, it was adopted in many preparatory programs. The reason for its popularity stemmed from its intuitive and experiential validity for ESL teachers and researchers, who are in most cases NSs, that is, this is how they themselves learned to read and write academic texts, and thus, their L2 students also could. For example, Brinton et al. (1989) cited the experience of UCLA freshmen enrolled in a summer program, where the students were able to link the content of material on geography with the rhetorical modes of constructing text. However, the proposed approach to teaching did not indicate whether university-level ESL students can be similarly enabled to read academic texts and produce research papers in the disciplines, such as the sciences, engineering, and urban planning.

THE OUTCOMES

In the 1990s, research continued into the types and ranges of skills necessary for NNS students' effective functioning in academic studies. Two trends have emerged as particularly prominent, English for academic purposes (EAP) and English for specific purposes, which has gained sufficient recognition to publish its own journal. The former deals with general academic preparation of ESL students for studying in colleges and universities in English-speaking countries and includes the teaching of various academic skills, such as reading, writing, listening, speaking, and note taking (Flowerdew, 1995; Jordan, 1997). However, in most programs, the L2 writing pedagogy is process oriented with the instructional goal of preparing students for English composition courses. The latter narrowly addresses writing skills in the disciplines, such as exact and natural sciences, engineering, and law (Berkenkotter & Huckin, 1995; Dudley-Evans & St. John, 1998).

Johns (1997) found that even advanced and highly trained NNSs enrolled in U.S. universities continue to struggle with language-related problems in their writing. She cited many examples of graduate and undergraduate students who, after years of ESL training, fail to recognize and use appropriately the conventions of academic written discourse. Johns pointed out that NNS students often produce academic papers and essays that faculty perceive to be vague and confusing, without an explicit thesis, rhetorically unstructured, and overly personal. In the view of many faculty she interviewed, in addition to discourse-related problems, the writing of NNSs lacks sentence-level features considered to be basic, for example, appropriate uses of hedging, modal verbs, pronouns, the active and passive voice (commonly found in texts on sciences), balanced generalizations, and even exemplification. As an outcome of the faculty views of the NNSs' overall language and particularly writing skills, Johns pointed out the sense of frustration and alienation that many NNS university students experience because they often believe the faculty to be unreasonably demanding and exclusive, and their own best efforts unvalued and unrecognized.

The effectiveness of EAP writing courses in preparing NNS students for actual academic writing in universities was discussed by Leki and Carson (1997). They found that "what is valued in writing for writing classes is different from what is valued in writing for other academic courses" (p. 64). Because many writing classes in EAP programs follow the methodologies developed for the composition teaching to NSs and focus on the writing process, Leki and Carson found that this type of teaching does not help ESL students "produce writing based on a reality external to their own thoughts" (p. 61). For example, in academic tasks that require students to work with texts, synthesis of information, or explanations related to their disciplines, the pedagogical approach of discovery and self-expression is not particularly helpful. Leki and Carson concluded that the teaching of writing in EAP programs needs to provide their students linguistic and writing skills that can enable learners to "encounter, manage, and come to terms with new information" (p. 61) and expand their knowledge base.

From a different vantage point, Chang and Swales (1999) investigated specific discourse and sentence-level writing skills of highly advanced NNS students, many of whom had spent years writing academic papers and graduate theses. These students reported that they had considerable difficulty "learning the rules of formal academic English" (p. 166) and distinguishing formal and informal registers in writing. In addition, the advanced NNSs were surprised to learn that sentence fragments, direct questions, first-person pronouns, and imperatives were not considered appropriate in most types of formal academic writing. The authors concluded that academically oriented NNSs need to be made aware of the rhetorical and sentence-level features and constraints prevalent in formal written discourse. An implication of the Chang and Swales findings is that even for advanced and highly literate NNSs, exposure to substantial amounts of reading and experience with writing in the relevant context does not ensure that learners become aware of discourse and sentence-level linguistic features of writing and acquire the necessary writing skills. The authors concluded that explicit instruction in advanced academic writing is needed.

THE CRUX OF THE ISSUE

The process-centered approach to teaching writing, however, seems to overlook the fundamental fact that NSs already have highly developed (native) language proficiency in English, whereas most NNSs dedicate years to learning it as a second language, in most cases as adults. Furthermore, as numerous studies in ESL learning and acquisition have shown, it is not clear whether a majority of NNS students in colleges and universities can succeed in attaining nativelike English proficiency even after years of intensive study that includes exposure to English language interaction, text, and discourse.

The model of the writing process developed by Bereiter and Scardamalia (1985, 1987, 1989) stipulates that recounts of experiences represent a form of text production that is accessible to practically all language users, and such narratives usually take place in conversations. Writing assignments as, for example, *What I did last summer* or *My vacation in my country* differ little from those that take place in conversational narratives and represent knowledge telling. What is required of the writer working with such assignments is to think about what they personally or someone else did during the summer or a vacation and write down their thoughts, often in chronological order. Another type of writing assignment that also requires writers to engage in knowledge telling deals with what Bereiter and Scardamalia (1987) called "opinion" essays that contain only two main elements: the "statement of belief and reason" (p. 8). Some of these essays may require multiple reasons, and at slightly more advanced levels of writing, anticipation of counterarguments, as is often expected of ESL writers when they need to construct balanced points of view and develop argumentative essays (Leki, 1999). Bereiter and Scardamalia (1987) also pointed out that knowledge-telling type of writing expects students to simply narrate what they already know, that is, retrieve the content from memory based on the prompt cues. As the next step, they need to organize the retrieved information according to a form appropriate within the structure of composition and in accordance with a few prescribed conventions for discourse organization, for example, overt topic markers and/or lists of reasons *(my first reason, the second reason, the third reason, . . . in conclusion . . .)* that are also retrieved from memory.

Knowledge telling represents the simplest type of essay writing because it necessitates little information or information processing beyond the writer's personal memories, experience, or thoughts. In this type of essay production, writers can generate text on practically any topic that they are familiar with without external information or support. Furthermore, according to Bereiter and Scardamalia, such text, based on readily available knowledge and reports of personal experience, usually conforms to the expectations of the genre and formal features of written discourse because it relies on already accessible discourse-production skills and contextual cues available in the prompt. The authors' research shows that when it comes to knowledge-telling essays, writers can get started in a matter of seconds and quickly produce essays on many topics available in their personal experience.

In the case of L2 learners, who also have access to L1 discourse organization skills such as the eight-legged structure in the classical Confucian rhetorical tradition or the description/generalization rhetorical patterns of Arabic prose, writing a L2 essay that conforms to the norms of L1 discourse paradigms based on personal experience or the statement of opinion represents a direct knowledge-telling task. Furthermore, advanced, trained, and experienced NNSs, as the student writers in this study, would have little trouble producing text according to the norms of the process-centered teaching of writing, to which most are exposed for a number of years during their intensive and academic writing instruction.

There is little doubt that most essays written in standardized testing or placement tests are often limited to the types of writing that induce knowledge telling (or statements of belief and reasons). The process-centered teaching of both L1 and L2 writing also promotes self-expression and discovery of personal feelings in types of written discourse that promote knowledge telling, that is, the simplest and most immediately available recounting of memories, experiences, and opinions, not supported by external information. To compound the problem, the NNSs who are trained within the process-centered paradigm arrive at the conclusion that this is what is expected of them in writing in the disciplines (Johns, 1997).

The Bereiter and Scardamalia model of composing and the psychological variables that are involved in the process also account for another type of writing that they called knowledge transforming. In knowledge-transforming writing, writers are necessarily involved in thinking about a problem, obtaining the information needed to analyze it, reworking their thinking as an outcome of having information, and thus, analyzing it. In writing assignments that lead to transforming knowledge, the writing assignment is the reason that writers expand and process new knowledge obtained as an outcome of writing. Knowledge transforming is considerably more cognitively complex than knowledge telling, because writers are not involved in merely retrieving information already available to them but derive it from content and integrate with that already available to become obtained knowledge. The process-centered methodology with its focus on self-expression and self-discovery does not provide an opportunity for writers to transform and expand their knowledge.

In addition, Bereiter and Scardamalia emphasized that knowledge transforming is also fundamentally different from knowledge telling in regard to the rhetorical and text-generating skills involved in producing written discourse. Such important considerations of writing as content integration, expectations of the audience, conventions and form of the genre, the use of language and linguistic features, the logic of the information flow, and rhetorical organization are integral components of knowledge transforming. Essentially, knowledge transforming becomes a problem identification, problem-solving, and analytical activity that takes place during the writing process. According to the Bereiter and Scardamalia model, knowledge telling and knowledge transforming describe the cognitive processes entailed in generating discourse and text in composing a piece of writing. They pointed out that the cognitive and mental processes that take place in knowledge transforming also apply to reading and other types of text processing, such as identifying contextual clues, definitions of terms, idea explication, and clarification.

The far more cognitively complex process that Bereiter and Scardamalia called knowledge transforming clearly requires information gathering and processing that cannot occur in the process-centered teaching of writing, which does not involve reality external to writers' own thoughts (Leki & Carson, 1997). Furthermore, the teaching of the writing process in effect discourages knowledge transforming because it is centered on self-expression rather than knowledge gathering. In this sense, it is counter to the classical academic model of writing expected in the disciplines when students are required to obtain, synthesize, integrate, and analyze information obtained from various sources, such as published materials, textbooks, experiments, and the like.

CURRICULA IN L2 COLLEGE-LEVEL WRITING/COMPOSITION COURSES

Between the late 1970s and early 1990s, a large body of work was published devoted to developing curricula for L2 writing classes at the college level. In fact, a concern with the product of writing not only disappeared from student and teacher-training textbooks, but product-oriented teaching of composition became associated with reactionary ultraconservativism. Several publications, for example, Leeds (1996) and Zamel and Spack (1998), include no original papers but reprints of articles published by such renowned proponents of writing process instruction as Peter Elbow and Linda Flower, who are actually not specialists on L2 learning or writing, but developed composition teaching methodologies for NSs.

The process-centered curriculum for ESL writing and composition classes usually includes such ubiquitous components as free writing, invention techniques, reflection, prewriting, rewriting, peer feedback, and revising (Ferris & Hedgcock, 1998). In fact, Sternglass (1997) described a sequence of composition courses in which NS and NNS students were mixed together and wrote on topics dealing with personal identity, complexity of asserting identity, race, ethnicity, and gender and sexual orientation. The curriculum does not include the issue of language development, lexicon expansion, or sentence construction for NNSs. Sternglass commented, however, that "[s]econd-language users may have more difficulty in conveying their meanings to readers than second-dialect writers. . . . Some features in second-language development can only be acquired over time. To expect a student to master all the particulars of tense, subject–verb agreement, and use of plurals . . . " would delay their academic progress (pp. 155–156). Although there is little doubt that expanding one's lexicon and syntactic range takes time, it is not clear, for example, why writing and composition courses cannot expedite students' progress. Furthermore, if students enroll in mainstream classes with limited linguistic range, their lack of language skills may prove to be a serious handicap in their academics. It is not at all surprising that L2 learners have greater difficulty conveying "their meanings" when they rely on a limited repertoire of lexis and syntax with which to express their meanings.

In a similar overview of composition curricula, Weese et al. (1999) described a series of composition courses for NS and NNS students at several colleges and universities. These writing programs are focused on the writing process that includes such classical features as collaborative tasks, peer-group feedback, and self-exploration. Some of the course assignments are based on external sources and reading. However, it seems somewhat ironic that students are taught to prepare formal academic papers based on such topics as "Literacy Autobiography," Richard Rodriguez's "Hunger of Memory," which describes how he became a writer, or "Song of Solomon." The program does not include grammar or vocabulary curricular tasks, for example, summaries or academic text conventions, because in the process-focused teaching of writing, the assumption is that students will attain developed language skills over time. It is difficult to imagine, however, that Chinese, Laotian, or other NNS students enrolled in the program can benefit more from working on their autobiographies, experiences of writers, or biblical love songs than from expanding their ranges of academic lexical or syntactic skills.

In his very short piece on current development in U.S. education, Wildavsky (2000) summarized the situation as follows (the text is cited in full): "Crossed signals: College professors demand correct grammar from incoming students, according to a new survey by the entrance-exam firm ACT Inc. But high school teachers rank that skill last. They care how students organize their writing" (p. 12). From the overview of curricula in process-centered teaching of writing, it appears that NNS students are not likely to do well in courses where professors demand correct grammar. They may do much better in classes where they need to engage in invention, explorations of their identities, or examinations of excerpts from literary memoirs. As has been mentioned, the teaching of the writing process may overlook the key difference between basic writers who are native speakers of English and L2 learners who may not have the language skills to understand their readings very well, not even to mention writing papers on such complex sociological phenomena as ethnicity, racism, or sexual orientation.

5

The Study of Features of Second Language Text: Essays, the Data, and Methods of Analysis

THE PRESENT STUDY

In his noteworthy study of differences between intuition-based and observation-based grammars, Aarts (1991) distinguished between grammatical and acceptable structures and those that reflect actual language use. He pointed out that, for example, prescriptive grammar rules do not account for a wide range of language structures and uses that would be considered grammatical but not necessarily acceptable in real communication. In addition, "language attitudes" (p. 51) often cause evaluative reactions that are not only disparate among native speakers of a language but also that do not necessarily deal with grammaticality or acceptability of particular structures. For example, intuition-based acceptability of sentence- and phrase-level structures does not reflect their acceptability in actual language use, which must be investigated by means of observation-based research and corpus analysis. Therefore, it appears that a detailed analysis of L2 texts is needed to determine their specific features that may affect their quality and, and therefore, evaluation.

The present study combines the methodological advantages of comparative analysis of L1 and L2 texts prevalent in contrastive rhetoric and new developments in corpus analysis developed for published texts. Specifically, the analytical approach based on contrastive rhetoric theory postulates that because discourse and contextual and appropriate uses of language to express meaning in communication, rhetorical traditions and the attendant features of discourse and text are a part of the L1 socialization process. Thus, L2 written discourse and text in the writing of NNSs frequently reflect sociocultural, rhetorical, and textual features prevalent in the L1 discourse paradigms of NNSs in addition to those found in L2. For this reason, by identifying discourse and textual features in the NNSs' L1 discourse frameworks, it may be possible to gain insight into systematic differences between the uses of L2 syntactic, lexical, and rhetorical features and those found in the L1 text of NSs. The empirical research methodology in corpus analyses relies on frequency counts of particular features in large amounts of text. For example, by comparing normalized frequency counts across various text genres, such as newspaper gossip columns and academic articles, the specific features of the genre can be identified and analyzed.

The detailed comparisons of L1 and L2 academic texts written by NSs of American English and NNS students provides a means of identifying the specific divergencies in uses of linguistic and rhetorical features in texts written in proximate contexts and in response to identical prompts. Unlike impressionistic rater-based evaluations of essays, the textual analysis of the essays in this book is structured around the objective features and common characteristics of academic text. Specifically, the text analysis in this study compares the frequencies of use of 68 linguistic and rhetorical features in 1,457 NS and NNS essays written in response to six prompts in placement and diagnostic tests.

In addition to identifying the important textual characteristics of NS and NNS text and the divergences in their uses, however, it is also important to note the characteristics of text and discourse that frequency counts do not identify. For example, frequency counts of linguistic, syntactic, and cohesive features of text say nothing about the discourse structure and organization in L1 or L2 essays. Frequency counts are also not intended to analyze the ideational quality of propositions, their sequencing, or clarity and, hence, contextualization. Similarly, absent from feature counts is information about use of topicalization markers (topic sentences), topic elaboration and progression, as well as evidence for or against argumentation development. However, it should noted that analyses of these features of discourse may simply not be possible to account for in a large corpus of data.

Counting the occurrences of particular features also provides no evidence regarding their correctness or errors in student sentence- or phrase-level syntax. In fact, one of the benefits that frequency counts allow is avoiding the definition of error that has created much debate and controversy in the teaching of L2 grammar (James, 1998). In general terms, analysis of frequency counts of features in a large text corpus and their comparisons provide empirical information about similarities and distinctions between feature uses and, by implication, their prominence in text. Quantitatively looking at usage in a large data set can, however, identify various patterns in language that go beyond idiosyncrasies of individual essays to definite and clear-cut trends in L2 use in written text to guide L2 teaching.

FIRST AND SECOND LANGUAGE ESSAYS AND THE DATA

The Writers

Of the NSs of American English whose writing is included in the data, 89% attended private universities and were first-year students enrolled in required composition classes.[1] The other 11% attended a small public mid-western university and were similarly enrolled in first-year composition classes. Because the placement and diagnostic tests were administered to NSs at the beginning of their first required composition and writing classes, the students had not received prior writing instruction at the university level. Thus, the NS students had not obtained a great deal of experience in formal academic writing beyond instruction typically offered in U.S. high schools in combination with the teaching of basic literature.

All of the 1,215 NNSs had achieved a relatively high English language proficiency, and their TOEFL scores ranged from 520 to 620, with a mean of 563. All NNSs had been admitted to undergraduate and graduate programs in four U.S. universities and pursued studies toward their degrees. About 67% held Associate's degrees awarded by community colleges prior to their entrance to 4-year universities, and the remaining 33% were divided almost equally between first-year (17%) and graduate students (16%).[2] The fact that the majority of the students successfully completed their studies in community colleges, were awarded Associate's degrees, and received admission as juniors in a 4-year university attests to their substantial exposure to U.S. academic frameworks and training. Similarly, the NNS first-year students had been enrolled in U.S. high schools for 3 to 4 years, and some had spent up to 9 years in U.S. schools. It is important to note that relatively few were new arrivals in the United States, and almost all college graduates and graduate students had spent an additional 6 months to 3 years studying English in various intensive and academic ESL programs to prepare for their entrance to colleges and universities.

---

[1]In general, of the 1,481 accredited 4-year universities in the United States, only 453 (30.6%) are public, and 1,028 (69.4%) are private (*World Book Almanac*, 1998).

[2]Among community college graduates, no distinction is made between international students, who are holders of student visas, and immigrant students because all were verifiably successful in their studies, earned college degrees, and were admitted to 4-year universities; that is, regardless of their visa status, they had equal academic standing and credentials required for admission.

All NNSs had received substantial instruction in EFL and ESL and L2 reading and writing, for periods of 4 to 15 years, with a mean of 9.8 years. Their residence in the United States typically fell within 2 to 6 years, with a mean of 3.8. Due to their earlier language training and education in the United States prior to their enrollment at the universities, it follows that the NNSs had had relatively extensive exposure to L2 reading and writing in L2 academic environments (see chap. 4 for a detailed discussion). The graduates of community colleges had studied English in U.S. intensive programs, followed by composition classes in their 2-year colleges. Similarly, of the 23% of NNSs without college degrees, over half graduated from U.S. high schools, where they had also received L2 reading and composition instruction.

Their majors spanned a wide variety of disciplines, ranging from computer science and electrical engineering to accounting, management, marketing, education and educational leadership, the fine arts, history, psychology, sociology, musical composition, and voice studies. Fewer than 6% of the undergraduate students had not declared their majors and were enrolled in general education courses.

The Essays and the Prompts

The prompts for NS and NNS essays were identical in every way (see the list that follows). Because the essay corpus simply represents placement and diagnostic tests routinely administered to all students, no attempt was made to differentiate NSs or NNSs by gender or age.

Both NSs and NNSs wrote their essays in response to assigned prompts that were modeled on the Test of Written English, administered by the ETS, and the Michigan Test of English Language Proficiency, as well as topic prompts that are commonly found in ESL and L1 composition textbooks. In such prompts, as in those in this study, the intention is to elicit writing samples by providing context for the writers based on experiences characteristic of most young adults entering U.S. universities. However, as with all placement tests, it is not always possible to ensure essay contextualization. All essay prompts were designed to elicit writing in the rhetorical mode of argument/exposition with the purpose of convincing/informing an unspecified general audience (Hacker, 1994; Leki, 1995; Y.-M. Park, 1988).

Selecting essays written in response to several different prompts had the goal of reducing the effects of individual prompts on the quality of writing. For example, Carlson (1988) reported that in NNS writing in response to different prompts, the number of spelling mistakes varied in the essays of Chinese students, and frequency of uses of vague words, nominalizations, and passive constructions also fluctuated in the texts written by NSs and the speakers of Spanish. Similarly, Hamp-Lyons (1991) reported that some amount of variation was found in the writing of both NSs and NNSs in different writing tasks.

In the present study, the writing of NNSs is compared to that of NSs both singly in prompt-by-prompt examinations (see chaps. 11 and 12) and as a whole, based on the pooled data by combining frequency counts for all essays written by NSs, Chinese, Japanese, Koreans, Indonesians, Vietnamese, and Arabs to create a broader overview of L2 text features by speakers of various L1s. An additional analysis compares the uses of linguistic and rhetorical features of NSs and NNSs by L1 groups across the six prompts (listed as follows):

1. Some people believe that when parents make their children's lives too easy, they can actually harm their children instead. Explain your views on this issue. Use detailed reasons and examples.

2. Many people believe that grades do not encourage learning. Do you agree or disagree with this opinion? Be sure to explain your answer using specific reasons and examples.

3. Some of the wealthiest, most famous people in the world are musicians, singers, movies stars, and athletes. Do you think these performers and athletes deserve high salaries such as millions of dollars every year? Support your position with detailed reasons and examples.

4. Some people learn best when a classroom lesson is presented in a serious, formal manner. Others prefer a lesson that is enjoyable and entertaining. Explain your views on this issue. Use detailed reasons and examples.

5. Many educators believe that parents should help to form their children's opinions. Others feel that children should be allowed to develop their own opinions. Explain your views on this issue. Use detailed reasons and examples.

6. Some people choose their major field of study based on their personal interests and are less concerned about future employment possibilities. Others choose majors in fields with a large number of jobs and options for employment. What position do you support? Use detailed reasons and examples.

In the subsequent discussion, Prompt 1 will be referred to as the *Parents* prompt, Prompt 2 as the *Grades* prompt, Prompt 3 as the *Wealth* prompt, Prompt 4 as the *Manner* prompt, Prompt 5 as the *Opinions* prompt, and Prompt 6 as the *Major* prompt.

All students were given 50 minutes, that is, one class period, to write the essays, but many did not take full advantage of the time. The issue of how much time should be allowed for placement essays has been somewhat controversial. For example, ETS currently limits the Test of Written English to 30 minutes. Kroll (1990b) found no important differences in either syntactic or discourse characteristics of student essays in L2 essays written during 60-minute testlike conditions or home essays, when students had written without the pressure of time.

Corpus Description and Size

The corpus consists of 434,768 words and 1,457 essays written by speakers of seven languages: NSs of American English, Chinese, Japanese, Korean, Indonesian, Arabic, and Vietnamese. The breakdown of the corpus is presented in Table 5.1 by the number of essays, average number of words per essay, and the total number of words in the essays per L1 group. Excluding NSs, the L1 groups of students represented in the study have been identified as the largest among NNS populations in U.S. universities and colleges, with the possible exception of speakers of Spanish in such states as California, Florida, and Texas (*Open Doors*, 1997/1998).

As is apparent from Table 5.1, on average, Japanese produced the shortest texts with 262 words/essay, followed by Koreans (268 words/essay) and speakers of Arabic (298 words/essay). Those written by NSs and Chinese were of similar length at 294 and 297 words/essay, respectively. Vietnamese and Indonesians wrote the longest texts with 320 and 352 words/essay on average.

As has been mentioned, the essays analyzed in this study were collected during routine administrations of placement and diagnostic tests in composition classes required of all students in five comprehensive universities in the United States, located in Illinois, Ohio, Texas, and Washington, all with high rates of enrollment of NNSs. Although some amount of variation exists in the numbers of NS and NNS texts, the numbers of essays written for each of the six prompts are largely comparable and on the same order. The specific numbers of essays for each prompt are presented in Table 5.2.

TABLE 5.1
Corpus Data by L1 Groups of Writers, Essays,
and the Number of Words in the Sample

L1 Groups	Number of Essays	Number Words/Essay (mean)	Total Number of Words/Sample
NSs	242	294	71,153
Chinese	220	297	65,255
Japanese	214	262	55,996
Korean	196	268	52,489
Vietnamese	188	320	60,157
Indonesian	213	352	74,989
Arabic	184	298	54,729
TOTALS	1,457	295	434,768

TABLE 5.2
Corpus Size by Prompt

L1 Group	Prompt 1 Parents	Prompt 2 Grades	Prompt 3 Wealth	Prompt 4 Manner	Prompt 5 Opinions	Prompt 6 Major
NSs	44	36	36	40	47	39
Chinese	39	39	30	39	34	39
Japanese	32	35	30	34	41	42
Korean	32	33	30	33	32	36
Indonesian	35	35	30	37	35	41
Vietnamese	34	30	30	32	30	32
Arabic	30	32	30	32	30	30
TOTALS	246	240	216	247	249	259

METHODS OF DATA ANALYSIS

Linguistic and Rhetorical Features of Instructed Writing

The linguistic and rhetorical features of L1 and L2 essays discussed in this study include those identified in earlier analyses of corpora of published academic prose in English, and research in writing and composition, as well as features specific to L2 writing. Because the goal of the study is to determine specific differences between NS and NNS uses of a wide variety of linguistic and rhetorical features in L1 and L2 texts, including a broad range of features was given a priority. For example, nouns, pronouns, verb tenses and aspects, conjunctions, adjectives, and adverbs can be found in all texts, including essays. However, because it was not always possible to determine which specific features of text are of greater importance in essay texts, a decision was made to include as many of the linguistic and rhetorical features of text as could be potentially important, based on the findings of earlier research.

The methodology for comparative analysis of NS and NNS writing was originally developed for studies in rhetoric and discourse (Kaplan, 1966). Whereas it may be tempting to approach the analysis of feature counts in NS and NNS essays as an undertaking in contrastive rhetoric, the differences in L1 and L2 uses of features may not be easy to explain by means of L1 to L2 transfer of rhetorical and discourse paradigms. The greatest difficulty with such an explanation lies in the simple fact that many syntactic and lexical features of English do not exist in other languages, whose speakers wrote the essays. For example, Chinese, Japanese, Korean, Indonesian, and Vietnamese do not have inflectional markers of tense and aspect, whereas gerunds, *it*-cleft and existential *there* constructions, and reduced clauses are rare outside of Indo-European languages.

Another problem arises if the NNSs' length of study in the United States is taken into account. When Kaplan (1966) first proposed that speakers of different languages may organize their written discourse according to the norms and conventions found in the rhetorical traditions of cultures where they were socialized, his data included essays written by relatively new arrivals enrolled in an EAP program. On the other hand, the essay writers in this study represent academically advanced and fluent NNSs who had received years of training in the United States. Thus, it would be difficult to determine whether uses of syntactic and lexical features in NNSs' L2 essays hinge on particular characteristics of students' L1s or whether L2 language usage represents an outcome of L2 learning (or teaching) processes. In light of these complexities, the discussion of textual functions of features and their uses in student texts takes a broad-based approach.

In general terms, the selection of syntactic, lexical, and rhetorical features for the analysis of essays was based on four criteria:

1. Their textual functions, meanings, and the implications of their uses in text as identified in earlier research on English language grammar and lexis.

2. The prominence of their uses, meanings, and functions established in corpus analyses of published academic genre in English.

3. The prominence of particular linguistic and rhetorical characteristics found in composition instruction and assessment, as identified in instructional texts for NSs and NNSs alike, as well as research on writing assessment.

4. Whenever possible, consideration of the uses of proximate syntactic, lexical, and rhetorical features in NNSs' L1s: Earlier research in contrastive rhetoric has established that NNSs often employ linguistic and rhetorical features of their L1s in producing texts in L2, when proximate features are encountered in both L1 and L2.

An examination of the seminal works on the English language grammar and lexis by Quirk, Greenbaum, Leech, and Svartik (1985), Greenbaum and Quirk (1990), Brown and Levinson (1987), Chafe (1970, 1986, 1994), Leech and Svartvik (1994), and Halliday and Hasan (1976), corpus analyses carried out by Biber (1988, 1995), Channel (1994), Hoye (1997), and Moon (1998), and discussions of academic genre by Swales (1990a), Swales and Feak (1994), and other researchers resulted in identification of the linguistic and rhetorical features prevalent and expected in Anglo-American academic texts.

In all, 68 features are examined in this study in three categories: (a) Syntactic and Lexical, (b) Clausal, and (c) Rhetorical. Although this division of the textual features is somewhat artificial, it may be difficult to argue that the uses of hedges, rhetorical questions, emphatics, and exemplification markers play a smaller role in the syntactic and lexical structure of text than such features as generic nouns and verb tenses. To determine which features of text could be roughly labeled rhetorical, the work of Halliday and Hasan (1976), Halliday (1994), Huebler (1983), Hermeren (1978), McCarthy (1994), as well as other research on rhetorical markers was surveyed.

Another consideration for the inclusion of particular features in the analysis of the essay data had to do with earlier research on L2 text written by NNSs in contrastive rhetoric studies. For example, rhetorical questions or emphatics are not considered to be a common feature in formal prose or published texts in English. Nonetheless, earlier studies of L2 text and writing determined that NNSs frequently employ these features in formal academic prose, possibly due to their acceptability and prevalence in many rhetorical traditions other than Anglo-American (see chap. 2). For this reason, such rhetorical features of text as rhetorical questions, emphatics, and presupposition markers were also included.

The syntactic and lexical features included in the analysis are organized by their grammatical classes, beginning with nouns and pronominals as the first head constituents of sentences (Quirk et al., 1985) and followed by the verb phrase elements (such as tenses and aspects). The linguistic features are divided into 17 large categories, presented and exemplified in Table 5.3. It is important to note that some of the members of these categories can be ambiguous (e.g., *while* can mark temporal or concessive clauses). However, in the frequency counts, care was taken to distinguish the functions of the ambiguous features. A detailed discussion of their syntactic and lexical, as well as textual meanings and functions can be found in chapter 6. In addition, the study analyzes the uses of seven textual features that play prominent roles in such rhetorical textual constructs as cohesion, clarification, and hedging.

Statistical Analysis of Data

To determine whether NSs and NNSs similarly used the linguistic and rhetorical features in their writing, the number of words in each of the 1,457 essays was counted, followed by a count of the occurrences of each of the linguistic and rhetorical features (see chap. 6 for further discussion). For example, NS essay #1 for Prompt 1 consisted of 250 words and included one exemplification marker *(for example)*. To determine the percentage rate of exemplification markers used in the essay, a computation was performed (i.e. $1/250 = 0.4\%$), and then repeated for three occurrences of adjective clauses ($3/250 = 1.2\%$). The computations were performed separately for each linguistic and rhetorical feature in each of the NS and NNS essays.

TABLE 5.3
Textual Features of Essays Analyzed in the Study

I. Linguistic features

1. Semantic and lexical classes of nouns

   - Enumerative (e.g., *advantage, aspect, category, class, element*)
   - Advance/retroactive (e.g., *approach, background, incident, method, occurrence*)
   - Language activity (e.g., *account, controversy, debate, dispute, irony, language*)
   - Illocutionary (e.g., *answer, appeal, comment, complaint, denial, excuse*)
   - Interpretive (e.g., *analysis, attitude, belief, blunder, cause, concept, mistake*)
   - Resultative (e.g., *finish, effect, end, result*)
   - Vague (e.g., *human being, people, society, stuff, thing, whatever, world*)

2. Personal Pronouns

   - First-person singular and plural
   - Second-person singular and plural
   - Third-person singular and plural

3. Slot fillers

   - Nonreferential *it* in the clause subject position (e.g., *It was easy to see what he was thinking*)
   - Existential *there* in the clause subject position (e.g., *There is always a problem with teenagers in this country*)

4. Indirect pronouns

   - Universal and negative (e.g., *everyone, no one, nothing*)
   - Assertive (e.g., *anyone, some, something*)

5. Nominalizations (abstract generic nouns) (*-ion, -ment, -ness, -ity* suffixation)

6. Gerunds (*-ing* pronominals with noun functions)

7. Verb tenses

   - The past tense
   - The present tense
   - The future tense

8. Verb aspects

   - Progressive
   - Perfect

9. Semantic and lexical classes of verbs

   - Public (e.g., *admit, agree, argue, claim, complain, deny, declare, object*)
   - Private (e.g., *accept, assume, believe, decide, doubt, feel, know, learn, think*)
   - Suasive (e.g., *demand, determine, insist, intend, prefer, request, require*)
   - Logical/semantic relationships (e.g., *apply, cause, compare, conflict, prove*)
   - Expecting/tentative (e.g., *attempt, desire, expect, like, plan, try, want*)
   - *seem* and *appear*

10. Modal verbs

    - Possibility and ability (e.g., *can, may, might, could*)
    - Obligation and necessity (e.g., *must, have to, should, ought to*)
    - Predictive (e.g., *would*)

(Continued)

67

TABLE 5.3
(Continued)

11. The passive voice (with or without the *by*-phrase)

12. Copula *be* as the main verb

13. Infinitives

14. Participles as adjectival or adverbial pre- and postpositional forms

- Present participles (e.g., *an amusing story, a student studying for the test*)
- Past participles (e.g., *a trained musician, the book published last year*)

15. Adjectives

- Attributive (e.g., *a famous singer*)
- Predicative (e.g., *most people in my country are poor*)

16. Semantic and lexical classes of adverbs

- Time (e.g., *already, finally, immediately, now, soon, then, today, yesterday*)
- Frequency (e.g., *annually, daily, frequently, occasionally, usually*)
- Place (e.g., *here, there,* and prepositional phrases, e.g., *in the United States*)
- Amplifiers (e.g., *absolutely, completely, deeply, highly, hugely, severely*)
- Downtoners (e.g., *almost, barely, enough, fairly, merely*)
- Other adverbs (e.g., of manner, *brightly, evidently, quietly, specifically*)

II. Features of Subordinate Clauses

17. Noun clauses

- Noun (nominal) clauses in the subject or object position, with explicit or omitted subordinators (e.g., *What he said hurt my feelings* or *I think (that) professors should pay attention to their students*)
- Noun clauses as adjective complements (e.g., *It is very sad that people go hungry in our rich country*)
- Noun clauses as objects of prepositions (e.g., *So, he showed me in which order to put those things together*)

18. Adjective clauses

- Full adjective clauses with or without subordinators, including pied-piping adjective clauses (e.g., *The family that moved in next door had six children* or *I applied to the colleges in which they had my major*)
- Reduced adjective clauses in postnominal positions, postpositional adjectives, and appositives (e.g., *Parents trying to do the best for their children* or *I want to achieve something important in my life*)

19. Adverb clauses

- Full adverb clauses, marked by the subordinators of:
- Cause (e.g., *because*)
- Concession (e.g., *although, though, whereas*)
- Condition (e.g., *if, in case, unless, provided that*)
- Purpose (e.g., *so, so that*)
- Other adverb clauses (time, place, manner, comparative, sentential)
- Reduced adverb clauses (e.g., *While watching these pianists practice, I learned a lot*)

(Continued)

68

TABLE 5.3

(Continued)

II. Rhetorical features

20.   Coordinating and logical conjunctions/prepositions

  • Phrase-level coordinating conjunctions (e.g., *and, both . . . and, but, yet*)
  • Sentence-level coordinating conjunctions (e.g., *in the first place, to begin with*)
  • Logical/semantic conjunctions and prepositions (e.g., *as well, because of, unlike*)

21.   Exemplification (e.g., *for example, for instance, such as*)

22.   Hedges

  • Epistemic adjectives and adverbs (e.g., *according to, apparent(-ly), theoretically*)
  • Lexical (e.g., *kind of, maybe, sort of*)
  • Possibility (e.g., *hopefully, perhaps, possibly*)
  • Quality (e.g., *as we/you/all know, as the saying goes*)
  • Hedged performative verbs (e.g., *I mostly explained that he made a mistake*)

23.   Rhetorical questions and tags (e.g., *Do you think that children can learn this way?*)

24.   Demonstrative pronouns (e.g., *this, that, these, those*)

25.   Emphatics (adjectives and adverbs) (e.g., *a lot, for sure, great(-ly), outright*)

26.   Presupposition markers (e.g. *obvious(-ly), of course*)

27.   Fixed strings, including phrasal verbs, idioms, and collocations (e.g., *bring up, give the boot, on a shoe string*)

  For example, the sentence *Children grow up the way their parents brought them up* includes two fixed strings, *grow up* and *bring up,* which are counted separately.

Nonparametric statistical comparisons of the NS and NNS data were employed because the majority of the percentage rates were not normally distributed, and a large number of essays did not contain the entire set of the features analyzed in the study. The Mann–Whitney *U* Test was selected as a conservative measure of differences between the NS and NNS data. The Mann–Whitney *U* Test compares two groups of data based on their ranks below and above the median (in this study, NS and NNS rates of frequencies for each individual feature, e.g., NS percentage rates of first-person pronouns in essays written to the same prompt and those of Chinese, then those of NS and those of Koreans, then those of NS and those of Japanese, etc.). The reason that comparisons of averages were not employed in this analysis is that averages often obscure the distribution of frequencies in the sample. For example, if in one NS essay, the rates of first-person pronouns are 20% and in another only 2%, then the average rates of first-person pronoun uses in these essays would be 11%, which clearly does not reflect the frequency distribution accurately. The Mann–Whitney *U* Test ranks the rates in a combined array of NS and each group of NNS, one by one. In this way, it can be determined if, for example, the NS or

NNS rates of every feature are ranked in a cluster near the top or the bottom of the array, or if they are distributed more or less evenly.[3] The medians, ranges, and results of statistical tests are presented throughout the volume, as well as in Appendix B. The ranges are reported to reflect a frequency of use for each feature. Ranges are determined by subtracting the lowest percentages' rate value in a sample from the highest, for example, in the case of the two NSs essays mentioned earlier, where, in one 20.00 (20%) of all words consisted of first-person pronouns and in the other 2.00 (2%), the range would be 18.00 (18%).

Identifying the most common features in NS texts and corresponding features in NNS essays establishes priorities of syntactic, lexical, and rhetorical features in texts written by speakers of various languages. In addition, determining order ranks of features' median rates in NNS texts relative to those of NSs can provide important insights into L1 and L2 use with practical applications of the analysis applying to curriculum design and L2 teaching. Rank orders of median rates of textual features examined in this study were computed separately for each group of writers and are presented and discussed selectively in chapter 14 to focus on those of greatest interest and significance for pedagogical applications.

In addition, because each L1 group of NSs and NNSs wrote placement essays on six different prompts, the study allowed for comparisons of the language feature uses in essays dealing with different topics. The analysis of features used in the essays permits comparisons across prompts to determine whether some induce particularly high or low rates of uses of certain linguistic and rhetorical features, relative to essays written on other prompts by speakers of the same L1. The findings of these analyses are presented in Appendix B.

The Bereiter and Scardamalia theory (Bereiter & Scardamalia, 1985, 1987; Scardamalia & Bereiter, 1987) that accounts for the differences in the writing processes of skilled and less skilled writers was developed primarily for school-age developmental learners (see chap. 4 for a detailed discussion). Their theory distinguishes between the types of writing tasks that the writers are able to perform, among which experiential writing and knowledge telling is considered to be simplest, that is, when writers simply need to tell what they already know without transforming their knowledge to

---

[3]In the case when the frequency rates of an L1 group, NS or NNS, cluster at one end of the array and when the distribution of rates is significantly different, it can be called a one-tailed .05 level of significance. On the other hand, when the frequency rates of a group cluster at both ends of the array and when the distribution is significantly different, it can be referred to as a two-tailed level of significance. A two-tailed level of significance marks dramatically different distributions of feature rates in the array and represents particularly and notably different uses of linguistic features in NS and NNS essays.

address the rhetorical or cognitive complexities of the writing task (knowl-edge transforming). However, Grabe and Kaplan (1996) advanced an addi-tional argument that skilled writers are also able to distinguish between dif-ferent types of writing tasks and genre of text, and thus, they are able modify their writing to make it congruent with genre conventions.

According to earlier research findings, uses of certain syntactic and lexi-cal, and rhetorical features are commonly associated with formal academic prose (e.g., passive forms of verbs and third-person pronouns; Swales, 1990a), whereas other features are frequently encountered in personal and/or experiential writing (e.g., second-person pronouns and the uses of verbs with the progressive aspect). The data obtained from the essays of seven groups of NSs and speakers of Chinese, Japanese, Koreans, Indone-sian, Vietnamese, and Arabic allow determination of whether some prompts elicit various types of writing, such as experiential and/or knowl-edge telling, or knowledge transforming, associated with cognitively com-plex writing tasks, which are covered in chapter 4.

The subsequent chapters identify how various syntactic, lexical, and rhetorical features are used in text and discourse in the seven languages whose speakers wrote the essays. The data analysis presents the compar-isons of frequency rates of the feature use in student texts and determines their differences and similarities across texts written by speakers of these languages. Chapters 6–9 present an overview of uses of various phrase- and clause-level syntactic and lexical features, followed by a similar examination of rhetorical devices in chapter 10.

II

Common Linguistic and Rhetorical Features of Academic ESL Text

The data from the study reported in Part II are extensive, so the analysis approaches these data from a few different vantage points. This portion of the book looks at the pooled data from all essays written by all students in the seven language groups. In chapter 6, the discussion of the findings is structured to begin with a comparative analysis of nouns, pronouns, and nominals in NS and NNS essays, that is, semantic and lexical classes of nouns, personal pronouns, subject slot fillers, indirect pronouns, nominalizations, and gerunds. The discussion of nouns is followed by the analysis of verb-phrase features in chapter 7: tenses, aspects, semantic and lexical classes of verbs, modal verbs, the passive voice, *be*-copula as the main verb, infinitives, present and past participles. Chapter 8 presents the data dealing with attributive and predicative adjectives, as well as semantic and lexical classes of adverbs. This analysis is followed by an examination of frequency rates for subordinate clauses in chapter 9, that is, noun, adjective, and adverb, including adverb clauses of cause, concession, condition, purpose, and other (e.g., time, place, and manner), as well as reduced adverb clauses.

In the discussion, the rates of rhetorical/cohesive feature use (see chap. 10) start with phrase- and sentence-level coordinators and logical/semantic conjunctions and prepositions (e.g., *as well, because of, besides, in spite of, instead of*) that are very common in both NS and NNS text, and then move to exemplification markers (*for example, for instance, such as, like*), various types of hedges, rhetorical questions, demonstrative pronouns, emphatics (*a lot, completely, definitely, no way*), presupposition markers (*of course, obviously*), and fixed strings, that is, phrasal verbs, idioms, and collocations.

The comparisons of NS and NNS frequency rates of feature use are presented by L1 groups throughout Part II. The medians and ranges data tables in each chapter provide the basis for the full comparative analysis. Even at first glance, it becomes apparent from the data that practically all features in the NS and NNS essays were used significantly differently across all L1 groups. Although this finding in itself may not be surprising, the extent of the differences may be.

In general terms, the findings of the study show that in formal written text, highly advanced and trained NNSs employ the vast majority of language features in dramatically different rates than first-year NS students do. Although there is little doubt that some differences in NS and NNS language use can and should be expected, the extent of these differences may point to the possibility that NNS use syntactic, lexical, and rhetorical features of English text in ways distinct from those of NSs with similar academic standing.

In addition, NS and NNS student essays alike do not include notably high frequency rates of many features found in published academic texts, as identified in previous studies and corpus analyses, such as advanced and retroactive nouns, nominalizations, gerunds, participles, public verbs, and complex sentences. Both NS and NNS prose gravitates toward syntactically and lexically simple constructions usually marked by features of conversational and spoken genre, demonstrated by high frequency rates of vague nouns, universal pronouns, private verbs, *be*-copula verbs, amplifiers, and emphatics.

It is also clear, however, that NNS academic essays displayed many features of personal narratives (e.g., first-person pronouns and a preponderance of the past tense). In addition, the data obtained from a large number of L2 texts show that overall, the range and types of structures employed in NNS prose were limited in their syntactic variety and complexity, as well as indicative of a severely restricted lexical repertoire. Even though NS and NNS texts alike exhibited many features of informal speech, the rates of their uses in NNS texts greatly exceed those found in NS academic essays (e.g., vague nouns, coordinating pronouns, and predicative adjectives). L2 writers' accessible language base simply lacks the appropriate and varied syntactic and vocabulary arsenal available to NS students of similar academic standing.

To summarize findings for NS and NNS data in broad strokes, two tables are presented herein. The first enumerates the features with NNS median frequency rates significantly greater than those in NS text across all L1 groups:

Features With Significantly Higher Median Frequency Rates in NNS and NS texts

Interpretive nouns	Amplifiers
Vague nouns	Other adverbs (manner, conjunct, and
Assertive pronouns	adjective/verb modifiers)
Public verbs	Adverb clauses of cause
Private verbs	Phrase-level conjunctions
Expecting/tentative verbs	Sentence-level conjunctions (transitions)
Modal verbs of necessity	Exemplification markers (for example)
Be as a main verb	Emphatics
Predicative Adjectives	

On the other hand, the second table presents the features with NNS median frequency rates significantly lower than those in NS text across all L1 groups:

Features With Significantly Lower Median Frequency Rates in NNS than NS texts

It-cleft	Past participles
Perfect aspect	Reduced adjective clauses
Progressive aspect	Reduced adverb clauses
Predictive modal *would*	Fixed strings (idiomatic phrases and
Passive voice	collocations)
Present participles	

The analysis of phrase-level structures in NS and NNS text demonstrates that although some of the features (e.g., pronouns, infinitives, and adjectives) appear in practically all essays, others are distributed relatively unevenly in L1 and L2 texts (past and present participles, and gerunds). In general terms, however, phrase-level constructions crucially affect the quality of text and can reflect the extent of NS and NNS language skills in regard to grammar and lexical repertoire.

6

Nouns, Pronouns, and Nominals and Their Functions and Uses in Text

This chapter describes the textual functions and student usage of semantic and lexical classes of nouns, personal pronouns, slot fillers, indirect pronouns, nominalizations, and gerunds. In all, six classes of nouns, pronouns, and nominals are presented and are further divided into subsets. The discussion of each class of features is similarly organized: First, an overview of the research is presented to discuss textual functions of a particular set of features, and then the discussion moves to the analyses of their uses in student essays.

To highlight findings for NS and NNS uses of nouns, pronouns, and nominals, NNS median frequency rates were significantly greater than those in NS text across all L1 groups for: interpretive nouns, vague nouns, and assertive pronouns.

However, the analysis findings of the NS and NNS essays also indicate that *it*-cleft constructions were employed significantly less frequently in NS texts than in those of NNSs.

SEMANTIC AND LEXICAL CLASSES OF NOUNS

Textual Functions

Nouns traditionally have been divided into classes based on their semantic features and textual functions. The classification outlined herein is based on the analysis of corpora that include academic and published texts, and research into their enumerative, advance/retrospective, language activity, illocutionary, interpretive, and resultative functions (Biber, 1988; Francis, 1994; Quirk et al., 1985; Tadros, 1994) as well as those that convey meanings of textual vagueness and indeterminacy (Channel, 1994; Moon, 1998).

Enumerative: *advantage, angle, aspect, attempt, branch, category, circumstance, class, consequence, course [of action/to follow], criterion(a), deal, disadvantage, drawback, element, fact, facet, factor, form,[1] item, motive, period, plan, problem, reason, stage, term, type.* For example, (a) *When parents spoil their children, there are many disadvantages[2]* (Chinese), and (b) *Children who don't know how to spend money are a big problem in my country, Korea* (Korean).

Enumerative nouns are prevalent in academic texts. Corpus-based analyses of published academic papers in English point to the fact that they are an essential characteristic of academic discourse, as they signal an introduction of listed and elaborated information in text (Tadros, 1994). These nouns can be associated with analysis and clarification and function as text reference markers that present new content or restate information. According to Tadros, their primary textual functions are classification and categorization of points made in the text, and the use of enumerative nouns commits the writer to description, elaboration, or explication. In this sense, enumerative nouns have ideational, interpersonal (social, expressive, and attitudinal), and text-cohesive functions because they mark the clause rheme (new information about the topic) and as the focus of new or old information (Halliday & Hasan, 1976). In many cases, they are used in plural and accompanied by cardinal numerals, demonstratives, and indefinite pronouns. Some of these nouns play the role of abstract partitives and are used so frequently in writing and formal speech that many are often considered to be clichés and broad categories of nouns[3] (Quirk et al., 1985).

Advance/retrospective: *accident, advance, affair, approach, background, behavior, challenge, change, characteristic, compromise, context, contingency, deed, difficulty, device, dilemma, disaster, episode, event, evidence, exercise, experience, fate, feature, incident, issue, manner, method, news, objective, occurrence, policy, practice, process, program, project, purpose, scenario, shortfall, sign, step, system, subject, task, technique, tendency, topic, truth.* For example, (a) *This issue of choosing a major creates a conflict between parents and children if parents want to control them* (Vietnamese), and (b) *The topic of how young people should form opinions came up in research recently* (Indonesian).

---

[1]The enumerative noun *meaning* was counted in the category of gerunds, even though it can be considered lexicalized (Sinclair, 1991).

[2]All examples herein are extracted from student texts.

[3]These nouns are called *hypernyms*, and an example can be: *doctor—surgeon, pediatrician, podiatrist.*

Advance/retrospective nouns are similar to enumerative nouns and serve the function of markers to alert the reader that a particular type of information is coming or is being summarized (Francis, 1994). The main difference between enumerative and advance/retrospective nouns is that the former can be found in practically any type of speech and writing, from informal conversations to sports reportage to academic prose. However, the latter occur more frequently in academic writing because they are more context-specific (Halliday, 1994). In general terms, advance/retroactive nouns identify formal and written registers (Biber, 1995).

Language activity: *account, consensus, contrast, controversy, criticism, debate, defense, detail, dispute, example,*[4] *formula, heresy, image, imagery, instance, irony, language, metaphor, myth, nonsense, paradox, proof, quote, reference, sentence, story, summary, tale, talk, theme, verdict.* For example, (a) *And so we had a big <u>debate</u> and solved nothing in the end* (NS), and (b) *<u>Language</u> is important for international students to study, but teachers tell <u>stories</u> instead of teaching* (Chinese).

Illocutionary: *advice, answer, appeal, charge, claim, comment, complaint, denial, excuse, gossip, pledge, point, proposal, (re-)assurance, remark, reminder, reply, report, request, response.* For example, (a) *Students use these explanations as <u>excuses</u> for not doing their homework* (Arab), and (b) *I want to mention this <u>point</u> because to me, it is important* (Korean).

Language activity and illocutionary nouns refer to verbal processes, language use, and communication (Francis, 1994). They are often employed as a cohesive device of lexical substitution (e.g., *comment-remark-point* or *answer-response* can be used interchangeably in discourse) (Halliday & Hasan, 1976). An important difference between these two classes of nouns is that language activity nouns are largely used in text and stylistic operations and refer to language functions (e.g., *irony, criticism*) represented in written text. Illocutionary nouns, however, are associated with cognate illocutionary verbs (e.g., *to answer, to appeal*) (Quirk et al., 1985).

Interpretive: *analysis, attitude, belief, blunder, cause, concept, doubt, excess, failure, idea, influence, insight, (in/on the) terms (of), knowledge, mistake, motive, opinion, pattern, picture, philosophy, principle, quality, rationale, sense, source, success, theory, thesis, thought, trend, view.* For example, (a) *If he makes a <u>mistake</u>, his parents will solve it* (Indonesian), and (b) *Parents have a lot of <u>influence</u> on their children even after they are married* (Japanese).

Interpretive nouns refer to cognitive and inferential states that are a result of information, thought, and experience processing. These include verbal processes and cognition in spoken or written expression and outcomes of thought and analysis (Chafe, 1985; Francis, 1994).

---

[4]Excluding the exemplification markers *for example* and *for instance.*

Resultative: *finish, effect, end*[5], *outcome, result. For example, (a) The* _result_ *of his action was that he had to quit school* (Vietnamese), and (b) *My studying to get an A in this class gave me a good* _outcome_ (Indonesian).

Resultative nouns are relatively infrequent and refer to a completion of process, activity, or event (Chafe, 1970).

Vague: *boy, human(s), human being(s), girl, guy, nominal -ever forms (whatever, whichever, whoever), kid, man, people, person, society, stuff, thing(y), way, whatnot, woman, world. For example, (a) Parents should not buy for their children* _whatever_ *they want* (Japanese), and (b) *When they grow up, they have to live in the* _world_ *full of trouble and problems* (Chinese).

Vague nouns are generic (Quirk et al., 1985), and their meanings are rarely homogeneous and almost always depend on the contexts in which they are used. Their most prominent semantic feature is that they refer to objects, concepts, and events that may have little definition and few clear-cut boundaries in the nonlinguistic world (Channel, 1994). Some of these may actually lack many characteristics of nouns and function as nominal placeholders in phrases and clauses (e.g., *He thinks he can do whatever/whichever, She liked the thingy* [NS]). Bickner and Peyasantiwong (1988) found that vague nouns (e.g., *people, world, society*) are common in the L2 essays of Thai and Indonesian students, and their uses reflect the impersonal character of generalizations expected in formal writing.

The nouns in these classes were counted in all occurrences of singular and plural forms.[6]

Uses of Nouns in Student Texts

The NS and NNS usage rates of most semantic and lexical types of nouns were significantly different with a few exceptions, noted as follows (See Table 6.1).

Enumeratives. In all groups, with the exception of Korean and Indonesian speakers, NNSs used significantly more enumerative nouns (the NS median of 0.38 vs., e.g., 0.56 for Chinese, 0.65 for Korean, and 0.58 for Arab texts)[7]. Enumerative nouns are semantically and lexically relatively simple *(advantage, attempt, disadvantage, fact, plan, problem, reason)* and in academic and formal texts, they have the function of classifying and presenting new information (Tadros, 1994). For example, *Studying based on personal interest, there are more* _advantages_ *and less* _disadvantages_, *and we will do*

---

[5]Excluding those that occurred in sentence transitions *in the end* and *as a result.*

[6]All nouns ending in *-s/tion, -ment, -ness, -ure,* and *-ity* are included in the nominalization counts (see later discussion).

[7]NNS medians called out in this discussion are significantly different from the NS median for the same feature.

TABLE 6.1
Median Frequency Rates for Semantic and Lexical Classes of Nouns (Median %)

| | | NS | *L1* | | | | | |
			Chinese	*Japanese*	*Korean*	*Vietnamese*	*Indonesian*	*Arabic*
Enumerative		**0.38**	**0.56***	0.45	**0.65****	**0.52***	0.37	**0.52****
	Range	4.17	3.33	3.67	8.33	4.00	3.46	7.45
Adv./retroact.		**1.00**	**0.49****	**0.45****	**0.53****	**0.26****	**0.32****	**0.57****
	Range	7.95	4.36	7.41	5.28	5.00	8.18	8.59
Illocution		**0.00**	**0.00***	**0.00***	**0.00***	**0.00**	**0.00**	**0.00**
	Range	3.70	2.08	4.61	3.68	2.22	3.00	3.11
Resultative		**0.00**	**0.27****	**0.00**	**0.00***	**0.31****	**0.24****	**0.00**
	Range	2.17	2.80	7.94	5.00	2.90	5.09	1.71
Language activity		**0.00**	**0.39***	**0.45***	**0.32**	**0.51****	**0.44****	**0.36***
	Range	7.41	6.06	8.27	8.70	5.16	5.80	6.54
Interpretive		**0.48**	**0.95****	**0.95****	**1.14****	**0.74***	**0.76***	**1.19***
	Range	13.46	10.31	10.56	12.38	7.00	8.93	9.52
Vague		**1.39**	**2.72****	**2.22****	**3.49****	**2.16****	**2.22****	**2.54****
	Range	8.33	13.19	11.97	14.04	8.26	9.23	13.46

Note. All comparisons are relative to NSs.
*one-tailed $p \leq 0.05$. **two-tailed $p \leq 0.05$.

our best to find a solution to every problem we face (Indonesian). However, one reason for the disparity in the NS and NNS uses of enumeratives can be noted in the contexts where these nouns were employed. For instance, NSs employed these nouns to introduce points and lead to an elaboration of information, with more specific terms used in the elaboration of the points: *People choose their major for many reasons. Some choose it because of their interest in a particular field, and some choose their major because they want lucrative jobs. When choosing a major, though, the best way is to choose something that you love to do, so that you can enjoy your job for the rest of your life.* In NNS essays, these nouns are not necessarily employed to classify and present new information but to carry the ideational content of the text without informational specifics. For example, the following block of text was extracted exactly as cited: *International students face many problems when they arrive in the U.S., and this fact always causes them many disadvantages. It is a fact that international students have many disadvantages when choosing a major. These disadvantages make it difficult for international students to study because they often face many problems. These problems lead students into trouble when they choose their major, and international students experience many troubles* (Korean).

Advance/Retrospective Nouns. The NNS use of enumerative nouns as ideational content without elaboration or detailed discussion is also reflected in their uses of advance/retrospective nouns. The latter are very similar to enumeratives but have the cohesive function of connecting information mentioned earlier and/or later in the text (Francis, 1994; Hunston & Francis, 2000) (see the earlier NS example). However, for all groups, the NNS use of advance/retroactive nouns was significantly less frequent than that in NS text (NS median of 1.00, Chinese 0.49, Japanese, 045, Korean 0.53, Vietnamese 0.26, Indonesian 0.32, and Arab 0.51). Thus, it appears that in L2 essays, ideational cohesion by means of advanced and retroactive nouns is substantially weaker than in NS essays.

Illocutionary Nouns.   (e.g., *advice, answer, excuse, comment*) are not very common in either NS or NNS text. Compared to the frequency rates of NSs for illocutionary nouns, the rates of Vietnamese, Indonesian, and Japanese speakers' texts did not differ significantly.

Resultative Nouns.   Although fewer than half of all NS essays included resultative nouns *(finish, effect, end, outcome, result),* most Chinese, Vietnamese, and Indonesian writers used them to greater extents (NS median 0.00, and speakers of Chinese 0.27, Vietnamese, 0.31, and Indonesian 0.24), and Korean with greater frequency in individual essays (NS range 2.17, Korean 5.00, and Japanese 7.94). For example, *This result happens as an outcome when students neglect to pay attention to their studies. As a result, they cannot pass their exams, and they fail in the university in the end* (Korean).The reason that resultative nouns appear significantly more frequently in NNS essays is that in text, they are employed to mark logical outcomes of writers' arguments directly, whereas in NS texts resultative statements are not necessarily overt, for example, *when there is conflict in the family, children tend to rebel against their parents and get involved in drugs to escape from their misery* (Japanese). In this sentence, the result/outcome of a conflict in a family is implicit, that is, "children tend to rebel," but it is not indicated directly by means of a resultative noun.

Language Activity Nouns.   (e.g., *contrast, debate, language, proof, quote, reference, sentence, story, summary, tale, talk*) are also relatively semantically and lexically simple and very common in the teaching of ESL. Thus, it is not surprising that in ESL texts, these were used significantly more often than in NS essays (e.g., NS median 0.00 and NNS between 0.31 and 0.51).

Interpretive Nouns.   The frequency of interpretive noun use *(belief, cause, idea, influence, knowledge, mistake, opinion)* in NNS texts was significantly higher than that in NS essays (NS median 0.48 and NNS from 0.74 to 1.14). Interpretive nouns, such as *opinion,* were included in the wording of the Opinion Prompt (see chap. 5 for a complete list) and, thus, had a great deal of influence on the word choice in NNS essays. A detailed discussion of the effect of the prompt wording on lexical choices in NNS texts follows later in the discussion of essays written to individual prompts in chapters 11 and 12.

Vague Nouns.   From the data in Table 6.1, vague nouns *(human, human being, guy, -ever words, kid, life, man, people, person, society, stuff, way, woman, world)* in NNS texts were so frequent that they deserve a special mention (NS median 1.39, Chinese 2.72, Japanese and Indonesian 2.22 each, Korean 3.49, Vietnamese 2.16, and Arab 2.96). It is easy to see that NNSs used them practically two to three times more frequently than NS, for example, *The happiest person in the world does what he or she'd like to do. I think whenever or whatever people make a decision, they should look at the future and not at the present time. People can go all the way if they put their mind into something they are interested in or want to do* (Korean). According to Channel (1994), vague nouns refer to objects and events that have little definition and can be used to convey the impersonal character of generalizations without precision. An obvious explanation of the high rates of use of vague nouns in NNS texts is that L2 writers simply lack more advanced and sophisticated vocabulary to be able to choose more appropriate, varied, and complex lexis to express their ideas.

PERSONAL PRONOUNS (AND CONTRACTIONS)

Textual Functions

Personal pronouns play an important role in textual cohesion because they are deictic and specifically referential (Halliday & Hasan, 1976). Their use in written discourse is pervasive, and they unify the information flow by representing the discourse roles of the participants. Hoey (1991) explained that in written text, personal pronouns are treated as lexical entities and, thus, they have the function of lexical cohesive links. Because pronouns function as referential markers in the text flow, their appropriate use is deemed important in evaluations of both L1 and L2 writing skills (Hacker, 1994; Vaughan, 1991). For example, (a) *I think that you have to try really hard, and then they will see what you can do* (Arabic), and (b) *My father always told me that you need to see what people are doing, and if you do, they will also pay attention to you, when your time comes* (Vietnamese).

The contextual and discourse functions of personal pronouns in written academic text are complex. Various studies in text-referential deixis and cohesion in written discourse have demonstrated that their use is highly prevalent and that they are often treated as lexical entities in lexical cohesive links (Halliday & Hasan, 1976; Hoey, 1991).

First person: First-person pronouns *(I, me, my, mine, myself, we, us, our(s), ourselves)* mark interpersonal discourse focus and direct involvement of the writer, and they are usually more common in spoken rather than written registers (Biber, 1988, 1995). Myers (1989) found that first-person singular pronouns are relatively common in academic writing in English because writers' personal involvement with their text is expected. Based on their analysis of a large number of writing manuals and guidelines, Chang and Swales (1999) reported that the use of the first-person singular is discipline-specific and appears to be, for example, appropriate in philosophy, acceptable in linguistics, and discouraged in statistics.

In many writing traditions other than Anglo-American, the use of first-person singular pronouns is considered inappropriate and unacceptable because it is associated with the expression of individual, rather than the collective, identity or opinion (Ohta, 1991; Scollon, 1991, 1994). Maynard (1993) commented that using *I* to stand for the individual undesirably increases the writer's responsibility for the truth value[8] of the proposition and diminishes his or her solidarity with the reader. In Indonesian and Arabic writing, however, the written tradition of Koranic classical rhetoric plays an important role. Hence, the use of the first-person plural pronoun *we* appears to be particularly common (Ostler, 1987; Sa'adeddin, 1989) to promote group solidarity and establish the common ground between the writer and the reader. It is important to note, however, that in addition to the influence of the classical rhetoric of the Koran, the impact of Buddhist and Confucian rhetorical traditions can be also felt in Indonesian formal writing (Prentice, 1987). On the other hand, Indrasuta (1988) found a preponderance of first-person singular pronouns in the L2 essay writing of Thai students. She explained that in Buddhist rhetorical paradigms, the fact of writing reflects the writers' need to explain their position on the issue rather than describe the importance of the issue or its causes.

The use of personal pronouns is discussed in practically every textbook on writing or composition. However, the authors' views on their use do not appear to be uniform, in particular as they pertain to the first-person singular. Raimes (1992) and Swales and Feak (1994) explicitly stated that first-person singular pronouns should not be used in writing because their use interferes with the objective tone expected in academic writing. On the other hand, studies of written academic English-language corpora indicate that the first-person singular is used to present claims and opinions shared or assumed to be potentially shared by the writer and the reader (Biber, 1988; Myers, 1989; Poole, 1991).

According to some studies, first-person plural pronouns can also be used to stress writer–reader solidarity, construct group identity in formal speech

---

[8]Truth-value is a term that refers to the base meaning of a proposition, and truth value can be increased or diminished by means of, for example, adverbs or negatives, for example, *she likes cakes, she definitely likes cakes, she doesn't like cakes, she doesn't like cakes at all.*

and writing, and create in- and out-group boundaries (Johnson, 1995; Myers, 1989). Conversely, Swales and Feak (1994) advised against their use. Quirk et al.(1985) mentioned that in English, the occurrences of *we* are almost always inclusive. However, Atkinson (1991) noted that *we* and *us* mark formal but interactive contexts and pointed out that the uses of these pronouns are conventionalized in academic writing in English. In the assessment of writing skills in U.S. colleges and universities and in standardized testing, a frequent use of the first-person singular pronouns marks an essay as a highly personal narrative. This rhetorical mode weighs against the writer because it suggests the writer's lack of ability to produce appropriate academic text and argumentation (Johns, 1991, 1997; Vaughan, 1991).

Second person: Second-person singular and plural pronouns *(you, your(s), yourself, yourselves)* are often considered inappropriate in academic prose (Smoke, 1999; Swales & Feak, 1994). The use of these pronouns requires a specific individual to whom the text is addressed, indicates a high degree of the writer's involvement with the addressee, and marks the conversational register (Biber, 1988, 1995). On the other hand, in Chinese, Japanese, and Korean writing traditions, *you* is employed to elicit the reader's involvement and promote group solidarity between the writer and reader (Hinds, 1983; Hwang, 1987; Matalene, 1985). According to S.-H. Lee (1987), in the Chinese and Korean rhetorical paradigm, direct personal appeals to the reader and advice, based on common wisdom, have a persuasive weight, akin to that of objectivity in Anglo-American rhetoric. Nguyen (1987) emphasized that Buddhist and Confucian traditions of scholarship were preeminent in the Vietnamese writing tradition for over 800 years, and for this reason, the influence of classical Chinese rhetoric is prominently reflected in Vietnamese writing and style. He noted that practically all Vietnamese literary heritage and contemporary prose exhibit features of Chinese formal written discourse and include direct communication with and appeals to the audience, represented by the frequent use of *you* or imperatives and the avoidance of first-person singular pronouns. On the other hand, in classical Arabic rhetoric, addressing the reader directly is considered to be appropriate only when the writer is vested with a legitimate authority to do so (Sa'adeddin, 1989).

Third person: *Third-person singular and plural* pronouns *(she, her(s), herself, he, him, his, himself, they, them, their(s), themselves,* (referential) *it, its)* serve as markers of inexact reference to persons and objects outside of the immediate scope of the writer's view (Biber, 1988). These pronouns are common in past-tense narratives and exposition and frequently have the function of text-referential cohesion devices (Halliday & Hasan, 1976). For instance, referential *it* is a syntactically flexible pronoun that can refer to animate and inanimate objects, abstract concepts, and clauses (McCarthy, 1994). Similar to other third-person pronouns, *it* is not explicit and rare in published academic genre (Biber, 1988). In speech or writing in English, third-person pronouns identify group boundaries and belonging and define those who remain outside (R. Scollon, 1993b). The distinction between third-person singular and plural extends to the differentiation between the outsider individual or group and can determine the degree of the outsider influence (Johnson, 1995).

On the other hand, R. Scollon (1993b) and R. Scollon and S. W. Scollon (1995) pointed out that in the Confucian rhetorical tradition, the writer's detachment in addressing the reader can project an authoritative stance, and hence, the use of third-person pronouns marks the discourse for elevated style. Similarly, Maynard (1997) stressed that in general, in Japanese discourse, writers do not focus on themselves but the audience or individuals and events external to the discourse. Hence, in speech and writing second- or third-person pronouns are prevalent.

In composition writing, the use of third-person singular and plural pronouns is recommended because they impart formality, detachment, and objectivity to academic prose (Hacker, 1994; Leki, 1999; Smoke, 1999) and help create and maintain a text's referential frame (McCarthy, 1991).

Uses of Personal Pronouns in Student Texts

First-Person Pronouns.   As shown in Table 6.2, frequency rates for first-person singular pronouns (median 3.97) in the essays of Japanese speakers were almost twice as great than those of NS (median 1.95), and the Chinese, Korean, Vietnamese, and Indonesian texts also contained significantly more first-person singular pronouns (medians 2.63, 3.33 each, and 2.78, respectively). For example, *When I was in my music class, I could forget about all my troubles. I liked playing the violin so much that I couldn't wait to go to the university to study. But my father said that I had to be a doctor, and I wanted to run away from my house* (Chinese). On the other hand, in the essays of Arabic speakers, first-person pronoun rates were not significantly different from those of NS (medians 1.89). The essays written by all NNSs, except

TABLE 6.2
Median Frequency Rates for Personal Pronouns (Median %)

		NS	Chinese	Japanese	*L1* Korean	Vietnamese	Indonesian	Arabic
First person		**1.95**	**2.63***	**3.97****	**3.33***	**3.33****	**2.78***	**1.92**
	Range	15.41	17.65	20.59	13.68	21.76	18.21	14.67
Second person		**0.00**	**1.07****	**0.52****	**0.94****	**0.60****	**0.00**	**0.40***
	Range	9.14	18.25	21.54	18.10	9.06	10.98	8.48
Third person		**4.09**	**5.13****	**4.86**	**4.83***	**5.06***	**5.56****	**4.76***
	Range	18.75	24.34	19.08	19.05	19.00	17.26	17.02

Note. All comparisons are relative to NSs.
*one-tailed $p \leq 0.05$. **two-tailed $p \leq 0.05$.

speakers of Arabic, included sizeable portions of personal narratives and recounting of their own experiences, which helps to explain the frequent uses of first-person pronouns and past-tense verbs (see the Past Tense section to follow). On the other hand, these texts also contained many generalizations, vague assertions, and recounts of third-party experiences of friends and relatives (see Third-Person Pronouns in later discussion), for example, *Of course, to get a job in Korea is hard. However, I thought the concentration on a work would solve the problem. If someone had an interest in his/her[9] major, and tried his/her best in the major field, he/she would get a job for him/her* (Korean).

Second-Person Pronouns. In the NNS texts, practically all types of personal pronouns were employed significantly differently from those in the essays of NSs, with the use of second-person pronouns by Indonesian speakers being the only exception.

Second-person pronouns that mark direct appeals and communication with the reader and that are often considered inappropriate in formal academic writing (Hacker, 1994; Swales, 1990a) are also utilized significantly more commonly in the NNS than NS texts (e.g., NS median 0.00, and speakers of Chinese 1.07, Japanese 0.52, Korean 0.94, Vietnamese 0.60, and Arabic 0.40). Combining recounts of personal experiences with their educational value for the reader who is directly urged to learn from the writer's mistakes or avoid them causes the NNS essays to resemble interpersonal narrative and increases the uses of *I, we, you,* and imperative constructions. For example, *If you are an undergraduate student, you may have difficulty choosing a major field. You have to try to find jobs that have both your interests and can satisfy your living. You need to hear your parents' words, like I did, but you cannot let your parents control you. Remember, this is your life, and you need to do what you need to do* (Chinese). Based on the uses of second-person pronouns in the texts of Chinese, Japanese, and Korean writers, the precepts of Confucian rhetoric (Matalene, 1985; Oliver, 1972) and, for the speakers of Arabic, the value of past experience for learning in the Arab culture (Johnstone, 1989), directly addressing the reader to establish solidarity and communication may appear to be a reasonable approach to constructing text.

Third-Person Pronouns. These may be considered preferable to first-person pronouns because they help create an impression of the writer's distance from the subject matter and a sense of objectivity (Hinkel, 1999b). However, in the NNS texts in all L2 groups, third-person pronouns were also

---

[9]All third-person pronouns spelled out with a slash (he/she) or the conjunction *or* (he or she) were counted as one pronoun occurrence.

used in significantly higher rates than in the NS text (NS median 4.09 and
NNS between 4.78 and 5.56). It appears that although NNS writers strove to
establish cohesion in their texts, as has been mentioned, they may have
lacked the lexical repertoire to allow them to create cohesive discourse. In
particular, third-person pronouns were used to span several sentences,
where a NS would repeat or restate the noun phrase to reestablish the referential deixis. For example, in NS text a construction can be: *A job is a
method of economic support. Self-respect and self-esteem are the key to success in one's
work. Employment represents a way of paying bills or earning cash.* On the other
hand, in many cases, NNS text did not strengthen cohesive ties by means of
lexical substitution: *It will be wasting time of life if we choose majors by only con-
centrating on jobs. It might be easy to get a job, but it will not stay for a long time. It
does not give as much interests as they wanted to do, and it causes less patience and
confidence about what they are doing. And if this happens many times in their life,
they will want to give up what they were doing and seek what they wanted to do*
(Korean).

   The Confucian rhetorical tradition predominant in Chinese, Korean,
Japanese, and Vietnamese writing encourages the use of third-person pronouns in elevated and formal styles to focus the discourse on general truths
applicable to most readers. The high rates of third-person pronoun use
may also be explained by the fact that speakers of these languages transferred an appropriate means of focusing discourse on the common ground
between the writer and the reader and generalizable truths.

NOMINALS

Slot Fillers

Textual Functions

   In general terms, *it* and *there* in the nonreferential clause-initial position
are existential "'notional" subjects that have no lexical or semantic content (Quirk, et al., 1985, p. 1403); that is, they fulfill the syntactic role of
subjects but have no meaning. In sentences with the existential slot fillers,
in most cases, the predicate verb is copula *be* or textual linking verbs (e.g.,
It seems/appears), although other verbs are also possible (*exist, occur, rise,*
and modals, as in *It/There may become/come*). The use of slot fillers allows
writers to postpone propositional content to the secondary clausal position. In formal writing, such constructions allow the writer to introduce
the proposition or claim while maintaining their detachment from its contextual purpose (Biber, 1988). For example, (a) *It seems that these days everybody grades on everything, and it doesn't matter what people do with these grades*
(Chinese), and (b) *There are many children in my country who don't want to
study the major that their parents chose for them* (Indonesian).

It (nonreferential) has relatively little lexical content (Biber, 1988) and can be contextually ambiguous. In academic writing, *it* is employed to project impartiality, objectivity, and evidentiality when it refers to whole segments of the preceding text (McCarthy, 1994). Hence, the increased level of evidentiality leads to increased frequencies of its use in academic texts and lends implicit authority to the writer's claim because nonreferential *it* also functions as a complex hedging device (Huebler, 1983). In academic writing, the subject filler *it* depersonalizes text and creates a sense of hedged objectivity, particularly when it is used with private and perception verbs (e.g., *seem/appear*) that project evidentiality (Myers, 1989). However, in Scollon's (1994) view, in academic and "scientific" writing in English, the use of *it* is conventionalized to a large extent and marks the text for a relatively formal register. The findings of earlier research have established that these constructions are so syntactically complex that they may not be common in the texts of even proficient NNSs (Hinkel, 1999b).

There (existential[10]) can function like nonreferential *it* because it contributes to the depersonalization of text and removes the proposition to the secondary clause position (Jacobs, 1995; Quirk et al., 1985). According to Schiffrin (1987, 1994), in its existential uses, *there* followed by the verb *be* can have pronominal and presentative functions because it is employed to assert existence of a particular entity. In her view, *there* can be a useful way to introduce a referent into text without assuming prior knowledge on the behalf of the reader. Schiffrin noted that existential *there* constructions result in a very informative noun phrase, which occupies the last position in a sentence and has the function of the rheme, that is, new information with the highest communicative content.

Biber (1988), however, found that existential *there* constructions are relatively static because they introduce a new syntactic unit while generally reducing the informational and lexical load in a sentence. He noted that because *there* is used in lexically and syntactically simple structures, it is more common in spoken and informal rather than in written registers.

Uses of Slot Fillers in Student Text

It. In this examination of ESL texts, the slot filler *it* was used significantly more frequently in the essays of NSs (median 0.56) than in the essays of NNSs (medians between 0.00 and 0.38) (see Table 6.3).

Existential there. On the other hand, a different picture emerges in the uses of the meaning-empty slot filler *there* that was not frequent in either NS

---

[10]Existential *there* denotes only the "existence" of some object or entity that is named following the verb—usually *be* or *exist*, as in *There was a beautiful princess* or *There exist various definitions of human life.*

TABLE 6.3
Median Frequency Rates for Slot Fillers (Median %)

					L1			
		NS	*Chinese*	*Japanese*	*Korean*	*Vietnamese*	*Indonesian*	*Arabic*
It-subject		**0.56**	**0.29****	**0.38***	**0.00***	**0.35****	**0.18****	**0.36***
	Range	3.25	3.21	2.81	2.13	2.46	1.37	3.96
There-subject		**0.00**	**0.00**	**0.00**	**0.18**	**0.00**	**0.00**	**0.35***
	Range	1.70	2.48	3.03	4.07	1.52	3.55	2.52

Note. All comparisons are relative to NSs.
*one-tailed $p \leq 0.05$. **two-tailed $p \leq 0.05$.

(median 0.00) or NNS texts, with the exception of speakers of Arabic (median 0.36). According to Biber (1988), existential *there* is syntactically and lexically simple and is more specific to spoken rather than written register because it delays the ideational content of a proposition until the end. In general, neither type of slot fillers (*it* or *there*) was common in L2 texts.

Indirect Pronouns

Universal and negative: *all, each*[11]*, every-* pronominals (*everybody, everyone, everything*), *every, none, no one, nothing.* For example, *In my country, there are some parents who prepare <u>everything</u> for their children and their goal is to be sure that <u>nothing</u> touches them in real life* (Korean).

Assertive: *any-* words (*anybody, anyone, anything*), *any, some-* pronominals (*somebody, someone, something*), *some.* For example, *<u>Some</u> wealthy people can buy <u>anything</u> they want <u>any</u> time they want it* (NS).

Textual Functions

Quirk et al. (1985) and Greenbaum and Quirk (1990) defined two main classes of indefinite pronouns—universal and assertive/partitive (see Table 6.4)—and stated that these have a wide range of meanings and functions in text. Universals and negatives mark the extremes of the continuum of meanings expressed by indefinite pronouns. According to Brown and Levinson (1987) and Huebler (1983), their uses are often associated with overstatements and referential points on a deictic scale that is higher than the actual state of affairs. These authors commented that a speaker or writer can use an exaggerative strategy to make a point by inflating contextual circumstances.

Pronominals, such as *every-* and *no-*, are marked exaggeratives, and they are seldom employed in academic writing in English (Biber, 1988; Halliday

---

[11]The frequency counts of pronoun *all/each* included only elliptical pronominal substitutions (e.g., *all came to the picnic*). Adjectival occurrences of *all/each* (e.g., *all students*) were excluded from frequency counts of pronouns.

TABLE 6.4
Median Frequency Rates for Indirect Pronouns (Median %)

		NS	Chinese	Japanese	Korean	Vietnamese	Indonesian	Arabic
					L1			
Universal		**0.44**	**0.85****	**0.77****	**0.89****	**0.72****	**0.55**	**0.91****
	Range	3.52	5.71	6.67	5.00	4.58	5.20	5.77
Assertive		**0.50**	**0.97****	**0.77****	**0.84****	**0.61***	**0.82****	**0.79****
	Range	3.21	7.14	6.67	7.07	2.63	6.28	6.38

Note. All comparisons are relative to NSs.
*one-tailed $p \leq 0.05$. **two-tailed $p \leq 0.05$.

& Hasan, 1976;). However, Cherry (1988) found that in certain contexts, student academic writing contained a relatively high rate of overstatements to add the power of conviction to the writer's propositional stance. Creating a hyperbole allows the writer to make a point without being precise (Channel, 1994) because exaggeratives and overstatements can function as contextual devices inverse to understatement and are not intended to be taken literally. Leech (1983) pointed out that overstatements are prevalent in speech because they embellish the truth value of the proposition or claim.

Although exaggerations and overstatements are considered to be inappropriate in formal Anglo-American writing, they are considered acceptable in persuasive writing in Confucian and Koranic rhetorical traditions. In classical Chinese rhetoric, which is common in Japanese, Korean, and Vietnamese writing, as well as Chinese (Hinds, 1984, 1990; Nguyen, 1987; I. Taylor, 1995; Tsujimura, 1987), exaggerations and overstatements may be seen as a device of indirect suasion and even eloquence (Oliver, 1971). Matalene (1985) found that her Chinese students routinely exaggerated and overstated facts in their academic writing. In traditional Korean rhetoric, writers are inherently vested with the authority to persuade and can rely on various forms of ethos and overstatement if they deem it necessary (Yum, 1987). Similarly, Connor (1996) and Sa'adeddin (1989) cited various studies that describe Arabic rhetorical expression as exaggerative and overassertive. They explained that in various types of Arabic prose, the oral tradition finds many manifestations in writing, including the ethos of overstatement for the purpose of persuasion.

Assertive and nonassertive indefinite pronouns have different textual functions, some of which are to hedge or express indeterminacy, vagueness, and uncertainty. Greenbaum and Quirk (1990) and Quirk et al. (1985) indicated these two types of pronouns (also called partitive) are contextually and deictically marked with respect to noun phrases. They also stated that assertive forms can have positive presuppositions. According to Channel (1994), the meanings and functions of assertives can be similar to those of hedges, and they differ from those of universal or negative pronouns that imply total inclusion or exclusion. However, because assertive and nonassertive pronouns are often vague and do not carry precise lexical contents, they are not prevalent in academic writing in English and are a characteristic of spoken register (Biber, 1988, 1995).

Quirk et al. (1985) stated that a considerable variation is found in the use of indefinite pronouns in British and American written texts. In Chinese, Japanese, Korean, and Vietnamese writing, indeterminacy in pronoun reference decreases the writer's responsibility for the truth value and factuality of a proposition by attributing the claim to someone else, presenting it as a vague general truth or commonly held opinion, and displaying uncertainty and hesitation (Hinds, 1983, 1990; Oliver, 1971; Yum, 1987). According to Chafe (1994), the construct of indefinite reference is far more complex and prevalent in written text in such languages as Indonesian and Japanese than in English because only entities that are essential to the discourse flow are definitively marked. In these languages, indefiniteness markers can be highly diverse and have many different functions.

The textual functions of assertive pronouns are similar to those of hedges and do not carry precise lexical contents (Channel, 1994). However, as with universals, assertives have been identified as relatively common in ESL texts written by Chinese, Korean, Japanese, and Indonesian university students (Hinkel, 1999b) because their lack of specificity reduces the writer's responsibility for the truth value and factuality of the proposition. As has been noted, in Confucian rhetoric, displaying appropriate uncertainty and hesitation is viewed as an objective stance when the author presents general truths and commonly held opinions. For example, *Second, interest will give us energy that will make us successful. Suppose that you are doing* <u>something</u> *you hate to do? Can you do it well? Everybody can't. . . . Third,* <u>some</u> *bad major can destroy your life. . . . But no one knows what will happen tomorrow* (Chinese).

Indirect Pronouns in Student Texts

Universal Pronouns. Universals and their exaggerative function are often considered to be appropriate and even necessary in various discourse traditions other than Anglo-American. For example, *First, we should think about what is the ultimate goal of our life. What do we want indeed? Happiness or money? I think most people will choose happiness. Thus, to do what we really want is important. If these two types of life for us to choose one is life full of interest though the income is not much the other is a boring life full of money, I believe* <u>everyone</u> *will choose the former because* <u>everyone</u> *wants happiness* (Chinese). In texts of NNSs in all L1 groups, universal pronouns were used significantly more frequently than in NS texts, and in the cases of texts written by speakers of Chinese, Japanese, Korean, and Arabic, with frequency rates almost twice those in NS essays (NS median 0.44 and NNS medians between 0.77 and

0.93). As has been mentioned, in many rhetorical traditions other than Anglo-American, exaggerations and overstatements represent a hyperbolic persuasive device that is associated with higher ethos (Hinds, 1984; I. Taylor, 1995), and this finding comes as little surprise. Previous studies found the texts written by, for instance, Chinese and Arabic speakers to be overstated and overassertive, compared to NS texts, with the goal of persuading the audience and making their points convincing (Matalene, 1985; Sa'adeddin, 1989). It appears that in their academic essays in English, NNSs largely continue to rely on overstatements and exaggerations as a means of rhetorical persuasion common in other rhetorical traditions.

Assertive Pronouns. As with universals, the NNS frequency rates for the uses of assertives were significantly higher in all NNS groups (NS median 0.50 and NNS from 0.61 to 0.97). Assertive pronouns often function as hedging devices that have the goal of expressing vague general truths and common opinions, as well as hesitation and uncertainty. In the classical Chinese rhetorical tradition, indefiniteness and imprecision in discourse is considered to be a desirable characteristic because it allows writers to state their opinions indirectly without risking loss of rapport with the audience.

Nominalization (Abstract Generic Nouns)

These include all nouns ending in -s/tion, -ment, -ness, -ure, and -ity. For example, *Who can study in this environment when all students are talking in class?* (Vietnamese).

Textual Functions

Nominalizations of verbs and adjectives are ubiquitous in academic and professional discourse in English. Quirk et al. (1985) classified many nominalized forms as generic because their meanings are abstract and often vague. They are often used to expand an idea and integrate information laconically (Biber, 1988). Nominalizations often refer to abstract concepts and generalizations and can be overused in formal registers, when writers desire to give their text an elevated style (Bhatia, 1992). Bhatia (1993) noted that nominalizations represent one of the conventions of academic and formal writing, and their use requires familiarity with the discourse norms accepted in academia. Nominalizations express propositional relationships between two nouns or nouns and verbs, and their use can be collocational, when the meaning of this relationship has to be deduced from context (Sinclair, 1991), for example, *the computer/MTV generation or language competence/performance.* Swales and Feak (1994) noted that nominalizations and other abstract generic nouns are common in academic texts that deal with concepts, instruments, and devices.

Iwasaki (1993) explained that in written Japanese, nominalization is discourse-dependent because in explanatory and descriptive texts, nominalizations convey polite indirectness and vagueness. However, assertions and directives cannot be nominalized because they cannot be softened or hedged. Heycock and Y.-S. Lee (1990) similarly found that the uses of abstract generic nouns in Korean depend on the type of the illocutionary force in the context: Verbs and adjectives are nominalized in indirect and nonspecific discourse, but cannot be in other contexts. In Chinese and Vietnamese, nominalization is syntactic rather than morphological, and whether a verb or an adjective is nominalized depends on its position and syntactic function in the sentence. Chinese nominalizations, similar to those in English, convey abstract meanings that can refer to concepts and abstractions (Li & Thompson, 1981). In L2 composition writing, Carlson's (1988) study showed that no marked differences existed between NSs' and Chinese speakers' uses of nominalizations in academic essays. Arabic synthetic derivations operate on all word forms, including nouns, and such derivations can be prefixal and infixal. The elevated writing style in Arabic, similar to that in English, is often expected to demonstrate advanced literacy and includes a high number of abstract generic nouns (Sa'adeddin, 1989). Because nominalizations are generally vague and usually denote concepts and abstractions, they are often found in texts that deal with advanced subject matter and ideational content.

Nominalizations in Student Texts.   In earlier studies (Carlson, 1988), no pronounced differences were found in the NS and NNS use of nominalizations in academic essays. In this study, the frequency rates of NSs' and NNSs' uses of nominalizations were mixed, and the most pronounced differences can be found in the nominalization rates of NSs (median 1.74) and Vietnamese and Indonesian writers (medians 1.67 and 1.46), who used these structures at significantly lower rates. (See table 6.5.)

Gerunds

Textual Functions

Gerunds are usually considered to be deverbal nouns that are less gradiently nominal than, for example, nominalizations, and usually refer to processes rather than completed activities (Quirk et al., 1985). Gerunds are derived structures that represent reductions of nominal clauses, and they retain their nounlike features and functions. Meanings of gerunds are mostly abstract, although some can be concrete (e.g., *painting*[s], *knitting*[s], *cutting*[s]). Because they have functions similar to those of nouns and nominalizations, in general, they are used as nominals and play similar roles in grammar and text. For example, (a) *Learning needs to be enjoyable because if I don't have fun, reading all these books makes me bored and sleepy* (Arab) and (b) *Giving grades and evaluating students is the teacher's job, and they know it* (Korean).

Gerunds in Student Texts. Similar to the NNS uses of nominalizations, the frequency rates of gerunds were significantly lower than those of NSs in the essays of all groups, except Arabs. In many cases, the meanings of gerunds can be vague and abstract (*reading, computing, creating, deciding*), and their uses are often lexicalized. For example, most ESL grammar textbooks include a unit on their meanings and functions, despite the fact that their derivations are relatively simple (verb + *ing*). In general terms, the textual functions of gerunds are similar to those of nominalizations. In the essays of NSs and NNSs, substantial divergences were noted in the frequency rates of gerunds in NS essays (median 1.50) and those of NNSs (medians between 0.99 and 1.23).

As is shown in Table 6.5, overall, the use of nouns, pronouns, and nominals in NS and NNS student essays exhibits a tendency toward simple lexical constructions usually marked by features of conversational genre and personal narratives, such as vague nouns, and personal and indirect pronouns. Despite the fact that both NS and NNS texts include many features of informal speech, in NNS texts their rates of employment are significantly higher than those found in NS academic essays (e.g., second-person and universal pronouns).

On the other hand, the uses of nominalizations, commonly associated with published academic texts (Bhatia, 1993; Biber, 1988) are largely similar in NS and NNS texts. The frequency rates of other relatively advanced lexical items, such as advanced/retroactive nouns, gerunds, and *it*-cleft structures, in NS essays significantly exceeded those found in NNS texts. Thus, it seems clear that L2 instruction needs to focus on expanding the vocabulary range of NNS students, as well as identifying lexical features of formal academic texts that are distinct from those in employed in spoken register. An additional observation that can be made based on the data in chapter 6 is that familiarity with L2 conversational lexicon does not necessarily lead to the expansion of vocabulary employed in academic texts.

TABLE 6.5
Median Frequency Rates for Nominalization and Gerunds (Median %)

		NS	Chinese	Japanese	Korean	Vietnamese	Indonesian	Arabic
					L1			
Nominalizations		**1.74**	**1.92**	**1.92**	**1.67**	**1.67***	**1.46***	**2.04**
	Range	12.24	9.17	9.12	13.33	8.42	7.37	7.53
Gerunds		**1.50**	**1.23***	**0.99****	**1.05****	**1.00****	**1.13****	**1.67**
	Range	6.94	5.83	5.56	8.23	4.17	5.33	10.58

Note. All comparisons are relative to NSs.
*one-tailed *p* < 0.05. **two-tailed *p* < 0.05.

7

The Verb Phrase and Deverbals and Their Functions and Uses in Text

Teaching various elements of the verb phrase, such as the meanings and uses of tenses, aspects, or passive constructions, represents one of the most difficult and work-consuming tasks in L2 pedagogy. Nonetheless, the functions and uses of verb phrase components also constitute one of the most essential domains of a sentence/clause structure. Thus, due to the complexity of the verb phrase and its elements, chapter 7 includes several key verbal and deverbal features, without which no verb phrase can be constructed: verb tenses, verb aspects, which are examined separately, semantic and lexical classes of verbs (e.g., public, private, suasive, and tentative), modal verbs, the passive voice, *be* as the main clause verb, infinitive, and present and past participles. All these elements in some form can be identified in most L2 teaching materials. For this reason, the terminology adopted in this chapter follows that common in most ESL instructional texts and applied linguistic analyses of verbal constructions.

As in chapter 6, the discussion of the verb phrase features begins with a brief summary of the findings. The findings for NS and NNS employment of verb phrase elements show that NNS median frequency rates were significantly higher than those in NS essays across all L1 groups for:

- Private verbs.
- Public verbs.
- Expecting/tentative verbs.

- Modal verbs of necessity.
- *Be*-copula as a main verb.

On the other hand, the verb phrase features with NNS median frequency rates significantly lower than those in NS essays across all L1 groups include:

- Perfect aspect.
- Predictive modal *would*.
- Passive voice.
- Present participle.
- Past participle.

TENSES

Textual Functions of Tenses

In English, tenses represent a developed deictic and inflectional system that includes both tenses and aspects. Among others, Guiora (1983), Riddle (1986), Sharwood Smith and Rutherford (1988), and Deitrich, Klein, and Noyau (1995) pointed out that in general, L2 tenses, the concepts of temporality, and tense-related inflectional morphology are often difficult for NNSs to acquire. In written text in English, the tense system provides means of grounding discourse within a framework of temporality and often serves as an ideational cohesive device in the Hallidayan sense (Matthiessen, 1996).

As is the case with many Asian languages, Chinese, Japanese, Indonesian, and Vietnamese do not have tense systems or inflectional tense markers, and the time of actions and events is marked by means of adverbs and adjuncts (Nguyen, 1987; Norman, 1990). Chung (1988) and Hinkel (1992, 1997b) reported that speakers of languages without inflectional tense systems may continue to misidentify the meanings and forms of tenses in English, despite their relatively high overall L2 proficiency.

In composition instruction, the teaching of tenses is a requisite feature, and most textbooks on composition writing include at least one unit on their meanings and functions (Hacker, 1994; Leki, 1999; Lunsford & Connors, 1997). According to Vaughan (1991), NNSs' ability to use English tenses appropriately is an important criterion in the assessment of their L2 writing skills.

Past.   Quirk et al. (1985) and Schiffrin (1981) pointed out that the simple past tense is used to mark an event completed in the past time. They noted that the past tense is often found in narratives that recount past experiences or activities and establishes the past-time frame in discourse. In academic writing, the past tense is used in presentations of observations, results of studies, and conclusions (Swales & Feak, 1994), as well as examinations of work and events from a historical perspective (Swales, 1990a).

Japanese and Korean have verbal forms for indicating the past time. Japanese past-time markers can take the form of particles that are used in limited contexts and only with certain types of verbs (Shibatani, 1990). Korean has past and nonpast tenses that are inseparable from the perfective and nonperfective aspects. The Korean past tense divides time deixis relative to the present moment, and actions or events that have occurred before the moment of speaking are those that are marked for the past tense; all other tenses are considered to be nonpast (Sohn, 1995). Unlike uninflected languages, Arabic has three morphologically marked tenses, including the past, which is used in narrative and written discourse to describe actions and events preceding the present moment (Kaye, 1987). For example, *When I took the history class, my grade was terrible because I didn't enjoy that class* (Vietnamese).

In this study, past-tense forms of verbs were counted according to their identification markers in grammar texts (e.g., Quirk et al., 1985), including regular and irregular verb forms.

Present. In English, the present simple tense (the general present) refers to habitual actions and events and/or those that are generally true (Quirk et al., 1985). In academic writing, the use of the present tense is often conventionalized (e.g., citational present) (Swales, 1990a), and the present tense is predominantly used in references to current knowledge. The use of the present tense in context carries an implication that the reported information is close to the writer's own opinion and views (Swales & Feak, 1994). Swales (1990a) found that in the academic genre, the use of the present tense is associated with generalizations and is more frequently employed in some disciplines than in others. Similarly, McCarthy and Carter (1994) referred to what they called "the historical present" (p. 100), often considered requisite in introductions and citations from sources to indicate "the 'now-relevance'" (p. 102) of research and information.

Unlike languages without morphological tenses, Arabic has an inflectional present tense. However, its use is distinct from that in English because it refers to the true present time and has no conventionalized discourse uses.

The frequency counts in this study include all occurrences of present-tense verbs, that is, the base form (first- and second-person singular and plural, and third-person plural), the inflectionally marked third-person singular form, and present progressive and present perfect forms (see also the subsections Progressive and Perfect in the section Aspects), and contractions. For example, *So, in the classroom, the teacher talks and the students listen and take notes. In my country, students never talk in class* (Japanese).

Future.   *be going to, shall*[1]*, will* (and contractions). For example, *Children will not become independent, and they will think that life is easy,* (Indonesian).

Although *will* and *shall* are often identified as markers of the future tense in English (Chafe, 1994), some linguists (Leech & Svartvik, 1994) hold the view that there is no future tense in English and that *will* and *shall* are used as modals. For example, Palmer (1990) stated that *be going to* is a more appropriate marker of the future tense because *will* and *shall* rarely refer to "pure" future (p. 160). He acknowledged, however, that the differences between the predictive (and modal) and future meanings of *will* and *shall* are indeterminate and that little may be gained by attempting to define them. Nonetheless, Quirk et al. (1985) and Leech and Svartvik (1994) commented that *will* and *shall* identify the future reference in many contexts. According to Hoye's (1997) findings based on the Survey of English Usage Corpus of English, in written and spoken discourse, in a large majority of its occurrences, *will* is employed to express prediction and futurity, which may be indistinguishable. In academic texts, the predictive function of *will* can mark logical inferencing based in prior experience and involves only an element of futurity (Hyland, 1998). In composition writing, the future tense is described as indicating "actions that have yet to begin" (Lunsford & Connors, 1997, p. 115) or "that will occur in the future" (Hacker, 1994, p. 306).

The occurrences of *will, shall,* and *be going to* were counted inclusively as markers of the future tense without distinction.

ASPECTS

Textual Functions of Aspects

According to Quirk et al. (1985), in English, the progressive and perfect aspects are not deictic and, thus, unrelated to the time of an action or event. The aspects refer to the contrasting meanings of the action or time that is in progress or completed, respectively. Quirk et al. also emphasized that although in traditional grammars aspects are closely associated with tenses, tenses are realized morphologically, and aspects syntactically. Croft (1998) clarified that in English, aspects refer to the internal structure of events and identify their conceptual duration (or progression) or completion. For example, the distinction between the simple and the progressive tenses may mark the meaning differences between states, or processes. In

---

[1]Although *shall* is not typically used in American English, L2 students occasionally use it in their writing because of their ESL/EFL training obtained outside the United States.

the teaching of writing, aspects are discussed together with tenses because both are considered to be important in text development and cohesion (Hacker, 1994; Smoke, 1999). For example, (a) *So, when he was studying singing, everybody was laughing at him* (Japanese), and (b) *In this school, I have seen many things that I had never seen before, such as students are saying their opinions and arguing with the teacher* (Chinese).

Although Chinese and Japanese have durative, continuative, and completive meanings expressed by means of adverbials and particles (Norman, 1990), none have verbal aspect markers (Shibatani, 1990; Zhu, 1996). Korean has a perfective aspect in which the semantic implications are similar to those of the English past perfect. Korean nonperfective aspects include inchoative, iterative, habitual, and durative, the meanings of which may be quite distant from those of similar constructs in English (Sohn, 1995). Vietnamese has no conceptual or inflectional aspects (Nguyen, 1987). In Arabic, however, the perfective aspect is used to mark the completion of an action and the past time removed from the deictic focus, relative to the present moment (Kaye, 1987). However, the imperfective aspect is not equivalent to the iterative or habitual meanings of the English simple tenses and can also be employed to mark the progression or incompletion of an action.

Progressive.   In English, the progressive aspect is usually marked by auxiliary *be* + the *-ing* form of the main verb. It indicates the action in progress at a given time or at the moment of speaking (Quirk et al., 1985), with the exception of states *(know, believe, understand)* or habitual actions (see the subsection on the Present Tense). The use of the progressive aspect is largely associated with spoken and informal registers (Biber, 1995) and is often employed in personal and/or expressive narratives (Chafe, 1994).

Perfect.   The meanings of the simple past and present perfect are not always distinguishable in English, and both mark an action or event for completion (Quirk et al., 1985) without providing a specific time reference. The perfective aspect with the present tense may imply the current relevance of an event to the present moment and indicate that the action or event took place at an earlier time. Swales and Feak (1994) noted that the use of the perfective aspect with the present tense occurs in academic writing to mark a continuing action (research, discussion, project) and that its use is conventionalized. The occurrence of the perfective aspect with the past tense (the past perfect) indicates the meaning of "past in-the-past" (Quirk et al., 1985, p. 195), removed from the deictical present and current relevance. In academic writing, the past perfect is relatively rare as it occurs mostly in historical narratives.

The frequencies of the progressive and the perfect aspects were counted separately from those of tenses because some studies have shown that the meanings of aspects create an additional level of complexity for NNSs (Hinkel, 1992; Sharwood Smith & Rutherford, 1988).

Uses of Tenses in Student Texts

Much earlier research has been devoted to NNS uses of English tenses, and various studies have demonstrated that L2 learners do not use them in ways similar to those of NSs (Guiora, 1983; Hinkel, 1992; Riddle, 1986). The data in this study elaborate on that point.

TABLE 7.1

Median Frequency Rates for Verb Tenses and Aspects (Median %)

		NS	Chinese	Japanese	L1 Korean	Vietnamese	Indonesian	Arabic
Past		**1.52**	**2.90****	**3.37****	**3.57****	**2.86****	**2.78****	**0.56****
	Range	11.88	16.67	13.02	11.82	13.01	11.46	7.41
Present		**9.41**	**9.76***	**10.00***	**9.67**	**9.03**	**9.85**	**9.31**
	Range	31.88	14.62	17.42	27.33	13.78	25.24	19.97
Future		**0.38**	**0.74****	**0.23***	**0.44**	**0.45**	**0.69****	**0.55***
	Range	5.68	12.93	5.21	6.16	4.81	5.26	5.23
Progressive		**0.36**	**0.00****	**0.00****	**0.00****	**0.00****	**0.00****	**0.00***
	Range	3.54	3.85	2.04	1.57	2.14	2.66	2.50
Perfect		**0.32**	**0.00****	**0.00****	**0.00****	**0.24***	**0.00****	**0.00****
	Range	3.33	1.76	3.31	2.31	1.94	3.03	3.01

Note. All comparisons are relative to NSs.

*one-tailed $p < 0.05$. **two-tailed $p < 0.05$.

Past. In academic texts, the past tense is employed in discussing past-time events, such as observations, experiment results, cases studies, and conclusions (Swales & Feak, 1994). However, it is important to keep in mind that much of the NNS text in the essays was devoted to recounting personal past experiences and those of friends and relatives. For example, *I had this similar problem when I was deciding my major in the sophomore year. I wanted to major in fine arts, but I was worried about my job possibilities. I ended up studying in business but never liked it. Therefore, my grades were not very pleasant, also I did not learn much because I was not interested in business* (Japanese). The frequency rates of past-tense uses of NSs (median 1.52) and NNSs (medians between 0.67 and 3.57) differed significantly in the L2 texts of all groups. However, whereas speakers of tenseless languages, such as Chinese, Japanese, and Indonesian, used significantly higher rates of past-tense verbs, the texts of the speakers of Arabic included significantly lower rates of this tense. Among the languages whose speakers wrote the essays, only English and Arabic have a developed morphological system of marking tenses, and in fact, the past tense in these two languages is often used in similar contexts. For example, Hinkel (1992) found that speakers of Arabic had less difficulty with the English tense system and the past tense in particular than speakers of tenseless languages, such as Chinese, Japanese, and Vietnamese.

A more important issue, however, is the contexts in which the uses of the past tense are considered to be appropriate in text, and earlier studies have found that speakers of tenseless languages employ the past in contexts different from those in which NSs do. Furthermore, sweeping generalizations and formulaic expressions in the texts of Arabs (Ostler, 1987) differ from the recounts of experiences and storytelling mixed with general truths in the essays of, for example, Chinese or Japanese. In most cases, generalizations are marked by a predominant use of the present tense, and experiences and stories are usually narrated in the past. For instance, the personal narrative exemplified earlier is similar to this recount by a NS: *My mom is a secretary at an elementary school. When she was younger, she had no plans on being a secretary, and she wanted to do something bigger. But she got married and had no chance to go to college because she had to take care of my dad, me, and my brothers.*

On the other hand, essays of Chinese, Japanese, and particularly Arabic speakers devoted much text to generalizations that require the use of the present tense (see the subsection on the Present Tense in the subsequent discussion) with past tense interspersed occasionally: *If people choose their major field of study just because they can find jobs easily after graduation, they are wrong. They cannot survive in the field of study they choose as they don't like it. They don't enjoy learning and studying the field; as a result, they do not graduate. If they don't graduate, they cannot have the jobs. For example, I used to think that I am good at science. However, after I evaluate myself and receive some inputs from my teachers, I am convinced that science is not the study field I am good at. . . . My uncle studied hospitality in Switzerland. He just found out that hospitality does not fit him when he had the job in the field* (Chinese). In this text, several generalizations in the present tense are followed by two examples, one in the present where the past tense would probably be more appropriate in the context of the past-time self-evaluation and input from teachers. The other example employs mixed present and past tenses, even though the recounting of the uncle's experiences could also be better told in the past tense.

Present.   Uses of present tense are common in generalizations and reports of information that reflect the author's own opinion (Swales & Feak, 1994). In all language groups, present tense was the most frequently used language feature (see Table 7.1). As has been mentioned, the NS (median 9.41) frequency rates of the present tense differed significantly only from those in the essays of Chinese (9.76) and Japanese (10.00) speakers, whose texts included past-time personal narratives mixed with present-tense generalizations. In fact, it is interesting to note that overall, judging from the frequency rates of all tenses combined, the essays of Arabic speakers contained fewer verbs than texts of, for example, NS, Chinese, Korean, or Japanese speakers. Palmer (1994) pointed out that Arabic has few verbs similar to copulative *(be)* verbs in English, whereas Chinese, Japanese, Korean, and Vietnamese include several types of existential and copula-like verbs to express a variety of meanings, such as existence, liking, ability, or experientiality (Li & Thompson, 1981; Nguyen, 1987; Shabatani, 1990).

Future. In NNS essays, the future tense is often used to refer to events that can be possible or potential outcomes of the present situation: *Because, sooner or later one __will__ have enough money and after that she or he __will__ look for other values of life. If they don't have any job which reflects their interests, they __will__ find themselves in trouble because we spend most of our lives dealing with our jobs* (Arab). In this excerpt, the future marker *will* is used in the instances where a NS would use a modal verb (*may* or *might*) to express a possibility or *would* to express potentiality. For example, similar predictive meanings can be found in NS texts: *Although I know I __would__ be happier being a photographer and study* [sic] *the ocean, I feel the business world __would__ put out more opportunity for me.* The frequency rates of *will* in NS texts (median 0.38) were significantly lower than those of Chinese speakers (median 0.74), Indonesian (0.69), and Arabic (0.60). However, the NS rates of the future tense were significantly higher than those of Japanese (0.23) and similar to those of Korean (0.44) and Vietnamese (0.45) writers, whose essays tended to be recounts of personal experiences and included particularly high rates of the past tense.

Uses of Verb Aspects in Student Texts

Progressive. In research on the acquisition of tenses and tense inflections, the progressive aspect in the present tense has been noted as relatively easy for NNSs to acquire (Hinkel, 1992). Nonetheless, in the NNS essays, the issue of progressive aspect use is not so much the acquisition of this aspect as it is contextual meanings and uses in academic text. According to Biber (1988), the progressive aspect is considered to be appropriate in the spoken register and is relatively rare in formal academic discourse. Similarly, in composition instruction, the usage of the progressive aspect is often discouraged because it is seen as inappropriate in most formal essays (Raimes, 1992; Smoke, 1999; Swales and Feak, 1994).

From the data in Table 7.1, it is clear that the majority of NNSs did not use the progressive aspect a great deal (medians of 0.00 for all L1 groups), which differed significantly from the frequency rates of NSs (median 0.36).

Perfect. The meanings and uses of the perfect aspect in English are verifiably complex. They cannot always be distinguished from those of the simple past tense (Quirk et al., 1985) because both denote the completion of a past-time action or event. In academic texts, the perfect aspect in the present tense can refer to continuing events or projects, and its uses are usually conventionalized (Swales & Freak, 1994). Earlier research has shown that this aspect is also particularly difficult for NNSs to acquire and use in appropriate contexts (Hinkel, 1992; Sharwood Smith & Rutherford, 1988). Thus, as with the progressive aspect, NNS essays contained few occasions for perfect aspect use, which was significantly lower than that of NSs (median 0.32 vs. 0.00 for speakers of Chinese, Japanese, Korean, Indonesian, and Arabic and 0.24 for Vietnamese).

SEMANTIC AND LEXICAL CLASSES OF VERBS[2]

Textual Functions

Verbs are often divided into semantic classes according to their meanings and textual functions. Quirk et al. (1985) classified some factual verbs as public, private, and suasive.

Public: *acknowledge, add, admit, agree, announce, argue, assert, bet, certify, claim, comment, complain, concede, confess, confide, confirm, contend, convey, declare, deny, disclose, exclaim, explain, guarantee, hint, insist, maintain, mention, object, offer, predict, present, promise, pronounce, protest, remark, repeat, reply, report, say, show, speak, state, submit, suggest, swear, tell, testify, warn, write.* For example, *I definitely <u>agree</u> that parents should <u>explain</u> things to their children, but they can never <u>tell</u> them what to do.*

Public verbs refer to actions that can be observed publicly and that are used to introduce indirect (and reported) statements.

Private: *accept, anticipate, ascertain, assume, believe, calculate, check, conclude, consider, decide, deduce, deem, demonstrate, determine, discover, doubt, dream, ensure, establish, estimate, expect, fancy, fear, feel, find, foresee, forget, gather, guess, hear, hold, hope, imagine, imply, indicate, infer, judge, know, learn, mean, note, notice, observe, perceive, presume, pretend, prove, realize, reason, recall, reckon, recognize, reflect, remember, reveal, see, sense, suppose, suspect, study, think, understand.* For example, *They don't <u>realize</u> how hard these wealthy people work to show their audiences that they are the best* (Arab).

Private verbs express intellectual states (e.g., *know, learn, think*) and nonobservable intellectual acts that are "private," for example, emotive *(feel, hope),* mental *(realize, understand),* and cognitive *(foresee, recognize).*

---

[2]The lists of items herein are not exhaustive and are limited to those encountered in the corpus.

Suasive: *allow, ask, beg, command, demand, determine, grant, insist, instruct, intend, order, pray, prefer, propose, recommend, request, require, resolve, urge, vote.* For example, *I absolutely insist that classes should be entertaining.*

Suasive verbs can also function as causal or "mandative" (Quirk et al., 1985, p. 1182) and express a directive to or intention for change (e.g., *order, require*).

Logical-semantic relationships: *accompany, alternate (with), apply, approximate, arise (from), cause, combine (with), compare, complement, conflict, constitute, contradict, contrast (with), distinguish, follow, illustrate, lead, occur, precede, produce, prove, replace, resemble, reflect, result (in), sum.* For example, *These days parents treat their children like babies, and they cause their children's failure in their school work* (Japanese).

Halliday (1994) explained that, in formal academic texts, certain verb classes refer to causes, proofs, embodiments of knowledge or concepts, and other logical-semantic relationships between actions and within experiential contexts. Their function is to represent the construction of knowledge and value by establishing cause and/or providing proof for events.

Expecting/wanting/tentative verbs: *attempt, desire, expect, like, plan, try, want, wonder.* For example, *Some students try to pass their classes because they really want to, but others expect that grades just would be given to them* (Chinese).

Expecting/wanting/tentative verbs refer to the future time, and are often employed in tentative constructions that imply an element of uncertainty (Quirk et al.,1985). These verbs occur more frequently in speech and informal register than in writing, and it is often difficult to clearly differentiate between these and private and suasive verbs (Biber, 1988). Expecting/wanting/tentative verbs are relatively few compared to those in other classes. Johnson (1989) found that in their formal papers, NNSs use substantially more private and expecting/tentative verbs than NSs do because L2 writers rely on hesitation and hedging devices to project politeness and their humble stance in propositions and claims.

Seem/appear are considered to be evidential verbs, and they refer to the process of reasoning or conclusions from reasoning (Chafe, 1985, 1986). They are common in academic texts and are usually employed as hedges (Huebler, 1983; Hyland, 1998). The frequency counts of these verbs in this study include their occurrences of all tenses.

Uses of Various Classes of Verbs in Student Texts

Semantic classes of verbs in English are numerous but only a few are common in students' essays. In general terms, their frequency rates in texts provide evidence of the extents of the writers' vocabulary ranges. However, although the large classes of private, public, suasive, logical-semantic relationship, and expecting/tentative verbs include advanced items found in published texts (e.g., *acknowledge, advocate, certify, foresee, reckon*), these classes also include many relatively simple verbs *(argue, believe, decide, know, say, speak)*. It is important to note that in student essays, lexically simple verbs in these semantic classes occur with far greater frequencies than other more complex items.

Public.   Because some of the public verbs are very common and simple, their frequency rates in NNS essays exceeded those in NS texts dramatically: for instance, almost four-fold in texts of Chinese and Arabic speakers, compared to NS rates (NS median 0.36 and NNS between 0.88 and 1.39 (see Table 7.2). For example, *In the first quarter, she <u>complained</u> to me that it was a very difficult major. After several quarters she <u>told</u> me it was not as hard as the first time. She <u>said</u> it was the right major for her* (Indonesian).

Private.   Private verbs were also very common in the essays of NSs and NNSs, except those of speakers of Arabic (NS median 2.00 and NNS between 2.27 and 3.36). For example, *Some students think that it would easy for them to choose a major. They <u>think</u> it will be enjoyable for them to <u>study</u>, or probably they have their own ideas they <u>dream</u> about* (Indonesian), or *I <u>remember</u> the time my father asked me what I <u>think</u> about my major. So, I started to <u>think</u> about a major where employment is easy* (Vietnamese).

It is interesting to note (see Table 7.2), however, that in both NS and NNS texts, the frequency rates of private verb uses greatly exceeded those of public verbs, particularly in the case of NSs (e.g., NS public verb median 0.36 and private verb median 2.00, speakers of Chinese public verb median 1.33 and private verb median 3.30, Indonesian public verb median 0.88

TABLE 7.2
Median Frequency Rates for Semantic and Lexical Classes of Verbs (Median %)

		NS	Chinese	Japanese	*L1* Korean	Vietnamese	Indonesian	Arabic
Public		**0.36**	**1.33****	**0.92****	**1.00****	**1.00****	**0.88****	**1.42****
	Range	6.73	7.06	7.24	8.05	6.29	8.89	7.89
Private		**2.00**	**3.30****	**3.33****	**2.92****	**2.70***	**3.36****	**2.16**
	Range	10.81	9.52	9.23	10.39	8.42	13.33	9.47
Suasive		**0.20**	**0.33**	**0.28**	**0.00****	**0.47***	**0.30**	**0.55****
	Range	4.17	3.21	3.33	1.72	3.36	3.13	3.13
Log./sem. relat.		**0.47**	**0.57***	**0.43**	**0.36***	**0.52**	**0.58***	**0.51**
	Range	4.09	4.78	4.61	2.59	3.18	4.63	3.13
Tentative		**0.52**	**0.87****	**1.10****	**1.67****	**0.69***	**1.09****	**0.72****
	Range	3.41	6.55	7.64	8.55	5.39	5.69	4.76
Seem/appear		**0.00**	**0.00**	**0.00**	**0.00**	**0.00**	**0.00***	**0.00***
	Range	0.83	2.08	1.25	1.22	0.49	0.45	0.63

Note. All comparisons are relative to NSs.

*one-tailed $p < 0.05$. **two-tailed $p < 0.05$.

and private verb median 3.36). In all likelihood, this fact is a direct result of the types of essays that all students were required to produce and that necessitated their statement and explanation of their opinions. The wording of the prompts, modeled after those in standardized tests, such as the TOEFL and SAT, instructs writers to state and support their opinions on various issues.

Suasive. These verbs were not very common in NS (median 0.20) or NNS texts, and NS frequency rates did not differ significantly from those of Chinese, Japanese, or Indonesian speakers. In the essays of Korean speakers (median 0.00), suasive verbs were found significantly less frequently than in NSs texts. On the other hand, the frequency rates of suasives were significantly higher in essays of speakers of Vietnamese (median 0.47) and Arabic (median 0.33). However, the frequency rates of suasive verbs in the texts of Vietnamese and Arabic speakers were primarily determined by repeated uses of just a few items, such as *ask, prefer, require,* and *recommend,* for example, *History classes are <u>required</u>, but they have no connection to my major* (Vietnamese) *or All students <u>prefer</u> to take easy classes such as music or art* (Arab).

Logical-Semantic Relationships. Halliday (1994) found that these verbs appear predominantly in formal academic texts because they refer to causes, proofs, and constitutive knowledge and concepts, for example, *When the teacher teaches, he <u>leads</u>* students to knowledge, and students must *<u>follow</u>* the teacher (Chinese), or *In American universities, students need to <u>apply</u>* theory to real life, and this does not exist in my country (Indonesian). Although these verbs were used by the majority of students in all language groups, they were not nearly as common as public or private verbs. The comparisons of NS frequency rates (median 0.47) to those of NNSs were mixed: similar in the texts of speakers of Japanese, Vietnamese, and Arabic but significantly higher than those in essays of speakers of Korean (median 0.36) and significantly lower than in the texts of Chinese (median 0.57) and Indonesian (median 0.58) speakers.

Expecting/Wanting/Tentative Verbs. These are largely simple and very common *(expect, like, plan, try, want),* and this lexical class includes fewer than 10 items. Their frequency rates in NNS texts (medians between 0.69 and 1.67) were significantly higher than those of NSs (median 0.52). For example, *American companies <u>expect</u> students to have knowledge in business because <u>they</u> want them to solve problems that the company has* (Japanese), *Firstly, I <u>want</u> to give an example* (Korean), or *Thus, to do what we really <u>want</u> is important* (Chinese).

Seem/appear were not at all common in student essays, as can be seen from the medians of 0.00 for all groups. Despite the lack of popularity of *seem/appear* in the essays, texts of Indonesian and Arabic speakers employed hardly any of these evidential verbs at all; that is, significantly fewer than NSs did.

MODAL VERBS[3]

Textual Functions

In general terms, the meanings and functions of modal verbs can be divided into three classes: those that denote ability, possibility, and permission; those that refer to obligation and/or necessity; and those that mark volition and prediction (Hermeren, 1978; Quirk et al., 1985).

Possibility and ability: *can, may, might, could, be able to* (and contractions). For example, *Universities want to graduate students who are able to write a letter without making mistakes all over the place* (Japanese).

In academic texts, modal verbs of possibility can also have the function of evidentials (Chafe, 1985) and hedges (Hinkel, 1995c, 1997a; Hoye, 1997; Hyland, 1998). The pseudomodal of possibility and ability *be able to* (in all tenses) was included in the counts because this is how it is ubiquitously presented in grammar texts (Quirk et al., 1985) and pedagogical ESL/EFL grammars (Greenbaum & Quirk, 1990; Leech & Svartvik, 1994). Palmer (1990) pointed out that *be able to* always indicates ability that is subject oriented and is frequently used as an implicative case of *can*.

Obligation and necessity: *must, have to, should, ought, need to, to be to, to be supposed to* (and contractions). For example, *People should study what they like, and they don't need to worry about getting a job because who knows what field will be popular in the future* (Indonesian). Necessity modals can refer to reasoning and conclusion making (Chafe, 1994).

In Japanese and Korean, modal verbs of obligation and necessity can also function as evidentials and hedges (Hwang, 1987; Maynard, 1993). In Chinese, however, modals are divided into two large classes that have the meanings of possibility and necessity. The modals of possibility include additional subclasses of ability, permission, and probability. Necessity modals refer to inclination, obligation, and certainty (Zhu, 1996). In writing, they can be used in contexts similar to those of English modals but cover a wider range of meanings and contextual implications, such as insistence, intention, willingness, compulsion, and occasionality. In Vietnamese, meanings similar to those expressed by necessity and possibility modals are usually conveyed by means of particles and/or action verbs (Nguyen, 1987). On the other hand,

---

[3]Some types of modals without an explicit or implicit lexical verb are called modal auxiliaries in Biber et al. (1999).

in Arabic these meanings are expressed through stative adjectives or adverbs (Kaye, 1987). Hinkel (1995b) reported that in formal texts, speakers of Asian languages, such as Chinese, Korean, Japanese, and Vietnamese, use modals of obligation and necessity in contexts different from those in which NSs consider them to be appropriate.

Predictive: *would* (and contractions). The predictive modal *would* in English may also have the function of a hedge in formal and informal academic writing, and it conveys hypothetical and presuppositional meanings (Huebler, 1983; Tadros, 1994). In addition, it may serve as a means of reducing the writer's responsibility for the truth value and accuracy of evidence in a piece of writing (Chafe, 1986). Palmer (1990) specified that the predictive conditional *would* refers to future events that are contingent on a particular proposition that may be unreal or counterfactual. The predictive conditional with real or unreal meanings refers to the future in complex ways and depends on particular mixed time relations that preclude the use of the future tense maker *will*.[4]

Although many researchers recommend that both NSs and NNSs be taught their meanings and uses (Channel, 1994; Coates, 1983; Tadros, 1994), in L1 and L2 composition instruction, explanations of modal verb uses and functions are often vague. According to Smoke (1999) and Raimes (1992), in composition writing, the line between the meanings of modals of possibility, necessity, and prediction can be blurred. L2 writers are often advised to demonstrate good judgment and use modal verbs appropriately to moderate their claims and to avoid strong predictives and implications of certainty (Swales & Feak, 1994). In published academic texts in American, Australian, and British English, the meanings of modals are indeterminate, frequently culturally stereotyped, and convey normative and referential relationships that differ across the dialects, discourse genre, and social structures in English-speaking communities (Collins, 1991). Together with other prevalent features of academic writing in English, modal verbs occupy a prominent place in composition and writing instruction, and college-level writers are expected to be familiar with their appropriate uses (Hacker, 1994).

The pseudomodals *need to* and *have to* were also included in the counts of necessity modals.

Modal Verbs in Student Texts

Much research has been devoted to the meanings, uses, and textual functions of modal verbs. In general, they are common in spoken and written registers in practically all types of texts (Biber, 1988).

---

[4]The frequency counts of the future auxiliary *will* are not included in those of predictive modals (see previous subsection entitled Future).

Possibility. In NS (median 0.97) and NNS texts, possibility, ability, and permission verbs appear to be quite common, and their frequency rates did
not differ significantly in NS, Vietnamese, Indonesian, and Arab essays. On
the other hand, texts of speakers of Chinese, Japanese, and Korean contained significantly higher rates of these verbs (medians between 1.26 and
1.41) than NS texts (see Table 7.3). Several studies have demonstrated that
these verbs express hesitation and uncertainty (Hinkel, 1995c, 1999b)
appropriate in classical rhetorical traditions other than Anglo-American
and common in the ESL essays of Chinese, Japanese, and Korean speakers.
For example, *There are so many faculty positions in universities in China, whether
you <u>can</u> get it or not depends on your current level* (Chinese), *People <u>cannot</u> work
in one field for a long time, if they don't like it* (Korean), or *First of all, if people
choose a major which interesting for them, they <u>can</u> get a job which is also interesting
for them. They <u>can</u> enjoy their life all the same* (Japanese). In many NNS essays,
possibility modals *may* and *might* were not as common as *can* and *could,*
because the distinctions in the meanings of permission/possibility and pos-
sibility/ability implicit in *may/might* and *can/could* are not always easily
apparent to NNSs (Hinkel, 1999b).

Necessity. Modal verbs of obligation and necessity *(must, should, need to,
have to)* are far more common in NNS than in NS texts, and earlier studies
have shown that the frequency rates of their uses are topic-dependent
(Hinkel, 1995b). Specifically, in NNS essays that discuss family obligations
and responsibilities and the role of an individual in society, Chinese, Japanese, Korean, and Vietnamese learners, socialized according to the Confucian norms of familial loyalty and appropriate conduct, employ the verbs of
obligation and necessity far more frequently than NSs do in similar discourse contexts. For example, *The children's duty is to support their parents
when they get old, and we <u>must</u> do our best to be good children to our parents* (Chinese) or *Because I am the oldest son, I <u>have to</u> do as my father says. If he chooses for*

TABLE 7.3
Median Frequency Rates for Modal Verbs (Median %)

		NS	Chinese	Japanese	Korean	Vietnamese	Indonesian	Arabic
					L1			
Possibility		0.97	1.26**	1.41**	1.33**	0.98	1.00	1.08
	Range	5.00	7.14	5.51	4.39	5.71	5.71	4.50
Necessity		0.60	1.36**	1.34**	1.37**	0.99**	0.83**	0.84*
	Range	4.81	7.94	6.02	8.99	4.43	5.00	5.12
Predictive		0.38	0.00**	0.00**	0.00**	0.00**	0.00**	0.21*
	Range	4.14	3.34	3.79	3.51	4.43	2.18	3.76

Note. All comparisons are relative to NSs.
*one-tailed *p* < 0.05. **two-tailed *p* < 0.05.

me to study engineering, I <u>have to</u> do it because I <u>need to</u> give honor to my family (Korean). In this study (see Table 7.3), the NNS frequency rates of modal verbs of obligation and necessity (medians between 0.78 and 1.37) in some cases were twice as high as those of NSs (median 0.60). Although in light of the findings in previous studies this finding is not particularly surprising, because some of the essay prompts were associated with family and education issues, the high rates of NNS use of obligation and necessity verbs may have been induced by the essay topics. It is important to mention, however, that overall, topics dealing with education and family are common on standardized tests because they are believed to be easily accessible to ESL students in various geographic locations.

Predictive. The predictive modal verb *would* is complex both lexically and syntactically because its meanings are ambiguous and variable, depending on the context; for example, in *I <u>would</u> like to say that . . . , If the teacher knew what I am thinking, he <u>would</u> understand,* or *My father said that he <u>would</u> give me money, would* has distinct functions of a politeness device, an auxiliary verb of the hypothetical present tense, and the future-in-the past tense marker associated with reported speech (Quirk et al., 1985). Because the meanings and uses of this verb are conceptually advanced, in all NNS groups (medians from 0.00 to 0.19), its frequency rates were significantly lower than those of NSs (median 0.38). Essentially, NNSs did not use *would* a great deal.

THE PASSIVE VOICE (+ *BY*-PHRASE)

Textual Functions

Passive constructions have been identified as one of the prominent features of academic and composition writing. Use of the passive voice is often intended to create an impersonal, indirect, and detached style and project the writer's objectivity (Biber, 1988; Myers, 1989; Swales, 1990a). Agentless passive is prevalent in structures that front thematic information and/or remove the agent from the prominent sentence position (Huebler, 1983; Jacobs, 1995).

Atkinson (1991) explained that scientific passive is often conventionalized in the rhetorical constructs of Anglo-American academic texts. Similarly, Swales and Feak (1994) noted that traditionally in academic writing, passive is often more suitable than active voice and is often considered to be requisite in written genres in such disciplines as natural sciences and engineering. In reaction to the conventionalized use of passive in academic texts, in the United States, much L1 writing instruction and many composition texts discourage the use of the passive voice, except on rare occasions (Hacker, 1994; Lunsford & Connors, 1997).

On the other hand, Owen (1993) showed that the uses of the passive in English can be severely lexically constrained and idiomatic and may not necessarily be learned from L2 instruction. He asserted that many uses of the passive can be pragmatic and discoursal, and in some cases, unacceptability of the passive can be subjectively gradient, ranging from nonidiomatic to idiomatic.

Although passive constructions are found in many languages, their meanings and functions are highly diverse, and they cannot be systematically translated from one language to another. For example, in Chinese, the passive is marked by means of a particle and, in some structures, also requires subject and object transformations (Li & Thompson, 1981). In Japanese, both direct and indirect passives are employed, and they can have resultative and theme- (topic) fronting meanings. Hoshi (1993) commented that in Japanese, subject-oriented adverbials require passive in subject- and rheme-fronted constructions that project imprecision and indirectness by avoiding direct subject references. In Korean, the passive is also prevalent in structures that differentiate between theme and rheme fronting, and can be used to avoid directly mentioning the subject of the clause (Kitahara, 1993). As in English, the Korean passive is often idiomatic and lexicalized, and in writing, the passives are employed to convey the author's respect for and solidarity with the audience (Hwang, 1987).

Indonesian passives necessarily distinguish between the beneficiary and the recipient of the action expressed by the verb and are overt markers of indirectness and detachment (Palmer, 1994). In Vietnamese, passive constructions do not exist, and passive meanings are expressed through verbs of experiencing and becoming, as well as subject or topic markers (Palmer, 1994). Nguyen (1987), however, pointed out that the passive voice in Vietnamese can be also expressed by means of clause subordination and topicalization[5] that depend on whether the action of the clause has benefective or adversative outcomes to the clause subject or topic. He stated that although topicalization "is sometimes translatable into English as passive" (p. 787), most types of the Vietnamese passivization are not.

On the other hand, Arabic has morphologically derived passive constructions that, as those in English, require the object promotion to the clause subject position. In addition, however, Arabic distinguishes between object-passive, and temporal-/locative-passive (e.g., *"Ramadan was fasted";* Palmer, 1994, p. 118) that are often requisite in formal and written registers.

The counts of passive voice in this study include all passive verbs with or without the *by*-phrase and as marked by the presence of the auxiliary *be* in all

---

[5]The fronting of the topic phrase, as in *For students, they need to follow the teacher* or *For Bob to win the race is quite a coup.*

tenses (and contractions). For example, *Because of the one-child policy, many young people in my country <u>are spoiled</u> because everything in their life <u>is prepared</u> by their parents. In some families, even their homework <u>is done</u> for them* (Chinese).

Uses of the Passive Voice in Student Texts

In all groups, the frequency rates of NS passive uses (median 1.19) was significantly greater than and occasionally two-fold of that of NNSs in all groups (medians from 0.49 to 0.80). In the studies of L2 learning, the passive voice has been proven to be particularly difficult for speakers of Chinese, Japanese, or Korean to acquire because in these languages, the passive voice has dramatically different conceptual and cognitive parameters, compared to those of the passive voice in English (Hinkel, in press; Master, 1991). Furthermore, the meanings and contextual uses of passive structures are severely lexicalized and idiomatic, thus making them prohibitively difficult to learn (Owen, 1993).

BE-COPULA AS THE MAIN VERB

Textual Functions

Be as the main verb has copula and existential functions and often marks stative constructions (Quirk et al., 1985). It conveys existential meanings of supplying and/or presenting information, and it is common in descriptive and expository writing. Structures with *be* as the main verb are somewhat simpler than those with verbs that have higher semantic and lexical content. For this reason, they are more characteristic of spoken than of written discourse and can serve as alternatives to attributive descriptions (e.g, *Baseball players are wealthy—Wealthy baseball players*) (Biber, 1988). For example, *He <u>was</u> terrible in chemistry, but his parents thought that he should <u>be</u> a doctor like they <u>are</u>* (Korean).

In general terms, copula *be* proper is a feature mainly of Indo-European languages. However, existential and copula-like verbs play a somewhat similar role in Chinese, when their function is to ascribe certain roles and attributes to the sentence subject, for example, *Ming* copula *my brother* (Norman, 1990). A range of existential and copula-like verbs can be found in Japanese, Korean, or Vietnamese, and they often have various grammatical and discourse functions, for example, possessive, adjectival predicate, or nominative and accusative distinctions. In these languages, the use of existential verbs depends on the animacy of the subject nouns, and some have the discourse functions of expressing liking, necessity, ability, and experientiality (Li & Thompson, 1981; Nguyen, 1987; Shibatani, 1990). Aoki (1986) emphasized that Japanese existential or copula-like verbs can also function as hedged evidentials when describing inner emotions and sensations of an experiencer removed in time and space, and hence, are prevalent in narratives and writing. Existential verbs in Arabic are few, and their meanings and functions are closer to those of the English *exist* and *have* than to copula *be* (e.g., *There exists money for him*) (Palmer, 1994). Indonesian has no copulative verbs (Sneddon, 1996).

The counts in this study include all forms of *be* as the main verb in all tenses (and contractions).

Uses in Student Texts

Due to its prevalence in attributive constructions, *be*-copula is largely associated with predicative adjectives in ideationally simple propositions that mostly consist of a subject and a predicate, such as *The money-making is very important, of course* (Korean), *The contents in University are very difficult* (Japanese), or *From above, my view is very clear. Being honest is more important than money. Students who are loyal to their interests are happy in their study* (Chinese).

As the data in Table 7.4 demonstrates, the frequency rates of *be*-copula in NNS texts (medians between 3.23 and 3.70) were markedly higher than those in NS essays (median 2.09), and in the essays of, for example, Korean speakers, the range of *be* frequencies included an upper bound of almost 15% of all words in the text. Another important issue to note is that the high frequency rates of this verb in NNS texts are closely tied with those for predicative adjectives (see chap. 8) that were employed at far greater rates than in NS texts.

INFINITIVES

Textual Functions of Infinitives

Infinitives are the base form of verbs that can be complements of nouns, verbs, and adjectives. According to Quirk et al. (1985), most infinitives

TABLE 7.4
Median Frequency Rates for Passive, *Be*-Main, and Infinitives (Median %)

		NS	Chinese	Japanese	Korean	Vietnamese	Indonesian	Arabic
					L1			
Passive		1.19	0.73**	0.80**	0.70**	0.49**	0.51**	0.65**
	Range	10.58	6.25	6.35	3.81	5.00	6.25	3.37
***Be*-main**		2.09	3.59**	3.70**	3.62**	3.23**	3.57**	3.53**
	Range	10.71	12.56	11.97	14.81	10.79	11.23	10.20
Infinitives		5.40	4.88*	5.38	2.87**	3.21**	3.44**	3.80**
	Range	24.11	11.52	14.58	11.67	11.11	11.26	12.86

Note. All comparisons are relative to NSs.
*one-tailed $p < 0.05$. **two-tailed $p < 0.05$.

represent reduced adverb clauses of purpose and retain their meanings. They can be marked or bare without the overt marker (as, e.g., those that follow modal verbs). Biber (1988) found that they often have the function of integrating and expanding idea units because they can allow for expressing ideas compactly. In his detailed study of the English infinitive, Duffley (1992) indicated that these constructions refer to an event as non-realized or yet to be realized with verbs of desire, endeavor, command, or requirement, but such events are understood as realized with verbs of accomplishment and achievement (e.g., *succeed, manage, persuade*). He further outlined the discourse functions of infinitives as those of purpose, reaction, and result (e.g., *I was surprised to see him fall*) and pointed out that infinitives in sentence subject positions can be used in depersonalized constructions. According to Duffley's findings, infinitives occur more frequently in written rather than in spoken English. These base forms of verbs have the syntactic function of noun, verb, and adjective complements, and their uses are often lexicalized. The textual functions of infinitives are relatively complex because in contexts with verbs of desire, endeavor, or requirement, they refer to actions and events that have not yet occurred. In addition, infinitives have the function of purpose, reaction, or result in impersonal constructions, common in formal written texts.

Uninflected Asian languages do not have infinitive verb forms. However, in Arabic, infinitives are marked by prefixes and are often used in contexts similar to those in English, for example, as clause subjects or verb complements (as in *He decided to go/promised to stay*) (Kaye, 1987).

The frequency counts in this study include marked and bare infinitives in all occurrences. For example, *His music teacher made him play violin eight hours a day, and he really hated to practice, but then he won the first prize and decided to be a professional* (Japanese).

Uses of Infinitives in Student Texts

Infinitives as such do not exist in many languages other than Indo-European (Palmer, 1994). In all NNS essays (medians from 2.87 to 4.88) with the exception of those of Japanese (median 5.38), infinitives were used substantially less frequently than in those of NSs (median 5.40; see Table 7.4). In NS texts, however, the range for infinitive usage went up to over 24% of all words. For example, *To spend eight hours a day at an abhorred occupation is a guarantee for misery. . . . Those who enjoy what they do for a living are more prone to strive to succeed, . . . but students today are beginning to lean more toward monetary benefits of any particular career* (NS).

PARTICIPLES

Textual Functions of Participles

Present participle: verb **+** *-ing.*
Past participle: verb **+** *-ed* or the past participle form of irregular verbs.

According to Quirk et al., (1985), in English, participles can perform the functions of nouns, verbs, and adjectives. Within the verb phrase, present and past participles can function as the main verb with progressive and perfect aspects, respectively. Past participles can be main verbs in passive voice constructions. Present and past participles can also be derived from complement, adjective, and adverb clauses. Because clausal participles represent a complex syntactic feature, they are more common in writing than in speech (Biber, 1988). In text, they function as a means of expanding ideas (Chafe, 1985) and creating textual unity and cohesion in elaboration and description (Halliday & Hasan, 1976). In English academic prose, amplification can take the form of evaluative adjectives (Swales & Feak, 1994). Present and past participles combine attitudinal and experiential meanings and refer to qualitative and emotive evaluations, size, age, and color (Poynton, 1996) (see also Amplifiers in chap. 8).

Participial forms do not exist in noninflectional languages. In Arabic, however, as in English, past participles are very common in passive voice and adjectival constructions when they have the function of attributive and/or predicative adjectives. Because in Arabic adjectives are postpositional and copulative verbs do not exist, it is not always possible to tell the difference between their attributive and/or predicative functions (e.g., *The book published*) (Palmer, 1994).

In this study, the counts of participles included only those found in full or reduced adverb (e.g., *While walking to the park, we saw John)* and adjective clauses *(The student sitting next to me is from Japan),* or fronted deverbal adjectives *(amused/amusing children).* Participles that function as main verbs in various tenses and the passive were excluded from the frequency counts of participles (see earlier sections Aspects and the Passive voice). For example, (a) *The formal manner <u>causing</u> students to take a nap during the lecture is normal in Korea* (Korean), and (b) *If <u>bored</u> and <u>tired</u>, students don't pay attention to the material, and then they miss the important points that they should know* (Arab).

Uses of Participles in Student Texts

In NNS essays, participles were not very common (medians between 0.00 and 0.60), compared to those in NS texts (medians of approximately 0.90 for both the present and the past; see Table 7.5).

TABLE 7.5
Median Frequency Rates for Participles (Median %)

		NS	Chinese	Japanese	Korean	Vietnamese	Indonesian	Arabic
					L1			
Present		**0.93**	**0.60****	**0.45****	**0.42****	**0.43****	**0.25****	**0.00****
	Range	6.15	4.81	5.26	3.81	4.94	5.68	3.23
Past		**0.89**	**0.43****	**0.36****	**0.34****	**0.24****	**0.28****	**0.28****
	Range	5.71	4.17	4.53	5.64	4.17	7.19	2.69

Note. All comparisons are relative to Nss.
*one-tailed $p < 0.05$. **two-tailed $p < 0.05$.

In general terms, as with the NS and NNS uses of nouns, pronouns, and nominals, the analysis of verb phrase elements in L2 texts shows that the more syntactically and lexically complex a particular verb phrase feature is, the less frequently it is encountered in NNS texts, compared to those of NSs. For instance, the frequency rates of the passive voice and participles were identified at substantially higher and *be* as the main verb at markedly lower rates in L1 than L2 essays. Similarly, the preponderance of past-tense occurrences in L2 texts points to the fact that many relied on past-time narratives as a means of rhetorical argumentation and providing evidence for their positions. This observation is further supported by the finding that uses of private verbs to refer to personal feelings and beliefs were also found in significantly higher rates in NNS than NS texts. Similarly, as with nouns and pronouns examined in chapter 6, the features of spoken genre, such as expecting/tentative verbs and modal verbs of necessity, were also common in L2 essays.

The findings in chapter 7 indicate that although NNS students have had a substantial exposure to spoken English, their familiarity with language features prevalent in formal academic written discourse is comparatively reduced. Together with expanding the NNS lexicon dealing with nouns, L2 instruction also needs to focus on additional work on increasing students' lexical variety of verbs. Furthermore, because in the course of daily communication in English advanced verb phrase constructions, such as the passive voice, the modal verbs of possibility, or participles may be relatively infrequent, it is important that NNS students work to increase their range of verbal constructions found in formal written text. In other words, whereas in L2 settings it is possible to attain conversational fluency without learning to employ advanced and academic language features, writing an academic essay may require a different set of vocabulary and syntactic constructions that are not found outside academic discourse and texts.

8

Adjectives and Adverbs and Their Functions and Uses in Text

Following the examination of nouns in chapter 6 and verbs in chapter 7, chapter 8 presents a discussion of adjectives and adverbs to outline their textual functions and uses in student texts. Combining the analysis of adjectives and adverbs into one chapter creates a slightly incongruous set of features because the two types of adjectives—attributive and predicative—are defined by their syntactic sentence/clause roles, whereas adverbs are classified based on their semantic and lexical properties. However, the redeeming quality of this organization is that both adjectives and adverbs represent secondary sentence elements, relative to noun phrase or verb phrase constituents. Each section is structured in the same way as the sections in chapters 6 and 7: First, the textual functions of adjectives or adverbs are presented, followed by a discussion of the study findings in regard to their uses in student texts.

The chapter begins with the discussion of two types of adjectives and then proceeds to the six most common lexical classes of adverbs: time, frequency, place, amplifiers, downtoners, and all other adverbs, such as manner and quality clustered into one category. As the data herein demonstrate, the combined uses of other adverbs were less frequently employed than, for example, adverbs of time or place.

To summarize the finding that follows, these features were used at significantly higher rates in NNS texts across all L1 groups:

118

- Predicative adjectives.
- Other adverbs (manner, conjunct, and adjective/verb modifiers).
- Amplifiers.

Among adjectives and adverbs, no features occurred significantly less frequently in NNS than NS text in all groups of texts.

ADJECTIVES

Textual Functions of Adjectives

The primary purpose of adjectives is description and elaboration. In this study, a distinction is made between attributive and predicative adjectives because they have different syntactic characteristics and textual functions. In English, attributive adjectives complement nouns and are a part of the noun phrase. Predicative adjectives belong among clause predication features and accompany copula *be* or linking verbs (e.g., *become, seem/appear, grow* + adjective). Although adjectives as a semantic and lexical class are found in most languages, the degree of their determinacy, syntactic roles, and discourse functions vary widely (Dixon, 1995). For example, in Chinese, adjectives similar to those in Indo-European languages do not exist (Li & Thompson, 1987), and they are considered to be a subset of verbs; for example, some researchers refer to them as verbs of state (e.g., *X content/difficult*) (Norman, 1990). In Japanese, they can be pronominal derivations that play the role of subject/object complements (e.g., *warmth* and *prettiness*) (Shibatani, 1990). According to Nguyen (1987), the structure of Vietnamese does not contain adjectives similar to those found in English. Rather, adjectival functions are performed by stative verbs or verbs of quality, and hence, most are predicative. In Arabic, adjectives are postpositional, and because there are no copula verbs, it is not always easy to distinguish between their attributive or predicative functions (as in *The boy tall* where the adjective can be both attributive and predicative). Furthermore, in Arabic, the forms of adjectives and adverbs are also indistinguishable, and have to be identified by their syntactic functions (Kaye, 1987).

In English discourse, adjectives play a role of deictic pre- and postnominal cohesive devices that can be anaphoric (Halliday & Hasan, 1976). In academic writing, attributive adjectives are employed for evaluation purposes, and the prevalence of particular types of adjectives appears to vary from discipline to discipline (e.g., *scholarly* and *rigorous* are common in humanities, and *elegant* and *economical* in physics) (Swales & Feak, 1994).

The frequency counts of attributive and predicative adjectives in this analysis included both simple and participial forms.

Attributive adjectives are those that are not a part of a clause predicate, for example, *a famous singer, an important class* (Quirk et al., 1985). Studies of academic corpora identify attributive adjectives as the predominant form of ideational and interpersonal modifiers that add information and definition to abstract nouns and often play attitudinal and classificatory roles in text cohesion (Francis, 1994). According to Chafe (1994), attributive adjectives have an important place in text flow because they provide sufficient or even unique definition and categorization to referents (usually, nouns) and increase their contextual salience. He also noted that although various types of referent modification can be used in text (e.g., possessives or prepositional phrases), attributive adjectives are relatively specific in their identification of referents and create for an easier text flow. In the frequency counts of attributive adjectives in this study, reduced adjective clauses and adjectival participles in postnominal positions were excluded. For example, *Famous artists in Indonesia don't make much money because people only want somebody to fix their economy.*

Predicative adjectives are those that are a part of a clause predicate, following copula *be* or linking verbs (e.g., *become, grow, seem/appear*). In written academic text, both attributive and predicative adjectives often function as lexical and strategic hedges that express a predicated state of affairs or a degree of variation relative to an expected norm (e.g., *it is possible/reasonable/relevant* or *two types of X are possible/applicable*) (Hyland, 1998). The use of adjectives as clause predicates allows for differentiation between theme/rheme and given/new information in nominal modification, when the clause subject usually refers to the given and the predicate to the new (Halliday, 1994). However, the employment of predicative adjectives imposes constraints on the range and type of information that can be conveyed because they require the presence of linking verbs and can only indicate states or particular properties of referents (Chafe, 1994). Hence, uses of predicative adjectives may signal a somewhat simplified clause structure and a stative/descriptive type of text. For example, *In my country, farmers are poor, their work is hard, and nobody cares if they are happy with their lives* (Vietnamese).

Uses of Adjectives in Student Texts

Attributive Adjectives. The employment of attributive adjectives in texts often necessitates a somewhat expanded range of vocabulary because these adjectives play attitudinal and classificatory roles in text cohesion (Francis, 1994). In the essays of speakers of Japanese, Korean, Vietnamese, and Indonesian (medians between 2.86 and 3.62), descriptive adjectives were used at significantly lower frequency rates than in those of NS (median 4.05). On the other hand, the attributive adjective rates in texts of Chinese and Arabic speakers did not differ substantially from those of NSs (see Table 8.1). For example, *Don't you think that is beautiful when a flock of birds fly across the <u>blue</u> sky? Don't you think you will be touched by when a <u>little</u> puppy or kitty looking into your eye?* (Chinese).

Predicative Adjectives. As has been mentioned, the usage of predicative adjectives often marks syntactically simple structures that distinguish between given/new information in propositions. The frequency rates of predicative adjectives (see Table 8.1) in NNS texts (medians between 2.78 and 3.41) were dramatically greater than those in NS texts (median 1.59). The NNS rates of predicate adjectives were almost twice the NSs' rates, and the data point to the fact that NNSs relied on simple syntactic structures and lexical means of conveying their ideas. For example, *When we are <u>young</u>, we have to make many important decisions, whether we are <u>ready</u> or not* (Indonesian), *I tried to study a doctor but it was too <u>difficult</u> for me* (Korean), or *Now computer industry is the most <u>popular</u> among students. Some of them are <u>enthusiastic</u> because they like to sit down in front of the computer for a long time* (Japanese).

TABLE 8.1
Median Frequency Rates for Adjectives (Median %)

		NS	Chinese	Japanese	Korean	Vietnamese	Indonesian	Arabic
					L1			
Attributive		**4.05**	**4.27**	**3.62***	**3.16****	**2.86****	**3.09****	**3.28***
	Range	14.34	13.28	13.84	14.81	15.97	15.97	14.31
Predicative		**1.59**	**3.33****	**3.41****	**3.24****	**2.78****	**3.17****	**3.13****
	Range	8.33	10.83	11.98	20.83	11.54	12.56	12.73

Note. All comparisons are relative to NSs.
*one-tailed $p < 0.05$. **two-tailed $p < 0.05$.

SEMANTIC AND LEXICAL CLASSES OF ADVERBS

Textual Functions of Adverbs

Adverbs are one of the largest word classes in English, and morphologically, three types can be determined: simple *(only, just)*, compound *(herewith)*, and derivational (those that are marked by the suffix *-ly*) (Quirk et al., 1985). Adverbs modify verbs, adjectives, whole clauses, and other adverbs, and their meanings are divided into semantic classes, such as time, place, frequency, and others. In text, adverbs play a variety of roles and can function as adjuncts, conjuncts, disjuncts, cohesive and referential devices, hedges, intensifiers, evidentials, diminutives, amplifiers, and downtoners (Halliday & Hasan, 1976). Because adverbs are ubiquitous in academic writing (Hoye, 1997), their occurrences in the corpus were counted according to the functions of their largest semantic classes (see also Epistemic Adjectives and Adverbs in chap. 10).

Adverbs and adverblike particles and adjuncts are also numerous in many Asian languages. In Chinese, semantic classes of adverbs include those with the meanings of time, location, direction, probability, certainty, and others (Zhu, 1996). Time adverbs are further divided into temporal adverbs, which locate an event on the time deixis and indicate how long it has been since it occurred, and durational adverbs, which refer to the length of time of an event. Japanese and Indonesian adverbs typically modify whole clauses and have meanings of time, manner, cause, frequency, and place. However, stative verbs and verb phrases can also be modified by adverbs (Prentice, 1987; Shibatani, 1987, 1990). In Korean, adverbs and adverb phrases can modify nouns, verbs, and whole clauses and are also divided into time, place, quantifier, nominalizer, and durational meanings (J.-H. Lee, 1993). However, because Chinese, Japanese, and Korean adverbs are often postpositional, it may be difficult to differentiate between locative, temporal, durational, and frequency adverbials, particles, and other type of markers in these languages (I. Taylor, 1995). In Vietnamese, adverbs per se do not exist, and instead, particles serve as markers of time, direction, orientation, result, and intensity (Nguyen, 1987). Arabic adverbs have functions and uses similar to those in English, but in form, they are not distinct from adjectives (Kaye, 1987).

The frequency counts in this study include all types of adverbs in each semantic class, including prepositional phrases.

Time: for example, *at last, already, finally, from now/then, immediately, just, now, nowadays, since xxx, soon, then, today, up to now/then/ xxx day, yesterday, last/next/past time/month/year/Monday, after/at/during/in/on/till/ until* (+ temporal/durational noun); prepositional phrases of time, marked by prepositions (e.g., *at about 5 o'clock*). For example, <u>*Nowadays,*</u> *investors put money into computer companies because they think that* <u>*in ten years,*</u> *they can be millionaires* (Arabic).

Time adverbs identify temporal, sequential, preceding, successive, and other relationships between actions and events in portions of text that range from phrases to sentences to whole sections of narratives. They establish and maintain temporal discourse deixis and play an important role in text cohesion (Halliday & Hasan, 1976). Chafe (1994) pointed out that adverbs of temporality and location are indices of the division of time and space. They indicate whether the deices time and space are of immediate and remote relevance to information flow and narrative development and orient the audience within the discourse framework. In written text, time adverbs determine the tenses appropriate in context and mark the temporality of objective and narrative events ("the construal of time," p. 77). In English, with its developed system of inflectional and morphological tenses, time adverbs frame discourse and, in this way, necessitate tense shifts (Croft, 1998)

Frequency[1]: for example, *annually, daily, frequently, monthly, per day/hour/year occasionally, often, oftentimes, seldom, sometimes, sporadically, regularly, usually, weekly.* For example, *They often don't know how to do anything or even how to think because their parents made their opinions for them* (Korean).

Adverbs of frequency often serve as hedges in written text and are employed in generalizations and evidential statements to reduce the writer's responsibility for the truth value of the proposition or claim (Chafe, 1986; Huebler, 1983). Based on the findings from her corpus data, Channel (1994) commented that the meanings of frequency adverbs are inherently vague and that they are used in similar contexts as other indefinite quantifiers and pronouns.

Place: for example, *here, there, in/at/from/to/into/out/out of/away/away from* + noun (phrase). For example, *When I came here, I could hardly speak any English at all* (Japanese).

Place adverbs establish the locational frame of a text (or narrative) and can be employed as a cohesive localizer (Halliday & Hasan, 1976). However, Biber (1988) and Francis (1994) found that they are also common in written academic corpora.

Amplifiers: *absolutely, a lot* (+ comparative adjective), *altogether, always, amazingly, awfully, badly, by all means, completely, definitely, deeply, downright, forever, enormously, entirely, even* (+ adjective/noun), *ever, extremely, far* (+ comparative adjective), *far from it, fully, greatly, highly, hugely, in all/every respect(s)/way(s), much* (+ adjective), *never, not half bad, positively, perfectly, severely, so* (+ adjective/verb), *sharply, strongly, too* (+ adjective), *terribly, totally, unbelievably, very, very much, well.* For example, *Parents love their children too much and totally spoil them. They never let them do anything by themselves* (Chinese).

Amplifiers are adverbs that modify gradable adjectives or verbs and advance their scalar lexical intensity (Quirk et al., 1985). The textual function of amplifiers is primarily that of exaggeratives and overstatements (see also Assertive and Nonassertive Pronouns discussed in chap. 6). In academic writing in English, such extreme amplifiers as *always* and *never* are considered to mark exaggerations, and their inclusion in essays is not advisable

---

[1]*Always* and *never* are located at the extremes of the continuum among frequency adverbs, and their meanings are different from those of other adverbs in this class because they are precise (Channel, 1994) and can be used for amplification (see Amplifiers).

(Smoke, 1999). As has been mentioned, in Chinese, Japanese, Korean, Vietnamese, and Arabic, amplification is seen as an appropriate means of expressing the writer's power of conviction, and it can take the form of adverbs or particles that convey a high degree of inclination, desirability, and/or expectancy (Connor, 1996; Sa'adeddin, 1989; Tsujimura, 1987; Yum, 1987; Zhu, 1996) or intensity and emphasis (I. Taylor, 1995).

Downtoners: *at all, a bit, all but, a good/great deal, almost, as good/well as, at least, barely, basically, dead* (+ adjective), *enough, fairly, (a) few, hardly, in the least/slightest, just, (a) little* (+ adjective), *merely, mildly, nearly, not a* (+ countable noun, e.g., *thing/person), only, partly, partially, practically, pretty* (+ adjective), *quite* (+ adjective), *rather, really, relatively, scarcely, simply, slightly, somewhat, sufficiently, truly, virtually.* For example, *Taking ESL classes helped me a bit, but mostly I studied by myself because I knew that I simply had to pass the TOEFL or my father wouldn't give me any more money* (Japanese).

The function of downtoners is the opposite of that of amplifiers, that is, to scale down the intensity of verbs and adjectives in text. Their purpose is to soften the meaning and reduce the qualitative and emotive implications of verbs and adjectives and to hedge the meaning of abstract nouns, adjectives, and verbs (Hyland, 1998, 1999). Hoye's (1997) findings indicate that formal downtoners (e.g., *fairly, merely, nearly, partly, partially, sufficiently*) are prevalent in formal and written text in English.

Other adverbs: *also, else, elsewhere, instead, rather, similarly, specifically, too,* and adverbs of manner, for example, *briefly, brightly, broadly, eagerly, enthusiastically, evidently, fast, frankly, generally, honestly, openly, privately, quickly, quietly, rightly, roughly, seriously, silently, sincerely, strictly, truly, truthfully, widely, wisely, wrongly.* For example, *He talked to his coach privately and decided that he couldn't make the team and meet his goal in soccer* (Arabic).

Adverbs of similarity, specificity, exceptionality, and manner refer to the particular features of modification of adjectives and verbs. They are common in written academic discourse in English and can also function as hedging and conjuncts (Hermeren, 1978; Huebler, 1983; Hyland, 1998).

Uses of Adverbs in Student Texts

Adverbs and adverbial particles are numerous in many languages, including Asian and Semitic. Overall, in academic essays, comparisons of NS and NNS frequency rates of adverb uses prove them to be mixed. In general terms, their uses in both L1 and L2 texts depend on their lexical meanings and textual functions.

Time Adverbs.   Adverbs of time *(then, immediately, soon, finally)* were common in NS (median 0.83) and NNS texts, but speakers of Chinese (median 1.00) and Korean (median 0.88) used them at significantly higher rates than NSs did. As the data in Table 8.2 shows, the medians in essays of Japanese, Vietnamese, Indonesian, and Arabic speakers did not differ substantially from NS texts. For example, *However, the iron industry has regressed recently* (Japanese) or *Last year, my father told me that I have to study engineering* (Arabic).

Frequency Adverbs. These adverbs (*annually, occasionally, usually*) are inherently vague, and are found in contexts similar to those of indefinite pronouns and quantifiers (Channel, 1994). The majority of NSs used frequency adverbs (median 0.00) similarly to the groups of NNS, with the exception of Vietnamese speakers (median 0.25), whose essays contained significantly more of these features (see Table 8.2).

Place Adverbs. (*in/at/from/to* + noun or noun phrase) were substantially more common than most other types of adverbs (NS median 1.48), and many NNS texts included them in similar frequency rates to NS (Chinese, Japanese, and Indonesian medians between 1.43 and 1.65). On the other hand, the frequency rates of place adverbs (Table 8.2) in the essays of Korean and Arabic speakers were significantly lower (medians of 1.25 each) or higher in Indonesian texts (median 1.94). For example, *In my country, students don't have to do homework. Their parents hire special servants who do all the homework for them. They go to the library to get books and even write papers for them. When these students come to the U.S., they are shocked that they have to do laundry for themselves, go to the store, and even drive to the mall* (Indonesian).

TABLE 8.2
Median Frequency Rates for Semantic and Lexical Classes of Adverbs (Median %)

		NS	Chinese	Japanese	Korean	Vietnamese	Indonesian	Arabic
					L1			
Time		**0.83**	**1.00****	**0.83**	**0.88***	**0.80**	**0.81**	**0.79**
	Range	5.00	6.54	3.92	4.86	4.00	3.44	3.85
Frequency		**0.00**	**0.24**	**0.00**	**0.00**	**0.25***	**0.22**	**0.18**
	Range	2.70	3.21	2.73	1.92	2.94	2.94	4.02
Place		**1.48**	**1.65**	**1.59**	**1.25***	**1.94***	**1.43**	**1.26***
	Range	4.76	5.68	6.25	7.02	5.72	5.91	6.05
Amplifiers		**1.73**	**3.17****	**2.94****	**2.81****	**2.14****	**2.67****	**3.03****
	Range	7.50	10.20	12.28	11.43	8.48	9.80	14.37
Downtoners		**0.48**	**0.42**	**0.43***	**0.33****	**0.42**	**0.60**	**0.55**
	Range	4.17	3.33	4.17	2.44	3.13	3.70	3.19
Other		**0.50**	**0.71****	**0.77****	**0.86****	**0.95****	**0.83****	**1.19****
	Range	3.57	3.93	5.29	5.46	4.17	3.70	3.96

Note. All comparisons are relative to NSs.
*one-tailed $p < 0.05$. **two-tailed $p < 0.05$.

Amplifiers.   Like downtoners, amplifiers modify gradable adverbs and verbs to add to the intensity of their meanings. For example, *Parents <u>always</u> encourage their children to study the major that will be needed by <u>a lot</u> more companies in the future, so that they could get jobs and earn a lot of money after they graduate from the university. There are <u>a lot</u> of people who <u>totally</u> hate their jobs, and they are <u>very</u> miserable* (Indonesian), or *I <u>completely</u> support that students should study to improve themselves. Their lives would be <u>totally</u> wasted if they don't learn new things every day* (Vietnamese). As noted earlier (see Universal Pronouns), in rhetorical traditions other than Anglo-American, exaggerations and overstatements are considered to be appropriate means of persuasion, when amplification is intended to convey a high degree of the writer's conviction. However, overstatements are discouraged in academic writing in English, and hedging one's propositions is deemed preferable in academic texts (Smoke, 1999; Swales & Feak, 1994). The reason that the frequency rates of amplifiers were so high in NNS texts may lie in the fact that, in general, NNS writers relied on restricted syntactic and lexical repertoires and, hence, employed other means of conveying their ideas and the degree of their conviction. This observation is further supported by very high frequency rates in the NNS usage of emphatics (see chap. 10).

Downtoners.   In academic texts, downtoners play the role of hedges and, in this capacity, are prevalent in formal writing (Hyland, 1998, 1999). In general, downtoners were not particularly common in NS (median 0.48) or NNS texts (medians between 0.42 and 0.60), and only the frequency rates of Japanese and Korean speakers were significantly lower than those of NSs. For example, *Students who have <u>a bit</u> of a financial problem have their limit to choose their fields of study. In an example, graduate student wants to study a field under a professor. A professor doesn't have <u>enough</u> money to support him* (Korean).

Other Adverbs.   Adverbs that confer things such as similarity, specificity, and manner are also common in formal academic writing because they often play the role of hedges and cohesive conjunctions (Huebler, 1983). Although NS texts (median 0.50) did not contain a high frequency of these adverbs (see Table 8.2), NNS frequency rates were significantly higher (medians between 0.71 and 1.00). For example, *<u>Instead</u>, another professor has got a project relating to another field so he can support him* (Korean), or *I feel much more comfortable in a classroom where I can <u>easily</u> express my thoughts without worry* (Chinese).

Overall, the two most prominent differences in the NS and NNS usage of adjectives and adverbs is the markedly high rates of predicative adjectives and amplifiers in L2 texts. In fact, NNSs in all L1 groups employed predicative adjectives at twice the rate of NSs, and amplifiers at the rate of at least 50% greater than NSs did. The high rate of predicative adjectives points to the fact that L2 texts contained many syntactically simple constructions, whereas the preponderance of amplifiers indicates that NNS students are faced with limited lexical means of expressing their convictions.

Another notable finding is that the adverbs of manner, conjuncts, and adjective/verb modifiers (clustered as other adverbs) were also employed significantly more frequently in NNS than NS essays. Because adverbs of manner and adjective/verb modifiers are common in spoken genre (Channel, 1994), their prevalence in L2 academic texts is not particularly surprising.

9

Subordinate Clauses and Their Functions and Uses

Subordinate clauses can function as nouns (i.e., subjects, objects, complements, or appositives), adjectivals, or adverbials. In general, in academic text of various types, the use of subordinate clauses is prevalent, and they are identified as markers of textual and structural complexity. Analyses of academic corpora point to the fact that they are more common in writing than in speech (Biber, 1988; Ford, 1993). Investigations into the types of subordinate clauses employed in writing distinguish between noun, adjective, and adverb clauses because they have different textual and structural functions (Chafe, 1986, 1994; Swales, 1990a). For example, noun clauses can play the role of key elements in sentence structure, and in most cases, adjective clauses and reduced adjective clauses modify nouns. Adverb clauses also play important roles in text when they modify whole independent clauses and indicate meanings of cause, concession, condition, and other relationships between sentences or portions of text. In general, subordinate clauses occupy a prominent place in discourse cohesion because they allow for ellipsis and substitution of lexical and syntactic elements (Halliday & Hasan, 1976).

Subordinate clauses are found in all the languages discussed in this study. However, the forms they take differ from those of dependent clauses in English. In Chinese, Vietnamese, and Indonesian, subordinate clausal relationships are inferred when they are overtly marked by particles with temporal, conditional, causal, resultative, and other adverbial meanings (Li & Thompson, 1981; Nguyen, 1987). In these languages, a sentence can contain as many clauses as there are action and stative verbs arranged in what Li and

Thompson called "serial verb construction" (p. 825), for example, *I have one apple very good to eat,* or *He told me (I) need to buy oranges.* R. Scollon (1993a) pointed out that the use of conjunctions in Chinese serially linked constructions can result in ambiguous textual meanings that allow the writer to avoid being direct and explicit. In Scollon's view, ambiguity and indirectness are valued highly in Chinese rhetorical tradition because they serve to protect both the writer's and the reader's "face." In Vietnamese, noun clauses exist only as objects of main clauses and are linked to them by means of particles (Nguyen, 1987). Adjective and adverb clauses have modifying functions and are marked by linking conjunctions and particles.

On the other hand, Japanese noun clauses are relatively rare, adjective clauses are premodifiers that precede the nouns they describe (Shibatani, 1987, 1990), and adverb clauses proper do not exist. Korean clausal relationships are marked by a system of particles that arrange serial sentence constructions functionally relative to one another, for example, *(time/when) Mary went home, met a mailman* (Kim, 1987). In Korean, adjective clauses follow the noun they modify in similar sequential structures, in which subordination is identified by particles. According to Kaye (1987), subordinate clauses in Arabic, however, can be only adjectival or adverbial, and are distinguished by their meanings and placement within the sentence structure. Noun modification is accomplished by means of compound noun structures or appositive relationships between noun phrases (Ostler, 1987). Arabic does not have noun clause constructions. None of these languages include structures that resemble reduced clauses.

In the assessment of writing on standardized and placement tests requisite in many U.S. colleges and universities, the types, frequencies, and accuracy of subordinate clauses used in L2 essay writing plays a major role (Davidson, 1991; Vaughan, 1991). Hamp-Lyons' (1991) survey of scales employed for rating NNSs' academic writing shows that subordinate clause use represents a crucial gauge of L2 proficiency. In writing instruction, many texts provide recommendations and directions for the use of subordinate clauses in academic prose (Raimes, 1992; Scarcella, 1994; Smoke, 1999) to improve the flow of text and facilitate connections between ideas (Swales & Feak, 1994). However, in their corpus analysis of academic writing in various disciplines, such as statistics, linguistics, and philosophy, Chang and Swales (1999) found that the use of clause subordinators seems to vary, with their occurrences least common in philosophy and most prevalent in statistics.

The findings of the study indicate that no clause type was used in NNS texts significantly more frequently than in those of NSs. However, two types of clauses were used at significantly lower rates in all NNS texts:

- Reduced adjective clauses.
- Reduced adverb clauses.

NOUN (NOMINAL) CLAUSES
(INCLUDING PREPOSITIONS):

Noun, or nominal, clauses are marked by:

1. Explicit or omitted *that-* or *wh-* complement clauses following main-clause verbs, such as public (reporting), private, suasive, *seem/appear*, mental (e.g., *believe, know, think, understand*), emotive (e.g., *feel, hate, like, love*), and performative (e.g., *announce, ask, claim, comment, indicate, propose, say, state*). For example, *I think parents need to be guides for their children, but children should find their own destiny*[1] (Korean).

2. *that/wh-*clauses in clause-initial position (including *wh-*clauses as objects of prepositions), for example, *That/What/When/Where/Why his parents told him to study (xxx) was very unfortunate* and *For what reason he came to see his professor is not important* (NS).

3. Adjective complements, including clauses with explicit or omitted *that*, for example, *He was happy (that)/when/where he got admitted to an American university*.

4. *wh-*clauses following the verb in the independent clause (see Item 1) as objects of prepositions, for example, and *I don't know in which house/for what purpose/ (to)what/who(m) he said that*.

Textual Functions

Noun clauses, including appositives, are particularly prevalent in written academic texts when they follow reporting verbs in summaries, restatements, and citations (Leki, 1999; Swales & Feak, 1994). In such structures, they often allow the writer to display knowledge and/or provide an evaluation of the proposition expressed (Swales, 1990a). In formal writing, noun clauses often have the function of removing the writer from the truth value of the proposition by attributing it to someone else and, in this way, noun clauses impart detachment and objectivity to text (Tadros, 1994). *That-*clauses following public, private, suasive, and other types of verbs are far more common in formal prose than other types of noun clauses. For instance, *wh-*clauses in the sentence subject position are more characteristic of speech than of writing (Biber, 1988). Another function of noun clauses is to provide for extensive cohesive ties by means of recapitulation of the information stated earlier (e.g., *It was stated/mentioned previously/above that . . .*) or predicting the development of discourse/argumentation moves, particularly in introductions (e.g., *This essay/I will show/argue/prove that . . .*). *Wh-* noun clauses

---

[1]As in the previous chapters, all examples are extracted from student texts.

that represent embedded *wh*-questions also serve to delay the proposition to the secondary clause position and lead to the topic the writer intends to introduce and address (Francis, 1994).

ADJECTIVE CLAUSES

Full Adjective Clauses[2] and Their Functions

Explicit or implicit subordinating conjunctions, marked as follows:

1. *that* and *wh*-words (excluding those in noun clauses; see previous section), following the subject or the object noun of the independent clause (Quirk et al., 1985), for example, *The picture that/which he painted sold for a lot of money* or *He bought a car that/which needed a lot of work*. These also included adjective clauses in the subject or object position within the subordinate clause (e.g., *that needed work* or *which he painted*).

2. Pied-piping adjective clauses with explicit or implicit prepositions (e.g., *This is house in which I was born/where I was born/which I was born in, to whom/whom/to who/who . . . to,* etc.).

3. Ellipsis of the subordinating conjunctions, for example, *The doctor I saw was pretty good.*

The syntactic and discourse function of adjective clauses is that of postpositional noun modifiers, similar to that of attributive adjectives, that is, to identify a referent in discourse (see also Reduced Adjective Clauses, which follows). However, because the amount of information included in a clause can be greater than that conveyed by an attributive adjective, the use of clauses allows for a more precise referential identification (Chafe, 1994).

Reduced Adjective Clauses and their Functions

Reduced adjective clauses include the following:

1. Present or past participles in post-nominal positions, accompanied by other types of modifiers, such as prepositional phrases and/or adverbials (e.g., *the student enrolled in my class/arriving next week*) (Quirk et al., 1985). Participles in prenominal positions without prepositional phrases

---

[2]In this study, relative clauses that can be both nominal and adjectival in their syntactic functions were distinguished as noun and adjective clauses to avoid confusion. In addition, because a vast majority of ESL/EFL grammar-training texts also separate between noun and adjective clauses, it may be that NNSs conceptualize them in this way.

and adverbials were counted separately and included in the counts of attributive adjectives because postpositional modifiers are more complex and syntactically sophisticated, and thus, in the case of NNSs, require a relatively higher L2 grammar proficiency. For example, *My big brother <u>studying in New York</u> always buys me things because he still thinks that I am his little brother* (Indonesian).

2. Prepositional phrases in postnominal positions, modifying single or multiple noun phrases (Biber, 1995). For example, *The study room reservation <u>at 10 o'clock</u> was cancelled, and we had no place to study* (Arabic).

3. Postpositional adjectives with or without prepositional phrases, for example, *I decided to do something <u>important/better</u>* (with indefinite pronouns as modified constituents; Quirk et al., 1985), *the actor <u>popular in my country</u>.*

4. Pre-/postpositional full and partial appositives, modifying the subject or the object of the independent clause (Quirk et al., 1985) (e.g., *My brother, <u>the scientist</u>, loves horses; I gave all the money to my father, <u>the ruler of the family</u>* [NS]), and explicit apposition markers: *that is (to say), i.e., including, or better yet/to say, or rather, as follows, in particular.*

Reduced adjective clauses are complex modifying structures that are derived from full adjective clauses. Adjective clause reduction in most contexts is considered to be optional and can be applied when the overall meaning of the clause is not affected (Chafe, 1970). Biber (1995) found that in formal genre of English written discourse, adjective clause reduction occurs substantially more frequently than in informal varieties, although the frequencies of occurrences of full adjective clauses do not exhibit a great deal of difference. In text, reduced adjective clauses are largely employed in highly informational discourse because they allow for a more integrated and compact structure than full adjective clauses (Biber, 1988). In his examination of apposition in several large written corpora, Meyer (1991) found that it most often takes the form of reduced adjective clauses that function as modifiers, complements, and attributives of subject and object nouns. Specifically, according to his findings, written academic prose contains high frequencies of attributive appositions in sciences and humanities alike.

Uses of Noun Clauses in Student Texts

Noun clauses are very common in written academic texts and usually accompany reporting verbs in summaries, citations, and paraphrases (Leki, 1999; Swales & Feak, 1994). In general terms, noun clauses are relatively uncomplicated and have been identified as ubiquitous in academic ESL

essays (Carlson, 1988). In the NS and NNS essays, these subordinate clauses were also relatively common: NS median 1.50, and NNS texts of all
groups included them at significantly higher rates (medians from 1.89 to
2.08). As the data in Table 9.1 demonstrates, the frequency rates of noun
clauses in Korean and Vietnamese speakers' essays were similar to those of
NS (medians 1.75 and 1.58, respectively). For example, *She strongly opposed
her daughter's decision because she thought it was good for her daughter. This example shows that there is gap between my friend's mother's consideration to her and my
friend's feeling* (Japanese) or *Parents have already decided what kind of clothes
their children should wear, what kind of friends their children should make, or even
have decided what kind of jobs their children are going to do in their future lives*
(Chinese).

Uses of Full and Reduced Adjective Clauses

All adjective clauses are far more common in formal written text than in
the informal register (Biber, 1988). However, reduced clauses are far more
compact than full and in their function of appositives are prevalent in academic texts.

Full adjective clauses are not syntactically and lexically complex, and
their frequency rates were relatively high in NS (median 1.11) and NNS
(medians between 1.58 and 2.08) texts (see Table 9.1). In fact, essays of
speakers of Chinese, Japanese, Indonesian, and Arabic contained significantly more of them than NS texts did. The frequency rates of full adjective
clauses in Korean and Vietnamese speakers' essays did not differ significantly from those of NSs. For example, *Nowadays, the world is time of competition. The men who have competitive power survive in our society* (Korean) or
*When children are like king in their house, this is not good for children, especially
when they will face the true world that is not as kind as their parents in the future*
(Chinese).

TABLE 9.1
Median Frequency Rates for Noun and Adjective (Median %)

		NS	Chinese	Japanese	Korean	Vietnamese	Indonesian	Arabic
					L1			
Noun		**1.50**	**2.00****	**2.08****	**1.75**	**1.58**	**2.08****	**1.90****
	Range	8.33	5.95	6.67	8.75	5.88	7.14	5.56
Full adjective		**1.11**	**1.07**	**1.00**	**0.84***	**0.74***	**1.18**	**1.43****
	Range	4.52	7.14	5.41	4.44	4.09	5.00	7.74
Reduced adjective		**0.00**	**0.00***	**0.00****	**0.00****	**0.00****	**0.00****	**0.00****
	Range	2.94	1.82	1.93	2.69	1.43	0.93	1.43

Note. All comparisons are relative to NSs.
*one-tailed $p < 0.05$. **two-tailed $p < 0.05$.

Reduced adjective clauses, however, are far more advanced, and their NNS frequency rates were significantly lower than those of NSs (medians 0.00 in all groups). As is apparent from Table 9.1, overall, reduced adjective clauses were not common in student essays.

ADVERB CLAUSES

Textual Functions of Full Adverb Clauses

Syntactically, adverb clauses are peripheral to the structure of the independent clause that they modify and play an important role in determining informational relationships in text (Quirk et al., 1985). In general terms, adverb clauses are used to frame discourse and present background information relevant to that in the independent clause. Adverb clauses express a variety of contextual relationships, some of which refer to cause, concession, condition, purpose, temporality, locations, and others, and their meanings in discourse can be ambiguous (Leech & Svartvik, 1994). For example, subordinators *since* and *as* can be found in adverb clauses of time, cause, and comparison, and *however* can be adjunctive and disjunctive, depending on the construction.

Biber (1988) found that in general adverb clauses are more common in speech than in writing. On the other hand, in instruction in academic writing and argumentative writing in particular, the uses of various types of adverb clauses, such as causative, concessive, condition, and purpose, are often recommended in explication, reasoning, and analysis (Hacker, 1994; Raimes, 1992; Scarcella, 1994; Smoke, 1999, Swales & Feak, 1994). For this reason, in this study these clauses were identified separately from those conveying meanings of time, place, manner, and comparison.

Cause: *as* (causative distinguished from temporal), *because, for, since*. For example, *They make so much money <u>because they work hard every day to stay in shape and give people entertainment</u>* (Vietnamese).

According to R. Scollon and S. W. Scollon (1995), causative conjunctions are prevalent in the English language use of speakers of Asian languages, who employ them substantially more frequently than do NSs of English. Specifically, the authors noted that *because Y, X* structures may represent a means of organizing information in text influenced by the subject-topic constructions in such languages as Korean, Chinese, and Japanese. Scollon and Scollon explained that, in addition, the use of multiple causative constructions *(because Y, because X, Z)* by speakers of these languages can create English language sentences and textual organization that NSs find particularly confusing.

Causative adverb clauses are prevalent in speech, although, for example, *as* is more frequently found in formal writing (Biber, 1988). On the other hand, composition instruction almost always includes rhetorical modes that deal with identifying causes of events or developments. Such pieces of writing require the traditional "cause-and-effect" structure also characteristic of essay tests of practically any kind (Hacker, 1994; Leki, 1999; Lunsford & Connors, 1997; Smoke, 1999). The overarching goal of cause-and-effect rhetorical instruction is to develop students' academic argumentation skills often considered essential for their college careers and writing in the disciplines (Hamp-Lyons, 1990, 1991; Johns, 1991, 1997).

Concession: *although (even) though, whereas, while* (excluding temporal meanings). For example, <u>*Although my father never finished high school*</u>, *he is the smartest man I know, and I always listen to his advice* (Korean).

As is typical of adverb clauses, concessives can be used to introduce background information (Leech & Svartvik, 1994). Concessive clauses usually include a proposition that is counter to that expressed in the independent clause. However, the proposition in the subordinate clause is seen as less contextually important than that in the independent clause (Quirk et al., 1985). For this reason, in academic writing, these clauses serve as a means of presenting a balanced position, which accounts for opposing views and provides evidence of the writer's credibility (Hinkel, 1999b). For example, Leki (1999) suggested a "formula" (p. 129) using *although* for creating a balanced thesis statement and presenting the writer's position objectively. Jacobs (1995) stated that concessive clauses can be employed to contrast ideas in order to advance a line of argument with the advantage of appropriate hedging.

Condition: *as/so long as* (excluding temporal meanings), *assuming that, given that, if, in case, provided that, supposing that, unless*, and implicit conditionals (e.g., <u>*Had he asked me*</u>, *I would have given it to him*).

Conditional clauses express a direct condition, and the action or the event in the independent clause is explicitly contingent on whether the condition expressed in the subordinate clause is or becomes true (Quirk et al., 1985). They can be used for framing discourse and can have different functions when they are placed before or after the independent clause (Biber, 1988). Conditional clauses belong in several classes: counterfactual present or past (e.g., <u>*If she were here*</u>, *I could be happy* and <u>*If he had studied*</u>, *he would have passed the test*) and real (e.g., <u>*If he buys this car*</u>, *he'll have to get another job to make the payments*). In academic texts, all types of conditional clauses are often used for hedging propositions and claims (Huebler, 1983) or soliciting agreement with a proposition that the writer believes to be risky (Myers, 1989; Swales & Feak, 1994). However, Ford (1993) found that conditional clauses are predominantly identified in informal conversations. She stated that they are rarely effective as a persuasion device because they tend to mark a proposition as questionable or problematic. In the frequency counts, in this study conditional clauses were included without distinction by type.

Purpose: *so, so as, so/such that.* For example, *People work hard <u>so that they can finance their children education as an investment for the future</u>* (Chinese).

Clauses of purpose are usually putative and require modal verbs, such as *can, could, may, might, should,* and *would.* In academic writing, they are used in statements of purpose, summaries, explanations, and conclusions (Swales & Feak, 1994). Full clauses of purpose are comparatively rare and, in most cases, reduced to infinitives or phrasal infinitives (Leech & Svartvik, 1994) (see Infinitives in chap. 7).

Other adverb clauses, with the meanings of: **time** (*after, as, as long as* [excluding conditional meanings], *as often as, as soon as, before, now that, once, since* [excluding causative meanings], *till, until, when, whenever, while*); **Place** (*where, wherever*); **Manner** (*as, at what* + time/place, [*in*] *the way* [*that*], *where* (*it* + verb, e.g. *counts/matters*] [excluding noun clauses]); **Comparative** (*as* [excluding temporal meanings], *as . . . as, as if, like*)*;* and **Sentential** (*which,* preposition + *which,* similar to adjective piped-piping clauses; e.g., *He went with us, <u>which I didn't appreciate/which did not sit well with me/which I was not comfortable with</u>*).

Adverb clauses of time establish a temporal connection between the time of the action or event in the independent and subordinate clauses, and they can be successive and/or simultaneous, depending on the meaning of the subordinator and the tense and aspect in either clause, for example, *<u>After he graduated from high school</u>, he was discovered by a basketball scout* (NS) or *<u>Before she became famous</u>, she was working as a waitress* (Chinese). The ordering of actions and events relative to the general temporal discourse frame and the time deixis in the subordinate and the independent clause is one of the ubiquitous cohesive devices in narratives and written exposition (Halliday & Hasan, 1976). Time clauses can be the locus of the more important action or event that occurs during the time frame specified in the independent clause, or vice versa (Quirk et al., 1985).

Clauses of place (locative) also serve to locate the events or action of either the subordinate or the independent clause, respectively, along the deixis established in the context of narrative, explication, or exposition. In general, in academic texts, clauses of place are not very frequent (Halliday, 1994).

Clauses of comparison can be employed to establish similarities or dissimilarities that can be both real or hypothetical (e.g., *as if he knows/knew everything*) and to construct analogies. These structures may have a cohesive purpose when they are used to compare the information provided earlier in discourse (Halliday & Hasan, 1976). In composition instruction, comparisons and analogies are frequently encouraged as an explication device and recommended for clarification (Hacker, 1994; Leki, 1999; Lunsford &

Connors, 1997; Raimes, 1992; Scarcella, 1994). However, they are relatively rare both in L1 and L2 academic essays (Hinkel, 1999b).

Clauses of manner are comparatively infrequent, as well. They represent an ambiguous blend of comparative and attributive functions and meanings of adverbs, and they have the meaning of *how*. The markers of these clauses can be paraphrased by *in a (. . .) manner* or *in a (. . .) way* (Quirk et al., 1985), for example, *My mother cooks my food how I like it*.

Sentential clauses refer back to the predicate of or the entire independent clause. They are placed in postmodifying positions, following the independent clause and, in most cases, marked by the relative pronoun *which*, with or without a preposition. The relative pronoun *which* is characteristically associated with adjective clauses, and its use in sentential clauses is considered to be "somewhat anomalous" (Quirk et al., 1985, p. 1120). It is important to note that the use of *which* in adverb clauses customarily marks informal conversational register (Biber, 1995) and, until very recently, has been viewed as inappropriate in formal prose, and particularly so, in academic writing (Lunsford & Connors, 1997).

REDUCED ADVERB CLAUSES

Textual Functions

Reduced adverb clauses include present or past participles with or without prepositional (or adverbial) phrases and/or adverb clause markers, external/peripheral to the independent clause structure, for example, *The professor looked at me, smiling broadly*, or *While walking to class that night, I noticed this poster*, or *After releasing her first CD, she made a hit movie* (NSs). With full or reduced adverb clauses, the independent clause retains its structure and meaning if the subordinate construction is completely omitted (Leech & Svartvik, 1994). In academic texts, reduced adverb clauses integrate information compactly, while retaining the meanings and functions of full adverb clauses (Biber, 1988). In general, they mark formal and written registers and are particularly seldom employed in speech.

In reduced adverb clauses, the subject is not present in the subordinate structure and is assumed to be the same as that in the independent clause. However, the constructions in which the subjects are not the same abound in both L1 and L2 writing and are considered to be questionable (if not outright unacceptable) (Quirk et al., 1985). For NNSs, reduced adverb clauses represent a structure indicative of an advanced language proficiency and sophisticated levels of language use and discourse fluency (Leki, 1999). However, their use is highly problematic for NNSs who make various types of errors, including wrong forms of participles, subject ellipsis without an alteration of the verb form, and verb ellipsis without the omission of the subject (Hacker, 1994). In general terms, uses of subordinate clauses in students' essays are often viewed as manifestations of relatively advanced language control and development (Hamp-Lyons, 1991).

Uses of Full Adverb Clauses in Student Texts

As simple adverbs, adverb clauses have many contextual functions and can express a variety of meanings, such as cause *(because, since, for)*, concession *(although, though)*, condition *(if, whether, unless)*, purpose *(so, so that)*, and others (e.g., time—*when, while, as soon as*; manner—*as, in the way that*; or comparison—*as . . . as, like*). In general terms, full adverb clauses are more common in informal than in formal language uses.

Cause clauses are prevalent in speech in English and are often associated with cause-and-effect essays popular in academic writing tasks that have the goal of developing argumentation and persuasion skills (Hacker, 1994; Leki, 1999). Causative structures and conjunctions are also prevalent in the English use of speakers of Asian languages, such as Korean, Chinese, and Japanese, due to the influence of the subject-topic syntactic constructions in these languages (R. Scollon & S. W. Scollon, 1995). For example, *According to my experience, <u>since I am the only child in my family</u>, my mother usually helps me to do my homework which is supposed to be finished by myself* (Chinese) or *For a child, education in the early age is very important <u>because it can help their future</u>* (Indonesian).

In all L1 groups (see Table 9.2), the frequency rates for adverb clauses of cause were significantly higher in NNS (medians from 0.42 to 0.53) texts than in those of NS (median 0.30). Cause clauses represent the most direct means of indicating causal relationships between actions and events in context, in addition to those referred to by resultative nouns *(result, outcome)*. As has been noted, in many cases, NNS writers often relied on restricted syntactic, semantic, and lexical means of conveying their ideas in written text and, for this reason, the preponderance of causal clauses, as well as resultative nouns, in their text points to their shortage of accessible linguistic repertoire.

Concession clauses, unlike adverb clauses of cause, are somewhat sophisticated due to the complexity of the notion of concession in written text and text cohesion. The function of concession clauses in discourse is to present ideational content in a balanced fashion to provide evidence of the writer's credibility (Hinkel, 1999b). For example, *They suggest that parents should try their best to ensure their children's opportunities to gain as much experiences as they could <u>even though there are some arguments about this issue</u>* (Chinese). As is shown in Table 9.2, concession clauses were not common in the text of NSs or NNSs (medians 0.00 for all groups), but their cluster-

TABLE 9.2
Median Frequency Rates for Adverb Clauses (Median %)

		NS	Chinese	Japanese	Korean	Vietnamese	Indonesian	Arabic
					L1			
Full: Cause		0.30	0.45**	0.53**	0.48**	0.42*	0.57**	0.38*
	Range	2.72	2.42	4.17	2.31	2.53	3.20	3.47
Concession		0.00	0.00	0.00	0.00*	0.00	0.00	0.00*
	Range	0.96	1.47	1.25	1.68	1.01	0.67	1.04
Condition		0.51	0.68*	0.48	0.53	0.32*	0.32*	0.33*
	Range	3.85	3.90	3.92	2.86	2.38	2.37	2.88
Purpose		0.00	0.00*	0.00*	0.00*	0.00*	0.00*	0.00**
	Range	2.08	2.66	1.74	1.06	1.74	1.19	1.04
Other		0.54	0.83**	0.58	0.59	0.60	0.73*	0.37*
	Range	4.17	4.80	2.78	3.86	3.38	3.27	4.26
Reduced adverb clause		0.31	0.00**	0.00**	0.00**	0.00**	0.00**	0.00**
	Range	3.95	2.38	1.67	3.70	1.12	1.37	0.96

Note. All comparisons are relative to NSs.
*one-tailed $p < 0.05$. **two-tailed $p < 0.05$.

ing in essays of several speakers of Korean (range 1.68) and Arabic (range 1.04) significantly exceeded that of NS (range 0.96).

Conditional clauses are more common in spoken than in written discourse (Ford, 1993). For example, *If their parents give the wrong education, they will follow the wrong way* (Indonesian), or *If parents make children's lives too easy, they can do everything they want, they can go everywhere they like, they will do the wrong things when they are growing up* (Vietnamese). The NNS frequency rates for conditional clauses (see Table 9.2) were similar to those of NSs (median 0.51) in the texts of speakers of Japanese (median 0.48) and Korean (median 0.53), significantly lower than those of NSs in compositions of speakers of Vietnamese, Indonesian (medians 0.32 each), and Arabic (median 0.29), and significantly higher in Chinese speakers' essays (median 0.68).

Purpose clauses were used in fewer than half of the essays in all L1 groups (medians 0.00), but however few NSs employed them in their essays, their frequency rates in NNSs essays were significantly fewer still. For example, *Children should learn to study hard before they mature so that they can be successful in the future* (Japanese).

Other types of adverb clause uses present a mixed picture. Whereas in essays of Chinese (median 0.83) and Indonesian (median 0.73) writers their frequency rates were significantly higher than those of NSs (median 0.54), those in the texts of Arabic speakers were significantly lower (median 0.34). For example, *So, as they grow up or when their parents are retired, their* *needs are gone, and the trouble will come to them* (Indonesian). No significant differences are noted in frequency rates for these types of adverb clauses in the compositions of NS, Japanese, Korean, or Vietnamese speakers.

Uses of Reduced Adverb Clauses in Student Texts

Reduced adverb clauses represent highly advanced syntactic structures that are used in formal written texts (Biber, 1988). In standardized tests, such as the TOEFL, questions with reduced adverb clauses are often employed to indicate advanced language proficiency (Hamp-Lyons, 1991), and in academic ESL texts, they are viewed as markers of sophisticated language use and discourse fluency (Leki, 1999). Although they were found in most NS essays (median 031), fewer than half of all NNS used them in their texts (medians 0.00 for all NNS groups). For example, *When being raised in my family, I was not spoiled at all, and when I looked at my friends driving their nice cars, I wished I could be in their family* (NS), or *After living by themselves, they would feel helpless and clueless when they want to do something individual* (Chinese). The frequencies of reduced adverb clause use in NS and NNS texts were significantly different for all L1 groups of NNSs (see Table 9.2).

Subordinate clauses are considered to be relatively advanced structures in L2 teaching. However, among various clause types, noun and full adjective clauses, as well as adverb clauses of cause, are considered to be syntactically simpler than, for example, reduced clauses, which were not particularly popular in either NS or NNS essays. In addition, the ideational functions of condition clauses are also relatively complex. It appears that in NNS texts, noun clauses were used at similar or higher rates than in NS essays, and full adjective clause rates were less frequent in L2 compositions of only speakers of Korean and Vietnamese. It would be fair to say that both NSs and NNSs could benefit from additional language instruction that focuses particularly on uses and functions of subordinate clauses in written academic text.

10

Text-Rhetorical Features and Their Functions and Uses

Rhetorical features of text primarily function in terms of discourse construction and text cohesion and flow. Although these features represent syntactic and lexical elements, their syntactic role is secondary to their rhetorical function. For example, the function of hedges, such as *maybe* or *perhaps* is to decrease the degree of certainty expressed in a proposition (*When I finish the university, it will be easy for me to find my future job* vs. *When I finish the university, perhaps it will be easy for me to find my future job*). It is not always possible to separate between rhetorical and syntactic functions of some of the features discussed herein. For this reason, their brief descriptions, based on earlier research, frequently include both rhetorical and syntactic functions of the textual devices.

The rhetorical features examined in this chapter by and large have the functions of cohesive and hedging devices in text and information flow, as well as text clarity and idiomaticity. Specifically, various types of conjunctions and demonstrative pronouns are important in text cohesion, whereas hedges, rhetorical questions, and presupposition markers represent lexical and syntactic means of reducing the truth value of propositions and adding to informational validity.

Following the discussion of the textual functions of features, their uses in student texts are examined. The important findings include those text-rhetorical features that were used significantly more frequently in NNS than NS texts:

- Phrase-level conjunctions.
- Sentence-level conjunctions (transitions).
- Exemplification markers (for example).
- Emphatics.

The features that were found significantly less frequently in NNS than NS essays:

- Fixed strings (idiomatic phrases and collocations).

COORDINATING AND LOGICAL CONJUNCTIONS/PREPOSITIONS

Phrase-level coordinating conjunctions: *also, and, both . . . and, but, either . . . or, neither . . . nor, nor, not only . . . but also, or, (and) then, yet.* For example, *Parents' generation grew up on strong cultural traditions <u>and</u> values. The responsibility of parents is to teach these traditions to their own children* (Arabic).

Sentence-level coordinating conjunctions (by frequency and meaning): <u>*Enumerative*</u>—*first(-ly), second(-ly), third(-ly), fourth(-ly) . . . , next, then; in the first/second/third . . . place; first/second/third . . . of all; for one thing, to begin/start with, in conclusion, to conclude, finally, last(-ly), at last.*[1] <u>*Additive*</u>— *above all, additionally, (once) again; in addition, likewise, similarly, in the same way, by the same token, even worse, furthermore, moreover, too* (in the sentence-initial position only); *also, and/ but (besides/then/still/yet/nevertheless/nonetheless), or (else/again), then (again),* (distinguished from phrase-level coordinators). <u>*Summative*</u>—*all in all, altogether, in sum, therefore, thus, to summarize, to sum up.* <u>*Resultative*</u>—*accordingly, as a result, as a/in consequence, consequently, hence, now, (and) so* (excluding adverbial subordinators). <u>*Concessive*</u>—*after all, all the same, anyhow, anyway(s), at any rate, at the same time, besides, else, however, in any case/event, for all that, nevertheless, nonetheless, on the other hand, (better/and) still, that said, though* (in the sentence final position only), *(but) then/yet* (distinguished from the phrase-level coordinator, in the sentence final or initial position only). <u>*Other*</u> (focusing, contrastive, replacive, temporal, transitional)—*as a matter of fact, by the way, conversely, incidentally, in contrast, in fact, meantime/while, in the meantime/while, eventually, originally, on the contrary, otherwise, rather, somehow, subsequently.*

Some examples of sentence-level conjunctions include: (a) <u>*Moreover,*</u> *mathematics is very important for freshmen to take* (Japanese), (b) <u>*Thus,*</u> *in this*

---

[1]In many L2 essays, although incorrectly used in place of *finally/last(-ly)*, this conjunction was relatively frequent.

class, students can improve their writing, speaking, and pronunciation skills (Chinese), and (c) *Firstly, I need to mention that I really hate accounting* (Indonesian).

Logical/semantic conjunctions and prepositions: *as well, because of, besides, despite, except* (+ noun phrase)*, for that reason, in contrast (to/with), in spite of, instead of, in place of, in that case, in the event of, in this/that way, like, too, unlike.* For example, *Besides that, they also learn to control, operate, and organize the American economy with its financial settings and problems* (Chinese).

Textual Functions of Conjunctions

Conjunctions are detached from the structure of a clause and play the role of semantic connectors of independent units such as phrases and clauses (Quirk et al., 1985). Their function is to establish connectivity between ideas in the discourse flow, and they can operate on multiple levels of text, such as phrasal, sentential, and logical/ideational (Halliday & Hasan, 1976). However, coordinating conjunctions are distinct from subordinators because they assume a certain degree of syntactic and systematic relationship between phrases and sentences to allow for parts of text to be connected in meaning. According to Halliday and Hasan, conjunctive relationships between ideas are derived from the functional and meaningful basis of the text flow, that is, the content and ideas in text, rather than merely issues of punctuation or other conventions of text parsing. Halliday (1994) observed that logical semantic conjunctions are particularly useful in academic texts where they can establish meaningful connections between ideas based on logical and semantic relationships, such as causal, evidential, equivalent, or partitive. However, Chafe (1985) pointed out that the mere inclusion of coordinating conjunctions in the text without connectivity of textual meanings results in a chaining of ideas and fragmented writing style.

Corpus analysis of various types of writing has demonstrated that the employment of conjunctions is relatively common in academic prose, compared to, for example, editorials, fiction, or correspondence (Biber, 1988). In her analysis of written academic discourse, Tadros (1994) found that sentence-level conjunctions play the role of "textual modifiers" (p. 98) when they are used as direct discourse organizers that order messages with respect to each other and signal the semantic or structural relationship between them. She also commented that they are almost always employed to present new information or discourse themes that are, however, not necessarily coreferential with the preceding text and can appear to be chainlike sequences throughout a text.

In many languages, phrase- and sentence-level coordination represents one of the most prevalent means of textual cohesion and organization of the information flow (Chafe, 1970, 1986, 1994). R. Scollon and S. W. Scollon (1995) reported that the use of coordinators, such as *but* and *and* in the English texts produced by speakers of Korean, Japanese, and Chinese often results in confusing textual organization and a general sense of incoherence because these coordinators are employed in contexts where other types of cohesive devices are expected (such as, e.g., subordinators).

In Chinese, Japanese, Korean, Indonesian, and Vietnamese, coordination may be difficult to distinguish from subordination because both types of structures employ sentence linking by means of particles and conjunctions to connect the information flow in text (Li & Thompson, 1981; Scollon, 1993a). Nguyen (1987) pointed out that in Vietnamese, several independent clauses can be linked by a connective *(and, but, yet, however, nevertheless)* or may be conjoined without it in an unmarked sequence. In Japanese and Korean, coordinating relationships are also common and can be explicitly or implicitly marked by conjunctions and particles (Kim, 1987; Shibatani, 1987). Similarly, Ostler (1987) found that in formal Arabic prose, coordinating relationships between phrases and sentences predominate in text. She pointed out that Arabic rhetoric places high value on parallel and balanced constructions of phrases and sentences, and relative markers are in fact demonstrative-referential determiners (e.g., *We rely on our teachers that they teach us <u>this</u> we need to know* [Vietnamese]). Parallel coordinating conjunctions, such as *and* and *or,* are employed to link any parallel structure, for example, nouns, verbs, phrases, and sentences. These must be present for the structures to be explicitly linked and create a formal (elevated) style and balanced text flow.

In research on rhetoric and composition, a distinction is made between conjunctions that connect phrases and those that connect independent clauses. The former are traditionally called coordinators, and the latter, sentence transitions (Hacker, 1994). In writing instruction, coordinating and transitional conjunctions are explained and discussed in a vast majority of composition texts and writing guides (Leki, 1999; Lunsford & Connors, 1997) because they are necessary to "maintain flow and establish clear relationships between ideas" (Swales & Feak, 1994, p. 22). Most instructional texts in academic and college writing contain lists of phrase- and sentence-level conjunctions, explain their meanings and functions, and strongly emphasize the importance of their use in academic writing (Leki, 1999; Raimes, 1992; Swales & Feak, 1994). According to Davidson (1991), the presence and the uses of coordinators, among those of several other cohesive devices, can be used as a statistically reliable measure of discourse cohesion in the assessment of L2 writing on standardized tests.

Uses of Coordinating and Logical
Conjunctions in Student Texts

Conjunctions establish connections between ideas in discourse and text, and coordinating conjunctions in particular determine a parallel relationship of ideas and syntactic units. They are the most ubiquitous and probably the most lexically simple means of developing text cohesion (Halliday & Hasan, 1976).

Phrase-level conjunctions *(and, but, yet, both . . . and)* are often the simplest and the most common of all types of cohesive devices. For example, *First of all, I think that children need to learn about what is good _and_ what is bad _and_ what is world like. Some children would distinguish what is good _and_ what is bad _and_ when they get experiences. Other children would not distinguish what is good _or_ bad because they are too young to classify things _or_ other reasons* (Korean) or *If a child asks his father _or_ mother for some money _and_ they give him the money right away without asking him what he is going to buy with this money is going to affect the child's attitude, _and_ the parents will never know what the child is going to buy, _but_ it could be drugs _or_ it could be a gun, _but_ if the parents ask their child what he is going to buy with the money, _and_ as soon as he buys the thing that he wanted, the parent must check _or_ make sure that their child bought the right thing, _and_ if the child asks for money to buy something _and_ the parents see that the thing that the child bought . . .* (this sentence, from an Arabic-speaking student's essay, continues for 15 more lines). In the essays of speakers of Chinese (median 4.39), Korean (median 4.20), Vietnamese (median 4.24), and Arabic (median 5.36), phrase-level conjunctions were employed in frequency rates significantly higher than the rates in NS texts (median 3.62). On the other hand, in the essays of Japanese writers (median 3.72) and Indonesians (median 3.51) the frequency rates of these cohesive devices did not differ significantly from those in NS essays. According to the values of ranges for Arabic and Chinese speakers' texts presented in Table 10.1, at their maximum frequencies, phrase-level coordinators represented approximately 16% to 18% of all words in some essays.

Sentence-level conjunctions (transitions) *(first, second, third, moreover, however, thus, therefore)* connect the ideas in propositions or sentence units. For example, *As a result, there are many young generations who spend their time with drinking and gambling* (Indonesian), or *First of all, parents should be teaching how to help people or how to be accepted in society by using their home. However, as I grow up, I come to need many things that are necessities. Therefore, I want something* (Japanese). Sentence transitions are listed and their functions explained in practically all composition textbooks and style guides (Hacker, 1994; Leki, 1999; Lundsford & Connors, 1997). These books, however, do not explain how transitions need to be paced and distributed in text.

TABLE 10.1

Median Frequency Rates for Coordinating and Logical Conjunctions/Prepositions
and Exemplification (Median %)

		L1						
		NS	*Chinese*	*Japanese*	*Korean*	*Vietnamese*	*Indonesian*	*Arabic*
phrase-level		**3.62**	**4.39****	**3.72**	**4.20****	**4.24****	**3.51**	**5.44****
	Range	9.45	17.84	10.32	12.70	13.49	10.02	15.83
Sentence-level		**0.64**	**1.59****	**1.92****	**1.95****	**1.33****	**1.43****	**1.43****
	Range	4.81	5.56	8.40	9.17	4.55	5.36	6.88
Log/sem conjunctions		**0.57**	**0.70***	**0.77***	**0.58**	**0.67**	**0.75***	**0.91***
	Range	3.85	5.19	4.65	2.22	2.92	3.41	3.13
Exemplification		**0.19**	**0.49****	**0.48****	**0.47****	**0.52****	**0.58****	**0.43****
	Range	3.41	3.03	2.86	2.86	2.70	2.78	3.81

Note. All comparisons are relative to NSs.

*one-tailed $p < 0.05$. **two-tailed $p < 0.05$.

According to the data in Table 10.1, in NNS essays of all L1 groups, their frequency was significantly greater (medians between 1.33 and 1.95) than that in NS essays (median 0.64). The ranges further point to the fact that, in some NNS essays, such as those of speakers of Japanese and Korean, 8.4% to 9.2% of all words consisted of sentence transitions.

Logical/semantic conjunctions include a mixture of those that are lexically and syntactically simple (e.g., *because of, except, instead, like, too*) and those that are somewhat more complex *(in spite of, in place of, in the event of)*. For example, *Because of that, I lost a vast amount of chance to learn how to do things without being helped by others. . . . Generally speaking, doing jobs for your kids is not only time-consuming but also gain more troubles because of that from time-wasting* (Chinese). *There are like constitutions or laws which are visible, and there are also rules which [are] invisible* (Japanese). The frequency rates of logical/semantic conjunctions in the essays of speakers of Chinese (median 0.70), Japanese (median 0.77), and Indonesian (0.75) were significantly higher than those in NS texts (median 0.57). On the other hand, the frequency rates in the essays of Korean, Vietnamese, and Arabic speakers did not differ substantially from NS rates (see Table 10.1).

EXEMPLIFICATION

Example markers: *as* (+ noun phrase), *(as) an example, for example, for instance, especially, in (my/our/his/her/their) example, in particular, like, mainly, maybe* (+ clause/noun, e.g., *So, he makes all this money and buys maybe a sports car, a house with a pool, or goes gambling* [NS]), *namely, particularly, such as . . . , that is (to say).*

Textual Functions

Exemplification in written academic prose is considered to be one of the most valuable elucidation devices, and examples can be marked or unmarked (Biber, 1988). Although a majority of marked examples consist of whole clauses and even short descriptive narratives, some (e.g., those marked by *especially, mainly, namely, particularly, in particular,* or *such as*) can be as short as appositive noun or adjective phrases (Quirk et al., 1985). Channel's (1994) examination of spoken and written corpora points to the fact that exemplification is far more common in speech than in writing and can be very vague.

In instruction, exemplification is considered to be advisable or even necessary when the writer seeks to expand or clarify the meaning of a proposition by giving a more precise description or illustration of the ideas, concepts, or objects referred to (Greenbaum & Quirk, 1990). Many composition and writing textbooks recommend that examples be used when writers need to convey their ideas clearly and explicitly or when they believe that the audience would not be familiar with the events, activities, or concepts discussed in text (Hacker, 1994; Leki, 1999; Raimes, 1992; Smoke, 1999). In the assessment of L2 writing, in general, exemplification to clarify a point in the line of argument is often considered to be an important skill that adds to the quality of an essay (Vaughan, 1991). Earlier studies, however, demonstrated that in L2 essay writing, Chinese, Japanese, and Korean students frequently use brief mentions of situations or events rather than elaborated examples expected in formal college-level compositions (Hinkel, 1994).

Uses of Exemplification in Student Texts

In composition and writing instruction, giving examples is considered to be desirable and advisable to clarify the writer's meaning, provide an illustration, or simply describe an event. For example, *For example, they spend a lot of time in the entertainment instead of doing their homework, such as math and reading* (Vietnamese), or *For instance, when our children go to school every day, the time of our children with their classmates must be longer than ours* (Chinese). In their essays, however, it appears that NNSs used a large number of example markers (median frequency rates between 0.47 and 0.58) that significantly exceeded those of NSs (median 0.19). If examples are intended to explain and clarify information, they can also be used to excess when it is not easy to tell what the reader can or cannot be expected to understand from the text. Similarly, if examples are considered to be desirable and are encouraged in essay writing, the writer may attempt to use more of them to make the ideas very, very clear to the reader.

HEDGES

Epistemic adjectives and adverbs: *according to* (+ noun), *actually, apparent (-ly), approximate(-ly), broad(-ly), clear(-ly), comparative(-ly), essential(-ly), indeed, likely, most* (+ adjective), *normal(-ly), potential(-ly), presumably, probable(-ly), rare(-ly), relative(-ly), somehow, somewhat, theoretically, the very* (+ superlative adjective + noun, e.g., *the very best/last minute/moment/dollar/penny/chance), unlikely.* For example, <u>*Actually,*</u> *when the French teacher asked me if I wanted the book, I said no* (Arabic).

    Lexical: *(at) about, in a way, kind of, maybe, like, more or less, more, most, something like, sort of.* For example, *But he gave it to me for my birthday, and I liked it* <u>*in a way*</u> (Arabic).

    Possibility: *by (some/any) chance, hopefully, perhaps, possible, possibly, in case (of), if you/we know/understand (what* [pronoun] *mean[s]), if you catch/get/understand my meaning/drift, if you know what I mean (to say).* For example, *This girl was looking at me in a funny <u>sort of way</u>, so I thought there were possibilities in this situation, if you know what I mean* (NS).

    Quality: *(as) we all know, as far as we/I know, as is (well) known, as you/everyone/the reader know(s), as the saying goes, (as) everyone/people/they say(s), from what I hear/know/see/understand, one/you/they say(s)/tell(s) (it).* For example, <u>*As we all know,*</u> *rich people are different because they think they are special* (Indonesian).

    Hedged performative verbs: *(would) like to/want to/can/may* + performative verb (e.g., *ask/comment/discuss/explain/mention/ note/point out/remark/ say/state/tell), (I/we/one/people/reader/they)* + hedge (e.g., *perhaps, like, mostly, sometimes)* + performative verb. For example, *I <u>would like point out</u> that there is serious problem with the homeless in this country, and if every baseball player gave just a portion of what they make, we could eliminate homelessness and hunger* (NS).

Textual Functions

A great deal of research has been devoted to hedging in academic prose, among other types of discourse (Channel, 1994; Hinkel, 1995a, 1997a, Holmes, 1984; Huebler, 1983; Hyland, 1998; Kay, 1997; Pagano, 1994). Although many studies are based on researchers' observations, others support their conclusions by means of large-scope corpus analyses (Biber, 1988; Biber & Finegan, 1991; Hoye, 1997), and today much is known about the meanings and types of hedges in academic discourse. In general terms, hedging represents the use of linguistic devices to decrease the writer's responsibility for the extent of and the truth value of propositions/claims, to show hesitation or uncertainty, and/or to display politeness and indirectness in order to reduce the imposition on the writer or the reader

(Hinkel, 1996, 1997a). However, hedging has numerous purposes, and it can take many forms, including conditional and concessive clauses, modal and private verbs, and conjunctions. In English, as well as in other languages, hedging devices are numerous and their meanings and contextual functions are complex. In part for this reason, various definitions and classifications have been developed to account for their uses and contextual implications. The types of hedges discussed in this study rely on the systems outlined in Brown and Levinson (1987), Huebler (1983), and Quirk et al. (1985) and are limited to those identified in the students' writing.

In Anglo-American written prose, hedges are used extensively with the general goal of projecting "honesty, modesty, proper caution," and diplomacy (Swales, 1990a, p. 174). Myers (1989) pointed out that hedging is conventionalized in academic writing and appears to be requisite in expressions of personal points of view. However, the appropriateness of its uses depends on the norms of a particular discourse community and the context of writing (Swales, 1990a). For example, Biber (1988) found that the frequency of hedges in written prose differs substantially between such genre as editorials, academic texts, fiction, and official documents.

As Huebler (1983) observed, the diversity of text functions associated with many types of hedges makes them flexible and effective as a system of socially expected uncertainly, doubt, hesitation, indirectness, and politeness. Channel (1994) explained that in the academic and scientific communities, hedges have the function of face-saving devices to "shield" (p. 17) the writer from the commitment of the truth value of the proposition, particularly when it applies to phenomena of which the existing knowledge is vague. Based on his corpus analysis of published academic prose, Hyland (1998) confirmed that "hedges were by far the most frequent features of writer perspective" (p. 106) and stated that in academic writing, this finding reflects the critical importance of distinguishing fact from opinion and the need to persuade the writer's peers and to present claims in ways that are deferent to the views of others. In composition instruction, however, hedges, often called "limiting modifiers" (Hacker, 1994; Lunsford & Connors, 1996) are not discussed in detail, save the descriptions of their placement in a sentence.

Hedging propositions and claims in order to decrease one's responsibility for their truth value and project politeness, hesitation, and uncertainty is a characteristic of many rhetorical traditions. In Chinese, hedging devices play an important role in conveying the writer's attitude to the claim (Biq, 1990). For this reason, hedges are ambiguous and can perform several discourse functions simultaneously, thus increasing overall discourse ambiguity and shifting the responsibility for inferring contextual meanings to the reader. Oliver (1971) similarly noted that hedges are requisite in Chinese written discourse to decrease the responsibility placed on the writer. Maynard (1997) and McGloin (1984) described the functions of an elaborate framework of hedges, uncertainty markers, and softeners in Japanese. They reported that in Japanese discourse hedges often play a role similar to the role they play in English. Hedges are a very common characteristic of Japanese discourse, particularly as they refer to possibility or probability, and because their number and variety is comparatively large, several can be employed in a proposition, depending on the writer's perceived or potential imposition on the reader (Maynard, 1993). According to M.-R. Park (1990), in Korean, hedges are employed as a strategy to minimize potential disagreements, and lexical, phrasal, and structural hedges can be employed to soften propositions or claims. She commented that in Korean the use of hedges can involve a great deal of subtlety and deep understanding of contextual or situational politeness in discourse. As has been mentioned, the Vietnamese rhetorical tradition closely adheres to classical Confucian rhetoric, and many similar features are found in Vietnamese and Chinese written prose (I. Taylor, 1995). On the other hand, classical Arabic prose does not place high value on hedges and understatements, and amplification and exaggeration are considered to be an appropriate means of persuasion (Sa'adeddin, 1989).

Epistemic adjectives and adverbs are among the most frequent hedging devices in published academic texts (Hyland, 1998, 1999), and of these, adverbs are more numerous than adjectives (in this study, epistemic adverbs are distinguished from other classes of adverbs). Lexical hedges, however, are more prevalent in informal speech, which is often characterized by vagueness (Channel, 1994). According to Kay (1997), this type of hedges includes prepositional modifiers of nouns, verbs, and whole clauses that are particularly unspecific and can mark a shortage of factual knowledge. Possibility hedges are also common in academic texts, and because they are often gradable, the use of a particular hedging device often depends on the formality or informality of the discourse, collocational restrictions, and the implied objectivity of the writer (Hoye, 1997).

Quality hedges have a distancing function that separates the writer and the truth value of the proposition (Quirk et al., 1985) by attributing it to an external source of information, such as assumed common or shared knowledge (Brown & Levinson, 1987). The quality hedges included in this study are a feature of informal writing, and studies of L1 and L2 composition indicate that NNSs employ them in their academic essays more frequently than NSs do (Hinkel, 1995a, 1997a). Their frequent use in academic compositions (particularly when it comes to references to common or shared knowledge) may create an impression of unequivocal generalization and unwarranted certainty and in the assessment of writing weigh against the writer (Milton, 1999). Hedged performative verbs often convey indirectness by shifting the deictic center of the proposition to embedded clauses (Quirk et al., 1985). Their purpose is to soften the claims in the embedded clause by hedging the illocutionary force of the performative verb and convey a degree of hesitation (Brown & Levinson, 1987).

In the frequency counts in this study, these types of hedges were compiled and analyzed separately.

Uses of Hedges in Student Texts

Hedging is common in academic prose in English and other rhetorical traditions, such as Confucian, where it is usually required in a well-written text (Oliver, 1972). Previous research has shown that academic essays written by speakers of Chinese, Japanese, and Korean are often overhedged and that they exhibit a great deal of hesitancy and uncertainty by means of various types of hedges (Hinkel, 1997a).

Epistemic hedges that consist of adjectives, adverbs, and collocational phrases *(according to, actually, normal[ly], probably, somehow)* are the most prevalent variety among a diverse array of hedging devices in English. For example, *According to that example, a lot of problems are created only because parents want their children's lives easier* (Indonesian), or *I actually don't know what to do, and also I was afraid to make any decision because if I make a wrong decision, there is nobody going to tell me I did wrong or anything* (Korean). Epistemic hedges are far more common in written academic texts than in informal speech. As the data in Table 10.2 shows, in the student essays, NSs (median 0.56) employed them at significantly lower frequency rates than did speakers of Korean (median 0.67) and significantly higher rates than Vietnamese (median 0.38) or Arabic (median 0.21). No marked differences in the rates of epistemic hedges were found in NSs' compositions and essays of speakers of Chinese, Japanese, and Indonesian.

Lexical hedges *(in a way, kind of, maybe, like, something like, sort of)* are relatively lexically simple but can be syntactically complex because they represent prepositional modifiers and/or lexicalized phrases derived from reduced subordinate clauses (Kay, 1997). Such lexical hedges as *maybe*, for instance, can be confused with verb phrases. For example, *Maybe, if I want something, I have to be a good kid, got good grades, or do my best for everything. . . . It sounds like it is my duty, it is my density* [sic] (Chinese), or *If parents try to act or play games with children, children will not trust parents and maybe other people anymore. . . . In a way, I think that parents change their attitude suddenly because they were so easy on children, children wouldn't understand why* (Japanese). In all

TABLE 10.2
Median Frequency Rates for Hedges (Median %)

		NS	Chinese	Japanese	L1 Korean	Vietnamese	Indonesian	Arabic
Epistemic		**0.56**	**0.54**	**0.57**	**0.67***	**0.38***	**0.56**	**0.00****
	Range	3.83	4.17	4.38	4.86	6.46	5.38	2.13
Lexical		**0.83**	**0.63***	**0.53****	**0.74**	**0.50****	**0.30****	**0.33****
	Range	7.58	6.38	3.53	12.50	5.24	5.24	5.25
Possibility		**0.00**	**0.00***	**0.00****	**0.00****	**0.00***	**0.00***	**0.00**
	Range	1.56	1.89	0.95	1.14	0.89	0.93	1.92
Quality		**0.00**	**0.24***	**0.00***	**0.00***	**0.00**	**0.26***	**0.16**
	Range	4.81	2.16	1.30	2.38	1.55	2.40	1.94
Performative		**0.00**	**0.00***	**0.00***	**0.00**	**0.00***	**0.00***	**0.00****
	Range	3.70	1.01	1.85	0.95	0.91	1.71	0.84

Note. All comparisons are relative to NSs.
*one-tailed $p < 0.05$. **two-tailed $p < 0.05$.

NNS essays (medians between 0.30 and 0.63), with the exception of those of speakers of Korean (median 0.74), lexical hedges were used at significantly lower frequency rates than in NS texts (median 0.83). In most cases, however, the types of lexical hedges used in NNS texts (see Table 10.2) were limited to about two or three (*maybe, like,* and *more*).

Possibility hedges (*as you/one know[s], by [some] chance, perhaps, possible, if you/we know/understand, if you know what I mean*) are largely collocational and can consist of entire lexicalized clauses (Hoye, 1997). For example, *If by chance you meet a person you want to marry, they will say no if they don't like her parents* (Indonesian), or *Perhaps, children have a talent to create something. However, parents make them lose this talent* (Japanese). These structures were not used by a majority of students in all L1 groups (medians 0.00), and their frequency rates in NNS texts were significantly lower than those of NSs, with the exception of Arabic speakers.

Quality hedges (*[as] we all know, as the saying goes, as people say, from what I hear*) have a distancing function that is employed to reduce the writer's responsibility from the ideational content of propositions by attributing it to someone else or to assumed common knowledge. For example, *As the good saying goes "Teaching your child how to fish instead of giving him fish"* (Chinese) or *As we know, it is not so good if you waste your money every day* (Korean). However, by virtue of their form, meaning, and function, quality hedges approximate those found in the classical Chinese rhetorical tradition. Thus, their frequency rates in the essays of Chinese, Japanese, Korean, and Indonesian speakers (see Table 10.2) were significantly higher than those in NS texts (median 0.00). In Vietnamese and Arab student essays, their rates were similar to those in NS texts.

Performative verb hedges *(like to/want to/can/may say/mention/point out/ tell)* were least common of all types of hedging devices, and they were not used by many students in all groups (medians 0.00). However, because their syntactic construction resembles that of clauses and often includes infinitives and modal verbs, NNS texts included significantly fewer of them than those of NSs, apart from those of Korean writers. For example, *When people say it harms the children, I'd <u>like to say</u> that it is the parents* [sic] *fault* (NS) or *I <u>want to mention</u> that my parents are not like that, they love me, but they don't spoil me, and I know that the value of money is different than the children who just get money without doing anything* (Indonesian).

RHETORICAL QUESTIONS AND TAGS

Textual Functions

In general, rhetorical questions are not considered to be appropriate in written academic texts in English because they can be excessively personal and subjective (Swales & Feak, 1994). Myers' (1989) study indicates that direct questions in writing are often viewed as personal and artificial, and Biber's (1988) analysis of published English language corpora indicates that they are rare in formal writing. The use of direct questions in formal prose in English can also play the role of hedging, so that a proposition is not expressed in the form of an overt claim or a statement (Huebler, 1983). Chang and Swales (1999) found that direct questions are actively discouraged in academic prose in many disciplines, but nonetheless, they seem to occur quite frequently in texts published in philosophy and linguistics, and less so in statistics. Direct questions can also be employed as introducers or predictors, particularly in section headings in academic texts (Tadros, 1994).

In Chinese, Japanese, Korean, Indonesian, Vietnamese, and Arabic, rhetorical questions are an appropriate device to convey hesitation and/or uncertainty of facts, and their discourse function can be compared to that of hedging devices in English (Biq, 1990; Hwang, 1987; Ohta, 1991; Sa'adeddin, 1989; I. Taylor, 1995). In Chinese formal writing, rhetorical questions perform various functions, such as hinting about the purpose of the text, and thus replacing a direct thesis statement and avoiding assertion. Wong (1990) noted that in the classical Chinese rhetorical tradition, questions are used to involve the audience and to promote its participation, as well as to seek an understanding of the writer's position. Another prominent use of direct questions in several Asian writing traditions is to display the author's authoritative stance and the broad applicability of his or her propositions (G. Taylor & Chen, 1991). On the other hand, in Japanese speech and writing, rhetorical questions, such as commentary questions, are employed to convey the writer's attitude, for example, emphasis, accusations, or persistence, and half- (tag) questions convey uncertainty or hesitation at the end of a statement (Maynard, 1993).

Uses in Student Texts

In written academic discourse, rhetorical questions are rare and are usually perceived to be inappropriate and excessively personal (Swales & Feak, 1994). However, in Confucian rhetoric, questions often play the role of hedging, hints, and direct appeals to the reader. For example, *As a result, parents should put on regulation to educate them: <u>what is right</u>? and <u>what is wrong</u>?* (Vietnamese), *<u>Why too much easy lives will harm the children</u>?* (Chinese), or *<u>Who can help them</u>?* (Japanese). Not surprisingly, rhetorical questions in NNS texts (medians from 0.00 to 0.24) were used at significantly higher frequency rates than in NS essays (median 0.00), with the exception of Indonesian compositions (see Table 10.3).

DEMONSTRATIVES

Markers: *this, that, those, these* (+ one[s]), excluding *that* used as a subordinator, relative pronoun, or complement, for example, *<u>That</u> day, I drove 700 miles just to see her because I thought that I will never see her again* (Korean).

Demonstrative pronouns belong in the class of determiners and play a prominent role in text cohesion and have indexal, referential, deictic, and experiential functions in written English (Halliday & Hasan, 1976). Quirk et al. (1985) identified several functions of demonstratives in discourse and point out that these pronouns are often ambiguous in their referential and

TABLE 10.3
Median Frequency Rates for Other Rhetorical Features (Median %)

		NS	Chinese	Japanese	Korean	Vietnamese	Indonesian	Arabic
					L1			
Rhetorical Questions		0.00	0.24**	0.19**	0.00**	0.00*	0.00	0.21**
	Range	2.07	4.26	3.17	5.71	2.46	3.91	5.47
Demonstrative		0.91	1.28*	0.88	1.42**	0.99	0.88	1.90**
	Range	4.46	8.44	8.76	10.00	6.03	5.14	14.06
Emphatics		1.22	2.83**	2.26**	1.97**	2.68**	1.92**	2.77**
	Range	5.77	7.74	12.50	10.92	6.85	7.91	13.01
Presupp. Markers		0.00	0.00	0.00*	0.00*	0.00	0.00	0.00**
	Range	1.10	2.10	1.71	1.39	1.03	0.81	3.01
Fixed Strings		3.76	0.96**	1.19**	1.03**	1.20**	0.80**	1.18**
	Range	20.19	4.76	8.70	4.55	6.41	3.85	4.61

Note. All comparisons are relative to NSs.
*one-tailed $p < 0.05$. **two-tailed $p < 0.05$.

determinative properties. According to McCarthy (1994), *this, that, these,* and *those* can perform the function of hedges because they are vague and, for this reason, are generally discouraged in Anglo-American written discourse. On the other hand, Biber (1988) and Myers (1989) found that demonstratives are common in academic writing precisely because of their hedging qualities and lack of specificity and because they serve to attribute an assertion or proposition to an impersonal agency external to the writer.

Levinson (1983) commented that in English the shift from the removed *that* to the proximate *this* marks an empathetic deixis. However, he noted that the use of demonstratives in such languages as Chinese, as well as Vietnamese (Palmer, 1994), can be a great deal more elaborate, when demonstratives can be organized with respect to the role of discourse participants, such as the writer and the audience, and carry meanings far more pragmatically and contextually marked. In Japanese, for example, demonstratives are not deictic but are objects of singular reference and can refer only to certain designated "objects in the world" rather than in context (Watanabe, 1993, p. 304). Ostler (1987) noted that in formal Arabic prose, demonstratives and other text-referential pronouns are one of the prevalent means of establishing syntactic cohesion and parallelism in text and information flow. According to McCarthy (1991), L2 learners frequently transfer the meanings of demonstratives from L1 and may attribute to these markers more referential implications than they actually have in English.

Uses of Demonstratives in Student Texts

Demonstratives are one of the simplest cohesive devices in English, but their referential functions can be ambiguous (McCarthy, 1994). For this reason, they are discouraged in academic writing. However, they are far more complex and prevalent in Chinese and Arabic written texts than they are in English (McCarthy, 1991) because they play an important role in developing textual parallelism and syntactic cohesive ties. For example, *First, this is because children are not complete adults and need parents' help to thrive. This assistance is not only teaching whatever they need but also giving plenty of love to them. . . . These children feel nervous and they become difficult to thrive well* (Japanese), or *I know many situations like this in my country. Children go to school but when they arrive to college, they drop out because they don't know anything about that. . . . That is a bad situation for children and also his parents but I don't know how about United States or North America. This is my opinion about my experience* (Arabic). The frequency rates of demonstrative pronouns (see Table 10.3) were significantly higher in essays of Chinese, Korean, and Arabic speakers (medians 1.28, 1.42, and 1.94, respectively) than in those of NSs (median 0.91). In the texts of Japanese, Vietnamese, and Indonesian speakers, however, demonstratives were used at rates similar to those of NSs.

EMPHATICS

Markers (adjectives and adverbs): *a lot* (+ noun/adjective), *certain(-ly), clear(-ly), complete(-ly), definite(-ly), exact(-ly), extreme(-ly), for sure, great(-ly), indeed, no way, outright, pure(-ly), real(-ly), such a* (+ noun), *strong(-ly), sure(-ly), total(-ly),* for example, *Indeed, everyone controls children's opinions, parents, schools, teachers, and even their friends* (Indonesian).

Textual Functions

The textual purpose of emphatics is similar to that of amplifiers and has the effect of reinforcing the truth value of a proposition or claim. The use of emphatics does not necessarily assume that the clause constituent that is emphasized needs to be gradable, but it becomes gradable with the addition of emphatics (Quirk et al., 1985). In discourse, emphatics identify an informal register and are more characteristic of speech than of formal writing (Chafe, 1985), and Biber (1988) found that emphatics and hedges co-occur in conversational genre. On the other hand, Hyland's (1998, 1999) corpus analysis of published academic papers shows that emphatics are relatively frequent in published texts in such diverse disciplines as philosophy, marketing, applied linguistics, physics, mechanical engineering, and sociology, but less so in biology and electrical engineering.

Uses in Student Texts

Emphatics, as amplifiers, have the purpose of emphasizing and strengthening the truth value of propositions and claims to display a high degree of the writer's conviction (*a lot, exact[ly], indeed, real[ly], no way, strong[ly]*). For example, *No way they can apply what they learn to the real world* (Vietnamese), or *Moreover, they may also [be] less competitive in searching [for] jobs. Their strong dependence really makes them lack competitiveness and confidence, and finally defeated easily* (Chinese), or *What children were taught affects a lot when they grow up. . . . To be a good adult or a good person, it's really important that children experience a lot of things, all things that they need to know about. Indeed, what is life without experience?* (Japanese).

However, it is important to distinguish between emphatics that are lexically simple and ubiquitous in informal speech, such as *a lot, really, no way,* and *sure(ly),* and those that are semantically and syntactically more advanced, for example, *indeed, outright,* and *such a +* noun. Furthermore, because the textual purpose of emphatics is to express the high degree of the writer's convictions, their simpler variants represent a more accessible means of persuasion than, for instance, detailed argumentation. In all NNS texts (medians between 1.97 and 3.26), the frequency rates of emphatics (see Table 10.3) exceeded that in NS texts (median 1.22). The rates of emphatics in the compositions of Chinese, Vietnamese, and Arabic speakers were two to three times those in NS texts.

PRESUPPOSITION MARKERS

Markers: *obvious(-ly), of course,* for example, *Of course, children don't know any-thing, and how can they, if their parents don't teach them!* (Chinese).

Textual Functions

According to Halliday and Hasan (1976), assumption markers indicate contextual propositions that the writer takes to be factual, and in this sense, they are presuppositional. They noted that in formal writing, these markers imply a slightly adversative force because they suggest that something is or should have been obvious, but may have been overlooked. Sinclair (1991) explained that the uses of *of course* have become largely idiomatic in English because it functions as a one-word marker similar to other clichés of indeterminate meaning that refer to assumed presuppositions. Presupposition markers and similar references to shared knowledge make spoken or written texts particularly prone to misunderstandings and negative evaluations (Chafe, 1994). In persuasive writing in particular, these markers are employed as a preface to an opinion or a line of argument, and preempt disagreement by appealing to shared presuppositions and values (Moon, 1994) and occur very frequently (Moon, 1998). In academic and composition writing in English, *of course* and *obviously* often indicate flawed organization of information into given and new because in the Anglo-American rhetorical tradition, the writer is responsible for text clarity, and minimal shared knowledge is customarily assumed (Tickoo, 1992).

Uses in Student Texts

Presupposition markers *(of course, obviously)* refer to shared knowledge and common assumptions that the writer believes to be factual and obvious. For example, *Of course, as a way of real life is not easy, parents know this, and children do not* (Chinese), or *Of course, parents still can give these quality of lives to their children but not just give money to them* (Vietnamese). These markers are strongly discouraged in academic writing instruction because in Anglo-American rhetoric, the writer can assume little common knowledge on the behalf of the reader. In composition research, presupposition markers have been identified as features of basic information organization and argument development. However, they were rare in both NS and NNS essays (see Table 10.3). The ranges of presupposition markers in text indicate, though, that they were used significantly more often in the essays of speakers of Japanese (range 1.71), Korean (range 1.39), and Arabic (range 3.01) than in NS prose (range 1.10).

FIXED STRINGS

Textual Functions

Fixed strings include phrasal verbs, idioms, and some common collocations, such as *foot the bill, toe the line, get the shaft, go by the book, kill two birds with one stone, up the creek* (Moon, 1994). They are characteristically culturally bound and assume a great deal of shared knowledge and values. In written texts, their use is so pervasive that without them a conveyance of ideas may not be easy, if at all possible (Owen, 1993). According to Sinclair (1990), they represent lexicalized and prepatterned "units of meaning" (p. 6) that cannot be constructed in other ways and that are sufficiently abstract so as not to be easily identifiable from the meanings of their words.

In her extensive study of fixed strings based on a written corpus of English texts, Moon (1998) pointed out that the density of fixed strings is very high even in nonfiction, although less so than in journalism. In her view, fixed strings are important in lexical cohesiveness in terms of synonymy and hyponymy but not necessarily in the general relatedness of topic and text.

In writing instruction and the assessment of L2 writing skills, the idiomatic use of vocabulary and lexis is considered to be one of the key measures of proficiency, fluency, and accuracy (Hamp-Lyons, 1990, 1991; Johns, 1991, 1997; Vaughan, 1991).

In the frequency counts in this study, fixed strings included phrasal verbs and idiomatic prepositional and noun phrases, typically contained in many ESL/EFL texts on vocabulary and idioms. Examples of fixed strings in text can be: (a) *After the last big fight, he got kicked out of school again, and his parents told him to move out or else* (Vietnamese); (b) *When they arrive in the U.S., they find out that they cannot even mail a letter because they don't know how to buy a stamp* (Chinese).

Uses in Student Texts

Phrasal verbs, idioms, and collocations are typically language-specific and culture-bound in that they assume a highly developed lexical repertoire, as well as shared knowledge and values. These examples of fixed strings are from NS essays: *When a teenage boy's car breaks down, and all he has to do is call his parents to get it fixed, he will never learn how to stand on his own two feet; I am happy to say that I have been able to live off the money my parents have given me all the way through; A child that has every need catered to at home is probably going to expect the same treatment at school. Chances are, though, that this spoiled child wouldn't be any fun to be around.*

Corpus analyses have found the uses of fixed strings to be predominant in both speech and writing (Partington, 1998). Among other researchers, Owen (1993) stated that it may be difficult to express most ideational contents in text without heavily relying on lexicalized and fixed meanings that cannot be constructed in other ways. Moon's (1998) study of fixed strings shows that they perform a vast number of textual functions, from cohesion to explication. In writing assessment, idiomatic lexis and vocabulary are often mentioned as one of the crucial measures of language proficiency and fluency. Although a majority of NNSs in all L1 groups used fixed strings in their texts, their frequency rates in NS essays (median 3.76) were two to four times those in NNS prose (medians between 0.80 and 1.20).

It seems clear that NNS texts overrely on simple phrase- and sentence-level conjunctions and exemplification. In fact, in many essays, these types of conjunctions, as well as demonstrative pronouns, represented the primary means of establishing text cohesion. Although Halliday and Hasan (1976) identified diverse cohesive devices commonly employed in English, it appears that a majority of them, such as lexical substitution and ties, and ellipsis, are not readily accessible even to advanced and trained NNSs.

In addition, personal and other types of examples represented practically the entire text of many L2 academic essays. Though giving examples in general and personal examples in particular is strongly encouraged in process-based composition instruction, personal narratives are rarely considered to be appropriate in formal academic discourse (Chang & Swales, 1999). However, beyond providing personal stories in lieu of evidence in argumentation essays, NNS writers may simply lack other means of supporting their main points. In light of the frequent usage of personal example, it appears that urgent instruction is needed in how rhetorical support can be developed in academic texts.

In NS and NNS texts alike (see Table 10.3), expanding the range of hedging devices seem to be another venue that should be addressed in language teaching. At the same time, the idiomaticity in NNS language use represents one of the most important issues. Clearly, NNSs who have resided in English-speaking environments for several years do not have the lexical arsenal proximate to that of NS first-year students. The general conclusion that can be made as a result of examining language features in L2 essays of advanced and trained NNSs is that they have a shortfall of syntactic and lexical tools to enable them to produce competent written academic text.

III

The Effect of Prompts on ESL Text

The three chapters in Part III examine the syntactic, lexical, and rhetorical features in the essays written for each of the six prompts in the order they were presented in chapter 5. Chapters 11 and 12 discuss the essays written on two groups of three prompts each. Chapter 11 covers the findings associated with texts on Parents, Grades, and Wealth prompts, followed by chapter 12 that reports the data from the essays written on Manner, Opinion, and Major topics. The rationale for dividing the essay prompts into the two groupings is, in fact, retrospective and is based on the findings of the essay text analyses. The results of the analysis, outlined later in this introduction, indicate that text features employed in essays on the first three prompts differed substantially from those identified in the second three prompts. Returning to the analyses of the pooled data reported in Part II, chapter 13 deals with comparisons of median frequency rates of features in essays written across prompts by speakers of the same language to identify the specific cross-prompt variations in usage rates.

In chapters 11 and 12, the comparisons of NS and NNS frequency rates of feature use are presented and discussed for each prompt, by L1 groups, in the same way the data were organized in chapters 6–10 for the pooled data. The medians and ranges provide the basis for a comparative analysis. However, because the data and results of the full analysis are discussed in Part II, the examination that follows highlights only the important differences in NS and NNS uses of textual features in essays written toward a particular prompt relative to those in the pooled data. The goal of this overview is to determine whether some prompts elicit fewer significant differences in L1 and L2 text and, hence, lead to more similar NS and NNS uses of syntactic and lexical features. Conversely, a comparison based on essay data for individual prompts can help identify a type of prompts that elicit a particularly frequent feature usage.

161

As in earlier chapters, the findings of the data analysis begin with a comparative analysis of phrasal feature uses in NS and NNS essays: nouns, personal pronouns, slot fillers *it* and *there,* indirect pronouns, nominalizations, and gerunds, then verb-phrase features (e.g., tenses, aspects, semantic and lexical classes of verbs, modal verbs, the passive voice, *be*-copula as the main verb), two types of adjectives, and lexical classes of adverbs. Again, phrasal features are followed by a discussion of frequency rates for various types of subordinate clauses and, finally, the rates of rhetorical, cohesive, and other text-construction features (see chap. 10). However, unlike the discussion in Part II, the examination here focuses only on the data of particular interest and importance to the analysis of NNS text. For instance, because the number of data points in the analysis is very large, only the 10 most frequently used features (see Appendix A) are examined in chapter 13 in the essays toward the six prompts, by L1 groups.

As has been mentioned, the NSs and NNSs prompts were identical in every way and modeled on the Test of Written English, administered by ETS, the Michigan Test of English Language Proficiency, and prompts typically found in ESL and L1 writing and composition textbooks with the goal of eliciting writing samples in the rhetorical mode of argument/exposition to persuade and inform a general audience, which is rarely identified (Hacker, 1994; Leki, 1995; Y.-M. Park, 1988).

The number of students who wrote essays toward a particular prompt was determined by its popularity among the writing and composition teachers who met to select prompts. Thus, if a particular topic was not considered to be relevant for students or had little to do with their experience, it was selected on fewer occasions than the topics that were deemed to be more accessible. For example, the prompts that had to do with the selection of one's Major (259 essays), the freedom of offspring to form their own Opinions independently of their parents (249 essays), the Manner in which classes are taught (247 essays), and the issue of whether Parents should make lives easy for their children (246 essays) were seen by the teachers as more appropriate and relevant to the experiences of students than, for instance, the matter of whether movie stars and sports figures deserved their Wealth (216 essays).

In the reality of placement essay tests, considerations of the prompt relevance to students' personal experiences and teachers' choices of essay topics based on these considerations have a great deal of bearing on the types of language features used in student texts. As the discussion in Part III shows, in many cases, the closer the prompts are to students' personal experiences, the more personal their essays become. In this case, if students are expected to demonstrate their skills in recounting personal stories and narratives, then topics that are directly relevant to students' experiences do their job well. Similarly, the prompts that require explicit statements of belief and opinion have little choice but to result in many statements of belief and opinion. On the other hand, if the purpose of the L2 placement essays is to elicit written text proximate to that of untrained NSs in its usage of syntactic and lexical features, then selecting directly relevant topics may be counterproductive. Specifically, as examination of features in texts written to particular prompts shows, the more distant the prompts are from students' personal experience, the closer to NS uses of language features the NNS text is.

However, this observation is likely to be true only if NS and NNS students are familiar with the topic on which they need to write the essays. That is, the fact that a particular topic does not lie within the domain of students' personal experience does not necessarily mean that it would represent a good writing prompt, because students who write essays need to have some degree of familiarity with the issue at hand. From this perspective, the topics in writing prompts need to be selected such that students have exposure to their subject matter but not necessarily be personally involved. For instance, few on university campuses would be considered famous athletes or movie stars, but many hear and read about popular figures in the media and thus become exposed to stories about the lives of the rich and famous accessible to many individuals in many geographic locations around the world. It may be that in general, essay prompts based on information external to writers' personal experiences and beliefs can lead to the production of less personal and more objective academic texts. In this sense, writing prompts about, for example, popular music, videos, movies, fashion, the Internet, computer technology, or TV shows may represent venues for the development of writing prompts.

In general terms, several important conclusions can be drawn from the analysis of NNS writers' essays on individual prompts. The most obvious finding is that the wording of the prompt, including the actual words in the prompt, as well as lexical classes of nouns, verbs, and adjectives, has a direct influence on NS and NNS essay texts, and many words from the prompts were repeated verbatim. However, the wording of prompts has a particularly great effect on NNS texts, because if these writers have limited access to L2 lexicon and syntactic structures they are more likely to copy the prompt lexis and syntactic constructions directly into their text. To some extent, they do what they are often instructed to do, that is, emulate how language is used in real life in their own text production.

The use of many features in L2 essays, such as lexical classes of nouns and verbs as well as complex syntactic structures, seems to reflect the paucity of the writers' repertoire in terms of the range of both accessible lexicon and grammatical constructions. Because the pooled data for all essays combined exhibit a large number of significant differences between NS and NNS uses of the lexical, syntactic, and rhetorical text features, the more congruent with the norms of academic discourse the student texts are, the fewer text features in student essays are similar to those in the pooled data. That is, significant differences between NS and NNS uses of lexical and syntactic features were noted in the uses of practically all cases in the data for all essays combined. Therefore, assuming that the goal of language instruction is to provide NNSs linguistic skills similar to those of NSs (or at least reduce the extent of differences between the native and non-native language proficiency), the greater the number of similarities between NS and NNS feature use, the more nativelike the L2 range of syntactic and lexical features. Overall, however, the data from the essays written toward various prompts show that the degree and the type of divergences between NS and NNS uses of linguistic and lexical features can vary substantially and that, to a great extent, the prompt wording and proximity to students' experiences can often determine the specific features employed in L2 academic texts.

11

The First Three Prompts

The discussion of text features in essays written toward each prompt begins with Parents, Grades, and Wealth topics. To avoid redundancy, the discussion of features in the three groups of essays touches only on those in which trends in median frequency rates were significantly different from the patterns in the pooled data reported in chapters 6–10. Because the examination of the text written toward the six prompts was divided into two halves in chapters 11 and 12, the study findings that pertain to all essays topics are included in the introduction to Part III.

THE PARENTS PROMPT

The text of the Parents prompt was as follows:

> Some people believe that when parents make their children's lives too easy, they can actually harm their children instead. Explain your views on this issue. Use detailed reasons and examples.

A total of 246 essays were written toward this prompt. This number included 44 NSs, 39 Chinese, 32 each of Japanese and Korean, 35 Indonesian, 34 Vietnamese, and 30 Arabic speakers. Of the 68 features analyzed in the corpus, 24 show interesting differences when compared to those addressed earlier, and these are dealt with in the discussion that follows.

The Noun Phrase

Semantic and Lexical Classes of Nouns.   In the essays for the Parents prompt, the NS and NNS usage rates differed significantly for enumerative, advance/retroactive, language activity, and vague nouns (see Table 11.1). As with the usage rates for the pooled data for all essays, NNSs in all groups employed significantly fewer advance/retroactive nouns and significantly more other types of nouns with simple lexical content, such as enumerative and vague nouns. In the essays of Japanese and Korean speakers, for example, the rates for resultative and interpretive nouns were also significantly higher than those in NS texts. For example, *We can often see such an example like this around us in the world. The reason is parents spoil their children* (Chinese).

Pronouns.   The use of pronouns in the essays on the Parents prompt differed somewhat from that in the pooled data (see chaps. 6–10). For example, in the pooled data, first-person pronouns are employed significantly more frequently by NNSs than NSs in all cases, with the exception of Arabic speakers. However, in the Parents essays, the NNS frequency rates of these pronouns were largely similar to those of NSs: Only texts of Korean speakers included first-person pronouns at significantly higher rates, and speakers of Arabic actually used substantially fewer of them (Table 11.1). On the other hand, NNSs in all groups used third-person pronouns dramatically more frequently than NS; for example, the median rates in essays of Korean, Vietnamese, and Arabic speakers on the Parents prompt are twice that of NSs. For example, *In fact, many of these children like to be alone and they don't like to talk to their friends. They always want to sit alone and think about their past days. Furthermore, they become more aggressive and want to fight with their friends. Also, they always need someone to help them and solve their problems* (Arab).

One explanation for the comparatively reduced rates of first-person pronouns and the increased rates of third-person pronouns may be that the wording of the prompt influenced the uses of syntactic and lexical features in student prose. In fact, this observation is further supported by other data in this chapter and is discussed in detail. For instance, the Parents prompt is worded in terms of parents—*they*—who can harm their children, thus, removed the context of the topic from the writers, who were not likely to be parents or have firsthand experience with parenting. Therefore, most pronoun references in the essays on the Parents prompt were third person.

Nominalizations and Gerunds.   In general terms, the frequency rates of nominalization uses did not differ in NS and NNS texts in the pooled data, except in the essays of Vietnamese and Indonesian speakers, who employed them at significantly lower rates (see Table 11.1). In the essays on the Parents prompt, NNSs used nominalizations and gerunds at significantly higher

TABLE 11.1
Frequency Rates for Features in Parents Texts (Median %)

				L1			
	NS	Chinese	Japanese	Korean	Vietnamese	Indonesian	Arabic

I. LINGUISTIC FEATURES

Semantic and Lexical Classes of Nouns

		NS	Chinese	Japanese	Korean	Vietnamese	Indonesian	Arabic
Enumerative		0.00	0.59**	0.54*	0.84**	0.38*	0.65**	0.76**
	Range	2.26	2.50	3.13	4.62	2.96	1.85	7.45
Adv./retroact.		1.80	0.00**	0.43**	0.42**	0.00**	0.57*	0.25**
	Range	7.95	1.43	3.48	3.70	5.00	8.18	1.52
Illocution		0.00	0.00	0.00	0.00	0.00	0.00	0.00*
	Range	0.38	1.00	2.20	0.55	0.66	0.86	0.87
Resultative		0.31	0.40	0.74*	1.59**	0.45	0.45	0.00*
	Range	2.17	2.50	7.94	5.00	2.90	5.09	1.01
Language activity		0.25	0.40*	0.87**	0.79*	0.43*	0.85**	0.00
	Range	3.55	2.08	8.27	8.70	3.85	5.09	1.58
Interpretive		0.00	0.00	0.41*	2.03**	0.24*	0.00	0.00
	Range	1.11	1.06	1.76	11.96	1.63	1.15	0.53
Vague		0.87	2.27**	2.20**	2.94**	2.58**	2.22**	3.12**
	Range	3.11	9.72	9.17	8.82	5.34	5.42	5.53

Personal Pronouns

		NS	Chinese	Japanese	Korean	Vietnamese	Indonesian	Arabic
First person		2.00	2.19	3.21	5.23*	2.38	2.29	1.04*
	Range	14.35	17.65	14.10	9.57	21.40	14.24	14.67
Second person		0.25	2.50**	0.72*	0.57*	1.10*	0.00*	0.55
	Range	2.61	8.73	5.63	18.10	5.41	5.12	7.54
Third person		4.09	7.03**	7.59**	9.32**	8.08**	7.84**	8.93**
	Range	7.93	22.20	12.13	15.58	12.18	12.45	13.14

Slot Fillers

		NS	Chinese	Japanese	Korean	Vietnamese	Indonesian	Arabic
It-subject		0.67	0.19**	0.43*	0.00**	0.53	0.51*	0.00**
	Range	2.67	2.04	1.45	1.19	1.85	1.37	1.14
There-subject		0.00	0.00	0.00	0.00	0.00	0.00	0.95**
	Range	1.23	1.09	3.03	1.09	1.02	1.15	2.23

Indirect Pronouns

		NS	Chinese	Japanese	Korean	Vietnamese	Indonesian	Arabic
Universal		0.71	1.47**	1.49**	1.47*	1.55**	1.41**	0.72
	Range	3.04	5.71	6.67	4.35	4.28	5.20	2.59
Assertive		0.28	0.97**	0.77*	0.65**	0.45*	0.73**	1.04**
	Range	2.22	5.82	2.59	4.26	2.57	2.73	6.38
Nominalization		0.98	1.62*	1.61*	1.76*	0.96	1.37	1.81*
	Range	4.76	4.55	5.83	5.82	3.62	6.25	3.38
Gerunds		0.83	0.63	0.72	1.00	0.74	1.22*	1.84**
	Range	2.27	2.65	2.88	4.02	3.03	2.78	6.25

(Continued)

TABLE 11.1
(Continued)

					L1			
		NS	Chinese	Japanese	Korean	Vietnamese	Indonesian	Arabic
Verb Tenses								
Past		**0.93**	**2.94****	**1.74**	**0.85**	**3.56***	**0.98**	**0.92**
	Range	10.95	7.27	6.92	7.64	10.71	8.79	5.30
Present		**8.26**	**10.00***	**12.30****	**11.96***	**11.60***	**10.42***	**9.39***
	Range	13.08	12.31	14.91	16.63	10.27	20.04	14.18
Future		**0.33**	**2.36****	**0.46**	**0.00**	**0.77***	**1.43****	**0.40**
	Range	3.24	12.62	4.40	2.20	4.81	5.26	2.38
Verb Aspects								
Progressive		**0.35**	**0.00***	**0.00***	**0.00***	**0.00**	**0.00***	**0.75***
	Range	2.10	2.65	1.67	0.88	1.07	1.96	2.00
Perfect		**0.33**	**0.00***	**0.00***	**0.00***	**0.00***	**0.00***	**0.00****
	Range	2.31	1.10	3.31	1.54	0.78	2.00	3.01
Semantic and Lexical Classes of Verbs								
Public		**0.21**	**1.82****	**0.53****	**0.57***	**1.19****	**0.80****	**1.75****
	Range	1.73	7.06	3.13	4.76	3.88	3.11	7.42
Private		**1.07**	**2.69****	**3.03****	**2.50****	**2.86****	**2.27***	**0.65***
	Range	4.09	8.47	6.30	8.20	7.10	7.27	2.41
Suasive		**0.00**	**0.00**	**0.00**	**0.00**	**0.00**	**0.00**	**0.00**
	Range	1.79	1.78	2.20	1.50	1.34	1.11	0.69
Log./sem. relat.		**0.46**	**0.23***	**0.38***	**0.28***	**0.00***	**0.20***	**0.00****
	Range	4.09	1.79	1.88	1.11	1.47	3.56	0.69
Tentative		**0.00**	**0.71****	**1.25****	**1.63****	**0.68***	**0.51***	**0.54***
	Range	2.39**	2.65	4.83	4.52	1.81	3.68	3.03
Seem/appear		**0.00**	**0.00**	**0.00**	**0.00**	**0.00**	**0.00**	**0.00**
	Range	0.60	2.08	0.96	0.77	0.43	0.00	0.43
Modal Verbs								
Possibility		**1.03**	**1.40***	**1.65***	**1.50***	**1.07**	**1.36***	**1.09**
	Range	4.29	3.79	5.26	3.78	4.61	3.27	4.22
Necessity		**0.43**	**1.85****	**1.45****	**1.16****	**0.78***	**0.88***	**0.53**
	Range	2.17	7.62	5.80	4.76	2.72	2.16	3.00
Predictive		**0.30**	**0.00**	**0.00***	**0.00***	**0.00****	**0.00****	**0.68**
	Range	2.31	2.78	1.79	1.74	1.00	1.92	3.76
Passive		**0.75**	**1.39***	**2.14****	**1.00**	**0.52**	**1.46***	**0.52**
	Range	3.03	6.25	6.35	3.81	5.00	6.25	3.19
Be-main		**2.01**	**3.03****	**3.23****	**3.43****	**2.75***	**2.94****	**3.23****
	Range	5.13	11.64	9.02	8.24	6.55	7.90	4.64
Infinitives		**2.36**	**3.00***	**5.02****	**4.73****	**2.67***	**2.38**	**5.98****
	Range	6.37	8.77	7.42	10.46	11.11	6.70	7.44

(Continued)

TABLE 11.1
(Continued)

		NS	Chinese	Japanese	Korean	Vietnamese	Indonesian	Arabic
					L1			
Participles								
Present		**0.00**	**0.50****	**1.06****	**1.10****	**0.30***	**0.61****	**0.00**
	Range	1.93	4.81	2.88	3.81	2.86	4.69	3.23
Past		**0.43**	**0.36**	**0.60***	**0.71***	**0.00**	**1.30****	**0.53***
	Range	5.71	4.17	2.88	3.00	4.17	7.19	2.69
Adjectives								
Attributive		**1.42**	**2.14***	**2.69****	**2.27***	**2.17***	**1.79**	**3.79****
	Range	4.92	6.09	4.42	7.14	7.14	8.85	9.39
Predicative		**1.49**	**2.73****	**3.23****	**3.30****	**2.36***	**2.90****	**3.01****
	Range	3.61	8.05	9.79	5.90	9.85	4.42	5.05
Semantic and Lexical Classes of Adverbs								
Time		**0.90**	**1.00**	**1.30**	**0.50**	**0.97**	**0.85**	**0.52**
	Range	3.78	4.36	2.36	4.86	3.24	2.60	2.59
Frequency		**0.00**	**0.00***	**0.00***	**0.37****	**0.00***	**0.00***	**0.43****
	Range	0.75	2.65	1.60	1.92	1.36	1.48	4.02
Place		**1.23**	**1.35**	**1.60**	**1.19**	**1.35**	**1.33**	**0.40***
	Range	3.91	4.38	3.46	4.76	5.09	5.91	4.02
Amplifiers		**1.40**	**2.60****	**3.08****	**3.09****	**2.88****	**2.38****	**4.29****
	Range	4.76	8.40	7.50	11.06	8.16	9.38	6.60
Downtoners		**0.43**	**0.00****	**0.40**	**0.29***	**0.36**	**0.33**	**0.00***
	Range	2.86	1.85	2.08	1.43	2.26	2.01	3.19
Other		**0.31**	**0.71***	**2.31****	**1.79****	**0.38**	**0.50**	**0.55**
	Range	2.45	3.07	5.29	5.46	4.17	2.73	2.23
Noun and Adjective Clauses								
Noun		**0.90**	**1.46***	**2.69****	**1.78***	**1.97****	**1.41***	**2.38****
	Range	3.91	4.64	4.62	5.27	4.09	4.58	5.32
Full adjective		**0.43**	**1.20****	**0.96***	**0.86***	**0.68***	**0.98****	**1.77****
	Range	1.44	4.00	3.41	2.69	2.73	2.78	7.74
Reduced		**0.00**	**0.00**	**0.00**	**0.00**	**0.00**	**0.00**	**0.00**
adjectives	Range	1.43	0.53	1.25	1.16	0.53	0.54	0.76
Adverb Clauses								
Full: Cause		**0.33**	**0.65***	**0.60***	**0.58**	**0.38**	**0.71***	**0.38**
	Range	1.43	2.14	1.65	1.26	2.03	2.94	1.90
Concession		**0.00**	**0.00**	**0.00**	**0.00**	**0.00**	**0.00**	**0.00**
	Range	0.70	1.43	1.25	0.95	1.01	0.36	0.60
Condition		**0.50**	**0.62**	**0.48**	**0.65**	**0.51**	**0.36**	**0.28**
	Range	3.04	2.78	2.75	2.20	2.38	1.82	1.50
Purpose		**0.00**	**0.00**	**0.00**	**0.00**	**0.00**	**0.00**	**0.00**
	Range	0.93**	0.69	0.83	1.06	0.53	0.55	0.00
Other		**0.90**	**1.04**	**0.89**	**0.86**	**1.07**	**1.00**	**0.72**

(Continued)

TABLE 11.1
(Continued)

		NS	Chinese	Japanese	Korean	Vietnamese	Indonesian	Arabic
					L1			
	Range	3.04	2.56	2.78	3.86	3.38	3.27	4.26
Reduced adverb clause		**0.00**	**0.00**	**0.00**	**0.00**	**0.00**	**0.00**	**0.00**
	Range	2.41	0.93	1.67	1.86	1.09	1.37	0.66

II. RHETORICAL FEATURES

Coordinating and Logical Conjunctions/Prepositions

		NS	Chinese	Japanese	Korean	Vietnamese	Indonesian	Arabic
Phrase-level		**2.00**	**3.81****	**3.29***	**3.50****	**4.00****	**3.69****	**4.23****
	Range	5.52	8.95	8.88	10.00	11.15	6.99	12.33
Sentence-level		**0.83**	**1.90****	**1.59***	**2.03****	**1.47***	**1.52****	**3.54****
	Range	2.27	4.05	3.47	4.86	2.82	2.30	4.89
Log/sem conjunctions		**0.00**	**0.38***	**0.38***	**0.33***	**0.48****	**0.25***	**0.00**
	Range	1.68	3.17	2.17	2.14	2.22	1.48	1.09
Exemplification		**0.00**	**0.48***	**0.43**	**0.77****	**0.48***	**0.60****	**0.00**
	Range	2.08	1.76	1.67	2.86	2.70	2.61	3.29

Hedges

		NS	Chinese	Japanese	Korean	Vietnamese	Indonesian	Arabic
Epistemic		**0.35**	**1.14****	**1.60****	**1.42****	**0.48***	**0.57***	**0.45**
	Range	2.10	3.13	4.38	3.70	2.50	2.67	2.13
Lexical		**0.48**	**1.40****	**0.53**	**0.37**	**0.34**	**0.40**	**0.38**
	Range	2.63	5.63	1.92	2.21	2.65	1.74	2.13
Possibility		**0.00**	**0.00**	**0.00**	**0.00**	**0.00**	**0.00**	**0.00**
	Range	0.91	0.95	0.48	1.14	0.89	0.65	1.20
Quality		**0.22**	**0.00**	**0.00***	**0.00**	**0.00**	**0.00**	**0.00***
	Range	1.20	1.06	0.52	1.68	1.55	1.46	0.48
Performative		**0.00**	**0.00**	**0.00**	**0.00**	**0.00***	**0.00**	**0.00***
	Range	0.87	0.78	0.79	0.74	0.53	0.98	0.46
Rhetorical Questions		**0.00**	**0.57***	**0.40***	**0.40***	**0.34***	**0.25***	**0.00**
	Range	1.43	3.40	3.17	5.71	1.25	1.31	5.32
Demonstrative		**0.95**	**0.79**	**0.43****	**1.47***	**0.45**	**0.49***	**2.11****
	Range	2.94	4.00	1.56	7.33	3.66	1.62	4.82
Emphatics		**0.98**	**2.32***	**2.65****	**2.67***	**2.02***	**2.27****	**5.00****
	Range	4.26	7.50	7.14	6.43	6.25	5.91	10.34
Presupp. Markers		**0.00**	**0.00***	**0.00**	**0.00**	**0.00**	**0.00**	**0.00***
	Range	0.38	0.71	0.48	0.53	0.74	0.81	3.01
Fixed Strings		**1.49**	**0.94***	**0.80***	**0.73***	**1.01***	**0.40****	**2.41***
	Range	7.14	4.23	4.76	3.81	2.66	1.78	4.11

Note. All comparisons are relative to NSs.

*one-tailed $p \le 0.05$. **two-tailed $p \le 0.05$.

rates. Interestingly, the rates of NSs and Vietnamese and Indonesian speaker compositions did not differ substantially. On the other hand, in the pooled data most NNS essays contained significantly lower rates of gerunds, but in the essays about Parents, NNS texts employed gerunds similarly to NSs, with the exceptions of Indonesian and Arabic speakers who used gerunds markedly more frequently. For example, *Usually, parents' generation was poor and had many children in their own families, so they knew the feeling to really want to have* (Korean) or *Taking care and growing up children is one of the most important parents' job in the family environment* (Indonesian).

The reason for the comparatively high frequency rates for nominalizations in NNS essays is that NNSs addressed the Parents topic in generalized ways that included abstract nouns, in addition to examples of their own families or those of their friends. On the other hand, many NSs relied on abstract nouns less and provided more examples and stories from various experiences. The median frequency rates for NS and NNS uses of tenses also attest to this development (see Tenses in the next section). Because gerunds usually refer to processes and nonfinite activities, NS and NNS rates for gerunds did not differ significantly in most cases. Notably, in essays of Arabic speakers the median rate of gerunds was twice that in NS essays about the role of parents; that is, Arabic speakers produced very many generalizations and were less inclined to storytelling, for example, *Raising children is like growing flowers in the garden, and parents' teaching is everything in children's upbringing.* As research indicates (Sa'adeddin, 1989; see also chap. 6), the use of abstract/generic nouns and generalizations is seen as a mark of elevated style in Arabic rhetoric, and in light of this information it is not particularly surprising that the rate of nominalizations and gerunds was high in essays of Arabic speakers.

Verb Phrase Features

Tenses. Contrary to rates in the pooled data, in Parents essays the NS frequency rates for the past tense were significantly higher than in those of NNSs for all L1 groups, except Arabic speakers, and only Chinese and Vietnamese speakers employed significantly more past-tense verbs than NSs (see Table 11.1). On the other hand, the NNS frequency rates of present-tense usage were significantly higher than those of NSs in Parents essays. In contrast, in the pooled data the differences between NS and NNS frequency rates for the present tense were not nearly as high. Because the past tense is a feature of past-time narratives and the present tense of general propositions and assertions, it follows that in Parents essays, NNSs recounted fewer past-time events than NSs did but generalized to a greater extent. For example, *I feel that a characteristic of a person does not only depend on easy life. . . . When parents love their children more than enough, the children also have*

*the responsibility to maintain the parent's trust. If children <u>are</u> able to be responsible
enough to fulfill their responsibility, then the positive outcomes <u>emerge</u> and positive
attitudes <u>happen</u> on the other side of the coin* (Indonesian).

The Passive Voice.   In Parents essays, Chinese, Japanese, and Indonesian
speakers relied on the passive voice to a greater extent than NS did, even
though overall, the frequency rates for passive were significantly lower in
all NNSs groups. Furthermore, unlike the median frequencies of the passive voice used in NNS essays in the pooled data (see also chap. 7), in NNS
Parents texts, there were no frequency rates significantly lower than those
in NS prose written to this prompt. This finding may have to do with how
relationships between parents and children are seen in various cultures
outside the United States. Specifically, in many Confucian, Taoist, and Buddhist cultures, parents have a much higher social status and control over
family matters, and children are widely expected to obey their parents'
wishes (Hinkel, 1995b). Thus, in many contexts, NNS students employed
the passive voice to assign the distribution of activities and situate the active
or passive personages in their narratives and explanations.

   The uses of the passive voice are complex in the various languages
whose speakers wrote the essays. In particular, some of these languages,
such as Vietnamese, do not have derived passive constructions, and, for
instance, in Japanese, the passive voice is obtained by means of syntactic
operations very different from those in English. Most important, however,
the meanings and functions of the passive voice in various languages have
different contextual implications and uses. For example, *As a result, I always
care about my parents and made a decision which I thought my parents <u>will be satis-
fied</u> [with]* (Japanese) *or She is <u>spoiled</u> by her parents to buy her the brand names
fashion and daily necessities. . . . As a result, she <u>is</u> directly <u>harmed</u> by her parents
and her life <u>will be ruined</u> after her parents die. In addition, the children <u>are spoiled</u>
if their parents do not correct their children's mistakes* (Chinese). In these examples, the Japanese student does an action that is evaluated by her parents,
and the Chinese student ascribes a passive role to her friend when she is
spoiled and harmed by her parents, and *her life is ruined.*

Infinitives.   As has been mentioned, most NNS Parents essays contained
significantly higher rates of nominalizations than NS essays did because
ESL texts included more generalizations and abstractions (see Table 11.1).
In many contexts, infinitives are also employed in general descriptions
when their contextual meanings convey purpose, reaction, or result.
Although in the pooled data the use of infinitives in NNS prose was significantly less frequent than in NS texts, this was not the case with Parents
essays. In fact, in the essays of all NNS groups, with the exception of
Indonesian, infinitives were used in significantly higher rates than in the

NSs essays. For example, *How to educate their children properly is not an easy job for every parent. They must be patient and attentive to notice their children's behavior, and they must choose a different way to direct them to the right way* (Chinese).

Present and Past Participles and Attributive Adjectives.

In the pooled data, the uses of present and past participles and attributive adjectives have significantly lower frequency rates in NNS essays than in those of NSs. As has been mentioned, both present and past participles in English often have the textual function of attributive adjectives (e.g., *spoiled children* and *hardworking parents*). In the essays on the Parents prompt, however, the rates of present participles in NNS texts significantly exceeded those of NSs, a majority of whom did not use them. Similarly, the frequency rates of past participles in the essays of Japanese, Korean, Indonesian, and Arabic speakers were significantly higher than in NS texts. As an outcome, attributive adjectives in NNS Parents essays were also used significantly more often than in NS essays. For example, *I have a spoiled cousin whose father is a famous doctor. This loved child is notorious in his school* (Korean) or *Furthermore, I agree with those saying that the parents control their children. . . . Spoiled and dependent children will not be healthy* (Indonesian).

However, it is important to note that the participles used in NNS texts were relatively few, and many were repeated, as in *spoiled children, loving parents*, or *protected children-protecting parents*. As has been mentioned, in many essays, the wording of the prompt strongly influenced the syntactic and lexical features in student writing, and the Parents prompt contained the phrases "make children's lives too easy" and "can harm their children," which found numerous variations: *easy lives, easy parents, hard lives, harmed children, harmed lives*, or *too easy lives*. It is important to keep in mind that such languages as Vietnamese and Chinese do not have attributive adjectives similar to those in English, and most descriptions are carried out by means of participial constructions or predicative adjectives. Similarly, in Japanese, adjectives can also perform the function of nouns and are used in different contexts than attributive descriptions in English (see chap. 8).

Full and Reduced Adjective Clauses.

The pooled data demonstrated significant differences in frequency rates for full adjective clauses only between NS and Korean, Vietnamese, and Arabic speakers' essays (see Table 11.1). However, in the essays written toward the Parents prompt, significant differences are noted between adjective clause frequency rates of NS and NNS texts in all L1 groups. In all cases, NNSs used significantly more full adjective clauses, in line with their high usage frequency of attributive adjectives. For example, *On the other hand, parents who make their children's lives too easy, will have an effect on their children's study. . . . Parents who really care about their children will teach their children how to use money. For* *instance, parents tell children to be wise with money and tell not to buy things <u>that</u>* <u>*are not essential for them*</u>. . . . *On the other hand, parents <u>who make lives easy for*</u> <u>*their children*</u> *will fulfill what they demand from the children* (Indonesian).

Another important difference between the pooled and the Parents data lies in the fact that in the former, NNS rates for the usage of reduced adjective clauses were significantly lower than in NS texts. In the essays written to the Parents prompt, the majority of all students in all groups did not use reduced adjective clauses (0.00 median frequency rates), and hence, there were no significant differences between them.

Cause, Purpose, Condition, and Reduced Adverb Clauses.   As has been noted, in the pooled data, adverb clauses of cause were employed at significantly higher frequency rates in NNS texts than in NS essays. On the other hand, adverb clauses of purpose and condition, as well as reduced adverb clauses were used significantly less frequently in ESL texts. In the Parents essays, only Chinese, Japanese, and Indonesian speakers employed cause clauses at significantly higher rates than NS did, and no significant differences in NNS and NS rates are noted in the frequency rates of purpose, condition, and reduced adverb clauses. The reason that fewer substantial differences are found in the usage of cause clauses is that most students did not address the prompt analytically and, thus, largely did not discuss causal relationships between the parents who make lives easy for children and the harm that can come to their children. Instead, many essays undertook to provide generalizations and narrative examples. On the other hand, although the majority of students in all groups used adverb clauses of condition, they were typically employed in line with general descriptions and prescriptions. For example, <u>*If parents make children's lives too easy*</u>, *they can go everywhere they like, they will do the wrong things, when they are growing up* (Vietnamese) or <u>*If children have a new*</u> <u>*problem*</u>, *they will ask their parents to help* (Indonesian).

Neither the purpose clauses nor the reduced adverb clauses were used by the majority of students in any group (medians 0.00), and therefore, there were no significant differences in the rates of uses of these features (Table 11.1).

Hedges and Frequency Adverbs.   Hedges and frequency adverbs have largely similar textual functions: They reduce the writer's responsibility for the truth value of a proposition and display an element of caution when presenting one's opinion. In the pooled data, few significant differences were noted between the rates of frequency adverbs in NS and NNS prose, as with the rates of uses of epistemic hedges *(according to, actually, apparent[ly], normal[ly], probable[ly])*. On the other hand, possibility hedges *(by chance, hopefully, perhaps, possible[ly])* and lexical hedges *(about, in a way, maybe, most)* were employed at substantially lower frequency rates in NNSs combined data than in the NS pool.

In the essays on the Parents prompt, though, frequency adverbs and epistemic hedges were used in markedly higher rates in practically all NNS groups than in NS texts. However, by and large, there were no significant differences between NS and NNS rates for both possibility and lexical hedges. The reason for these differences clearly lies in the context of the general descriptions prevalent in essays written to the Parents prompt. Because epistemic hedges and frequency adverbs are contextually useful and even necessary in generalizations, their use was more prevalent in NNS texts to reduce the writer's responsibility for the applicability of propositions to all situations and all people. On the other hand, lexical hedges were largely equally common in both NS and NNS essays (particularly, *like, maybe, more, and most*). Possibility hedges are more appropriate in hypothetical statements or conclusions, and such constructions were not used by a majority of students in any group (medians 0.00). Hedging devices are very common in Confucian and Buddhist rhetoric and are considered to be an essential component of written text. However, in many languages, such as Chinese, Japanese, and Korean, they do not necessarily take the form of lexical items as epistemic or possibility hedges in English. Instead, hedges can be represented in allusions, suggestions, hints, and rhetorical questions (Varley, 2000).

THE GRADES PROMPT

The text of the prompt reads as follows:

> Many people believe that grades do not encourage learning. Do you agree or disagree with this opinion? Be sure to explain your answer using specific reasons and examples.

Of the total 240 essays written toward the Grades prompt, 36 were written by NSs, and 39 by Chinese, 35 each by Japanese and Indonesian, 33 by Korean, 30 by Vietnamese, and 32 by Arabic speakers. As with the discussion of features in Parents essays, the examination of the Grades essays deals only with those features that were used differently compared to those in the data for all essays combined (see chaps. 6–10). Of the 68 features whose occurrences were counted in the corpus, 14 show divergent trends relative to the pooled data.

Noun Phrase Features

Pronouns. In the NS and NNS essays on the Grades prompt (see Table 11.2), fewer divergences are noted in the use of first- and third-person pronouns. Whereas in the pooled data, significant differences were identified in the frequency rates of the pronoun uses in NS and NNS texts, where they were employed at significantly higher rates, in Grades essays, first-person

TABLE 11.2

Frequency Rates for Features in Grades Texts (Median %)

					L1			
		NS	Chinese	Japanese	Korean	Vietnamese	Indonesian	Arabic

I. LINGUISTIC FEATURES

Semantic and Lexical Classes of Nouns

		NS	Chinese	Japanese	Korean	Vietnamese	Indonesian	Arabic
Enumerative		**0.43**	**0.89****	**0.65***	**0.93***	**0.34**	**0.79***	**0.36**
	Range	2.38	3.33	2.78	4.89	2.92	3.46	1.70
Adv./retroact.		**1.89**	**1.07***	**0.32****	**0.55****	**0.19****	**0.74***	**0.61****
	Range	6.80	4.36	1.59	3.25	2.16	5.12	8.59
Illocution		**0.00**	**0.00**	**0.00**	**0.00**	**0.00**	**0.27**	**0.00**
	Range	2.22	1.16	4.61	1.72	1.60	1.13	0.94
Resultative		**0.00**	**0.53****	**0.25***	**0.25***	**0.43****	**0.25***	**0.00**
	Range	0.87	1.96	1.36	1.37	1.36	1.82	1.07
Lang. activity		**0.00**	**1.07****	**0.38****	**0.46****	**0.34***	**1.27***	**0.00***
	Range	0.87	6.06	2.99	1.82	1.86	5.80	1.07
Interpretive		**0.55**	**0.56**	**0.28**	**0.00***	**0.00**	**0.70***	**0.35**
	Range	3.77	2.48	2.75	3.81	1.43	2.42	3.21
Vague		**0.52**	**2.33****	**1.62***	**3.38****	**1.67***	**1.45***	**3.51****
	Range	3.54	10.83	7.64	8.73	6.42	5.14	7.41

Personal Pronouns

		NS	Chinese	Japanese	Korean	Vietnamese	Indonesian	Arabic
First person		**3.57****	**4.58***	**4.76**	**3.33**	**6.23***	**3.55**	**1.42**
	Range	11.17	13.33	15.63	12.96	11.44	13.33	10.00
Second person		**0.64**	**2.66****	**2.27***	**1.82****	**1.04***	**1.57***	**0.00***
	Range	9.14	10.71	10.00	6.42	9.06	10.98	3.55
Third person		**2.87**	**3.03**	**2.47**	**2.92**	**2.56**	**3.02**	**4.76***
	Range	9.52	10.00	6.25	8.90	9.36	10.30	10.64

Slot Fillers

		NS	Chinese	Japanese	Korean	Vietnamese	Indonesian	Arabic
It-subject		**0.42**	**0.00***	**0.00***	**0.00***	**0.45**	**0.20***	**0.65**
	Range	2.78	0.95	1.36	0.65	2.46	0.67	3.96
There-subject		**0.00**	**0.00**	**0.21**	**0.29**	**0.29**	**0.00**	**0.00**
	Range	1.30	1.15	1.39	3.70	1.48	0.91	1.56

Indirect Pronouns

		NS	Chinese	Japanese	Korean	Vietnamese	Indonesian	Arabic
Universal		**0.71**	**0.82**	**0.85**	**1.30***	**1.30***	**0.79**	**1.56****
	Range	2.75	4.91	2.04	4.04	3.80	2.53	4.81
Assertive		**0.33**	**0.51***	**0.93****	**2.30****	**0.43**	**1.10***	**0.85***
	Range	1.73	2.27	3.18	7.07	1.71	6.28	5.47
Nominalization		**1.10**	**2.02***	**1.43***	**1.63**	**1.61**	**1.89***	**2.50****
	Range	6.92	9.17	6.25	6.43	5.42	6.67	6.61
Gerunds		**1.79**	**2.12**	**1.65**	**1.39**	**1.48**	**1.47**	**3.78****
	Range	5.24	5.83	4.86	5.52	3.33	4.32	9.70

(Continued)

TABLE 11.2

(Continued)

		NS	Chinese	Japanese	Korean	Vietnamese	Indonesian	Arabic
					L1			

Verb Tenses

		NS	Chinese	Japanese	Korean	Vietnamese	Indonesian	Arabic
Past		**1.25**	**3.92****	**3.70****	**5.80****	**3.67****	**3.44***	**1.33**
	Range	9.57	9.50	12.48	9.55	7.21	9.09	5.77
Present		**10.62**	**9.87**	**8.54***	**8.77**	**10.00**	**11.23**	**8.64***
	Range	13.88	10.55	14.84	10.06	13.51	12.27	10.56
Future		**0.63**	**0.41**	**0.00***	**0.00***	**0.20**	**0.68**	**1.59****
	Range	4.17	3.93	2.78	2.22	2.78	3.64	5.23

Verb Aspects

		NS	Chinese	Japanese	Korean	Vietnamese	Indonesian	Arabic
Progressive		**0.47**	**0.00***	**0.00***	**0.00**	**0.26**	**0.23***	**0.00***
	Range	2.31	0.92	1.19	1.43	2.14	1.93	0.71
Perfect		**0.42**	**0.00**	**0.00***	**0.00***	**0.36**	**0.00***	**0.00***
	Range	2.43	1.76	0.62	1.75	1.94	3.03	1.67

Semantic and Lexical Classes of Verbs

		NS	Chinese	Japanese	Korean	Vietnamese	Indonesian	Arabic
Public		**0.00**	**0.65****	**0.92****	**0.66****	**0.71****	**0.74****	**1.43****
	Range	2.76	3.75	2.86	5.56	3.74	7.25	6.25
Private		**2.86**	**4.25****	**3.83***	**4.44***	**2.56**	**3.85***	**2.86**
	Range	7.80	8.09	8.33	9.57	5.87	9.03	9.47
Suasive		**0.00**	**0.00**	**0.00***	**0.00**	**0.00***	**0.00**	**0.00**
	Range	1.39	0.91	1.39	1.59	1.36	0.89	1.20
Log./sem. relat.		**0.00**	**0.37**	**0.27**	**0.00**	**0.34**	**0.16**	**0.00**
	Range	1.89	2.92	1.74	1.43	1.71	2.73	1.60
Tentative		**0.57**	**0.89***	**2.16****	**1.85****	**0.82**	**1.33***	**1.00***
	Range	2.67	5.50	7.64	6.90	5.35	5.69	2.86
Seem/appear		**0.00**	**0.00**	**0.00**	**0.00**	**0.00**	**0.00**	**0.00**
	Range	0.57	0.36	0.46	0.48	0.42	0.45	0.43

Modal Verbs

		NS	Chinese	Japanese	Korean	Vietnamese	Indonesian	Arabic
Possibility		**0.83**	**0.91**	**0.85**	**1.39***	**0.87**	**1.14**	**1.28***
	Range	4.40	4.17	3.64	4.39	4.14	4.04	3.83
Necessity		**0.47**	**1.18****	**1.17****	**1.37****	**1.19****	**1.03***	**0.44**
	Range	2.20	5.00	4.94	6.43	4.43	3.33	2.88
Predictive		**0.42**	**0.00***	**0.00***	**0.00***	**0.00***	**0.00****	**0.00**
	Range	4.14	1.24	1.82	1.47	4.43	0.89	1.56
Passive		**0.96**	**0.36***	**0.55***	**0.34***	**0.51***	**0.30***	**0.59**
	Range	3.85	2.06	2.38	3.26	2.96	1.28	2.33
Be-main		**1.89**	**2.94****	**2.67****	**3.12****	**2.92***	**2.95***	**3.87****
	Range	4.17	9.42	6.83	5.93	4.02	6.14	8.73
Infinitives		**6.14**	**4.04***	**4.55***	**2.78****	**2.86****	**3.68***	**5.71**
	Range	9.65	11.50	11.90	5.16	7.13	11.26	10.46

(Continued)

TABLE 11.2
(Continued)

		NS	Chinese	Japanese	*L1* Korean	Vietnamese	Indonesian	Arabic
Participles								
Present		**2.67**	**0.50***	**0.00****	**0.00****	**0.49****	**1.27***	**0.00****
	Range	6.15	4.58	2.30	2.17	2.27	5.68	1.28
Past		**1.82**	**0.74***	**0.00****	**0.27****	**0.00****	**0.89***	**0.00****
	Range	4.44	2.30	0.91	1.07	1.07	3.03	2.48
Adjectives								
Attributive		**2.63**	**3.27***	**1.74***	**1.72***	**2.02**	**2.17**	**5.29****
	Range	6.73	12.42	6.77	6.06	5.60	9.77	12.79
Predicative		**1.33**	**3.12****	**2.08****	**2.02****	**1.56**	**2.35***	**3.17****
	Range	4.64	10.83	7.21	6.21	6.34	6.47	5.66
Semantic and Lexical Classes of Adverbs								
Time		**0.37**	**1.06****	**0.81***	**1.36****	**0.97***	**0.81***	**0.71**
	Range	2.08	6.54	3.85	4.76	4.00	3.01	3.49
Frequency		**0.25**	**0.24**	**0.00**	**0.00***	**0.00**	**0.23**	**0.30**
	Range	1.48	1.33	1.43	0.65	1.01	1.80	2.13
Place		**0.95**	**1.43***	**1.63***	**1.10***	**2.00****	**1.05**	**1.06**
	Range	2.86	3.92	4.83	5.45	5.45	3.86	4.69
Amplifiers		**1.60**	**3.52****	**2.30***	**2.64****	**2.73****	**2.70****	**2.92****
	Range	4.35	9.45	7.01	7.35	6.07	7.27	7.18
Downtoners		**0.36**	**0.00**	**0.00***	**0.00**	**0.32**	**0.20**	**0.53***
	Range	1.15	3.33	4.17	1.72	1.48	1.62	1.69
Other		**0.84**	**0.51**	**0.89**	**0.46***	**0.73**	**0.76**	**0.19****
	Range	3.57	2.82	2.36	1.90	2.27	3.51	2.08
Noun and Adjective Clauses								
Noun		**2.30**	**2.61**	**2.08**	**2.17**	**2.24**	**2.70**	**2.00**
	Range	5.19	4.99	6.25	4.42	4.38	4.57	4.82
Full adjective		**1.01**	**0.67**	**0.62**	**0.46***	**1.01**	**1.41***	**0.77**
	Range	2.93	2.30	2.19	2.38	1.95	4.67	3.33
Reduced adjective		**0.00**	**0.00**	**0.00***	**0.00**	**0.00**	**0.00***	**0.00***
	Range	2.36	1.05	0.46	0.93	0.64	0.81	1.04
Adverb Clauses								
Full: Cause		**0.28**	**0.34**	**0.32**	**0.44**	**0.46***	**0.33**	**0.29**
	Range	1.48	1.90	2.08	1.26	2.53	1.82	1.52
Concession		**0.00**	**0.00**	**0.00**	**0.00**	**0.00**	**0.00**	**0.00**
	Range	0.94	1.47	0.61	1.39	0.73	0.67	0.59
Condition		**0.70**	**0.53**	**0.32***	**0.33***	**0.46**	**0.30***	**0.33***
	Range	2.76	3.90	1.39	1.77	1.73	1.47	1.77
Purpose		**0.00**	**0.00***	**0.00***	**0.00***	**0.00**	**0.23**	**0.00***
	Range	1.79	1.00	1.44	0.65	1.38	0.89	1.04
Other		**0.57**	**0.53**	**0.48**	**0.51**	**0.49**	**0.45**	**0.00****
	Range	2.22	2.03	1.75	2.40	2.03	3.03	0.85

(Continued)

TABLE 11.2
(Continued)

		NS	Chinese	Japanese	L1 Korean	Vietnamese	Indonesian	Arabic
Reduced adverb clause		**0.30**	**0.00**	**0.00**	**0.00***	**0.00**	**0.27**	**0.00***
	Range	0.96	1.11	1.38	1.25	1.10	1.23	0.78

II. RHETORICAL FEATURES

Coordinating and Logical Conjunctions/Prepositions

		NS	Chinese	Japanese	Korean	Vietnamese	Indonesian	Arabic
Phrase-level		**3.07**	**3.53***	**3.69***	**4.29****	**3.43***	**3.90***	**5.72****
	Range	4.76	10.04	7.86	9.66	12.67	9.59	7.14
Sentence-level		**0.38**	**1.14****	**1.92****	**1.72****	**1.28****	**1.11****	**1.59****
	Range	3.08	4.17	3.85	5.08	4.55	3.59	4.06
Log/sem conjunctions		**0.00**	**0.95****	**0.62****	**0.46****	**0.42**	**0.77****	**0.00**
	Range	0.99	5.19	1.75	1.77	1.10	3.41	2.80
Exemplification		**0.30**	**0.65****	**0.44****	**0.55****	**0.86****	**0.48***	**0.53***
	Range	1.25	3.03	1.54	1.59	1.60	1.19	1.95

Hedges

		NS	Chinese	Japanese	Korean	Vietnamese	Indonesian	Arabic
Epistemic		**0.64**	**1.15***	**0.91**	**1.32***	**0.00****	**1.14***	**0.28****
	Range	2.66	3.69	2.78	3.90	3.23	3.67	1.15
Lexical		**0.29**	**0.41***	**0.30**	**0.00**	**0.49***	**0.25**	**0.66**
	Range	1.48	2.00	1.44	1.01	1.63	1.23	3.37
Possibility		**0.00**	**0.00**	**0.00**	**0.00**	**0.00***	**0.00**	**0.00***
	Range	0.91	0.79	0.45	0.53	0.53	0.55	0.52
Quality		**0.00**	**0.00**	**0.00**	**0.00**	**0.00***	**0.00**	**0.00**
	Range	0.30	0.91	1.19	2.38	1.20	0.51	0.38
Performative		**0.00**	**0.00**	**0.00**	**0.00**	**0.00***	**0.00**	**0.00***
	Range	1.07	1.01	0.91	0.95	0.91	0.51	0.78
Rhetorical Questions		**0.00**	**0.34***	**0.28**	**0.34***	**0.36***	**0.18**	**0.00**
	Range	2.07	4.17	1.46	2.05	2.46	2.11	5.47
Demonstrative		**1.19**	**1.10**	**0.40****	**0.94**	**0.63****	**0.76***	**2.40****
	Range	4.15	8.44	2.60	3.33	1.97	2.70	13.66
Emphatics		**0.71**	**1.90****	**1.49****	**1.32****	**2.33****	**1.03***	**4.76****
	Range	2.38	6.57	4.09	5.88	4.88	2.77	12.76
Presupp. Markers		**0.00**	**0.00**	**0.00**	**0.00**	**0.23****	**0.00**	**0.00***
	Range	0.36	0.48	0.45	1.39	1.03	0.59	1.77
Fixed Strings		**2.29**	**0.79****	**0.96****	**0.79****	**1.61***	**0.35***	**1.44***
	Range	5.65	3.81	2.73	3.33	4.74	2.23	4.28

Note. All comparisons are relative to NSs.

*one-tailed $p \leq 0.05$. **two-tailed $p \leq 0.05$.

pronouns were found at similar rates in both L1 and L2 prose, with the exception of Chinese and Vietnamese speakers. In addition, although in the pooled data, NNS essays contained significantly higher rates of third-person pronouns, in the compositions on the Grades prompt, such differences were identified only in essays of Arabic speakers.

The reason for the similarity in NS and NNS median frequency rates for pronoun use lies in the fact that both NS and NNS students often produced explanations of personal views and beliefs in response to this prompt, and hence, the usage of first-person pronouns was relatively high. For example, in the pooled data, the NS median rate of first-person pronouns was approximately half that in Grades essays (1.95 vs. 3.57, respectively), although the differences in the NNS rates between the two sets of data were not nearly as great. For example, *I disagree that grades do not encourage learning. But I think that the grades is just one information, not the ways of evaluating someone's thoughts. I think that grading is important in our education because it shows us our weak points that we need to improve* (Korean).

In their statements of beliefs and opinions, both NSs and NNSs described their views on how students learn and teachers teach, and most of their texts were written in terms of students/teachers—*they* or a student/a teacher—*he/she.* These texts also lead to an increase in third-person pronouns. *Teachers should give appropriate courage to them. If they express very high intelligence in some specific subject, teachers may keep in touch with their parents to see if there [is] any possible way to provide a better studying environment for them* (Chinese).

Gerunds.   As has been mentioned earlier, the wording of the prompt had a great deal of influence on the types of syntactic and lexical features that were encountered in both NS and NNS essays, but to a greater extent, in NNS prose. Although the pooled data show that the NNS frequency rates of gerund usage were significantly lower than in NNS texts, this is not the case in the Grades essay, where the NSs and NNSs employed gerunds at similar rates, and Arabic speakers actually used them significantly more frequently (see Table 11.2). It is important to keep in mind, however, that the wording of the prompt included the gerund *learning.* For example, *I couldn't tell her the real meaning of learning such as the enjoyment of learning new things, solving the problems alone because there kinds of things don't regard as an important in our society. . . . Therefore, I agree [with] the idea that grades do not encourage learning* (Japanese).

Verb Phrase Features

Modal Verbs of Possibility.   According to the pooled data analysis, most NNSs relied on modal verbs of possibility as one of the more common hedging devices in NNS texts, whereas other types of hedges were overall used at lower rates than in NS essays. However, in the essays on the Grades prompt, the modals verbs of necessity did not differ significantly in NS and NNS prose, and the uses of other hedges were actually used at significantly higher rates than in NNS texts (see later section Hedges and Time and Other Adverbs). For example, *As you <u>can</u> see, grades do encourage learning. The grades <u>can</u> push yourself to work as hard as you <u>can</u>.* (Vietnamese).

Noun Clauses

In essays on the Grades prompt (see Table 11.2), NS and NNS also used noun clauses at similar rates, despite the fact that in the pooled data, the NNS frequency rates for the uses of noun clauses significantly exceeded that of NSs. The reason for the similarity lies in the fact that in the essays written toward this prompt, NSs employed noun clauses at higher rates than the pooled data show (2.30 median vs. 1.50), and hence, equalized the disparity in their frequencies. Because many NS essays contained statements of belief and opinion (e.g., an increase in the use of private verbs that often determine the noun clause structure was also substantial relative to the pooled data—2.00 median vs. 2.86 median), noun clauses were the structure of choice in both NS and NNS texts. For example, *However, some people believe <u>that grades can encourage the learning</u>. When I think <u>it's wrong</u> because there [are] many aspects besides grades that encourage learning. . . . Maybe, they think <u>they are stupid or dumb</u>, and he/she will think <u>that they are dumb</u> when they fail a class* (Indonesian).

Reduced Adjective and Adverb Clauses, and Cause Clauses

Because reduced adjective and adverb clauses were not common in NS essays written toward the Grades prompt, fewer disparities in NS and NNS texts were noted in the frequency rates of these structures than in the pooled data. On the other hand, NNS essays about the importance of Grades in learning contained fewer adverb clauses of cause than the data for all essays combined. In fact, NNS texts written on the Grades prompt did not contain many cause/effect type of texts and consisted predominantly of statements of belief and recounts of personal experiences.

Hedges and Time and Other Adverbs

In the statements of belief and opinion in Grades essays (see Table 11.2), NNS employed time adverbs and other adverbs (e.g., manner and quality) largely in rates similar to those in the pooled data, whereas the NS rates for these adverbs fluctuated. Actually, the NS frequency rates of the uses of timed adverbs decreased but increased for other types of adverbs. As an outcome, the comparisons of NS and NNS frequency rates for time adverbs are significantly different for practically all NNS groups. This development is mostly determined by the fact that general statements of belief and opinion, unlike narratives that can be framed for time, do not require many adverbs of time. However, descriptions of general situations and opinions require many qualifiers, and hence, the NS frequency rates for adverbs of manner and quality increased from a 0.50 median in the pooled data to a 0.84 median in Grades essays.

On the other hand, compared to the pooled data, the NNS frequency rates for epistemic hedges *(according to, actually, essentially, probably)* in the Grades essays increased two-fold in the texts of Chinese, Japanese, Korean, and Indonesian speakers. In the Confucian rhetorical tradition, hedges play an important role in reducing the writer's responsibility for the truth value of propositions, as well as expressing doubt and uncertainty. Thus, as did NSs, L2 writers hedged their statements of belief and opinions, but did this by means of direct hedges, rather than qualifying adverbs. Together with this development, neither NSs nor NNS relied on lexical and possibility hedges, and the comparative frequency rates for these two types of features were far less pronounced in the Grades essays than in the pooled data. For example, *Presently, students sacrifice their free time to studying and learning* (NS) or *A student's grades can sometimes determine his or her ability to continue in class. According to me, I believe that grades do encourage learning* (Vietnamese).

THE WEALTH PROMPT

The text of the Wealth prompt is included in full:

> Some of the wealthiest, most famous people in the world are musicians, singers, movie stars, and athletes. Do you think these performers and athletes deserve high salaries such as millions of dollars every year? Support your position with detailed reasons and examples.

In all, the Wealth prompt was administered to 216 students. They consisted of 36 NSs and 30 students in all other L1 groups: Chinese, Japanese, Korean, Indonesian, Vietnamese, and Arabic. The examination that follows accounts for the uses of 30 features in Wealth essays in which median frequency rates were different in important ways from the picture in the pooled data (chaps. 6–10). Reasons for the fact that almost half of all features used displayed interesting characteristics and differed from the patterns in the combined data are also discussed. It is important to note, however, that the

Wealth prompt was administered to the smallest number of students during the placement and diagnostic tests because during the selection of essay prompts, the instructors in writing and composition classes criticized this topic of wealthy entertainment and sports stars as irrelevant for students and their experiences. Many writing teachers argued that university students may not be too interested in the salaries paid to the stars and may know little about them (and hence, would have little to say in their essays). The importance of this factor in prompt selection is further noted in the overview of the chapter's findings (see also introduction to Part III).

Overall, this discussion of the features in NNS essays on the Wealth prompt (see Table 11.3) focuses on those that L2 writers did not use in ways similar those in the pooled data and that were employed in rates similar to those of NS.

The Noun Phrase

Semantic and Lexical Classes of Nouns. The frequency rates for enumerative nouns in the NNS Wealth essays (see Table 11.3) were largely similar to those of NSs, even though according to the pooled data for all essays, enumeratives were used by NNSs at significantly higher rates overall. The only exception were Arabic speakers, whose Wealth essays contained a significantly higher number of these nouns. In addition, the frequency rates for resultative and language activity nouns were also similar in NS and NNS texts on the Wealth prompt, regardless of the significant differences between NS and NNS rates for these types of nouns in the pooled data. An implication of this finding is that both NSs and NNSs did not adhere to the traditional enumerating structure of their texts *(the first reason/advantage/ disadvantage, the second reason/advantage/disadvantage . . .)* nearly as much as in their essays on other prompts.

Personal Pronouns. Other important features of the essays written toward the Wealth prompt are that the frequency rates for first-person pronouns also did not differ significantly from NS usage in Chinese, Japanese, Korean, and Indonesian speaker essays, whereas in Vietnamese and Arabic speakers' texts they remained significantly higher than in NS essays, which represents no change from the usage reflected in the pooled data. Similarly, the frequency rates for second-person pronouns in NS and Chinese, Korean, and Vietnamese speaker Wealth essays were similar, and in fact, the rates for these pronouns were significantly smaller in Japanese and Indonesian speaker Wealth texts than in those of NSs. The only exception were the Arabic speaker essays, which employed second-person pronouns at significantly greater rates than NSs did. As an outcome, most NNS texts included significantly higher rates of third-person pronouns than NS essays on the Wealth topic.

TABLE 11.3
Frequency Rates for Features in Wealth Texts (Median %)

		NS	*Chinese*	*Japanese*	*Korean*	*Vietnamese*	*Indonesian*	*Arabic*
					L1			

I. LINGUISTIC FEATURES

Semantic and Lexical Classes of Nouns

		NS	*Chinese*	*Japanese*	*Korean*	*Vietnamese*	*Indonesian*	*Arabic*
Enumerative		**0.27**	**0.00**	**0.00**	**0.00***	**0.00**	**0.00**	**0.60***
	Range	1.89	2.14	1.73	0.82	2.66	2.10	4.35
Adv./retroact.		**1.92**	**0.71***	**1.42***	**1.23***	**0.20****	**0.00****	**0.00****
	Range	4.51	4.29	7.41	3.33	3.72	0.94	1.52
Illocution		**0.00**	**0.00**	**0.00**	**0.00**	**0.00***	**0.00***	**0.00**
	Range	1.06	0.53	0.83	1.06	0.47	0.45	0.81
Resultative		**0.00**	**0.00**	**0.00**	**0.00**	**0.00**	**0.00**	**0.00**
	Range	1.08	1.39	0.93	1.30	1.90	1.90	1.71
Language activity		**0.00**	**0.00**	**0.00**	**0.00**	**0.00**	**0.00**	**0.00***
	Range	1.14	0.83	0.40	0.43	0.74	0.46	1.68
Interpretive		**0.00**	**0.28***	**0.00**	**0.00**	**0.00**	**0.00**	**0.46***
	Range	1.14	2.60	2.65	1.14	0.95	0.88	1.85
Vague		**1.00**	**2.50***	**2.36****	**1.67***	**2.21***	**1.67***	**5.00****
	Range	6.43	13.19	7.81	4.68	7.34	5.42	12.85

Personal Pronouns

First person		**1.19**	**1.58**	**0.93**	**1.17**	**3.60****	**1.09**	**2.07***
	Range	5.00	4.76	13.49	9.03	16.77	9.60	7.50
Second person		**0.00**	**0.00**	**0.00***	**0.00**	**0.00**	**0.00***	**0.62***
	Range	3.70	2.16	1.26	5.73	3.92	2.30	7.64
Third person		**4.13**	**6.76***	**6.36***	**6.49***	**7.17***	**6.36***	**5.39**
	Range	10.29	9.70	12.24	9.02	13.21	9.69	13.62

Slot Fillers

It-subject		**0.57**	**0.51**	**0.50**	**0.41**	**0.00***	**0.24**	**0.81***
	Range	2.08	3.21	2.60	2.13	1.29	1.32	2.40
There-subject		**0.00**	**0.22**	**0.00**	**0.00**	**0.00**	**0.00**	**0.00**
	Range	0.76	1.07	1.48	1.62	1.52	1.67	2.52

Indirect Pronouns

Universal		**0.57**	**0.66**	**0.71**	**1.01**	**0.59**	**0.81**	**1.15***
	Range	2.09	3.13	2.78	2.96	3.26	1.81	3.85
Assertive		**0.47**	**0.69**	**0.43**	**0.62**	**0.38**	**0.28**	**0.46**
	Range	2.18	2.57	4.08	1.67	2.23	1.67	2.82
Nominalization		**1.12**	**1.28**	**1.32**	**0.63**	**1.27**	**0.91**	**1.78***
	Range	3.17	4.79	5.00	6.43	4.79	2.78	5.56
Gerunds		**0.95**	**0.71***	**0.50***	**0.53***	**0.76***	**0.59***	**1.08**
	Range	3.13	3.72	4.09	1.73	1.96	1.99	4.97

(Continued)

TABLE 11.3
(Continued)

		NS	Chinese	Japanese	Korean	*L1* Vietnamese	Indonesian	Arabic
Verb Tenses								
Past		**0.53**	**0.45**	**1.30***	**1.01**	**5.24****	**1.96****	**1.10**
	Range	4.48	4.56	7.29	7.22	12.43	7.43	7.41
Present		**10.23**	**11.15**	**10.00**	**11.69**	**9.52**	**9.24**	**10.00**
	Range	8.66	10.89	11.62	10.93	10.47	10.35	17.32
Future		**0.00**	**0.00**	**0.00**	**0.00**	**0.00**	**0.00**	**0.42***
	Range	0.76	1.19	1.01	1.82	0.49	1.32	3.85
Verb Aspects								
Progressive		**0.27**	**0.00**	**0.00**	**0.00***	**0.00**	**0.33**	**0.00**
	Range	1.89	3.85	2.04	1.48	1.86	1.65	2.50
Perfect		**0.28**	**0.20**	**0.00**	**0.00**	**0.30**	**0.36**	**0.00***
	Range	1.79	1.52	2.90	1.67	1.39	2.98	1.38
Semantic and Lexical Classes of Verbs								
Public		**0.00**	**0.00**	**0.00**	**0.00**	**0.00**	**0.00**	**0.43***
	Range	2.38	1.04	4.35	1.33	0.98	1.04	4.20
Private		**1.06**	**1.52**	**0.41****	**1.36**	**1.18**	**0.99**	**2.42****
	Range	3.85	3.21	6.12	5.70	2.93	2.93	9.24
Suasive		**0.00**	**0.00**	**0.00**	**0.00**	**0.00**	**0.00**	**0.00**
	Range	0.75	0.71	0.00	0.00	0.74	1.49	0.63
Log./sem. relat.		**0.00**	**0.32**	**0.00**	**0.00**	**0.00**	**0.00**	**0.00**
	Range	1.25	2.05	0.85	0.89	2.05	2.00	2.90
Tentative		**0.57**	**0.85***	**0.95***	**1.14**	**0.79***	**1.33***	**0.55**
	Range	2.09	2.56	1.99	3.51	5.39	4.78	4.08
Seem/appear		**0.00**	**0.00**	**0.00**	**0.00**	**0.00**	**0.00**	**0.00**
	Range	0.57	0.43	0.00	0.41	0.00	0.44	0.63
Modal Verbs								
Possibility		**0.78**	**0.83**	**1.00***	**1.02***	**0.68**	**0.78**	**0.68**
	Range	3.83	3.21	2.92	2.66	5.71	5.71	4.50
Necessity		**0.57**	**0.79**	**0.36**	**0.58**	**0.74**	**0.59**	**1.20**
	Range	3.76	3.72	2.50	5.56	4.29	3.53	5.12
Predictive		**0.38**	**0.00***	**0.00***	**0.00***	**0.00***	**0.00****	**0.00***
	Range	2.93	1.79	1.95	0.74	1.52	1.20	1.46
Passive		**1.03**	**0.43***	**0.43***	**0.00****	**0.59**	**0.57***	**0.38***
	Range	3.65	1.79	2.48	2.22	1.94	3.24	3.17
***Be*-main**		**1.86**	**2.50***	**3.17***	**2.92***	**2.30***	**2.67***	**4.19****
	Range	4.51	5.87	5.67	5.13	5.01	5.24	10.20
Infinitives		**5.07**	**3.58***	**4.41***	**2.38****	**3.35****	**2.10****	**5.62**
	Range	8.09	6.62	9.36	2.78	4.61	4.82	10.55
Participles								
Present		**1.73**	**1.07***	**0.93***	**0.56****	**0.59***	**0.00****	**0.00****
	Range	3.72	3.54	5.26	2.27	4.94	3.90	0.84
Past		**1.72**	**0.79****	**1.01***	**0.68****	**0.00****	**0.00****	**0.00****
	Range	5.26	2.83	3.01	2.22	1.90	0.91	0.93

(Continued)

TABLE 11.3
(Continued)

		L1					
		NS	Chinese	Japanese	Korean	Vietnamese	Indonesian	Arabic
Adjectives								
Attributive		3.76	4.78*	4.55*	7.20**	3.82	5.79*	6.44**
	Range	7.98	7.43	7.36	11.61	14.64	14.64	12.14
Predicative		1.14	2.78*	1.95*	3.19**	2.74**	2.00*	3.23**
	Range	3.92	7.69	10.91	10.28	8.49	8.60	10.94
Semantic and Lexical Classes of Adverbs								
Time		0.68	0.64	1.04	0.89	0.49	0.83	0.79
	Range	3.65	2.63	2.85	2.88	2.42	3.39	3.75
Frequency		0.45	0.69	0.29	0.43	0.98**	0.59	0.45
	Range	2.70	3.21	2.73	1.35	2.58	2.94	2.07
Place		0.75	1.20*	1.30*	1.62*	2.21**	1.25*	1.35*
	Range	2.50	5.26	5.45	7.02	4.35	3.61	6.05
Amplifiers		1.71	2.05	1.79	1.27*	2.05	1.71	3.12*
	Range	4.98	5.40	4.27	4.93	5.76	4.35	13.89
Downtoners		0.38	0.00*	0.00*	0.00**	0.00*	0.00*	0.48
	Range	1.16	2.14	1.67	0.41	1.21	0.91	2.50
Other		0.48	0.00*	0.63	0.00*	0.36	0.48	0.00**
	Range	2.26	1.43	1.90	1.25	2.78	2.78	1.22
Noun and Adjective Clauses								
Noun		1.38	1.42	1.72	1.30	1.08	1.24	2.07*
	Range	6.94	4.33	3.68	2.26	5.88	5.88	5.56
Full adjective		1.52	1.04*	1.14*	0.69**	0.74*	0.61**	1.80
	Range	2.90	2.63	2.26	3.06	3.68	3.68	4.17
Reduced adjective		0.35	0.00**	0.00*	0.00*	0.00	0.00*	0.00*
	Range	2.27	0.72	1.04	0.97	1.43	0.89	0.93
Adverb Clauses								
Full: Cause		0.29	0.42	0.48	0.38	0.36	0.61*	0.45
	Range	2.02	1.50	1.59	2.13	2.21	2.50	3.47
Concession		0.00	0.00	0.00*	0.00	0.00*	0.00	0.00
	Range	0.70	0.83	0.74	0.65	0.95	0.60	0.93
Condition		0.25	0.37	0.28	0.58*	0.00*	0.00	0.42
	Range	1.24	1.79	1.45	1.60	0.72	1.79	2.88
Purpose		0.52	0.00*	0.32*	0.00*	0.00**	0.00**	0.00**
	Range	2.08	2.66	1.74	0.67	1.74	1.18	1.04
Other		0.45	0.45	0.57	0.69*	0.93*	0.36	0.00**
	Range	1.50	4.80	2.38	2.16	2.21	2.21	1.32
Reduced adverb clause		0.49	0.00*	0.28*	0.00*	0.49	0.27*	0.00**
	Range	3.95	1.97	1.24	3.70	1.12	1.15	0.84

(Continued)

TABLE 11.3
(Continued)

		NS	Chinese	Japanese	Korean	Vietnamese	Indonesian	Arabic
					L1			

II. RHETORICAL FEATURES

Coordinating and Logical Conjunctions/Prepositions

		NS	Chinese	Japanese	Korean	Vietnamese	Indonesian	Arabic
Phrase-level		**4.17**	**3.57**	**3.90**	**4.67**	**4.50**	**3.64***	**6.28****
	Range	5.44	6.37	6.88	11.03	12.22	5.34	9.51
Sentence-level		**0.36**	**1.09****	**1.07****	**1.52****	**0.90***	**0.98****	**1.45****
	Range	2.26	2.69	4.23	2.81	3.92	3.27	6.64
Log/sem conjunctions		**0.38**	**0.22**	**0.36**	**0.00***	**0.30**	**0.39**	**0.62**
	Range	2.35	1.39	4.35	1.25	1.96	2.29	2.82
Exemplification		**0.00**	**0.32***	**0.40****	**0.32***	**0.60****	**0.74****	**0.97****
	Range	3.41	2.13	2.08	0.67	2.08	2.29	3.63

Hedges

		NS	Chinese	Japanese	Korean	Vietnamese	Indonesian	Arabic
Epistemic		**1.52**	**1.84**	**1.43**	**1.73**	**2.05**	**2.12***	**0.00****
	Range	3.83	4.17	3.64	4.86	6.46	5.38	1.78
Lexical		**0.43**	**1.09***	**0.87***	**1.48****	**1.50****	**1.33****	**0.89***
	Range	1.70	6.38	2.26	3.19	5.24	5.24	5.25
Possibility		**0.00**	**0.00**	**0.00**	**0.00**	**0.00***	**0.00***	**0.00**
	Range	0.75	0.60	0.95	0.44	0.38	0.43	1.03
Quality		**0.00**	**0.00**	**0.00**	**0.00**	**0.00**	**0.00**	**0.00**
	Range	0.75	1.60	0.51	0.00	0.98	1.30	0.63
Performative		**0.00**	**0.00**	**0.00**	**0.00**	**0.00**	**0.00**	**0.00**
	Range	0.68	0.71	1.85	0.89	0.00	1.71	0.84
Rhetorical Questions		**0.00**	**0.00**	**0.00***	**0.00**	**0.00**	**0.00**	**0.00**
	Range	1.15	4.26	1.48	0.89	0.98	3.91	2.08
Demonstrative		**1.68**	**1.26**	**1.05**	**1.30**	**1.08**	**1.30**	**2.88****
	Range	3.25	3.40	5.80	3.25	3.68	5.14	9.26
Emphatics		**0.77**	**1.30****	**0.93***	**0.00****	**1.76****	**0.84**	**4.38****
	Range	4.33	6.85	2.60	1.89	6.85	4.01	10.51
Presupp. Markers		**0.00**	**0.00**	**0.00**	**0.00**	**0.00**	**0.00**	**0.00**
	Range	0.33	1.04	0.91	0.74	0.49	0.31	0.63
Fixed Strings		**2.68**	**1.05****	**1.25****	**1.52****	**1.32****	**1.20****	**1.10****
	Range	5.80	4.76	8.70	2.27	3.42	3.85	4.20

Note. All comparisons are relative to NSs.
*one-tailed $p \leq 0.05$. **two-tailed $p \leq 0.05$.

It-Slot Filler.   As has been mentioned, constructions with *it*-cleft are relatively syntactically complex, and the pooled data demonstrate that NNS texts contain significantly fewer of them than NS essays do. In writing about the Wealth prompt, however, most NSs and NNS employed similar rates of these constructions, with the exception of Vietnamese, the majority of whom did not use *it*-cleft, and Arabic speakers, who actually used these slot fillers at significantly higher rates than NSs. For example, *I think it is difficult to determine whether athletes and movie stars should get paid high salaries or not, but all in all I think they don't deserve it* (Arab).

Indirect Pronouns.   Universal and assertive pronouns are found in both NS and NNS essays, and according to the data for all essays combined, NNSs employ significantly higher rates of them than NSs do. However, this finding does not hold true for Wealth essays (Table 11.3), in which NSs and NNSs largely use them at similar rates. It appears that overuses of the vague *some/any*-words and exaggerative *every/no*-words are not nearly as common in NNS texts on athletes and movie stars as they are in other types of essays combined.

Verb Phrase Features

Tenses and Aspects.   The NNS employment of various English tenses and aspects, that is, the past and the present, as well as the progressive and the perfect, for all essays combined was significantly different from that of NSs. However, in writing on the Wealth prompt, most NNSs, except Japanese and Vietnamese, used the past tense at frequency rates similar to those of NSs. In addition, despite the fact that in the pooled data, Chinese and Japanese speaker median rates for the present tense were significantly higher than NS rates, in their essays about wealthy performers, all groups of NNSs employed the present tense similarly. Furthermore, in the prose written to this prompt, the frequency rates for progressive and perfect aspects also showed no statistically significant divergences.

Semantic and Lexical Classes of Verbs.   The differences between NS and NNS uses of public and private verbs were also less common than in the pooled data. In fact, only the essays of Arabic speakers showed significantly higher rates of uses of these two verb classes. Japanese speaker essays actually contained fewer occurrences of private verbs than NS texts did. Notably, the majority of the students in all groups, except Chinese, did not rely on verbs that denote logical/semantic relationships (medians 0.00) and, therefore, no significant disparities are found in their uses.

Necessity Modals.   Modal verbs of necessity, which NNS employed significantly more frequently than NS did in response to most prompts in this study, were not used differently by any group of student writers. The pooled data show that in their texts written to other prompts, NNS used significantly higher rates of these verbs.

Attributive Adjectives.   Although in many cases, NNSs rely on predicative adjectives and use significantly fewer attributive modifiers of nouns, in writing about sports figures and singers and their salaries, L2 writers in all groups, except Vietnamese, used significantly more attributive adjectives than NSs. It is important to mention, however, that many attributive adjectives were repeated, because they were used in the prompt. Three attributive adjectives were included in the prompt wording, that is, *wealthy, famous,* and *high,* and many turned up in NNS student texts. For example, *Michael Jackson a very famous singer in the United States. He is rich; he owns a big and comfortable house by himself and he also has a private flight. Luise* [Carl Lewis?], *a famous sprinter in America. He can get his income about [a] million dollars per year; he owns private houses by himself* (Chinese), or *Some famous players make lots of money, but they start to be famous at a young age. They have a special ability and talent. A famous actor River Fenix became famous when he was twelve years old. He showed some good acting in his movies. He didn't know how to use big money and so he spent money for expensive drugs or alcohol* (Japanese).

Amplifiers and Other Adverbs.   Although the pooled data show that NNS writers employ amplifiers at significantly higher rates than do NS students (almost twice the median frequency rate in some cases), in Wealth essays, these types of exaggeratives were used in similar rates by NS and NNS, with the exception of Arabic speakers. Actually, Korean speaker prose on the topic of wealthy and famous stars contained significantly fewer amplifiers. In addition, adverbs of manner and quality were used in significantly lower rates in the texts of Chinese, Korean, and Arabic speakers, most of whom did not use them at all, than in NS essays.

Noun Clauses.   Unlike the uses of nouns clauses in the pooled data, the employment of these features in Wealth essays of L1 and L2 writers was largely similar. The essays of Arabic speakers, however, included significantly more noun clauses than NS essays, as they did in the data for all essays combined.

Full Adjective Clauses.   On the other hand, significantly lower median rates for the uses of full adjective clauses were found in NNS Wealth essays (Table 11.3), compared to those of NSs. Again, the texts of the Arabic speakers were different and included similar rates of these features. The data for all essays combined showed a lower median rate only in Korean and Vietnamese speaker texts, whereas the frequency rates for full adjective clauses in the essays of other writers were similar to those in NS texts.

Adverb Clauses of Cause and Condition.   The Wealth essay data demonstrate that NSs and NNSs in most cases used cause and conditions similarly. However, Indonesians employed cause clauses significantly more frequently than NSs did, and Vietnamese texts contained significantly fewer condition clauses.

Coordinators and Conjunctions.   Phrase-level coordinators and logical/semantic conjunctions in Wealth essays also display a great deal of similarity. The exceptions are the essays of Indonesians and Arabs, which included markedly higher rates of phrase-level coordinators than NS texts did, and Korean texts, most of which did not rely on the uses of logical/semantic conjunctions.

Rhetorical Questions.   Rhetorical questions were not common in the Wealth essays of either NSs or NNSs, and only Japanese text contained significantly higher rates of these features. In the pooled data, however, NNS writers in all groups relied on rhetorical questions to establish rapport with the reader at higher rates than NSs did.

Demonstrative Pronouns.   The uses of demonstratives in Wealth texts were also similar among texts of all groups of writers, except for Arabic speakers' prose, which contained significantly more of them than did NS text. The data for all essays combined showed significant divergences in the uses of demonstratives in NS and Chinese, Korean, and Arabic speaker texts.

As has been mentioned, the more divergences are identified in features uses between those in texts written toward a particular prompt and the pooled data, the more likely the essays are to include features of the conversational genre, personal narratives, or statements of belief and opinion without argumentation and support. Thus, among the essays written toward the three prompts, Parents, Grades, and Wealth, the texts on the last topic of Wealth were less prone to contain significantly higher or lower rates of features associated with spoken genre and personal stories.

12

The Second Three Prompts

Following chapter 11, this chapter continues with the analyses of features in essays written toward the second cluster of three prompts, Manner, Opinions, and Major. As in the discussion of the Parents, Grades, and Wealth prompts, chapter 12 focuses only on the features that are employed in median frequency rates markedly distinct from those noted in the pooled data discussed earlier in chapters 6–10. The findings of the analysis that pertain to all six prompts are noted in the introduction to Part III.

THE MANNER PROMPT

The text of the prompt read:

> Some people learn best when a classroom lesson is presented in a serious, for-mal manner. Others prefer a lesson that is enjoyable and entertaining. Explain your views on this issue. Use detailed reasons and examples.

Students in all L1 groups wrote 247 essays on the Manner prompt. In addition to 40 NSs, these students included 39 Chinese, 34 Japanese, 33 Korean, 37 Indonesian, and 32 each of Vietnamese and Arabic speakers. The discussion of the Manner essays deals with 17 syntactic, lexical, and rhetorical features that were used at importantly different median frequency rates compared to those in the data for all essays combined.

The Noun Phrase

Semantic and Lexical Classes of Nouns.   In the Manner essays (Table 12.1), the frequency rates of enumerative nouns were significantly higher and those of interpretive nouns markedly lower, compared to the rates of these nouns in the pooled data for most student groups (chap. 6). For instance, the frequency rates of NSs, and Chinese and Japanese speaker compositions did not differ significantly. On the other hand, the median frequency rates of these nouns in the Manner essays were twice those in the pooled data for texts of Korean, Vietnamese, and Arabic speakers. The reason for the discrepancy largely had to do with how Chinese and Japanese or Korean, Vietnamese, and Arabic speakers approached the prompt. Whereas most Chinese and Japanese speakers recounted real or imaginary examples of how classes can be taught, Korean, Vietnamese, and Arabic speakers largely provided statements of belief and discussed their reasons for having these beliefs. For example, *As a student, I know the <u>reason</u> why funny manner is so important in learning* (Vietnamese) or *So, each person has his own way of learning, and that's one of the <u>reasons</u>, too. There are many <u>reasons</u> why they like, they think that they learn more. <u>Types</u> of teaching are different in every class, and entertaining manner provides a lot of information* (Arab). It is also interesting to point out that although in the pooled data (chap. 6), the frequency rates for advance/retroactive nouns in essays of Korean and Arabic speakers were significantly lower than in NS texts, in the Manner essays, no significant differences were noted.

In addition, although the disparities in the NS and NNS frequency rates of interpretive nouns are significant in both the pooled data and Manner essays, NNSs employed fewer of them (with sometimes half the median rates observed in the pooled data) in texts written to this prompt. This observation is important later in the discussion of essays written on the Opinion prompts.

Personal Pronouns.   As has been mentioned, for all data combined, the median rates of first-person pronouns in NNS essays were significantly greater than those in NS texts. Whereas this finding holds true for Japanese and Indonesian speaker Manner essays, overall, no substantial disparities in the frequency rates of first-person pronouns were identified between first pronoun uses in NS Manner essays and those of Chinese, Korean, and Vietnamese speakers. In fact, Arabic speakers employed significantly fewer of these features in their essays on the Manner prompt. Notably, however, the median frequency rates for first-person pronouns in NS Manner essays

TABLE 12.1
Frequency Rates for Features in Manner Texts (Median %)

		L1						
		NS	*Chinese*	*Japanese*	*Korean*	*Vietnamese*	*Indonesian*	*Arabic*

I. Linguistic Features

Semantic and Lexical Classes of Nouns

		NS	Chinese	Japanese	Korean	Vietnamese	Indonesian	Arabic
Enumerative		**0.41**	**0.46**	**0.42**	**1.25****	**0.89****	**0.30**	**1.24****
	Range	2.63	1.74	3.67	8.33	1.42	1.53	3.65
Adv./retroact.		**0.82**	**0.65***	**0.73**	**0.47**	**0.43***	**0.28****	**0.78**
	Range	3.41	3.21	2.27	5.28	2.22	2.22	2.86
Illocution		**0.00**	**0.00**	**0.00**	**0.36****	**0.90****	**0.30***	**0.00**
	Range	0.93	1.63	1.63	3.66	2.22	2.67	0.56
Resultative		**0.00**	**0.00***	**0.00**	**0.00**	**0.30****	**0.00**	**0.00**
	Range	0.72	0.77	0.81	1.33	1.28	1.39	0.95
Language activity		**0.30**	**0.69***	**0.40**	**0.81***	**1.67****	**0.67**	**1.03***
	Range	3.57	4.42	4.00	2.36	1.93	2.73	6.20
Interpretive		**0.63**	**1.35****	**1.39***	**2.22****	**1.80****	**0.83***	**1.15****
	Range	2.22	2.89	3.64	7.01	2.88	3.33	6.25
Vague		**1.94**	**2.78****	**1.06***	**3.49***	**3.17***	**1.45***	**0.79**
	Range	6.25	6.62	5.08	13.29	7.94	5.86	6.07

Personal Pronouns

		NS	Chinese	Japanese	Korean	Vietnamese	Indonesian	Arabic
First person		**3.87**	**3.72**	**5.14***	**0.69**	**2.00**	**5.45***	**1.72***
	Range	9.69	9.05	16.06	11.82	8.93	14.47	5.42
Second person		**0.00**	**0.93****	**1.25****	**1.18***	**2.45****	**0.00**	**0.00**
	Range	6.11	6.55	21.54	14.15	6.41	7.78	2.43
Third person		**2.78**	**2.60**	**1.56***	**2.19**	**2.10**	**2.01**	**2.08**
	Range	7.50	11.15	6.18	5.22	4.48	8.84	12.10

Slot Fillers

		NS	Chinese	Japanese	Korean	Vietnamese	Indonesian	Arabic
It-subject		**0.56**	**0.00***	**0.19***	**0.00***	**0.43**	**0.00****	**0.24**
	Range	2.31	1.71	1.63	0.93	0.90	1.11	2.50
There-subject		**0.00**	**0.35***	**0.19**	**0.31**	**0.00**	**0.00**	**0.36***
	Range	1.70	2.48	2.23	4.07	0.60	1.10	1.38

Indirect Pronouns

		NS	Chinese	Japanese	Korean	Vietnamese	Indonesian	Arabic
Universal		**0.56**	**1.07****	**0.95***	**0.00**	**1.09***	**0.27**	**1.25***
	Range	2.50	4.30	2.86	5.00	3.85	2.14	4.92
Assertive		**0.72**	**1.39****	**0.56**	**0.93**	**0.30**	**0.82**	**0.83**
	Range	3.21	6.55	3.13	3.25	1.92	2.50	3.89
Nominalization		**2.50**	**1.67***	**1.56***	**1.01***	**1.82**	**1.52***	**2.10**
	Range	7.60	6.19	5.71	13.33	2.54	7.37	6.29
Gerunds		**2.08**	**1.35***	**1.11***	**0.83***	**1.39***	**0.88****	**1.70**
	Range	4.71	4.83	4.76	3.24	2.09	2.75	4.55

(Continued)

TABLE 12.1
(Continued)

					L1			
		NS	Chinese	Japanese	Korean	Vietnamese	Indonesian	Arabic
Verb Tenses								
Past		2.38	2.86	4.85**	5.08**	2.78	3.48*	0.00**
	Range	11.88	10.13	9.92	8.67	7.68	11.11	4.29
Present		8.48	9.63*	9.09	6.99*	7.74*	9.72	8.61
	Range	13.15	10.73	13.52	12.34	9.46	12.36	12.11
Future		0.38	1.01*	0.00	0.34	1.19*	0.34	0.21
	Range	5.09	5.00	1.56	2.29	1.50	5.21	1.70
Verb Aspects								
Progressive		0.39	0.00	0.00	0.00*	0.00*	0.00*	0.00*
	Range	3.54	1.35	2.04	1.57	0.64	1.58	1.11
Perfect		0.00	0.00	0.00	0.00	0.26	0.00	0.00
	Range	3.33	1.36	0.89	2.31	0.99	0.94	0.56
Semantic and Lexical Classes of Verbs								
Public		0.51	2.42**	1.54**	1.42**	1.49**	1.82**	1.82**
	Range	2.50	5.24	5.14	5.50	2.89	8.51	4.23
Private		2.94	3.80*	3.65	4.17*	2.72*	4.13**	2.99
	Range	10.42	7.27	7.21	9.01	3.19	11.11	5.44
Suasive		0.74	0.93*	0.57	0.00*	0.89	1.21*	1.11*
	Range	2.81	3.10	2.86	1.41	1.99	3.13	3.13
Log./sem. relat.		0.39	0.69*	0.38	0.47	0.67*	0.69*	0.71*
	Range	2.19	1.90	2.08	1.92	1.56	2.31	1.70
Tentative		0.48	0.77*	0.58	1.05*	0.00	0.91*	1.25**
	Range	2.22	6.55	2.92	8.33	2.99	5.56	4.76
Seem/appear		0.00	0.00	0.00	0.00	0.00	0.00	0.00
	Range	0.63	0.48	1.25	1.22	0.30	0.31	0.42
Modal Verbs								
Possibility		1.07	1.52*	1.06	1.69*	0.56*	1.03	1.80*
	Range	4.35	7.14	3.65	4.07	2.33	4.21	4.04
Necessity		0.46	1.11**	0.78*	1.01**	0.60*	0.51	0.55*
	Range	2.94	5.09	4.38	5.00	2.56	3.00	2.86
Predictive		0.64	0.24	0.00*	0.25*	0.00**	0.00**	0.26*
	Range	3.62	3.34	3.79	3.51	2.88	2.18	2.43
Passive		1.16	0.83*	0.57*	1.18	0.40**	0.29**	1.03*
	Range	4.12	2.28	3.00	2.78	1.11	2.90	2.50
Be-main		3.33	4.55**	4.86**	4.47*	5.36**	4.13**	4.53*
	Range	5.56	6.54	8.29	10.56	10.79	8.77	8.35
Infinitives		5.36	5.00	4.86*	3.72**	3.19**	2.75**	2.40**
	Range	6.30	8.13	13.85	11.67	3.62	3.65	7.31

(Continued)

TABLE 12.1

(Continued)

		NS	Chinese	Japanese	Korean	Vietnamese	Indonesian	Arabic
Participles								
Present		1.85	1.35*	1.04*	0.42**	1.39*	0.61**	0.43**
	Range	4.76	4.17	4.00	1.69	4.44	3.94	1.79
Past		0.77	0.30**	0.40*	0.00*	0.27*	0.00**	0.31*
	Range	3.33	2.02	2.65	1.75	1.33	1.16	1.56
Adjectives								
Attributive		8.50	7.05*	6.29*	3.85**	3.67**	3.33**	2.72**
	Range	11.57	10.50	12.01	13.07	3.60	9.18	6.62
Predicative		2.17	4.29**	3.99*	3.85*	3.60*	3.99**	3.85*
	Range	7.04	4.36	11.39	20.09	10.94	11.52	8.03
Semantic and Lexical Classes of Adverbs								
Time		0.50	0.98*	0.57	0.68	0.56	0.38	0.62
	Range	2.22	3.35	3.03	2.93	1.79	3.44	1.74
Frequency		0.00	0.00	0.27	0.00	0.20	0.28	0.27
	Range	1.49	1.39	2.00	1.36	0.89	1.00	0.78
Place		2.07	2.22	2.27	1.92	2.08	2.55*	1.58
	Range	4.31	5.68	6.25	6.10	4.22	4.96	4.34
Amplifiers		1.93	3.56**	2.86*	2.82*	2.38*	2.86**	3.06**
	Range	3.52	6.64	11.98	9.65	6.18	6.01	6.67
Downtoners		0.48	0.48	0.50	0.67*	0.64*	1.00*	0.62
	Range	1.43	2.22	1.63	2.44	1.92	3.70	1.96
Other		0.66	1.47**	0.73	1.56*	0.90	1.39**	1.86**
	Range	2.78	3.93	3.00	4.47	3.31	2.60	3.34
Noun and Adjective Clauses								
Noun		1.25	1.95**	1.56	1.25	0.89*	1.75*	1.52
	Range	5.41	5.60	3.50	7.08	2.39	5.00	3.89
Full adjective		1.43	1.85	0.83*	1.40	0.67*	1.13	1.81*
	Range	3.37	7.14	3.65	4.39	2.61	2.94	5.36
Reduced adjective		0.19	0.17	0.00	0.00*	0.00*	0.00*	0.00*
	Range	1.23	1.82	1.52	0.94	0.30	0.70	0.52
Adverb Clauses								
Full: Cause		0.00	0.43*	0.73*	0.35*	0.30	0.55*	0.79**
	Range	1.67	2.42	4.17	2.31	0.80	2.20	2.60
Concession		0.00	0.00	0.00	0.00	0.00	0.00	0.00
	Range	0.73	0.45	0.57	0.67	0.32	0.56	0.30
Condition		0.63	1.10*	0.48	0.31	0.20*	0.29*	0.00*
	Range	2.32	2.07	2.55	2.86	0.96	2.04	1.70

(Continued)

TABLE 12.1
(Continued)

		NS	Chinese	Japanese	Korean	Vietnamese	Indonesian	Arabic
					L1			
Purpose		**0.00**	**0.00**	**0.00**	**0.00**	**0.00**	**0.00**	**0.00**
	Range	1.11	0.60	0.36	0.91	0.64	0.46	1.04
Other		**0.51**	**0.66***	**0.41**	**0.69**	**0.41**	**0.77***	**0.33**
	Range	1.79	2.98	1.67	1.92	1.21	2.12	2.22
Reduced adverb clause		**0.00**	**0.00***	**0.00**	**0.00***	**0.00**	**0.00***	**0.00**
	Range	1.32	0.48	0.73	0.41	0.79	0.63	0.71

II. RHETORICAL FEATURES

Coordinating and Logical Conjunctions/Prepositions

		NS	Chinese	Japanese	Korean	Vietnamese	Indonesian	Arabic
Phrase-level		**4.08**	**5.14***	**4.00**	**4.20**	**4.34***	**4.01**	**4.91***
	Range	6.00	7.52	6.06	9.79	9.40	4.40	12.36
Sentence-level		**0.93**	**1.74***	**2.08***	**2.10***	**1.28***	**1.36***	**1.04***
	Range	2.35	5.56	5.87	8.85	2.75	2.82	2.22
Log./sem. conjunctions		**1.10**	**1.07**	**1.11**	**0.96**	**1.28***	**1.03**	**1.28**
	Range	2.63	2.88	3.65	2.00	1.71	2.81	3.13
Exemplification		**0.31**	**0.49***	**0.48***	**0.47***	**0.41***	**0.68***	**0.61***
	Range	1.24	1.73	2.86	1.92	1.06	2.78	2.38

Hedges

		NS	Chinese	Japanese	Korean	Vietnamese	Indonesian	Arabic
Epistemic		**0.50**	**0.00***	**0.00***	**0.63**	**0.00***	**0.00***	**0.00***
	Range	2.17	1.28	1.61	4.07	0.90	0.93	1.29
Lexical		**1.93**	**0.39***	**0.77***	**1.05***	**0.40***	**0.35***	**0.26***
	Range	5.99	1.79	2.92	4.17	2.22	2.68	1.11
Possibility		**0.00**	**0.00**	**0.00***	**0.00***	**0.00**	**0.00**	**0.00**
	Range	1.56	0.98	0.41	0.52	0.60	0.77	1.92
Quality		**0.34**	**0.48***	**0.00***	**0.31**	**0.00***	**0.90***	**0.67***
	Range	1.76	2.16	1.25	1.04	0.56	1.67	1.94
Performative		**0.00**	**0.00**	**0.00**	**0.00**	**0.00**	**0.00***	**0.00**
	Range	1.52	0.46	1.14	0.47	0.33	0.29	0.76
Rhetorical Questions		**0.00**	**0.00***	**0.38***	**0.34***	**0.30***	**0.00**	**0.26***
	Range	0.83	2.38	1.67	1.92	1.79	0.94	1.52
Demonstrative		**0.93**	**1.78***	**1.62***	**2.00***	**1.80***	**0.91**	**1.89***
	Range	2.68	5.32	8.37	10.00	4.57	3.45	6.62
Emphatics		**1.32**	**3.41***	**0.00***	**2.37***	**3.53***	**1.39**	**2.56***
	Range	3.54	4.06	3.41	9.38	6.09	4.48	6.89
Presupp. Markers		**0.00**	**0.00**	**0.00**	**0.00**	**0.00**	**0.00**	**0.33***
	Range	0.46	0.67	1.09	0.42	0.00	0.43	0.61
Fixed Strings		**5.50**	**0.78***	**1.60***	**1.40***	**1.20***	**0.69***	**1.56***
	Range	12.65	2.38	3.32	4.55	5.61	1.70	3.06

Note. All comparisons are relative to NSs.
*one-tailed $p \leq 0.05$. **two-tailed $p \leq 0.05$.

were more than twice that in the pooled data (chap. 6); that is, both NSs and NNSs included personal narratives and statements of personal belief in their essays because the prompt dealing with the distinctions between a serious and entertaining manner in classroom instruction was something familiar to all students. Thus, most writers had something to say or a story to tell about this topic. For example, *For me, I prefer a class which is more enjoyable and more interesting because I won't fall asleep, feel nervous, and the class will be more lively. The first reason why I like to take an entertaining class is that I will not fall asleep. I usually fall asleep while a professor gives a boring lecture; also I sometimes daydreaming because the lecture sounds like a broken radio* (Chinese).

On the other hand, the frequency rates for second-person pronouns were particularly high in NNS texts on the Manner prompt, compared to the pooled data (chap. 6). In Confucian and Buddhist rhetorical traditions, direct personal appeals to the reader add a persuasive weight to one's text because they conjure common wisdom and universally applicable truths in the writer's proposition. In the Arabic classical tradition, uses of second-person pronouns entail the writer's legitimate authority to address the reader directly, but the majority of Arabic and Indonesian speakers did not use these features in their Manner texts.

Assertive Pronouns. According to the combined data for all L1 groups, NNS texts contained significantly higher rates of assertive pronouns than NS prose. However, this finding is not reflected in the Manner essays (Table 12.1) because NSs employed more of these features and, thus, the distinctions between NS and NNS in the frequency rates for assertive pronouns were not nearly as great.

The Perfect Aspect. Unlike the NS and NNS frequency rates for the employment of the perfect aspect in the pooled data, rates in the Manner essays did not include significant differences because a majority of students in any group did not use this syntactic feature. As has been noted, most writers recounted past-time experiences and events or generalized in the form of opinions.

Semantic and Lexical Classes of Verbs. The wording of the prompt included a public verb *present,* a private verb *learn,* and a suasive verb *prefer.* In addition, because the Manner prompt (Table 12.1) deals specifically with teaching, other public verbs appeared frequently in NS and NNS essays on this topic, for example, *argue, discuss, explain, repeat, speak, say, tell,* and *write.* Thus, the median frequency rates for these three classes of verbs were higher in NS and NNS essays on the Manner prompt than in the combined data for all essays. However, the increase was not nearly as dramatic in NS as in NNS texts; for example, the median rates of public verbs in the Manner essays of Chinese, Japanese, and Indonesian speakers were almost twice as high as their respective rates in the pooled data. Similarly, the median rates for suasive verbs was three times as high in the Chinese and two times as high in the Japanese speaker Manner essays, relative to the data for all essays combined. For example, *I prefer a lesson that is enjoyable and entertaining because I think that teachers can explain the material in more flexible ways to reach the goal of education. So, why teachers have to use serious and formal manner to present a lesson that makes students bored? However, some people may think that if a lesson is not formal and serious, then they don't learn anything. But I don't think it is true. . . . To sum up, I prefer receiving education by funny ways. Compared to be taught by formal manner that makes me hate learning in the past, I think I'll be happy to learn by enjoyed manner* (Chinese).

Present Participles, Attributive Adjectives, Adjective Clauses, and Other Adverbs.   In addition to the various semantic types of verbs, the wording of the prompt also contained four adjectives, *serious, formal, enjoyable,* and *entertaining,* the last of which constituted a present participle. As an outcome, frequency rates for various classes of descriptors, including full and reduced adjective clauses in the essays of some writers were dramatically higher in Manner essays than in the pooled data (chap. 9). Specifically, NSs employed twice the rates of present participles and attributive adjectives in the texts written about instructional manners than in the data for all prompts combined. Similarly, the frequency rates for other (manner and quality adverbs) was two-fold in Chinese, Korean, and Arabic speaker essays, and the uses of present participles for all groups of NNSs was two to three times as great. For example, *The different people have their different approachment [sic]. One prefers to serious and formal manner than enjoyable or entertaining. These differences come because of their different background. For those people who like to study in serious manner tend to be focus what they received in the classroom. . . . I also believe that serious learners also need to be serious when they study. For serious learner, entertaining study is a waste of time. They learn easily in a serious manner* (Indonesian).

Conjunctions.   The frequency rates of phrase-level and logical/semantic *(besides, because of, in contrast, instead of)* conjunctions were also markedly higher in the Manner essays of all students, compared to the pooled data (chap. 10). It is also important to note that two sets of parallel adjectives *(serious/formal* and *enjoyable/entertaining),* as well as two juxtaposed complex parallel sentences were included in the prompt *(Some people learn best . . . /Other people prefer . . .).* In the Manner essays of students in all groups, the frequency rates of coordinating and logical/semantic conjunctions, including those with juxtopositional meanings, were substantially higher than the rates of these features in the pooled data. However, because the median rates of conjunctions increased in both NS and NNS texts, the differences between L1 and L2 frequencies largely remained similar to those in the data for all essays combined. For example, *Formal and serious technique for* *teaching __and__ learning is good in the classes __and__ materials which has many things to explain __and__ formulate. __But__, this method may result in the boredom to student who don't care about the subject. __Also__, it results in the alienation of teacher and student. __In contrast__, enjoyable __and__ entertaining style is suitable for the classes __and__ lectures where the teacher talks __and__ teaches* (Korean).

Epistemic and Lexical Hedges. In the essays written to the Manner prompt, NNS frequency rates for common hedges were particularly low for all L2 groups, possibly because in the view of NNSs, juxtaposed constructions and explanations provide sufficient and appropriate contextual means for reducing the writer's responsibility for propositional truth value and add a necessary duality to the claims. In classical Chinese and Confucian rhetoric, confuting a proposition by means of juxtaposing propositions is considered to be a common means of expressing hedging and ambiguity of claims (Hinds, 1984; R. Scollon, 1991). For example, *Some students are better able to learn in an enjoyable and entertaining environment, yet other students prefer that classes are taught in a serious and formal manner. . . . Not all courses are the same, some are more difficult than others. I want to study in an appropriate manner, sometimes serious and formal, and sometimes enjoyable and entertaining in different environment* (Chinese).

THE OPINIONS PROMPT

The text of the prompt was included as follows:

> Many educators believe that parents should help to form their children's opinions. Others feel that children should be allowed to develop their own opinions. Explain your views on this issue. Use detailed reasons and examples.

Of the 249 essays written toward the Opinions prompt, 44 were written by NSs, and 39 by Chinese, 42 by Japanese, 36 by Korean, 41 by Indonesian, 32 by Vietnamese, and 30 by Arabic speakers. Fourteen features are discussed in this section to account for the patterns of usage that were largely distinct from the trends in the pooled data (chaps. 6–10).

The Noun Phrase

Semantic and Lexical Classes of Nouns. In the frequency rates of semantic classes of nouns, the most prominent differences between the pooled data and the Opinions essay data (Table 12.2) are found in the uses of interpretive and language activity nouns. In particular, relative to the pooled data, NSs employed interpretive nouns at frequency rates seven times higher (medians of 0.48 vs. 3.81, respectively), and the rates for NNSs increased

TABLE 12.2
Frequency Rates for Features in Opinions Texts (Median %)

					L1			
		NS	Chinese	Japanese	Korean	Vietnamese	Indonesian	Arabic

I. LINGUISTIC FEATURES

Semantic and Lexical Classes of Nouns

		NS	Chinese	Japanese	Korean	Vietnamese	Indonesian	Arabic
Enumerative		**0.64****	**0.46**	**0.32***	**0.36**	**0.45**	**0.37**	**0.35**
	Range	4.17	1.72	3.17	4.87	1.28	1.79	1.44
Adv./retroact.		**0.50**	**0.40***	**0.37***	**0.35***	**0.00****	**0.43**	**0.72**
	Range	4.81	2.39	1.42	2.31	0.87	2.80	1.56
Illocution		**0.37**	**0.00**	**0.00***	**0.23***	**0.00**	**0.45**	**0.42**
	Range	1.92	2.08	1.36	1.72	1.39	3.00	3.11
Resultative		**0.00**	**0.00**	**0.00**	**0.00**	**0.45****	**0.26***	**0.36***
	Range	1.67	1.19	0.81	0.71	1.25	1.07	1.52
Language activity		**0.56**	**0.36**	**0.56**	**0.41**	**0.99**	**0.60**	**1.01**
	Range	5.77	3.33	3.38	2.11	1.79	2.14	6.54
Interpretive		**3.81**	**3.33**	**3.77**	**3.16***	**4.19**	**3.33**	**3.43**
	Range	12.93	10.31	9.20	6.85	5.52	5.97	6.02
Vague		**1.60**	**2.76****	**2.96***	**4.29****	**1.88***	**2.08****	**1.68**
	Range	5.00	7.47	11.97	7.84	4.40	6.41	3.20

Personal Pronouns

		NS	Chinese	Japanese	Korean	Vietnamese	Indonesian	Arabic
First person		**0.97**	**2.02***	**2.65***	**3.49****	**1.47***	**0.71**	**2.27***
	Range	9.64	17.04	11.74	13.15	10.19	9.09	5.62
Second person		**0.00**	**0.63***	**0.00**	**0.95***	**0.51***	**0.00**	**0.00**
	Range	6.35	7.05	7.95	6.35	4.50	6.40	2.17
Third person		**5.77**	**8.00***	**8.25***	**7.26**	**7.86***	**8.08***	**4.55**
	Range	16.80	10.25	17.56	11.40	17.90	14.09	11.81

Slot Fillers

		NS	Chinese	Japanese	Korean	Vietnamese	Indonesian	Arabic
It-subject		**0.56**	**0.00****	**0.47**	**0.35***	**0.28**	**0.00****	**0.21***
	Range	3.25	0.73	2.81	1.71	1.19	1.21	1.12
There-subject		**0.00**	**0.00**	**0.00**	**0.00**	**0.23**	**0.00**	**0.35***
	Range	1.67	1.00	1.39	1.23	0.52	1.00	1.54

Indirect Pronouns

		NS	Chinese	Japanese	Korean	Vietnamese	Indonesian	Arabic
Universal		**0.27**	**0.62***	**0.45**	**0.43**	**0.24**	**0.30**	**0.69***
	Range	3.52	2.11	2.23	2.14	2.00	4.40	3.13
Assertive		**0.64**	**1.14****	**0.57**	**0.73**	**1.28***	**0.48**	**0.79**
	Range	2.88	4.70	2.56	3.17	1.87	1.95	2.42
Nominalization		**2.20**	**1.01****	**1.48***	**1.71**	**1.26***	**0.94****	**1.74**
	Range	7.46	5.17	4.13	13.33	2.86	5.65	4.76
Gerunds		**1.50**	**1.28**	**0.63***	**1.25***	**0.65***	**1.00**	**0.93**
	Range	4.46	3.83	5.43	8.23	3.03	4.80	4.69

(Continued)

TABLE 12.2
(Continued)

		NS	Chinese	Japanese	Korean	Vietnamese	Indonesian	Arabic
					L1			
Verb Tenses								
Past		2.20	3.50**	3.04	4.73*	0.99*	0.00*	0.00**
	Range	9.62	13.56	8.05	10.92	9.00	6.46	3.41
Present		8.47	9.30	10.05*	9.14	9.29	9.29	9.23
	Range	31.63	8.98	9.00	11.50	5.82	8.47	8.64
Future		0.62	0.46	0.29*	2.12**	0.78	0.74	0.30
	Range	5.36	4.04	2.12	5.90	2.04	4.03	2.60
Verb Aspects								
Progressive		0.00	0.00	0.00	0.00	0.23	0.00	0.00
	Range	2.27	1.10	1.32	0.81	0.85	1.23	1.04
Perfect		0.32	0.00*	0.00	0.00	0.00*	0.00*	0.00*
	Range	2.00	0.95	0.96	1.28	1.11	0.93	0.57
Semantic and Lexical Classes of Verbs								
Public		0.81	2.50**	1.94**	2.65**	2.78**	2.04**	1.44**
	Range	6.73	4.60	7.24	6.96	5.67	4.17	5.69
Private		2.56	3.16*	3.29	2.74	2.96	3.36*	1.43*
	Range	8.33	5.56	5.77	7.75	6.02	11.51	5.38
Suasive		1.18	1.19	0.63*	0.29**	0.74	0.52*	1.77*
	Range	4.17	3.21	3.33	1.72	3.08	2.50	2.81
Log./sem. relat.		0.63	2.18**	1.12	0.86	0.91	1.82**	1.26
	Range	3.33	4.41	4.61	2.59	3.18	4.06	2.93
Tentative		0.43	0.91*	0.63*	1.05**	0.83*	0.40	0.42
	Range	1.35	2.47	2.27	4.21	2.53	5.36	2.38
Seem/appear		0.00	0.00	0.00	0.00	0.00	0.00	
	Range	0.83	0.38	0.40	0.49	0.25	0.00	0.48
Modal Verbs								
Possibility		1.02	1.05	1.32	1.28	1.52*	0.96	0.95
	Range	5.00	4.37	3.17	3.45	3.13	2.38	3.69
Necessity		1.42	2.02*	1.92*	2.96**	1.90*	1.49	1.47
	Range	4.81	4.81	4.76	8.35	2.71	2.70	5.00
Predictive		0.27	0.00	0.00*	0.16	0.00*	0.00	0.42
	Range	1.95	1.67	1.71	1.15	1.47	0.85	1.52
Passive		1.50	0.73*	0.90*	0.68**	0.50**	0.32**	0.71*
	Range	10.58	4.02	3.13	1.54	1.50	2.88	1.77
Be-main		2.50	4.17**	3.23*	4.95**	3.72*	3.64**	3.46*
	Range	10.71	8.89	11.02	12.82	6.22	7.24	5.73
Infinitives		7.33	7.41	7.39	2.99**	4.29**	3.64**	3.03**
	Range	22.07	9.67	10.89	8.05	5.48	8.64	8.29

(Continued)

TABLE 12.2
(Continued)

		L1						
		NS	Chinese	Japanese	Korean	Vietnamese	Indonesian	Arabic
Participles								
Present		**0.50**	**0.00****	**0.00****	**0.00****	**0.00****	**0.00****	**0.00***
	Range	2.03	1.15	1.14	0.71	0.76	0.89	1.04
Past		**0.44**	**0.00***	**0.00****	**0.00***	**0.26***	**0.00****	**0.23**
	Range	5.00	1.33	1.33	5.64	1.00	0.52	1.04
Adjectives								
Attributive		**5.13**	**4.29**	**2.84****	**2.18****	**1.48****	**1.77****	**2.42****
	Range	8.99	8.68	6.26	6.60	4.41	5.02	4.51
Predicative		**1.50**	**3.04****	**3.86****	**2.81****	**2.78***	**3.76****	**2.86****
	Range	8.06	6.10	10.55	6.96	4.29	8.00	3.76
Semantic and Lexical Classes of Adverbs								
Time		**0.88****	**1.01**	**0.57**	**0.70**	**0.94**	**0.64**	**0.85**
	Range	5.00	3.33	2.71	2.00	2.55	3.30	2.61
Frequency		**0.00**	**0.00**	**0.00**	**0.00**	**0.25***	**0.00**	**0.00**
	Range	1.83	1.67	1.97	0.85	0.94	0.63	0.61
Place		**1.89**	**1.28**	**0.96***	**0.94***	**1.39**	**0.89***	**1.26**
	Range	4.76	4.76	3.76	4.29	2.68	3.20	4.47
Amplifiers		**1.52**	**3.70****	**4.05****	**2.65****	**1.99**	**2.52***	**2.78****
	Range	7.50	4.91	8.45	5.26	4.35	6.85	8.30
Downtoners		**0.66**	**0.96***	**0.60**	**0.41**	**0.78***	**1.00***	**0.72**
	Range	4.17	3.13	1.97	2.12	2.76	2.92	2.99
Other		**0.57**	**0.50**	**0.47**	**0.87***	**1.39****	**1.11****	**1.89****
	Range	2.27	3.89	2.56	3.17	1.91	3.60	2.92
Noun and Adjective Clauses								
Noun		**2.02**	**2.43***	**1.52**	**2.30**	**2.27**	**2.81****	**2.17**
	Range	8.33	4.72	4.65	4.72	3.77	5.78	4.41
Full adjective		**0.81**	**0.63**	**0.89**	**0.85**	**0.48**	**0.74**	**1.24***
	Range	2.88	2.14	3.93	2.30	2.87	3.13	5.28
Reduced adjective		**0.00**	**0.00**	**0.00***	**0.00**	**0.00***	**0.00***	**0.00**
	Range	2.50	1.11	0.88	1.54	0.46	0.93	1.04
Adverb Clauses								
Full: Cause		**0.00****	**0.40***	**0.48***	**0.57****	**0.28***	**0.32***	**0.36***
	Range	1.67	1.56	1.97	1.71	1.52	3.20	1.54
Concession		**0.00**	**0.00***	**0.00***	**0.00**	**0.00***	**0.00****	**0.00***
	Range	0.96	1.00	0.86	0.82	0.51	0.30	1.04
Condition		**0.63**	**0.42**	**0.51**	**0.65**	**0.51**	**0.48**	**0.42**
	Range	3.85	1.56	3.15	1.39	1.25	2.02	2.17

(Continued)

TABLE 12.2
(Continued)

		NS	Chinese	Japanese	Korean	Vietnamese	Indonesian	Arabic
					L1			
Purpose		**0.00**	**0.00**	**0.00**	**0.00**	**0.00**	**0.00**	**0.00**
	Range	0.96	1.15	1.67	0.72	0.28	0.96	0.69
Other		**0.53**	**1.01***	**0.79***	**0.47**	**0.56**	**0.52**	**0.72**
	Range	4.17	2.69	2.52	3.29	2.22	2.56	1.90
Reduced adverb clause		**0.19**	**0.00***	**0.00***	**0.00***	**0.00***	**0.00***	**0.00***
	Range	2.88	0.60	0.85	0.36	0.31	0.60	0.23

II. Rhetorical Features

Coordinating and Logical Conjunctions/Prepositions

		NS	Chinese	Japanese	Korean	Vietnamese	Indonesian	Arabic
Phrase-level		**4.50**	**5.31**	**2.82****	**4.10**	**4.55**	**2.88****	**5.97***
	Range	8.55	13.10	6.55	12.23	5.23	3.02	12.78
Sentence-level		**0.66**	**1.25***	**2.12****	**1.51****	**1.73****	**1.60****	**1.05***
	Range	4.81	2.50	5.34	3.13	3.89	4.95	3.08
Log./sem. conjunctions		**1.11**	**0.76***	**0.56***	**1.09**	**0.76**	**0.84**	**1.20**
	Range	3.85	2.22	3.57	1.50	2.21	2.14	2.25
Exemplification		**0.27**	**0.46***	**0.50***	**0.44***	**0.71****	**0.51****	**0.30**
	Range	1.50	1.38	2.63	2.12	1.16	2.42	2.08

Hedges

		NS	Chinese	Japanese	Korean	Vietnamese	Indonesian	Arabic
Epistemic		**0.37**	**0.00***	**0.32**	**0.24***	**0.25**	**0.00***	**0.00***
	Range	1.35	0.93	2.56	0.70	1.79	1.23	0.77
Lexical		**0.83**	**0.54***	**0.38****	**0.32***	**0.25****	**0.00****	**0.00****
	Range	7.58	1.85	1.42	1.45	1.28	0.85	1.01
Possibility		**0.00**	**0.00**	**0.00**	**0.00***	**0.00**	**0.00***	**0.00**
	Range	1.01	0.67	0.85	0.32	0.63	0.93	0.51
Quality		**0.42**	**0.53**	**0.00****	**0.00***	**0.26**	**0.44**	**0.71**
	Range	4.81	1.72	1.30	1.29	0.79	2.40	1.56
Performative		**0.00**	**0.00***	**0.00**	**0.00***	**0.00***	**0.00***	**0.00***
	Range	0.96	0.00	0.87	0.00	0.00	0.23	0.00
Rhetorical Questions		**0.00**	**0.30***	**0.00***	**0.00**	**0.23***	**0.21***	**0.36****
	Range	1.92	1.67	2.56	0.73	0.78	0.96	4.32
Demonstrative		**0.68**	**1.48***	**0.83**	**1.42****	**0.77***	**0.67**	**1.44****
	Range	4.46	4.63	4.33	5.56	2.46	1.82	4.57
Emphatics		**1.71**	**3.85****	**3.83****	**3.71****	**2.95****	**2.60****	**2.10***
	Range	5.77	6.80	12.50	9.86	3.84	5.30	5.59
Presupp. Markers		**0.00**	**0.00**	**0.00***	**0.00**	**0.00**	**0.00**	**0.00**
	Range	1.10	1.00	1.71	0.51	0.96	0.31	0.42
Fixed Strings		**5.30**	**1.25****	**1.14****	**0.69****	**1.01****	**0.96****	**0.76****
	Range	20.19	3.68	3.95	1.81	3.24	2.38	2.00

Note. All comparisons are relative to NSs.
*one-tailed $p \leq 0.05$. **two-tailed $p \leq 0.05$.

two to six times as well. The wording of the prompt contained two mentions of the noun *opinion*. The reason for the increase in the rates of interpretives stems directly from the fact that the noun *opinion,* repeated in the prompt, is an interpretive noun, and hence, students in all groups employed it extensively in their texts. For example, *According to this <u>controversy</u>, I personally agree with the idea having parents help to form their children's <u>opinions</u>. . . . The first benefit is that children's <u>opinions</u> are going to be on the good track by having their parents' advice. Parents are more mature than children. So, they know what to do and how to think. Even though parents may not be true for all cases, at least they form their children's <u>opinions</u> to the best way they think. . . . The second benefit is that children learn and get the right <u>opinions</u> from the start. Children will transfer their parents' experiences to their <u>opinions</u>. This way, children can increase their <u>knowledge</u> without making <u>mistakes</u>. . . . Forming children's <u>opinions</u> doesn't mean dictating or limiting their <u>opinions</u>. . . . No parents want to see their children having wrong <u>opinions</u>* (Indonesian).

Similarly, language activity nouns *(controversy, debate, example, language, proof, story, talk)* also exhibited increased frequency rates in NS Opinion essays, and thus, the differences between the NS and NNS uses of these nouns were not as substantial as they were in the pooled data (chap. 6).

Assertive Pronouns.   As the pooled data in chapter 6 shows, assertive pronouns were employed substantially more frequently in NNS than in NS essays. However, in the Opinions essays, the NS frequency rate for assertive pronouns was higher, and thus, the differences in the frequency rates in NS and NNS texts for the use of this feature were not as prominent.

Verb Phrase Features: Tenses and Aspects.   Compared to the pooled data reported in chapter 7, the uses of the past and present tenses in both NS and NNS Opinion essays (Table 12.2) demonstrate a great deal of variability. Specifically, in texts of NS, Chinese, and Korean speakers, frequency rates for the past tense in Opinions essays are substantially higher than those in the pooled data, whereas Vietnamese, Indonesian, and Arabic speaker essays contained relatively few past-tense verbs. On the other hand, the NS frequency rates for the present tense were somewhat lower in Opinions essays and, thus, not particularly different from those in the NNS prose of most groups, except the Chinese. As has been noted, the differences in the uses of tenses generally stem from how students approached the prompts: Generalizations and assertions lead to an increase in present-tense frequency rates (as in the case of Vietnamese, Indonesians, and Arabic speakers), whereas recounts of past-time experiences result in higher frequency rates for past-tense verbs. For example, *By helping children to form their opinions, parents <u>can help</u> their children to stay on the right track. Everyone <u>experiences</u> more and more as they <u>grow</u>. Parents' experiences <u>are</u> very important for* *their children. By having the correct opinions, it <u>decreases</u> the chance of getting hurt and <u>reduces</u> the time of finding the right direction. Helping children to form their opinions also <u>helps</u> them develop a correct opinion process* (Vietnamese), or *My aunt's first daughter <u>read</u> books so much since she <u>was</u> 6 years old. She is very serious. One time she <u>told</u> me not to eat genetic beans because after watching TV she <u>learned</u> that genetic beans were wrong. I <u>was</u> so surprised by her* (Korean).

The frequency rates of progressive verbs in NS data for all essays combined were significantly higher than those in NNS texts. However, the majority of students in all groups did not use the progressive aspect in the Opinions essays, and the medians for all essays were 0.00.

Semantic and Lexical Classes of Verbs. The frequency rates for public, suasive, and logical/semantic relationship verbs in Opinion essays of all students showed dramatic increases (Table 12.2), compared to their rates of usage in the pooled data. Public verbs *(admit, agree, argue, explain, maintain, mention, object, suggest, warn)* in Opinion essays were employed two to three times as frequently, relative to the combined data for all essays. Suasive verbs *(allow, ask, demand, grant, insist, instruct, order, prefer, recommend, require, urge)* in Opinions essays showed up in rates two to six times higher than in the pooled data (chap. 7). Logical/semantic relationship verbs *(apply, cause, combine, contradict, follow, lead, occur, produce, resemble, result)* also exhibited frequency rate increases up to three times of those in the data for all essays. It is important to note that the prompt contained two private verbs *(believe* and *feel)* and a suasive verb *(allow).* There is little doubt that these increases in the frequency rates of various verbs, all of which refer to the activity of performing public acts and speaking and their effects, reflect students' views on whether or how parents impact their children's opinion forming. For example, *I <u>prefer</u> making decisions by myself even though my parents <u>say</u> it is wrong. If someone always <u>tells</u> us what we have to do, our ability to make decisions will get worse. If adults <u>explain</u> that some opinion is false, maybe, children will <u>listen</u>. Parents can <u>recommend</u> their children what to do but cannot <u>tell</u> them. I should <u>mention</u> my experience* (Japanese), or *Parents could <u>tell</u> children when some information they see on TV is wrong. They are always advisers to give suggestions and help making choices when children have problems. But they should be <u>allowed</u> to develop their own opinions even though it has become a controversial topic in education* (Chinese).

The frequency rates for private verbs in Opinions texts were higher than in the pooled data, although their increases were not nearly as great as those of public, suasive, and logical/semantic relationship verbs. A somewhat surprising finding in the Opinions texts of some students is that the rates of the expecting/tentative verbs *(attempt, plan, try, want)* decreased, compared to the pooled data. In fact, these verbs were used at almost half the median frequency in Japanese, Indonesian, and Arabic speaker texts.

On the other hand, the frequency rates for expecting/tentative verbs in NS, Chinese, and Vietnamese speaker essays largely remained similar.

Modal Verbs of Necessity. Another feature of text that showed large increases in Opinions essays, compared to the pooled data, are the modal verbs of necessity whose frequency rates were approximately double in NS, Korean, Vietnamese, Indonesian, and Arabic speaker texts. The prompt included two mentions of the necessity verb *should,* and most students in all groups interpreted the issue of parents' forming their children's opinions in terms of obligation and necessity. For example, *Children should be allowed to develop their own opinions. However, it is undeniable that parents need to take part in helping forming children's opinion. Unfortunately, sometimes children have no choice. They have to follow the rules that [are] set by their parents* (Indonesian), or *When we talk about something, we have to be always careful about a logical error. It is useless to say parents should help them or the opposite. I think we should think about how to help our children to form balanced and mature opinions* (Korean).

Adverb Clauses. A comparison of the pooled data to the Opinions data (Table 12.2) shows that the frequency rates of concession clauses in NNS prose were significantly lower than in NS texts in the Opinions data, and largely similar in the combined data. Conversely, the frequency rates of conditional and purpose clauses were used similarly in NS and NNS Opinions essays, even though they often differed significantly in the pooled data. The reasons for the data variability are that most NNSs did not employ concession and condition clauses in Opinions texts nearly as often as they did in essays written toward other prompts, and purpose clauses were far less common in NS texts on this topic. Hence, the NS and NNS frequency rates were less distinct than in the pooled data.

Possibility Hedges. Possibility hedges that are used significantly differently in NS and NNS pooled data also showed far fewer divergences in Opinions essays, mostly because they were not found often in the texts of any student group.

THE MAJOR PROMPT

The text of the prompt is presented in full:

> Some people choose their major field of study based on their personal interests and are less concerned about future employment possibilities. Others choose majors in fields with a large number of jobs and options for employment. What position do you support? Use detailed reasons and examples.

All in all, 259 essays were written on the Major prompt because it was one of the favorite among the ESL writing instructors who had input into the selection of prompts to be administered for the placement and diagnostic tests. The reason that most L2 teachers considered this prompt appropriate and suitable for essay tests is that the instructors believed that the Major prompt provided contextual and real-life relevance for students. However, as the analysis herein demonstrates, overall, this prompt, as the Parents prompt, elicited 12 divergently used features. The students who wrote the essays on about their choices of majors included 39 NSs and Chinese, 42 Japanese, 36 Korean, 41 Indonesian, 32 Vietnamese, and 30 Arabic speakers. In all, 10 of the 68 linguistic and rhetorical features are examined in this section.

The Noun Phrase

Semantic and Lexical Classes of Nouns. Unlike the frequency rates for enumerative and advance/retroactive nouns in the pooled data, in the essays written on the Major prompt (Table 12.3) , the frequency rates of these features in NS and NNS texts did not show many divergences. On the other hand, as with Opinion essays, the median rates for interpretive nouns in NNS but not NS texts showed a great increase, compared to those in the combined data. For instance, the interpretive nouns in Chinese, Japanese, Vietnamese, Indonesian, and Arabic speaker data had median rates two to four times those in the pooled data. The only exception were the NS and Korean speaker essays, in which interpretive nouns were used less frequently. However, in Major essays, the use of interpretive nouns did not concentrate so narrowly on just a few, but rather involved a broader range of these features. For example, *Being a professional is one of the most important principles of success. . . . Thus, strong competition makes only professional people to get a job and avoid failure. If students choose their major depend on their interests, their motive would help them overcome their mistakes* (Japanese), or *Therefore, they do not waste and forget the knowledge that they earned from school. We have to learn all the theories that they teach us here and create our idea for our future to choose a major that can lead us to success* (Vietnamese).

Personal Pronouns. Although students in all groups recounted personal experiences and provided generalized statements of belief and opinion, some groups wrote these types of text to a greater extent than others. The rates for the first-person pronouns were particularly high in Japanese and Indonesian essays, that is, twice the frequency rates for the pooled data, even when NNS rates in all groups significantly exceeded those of NSs. As was mentioned earlier, in Japanese and Indonesian written discourse, the use of the first-person singular pronouns is often considered inappropriate,

TABLE 12.3
Frequency Rates for Features in Major Texts (Median %)

		L1						
		NS	*Chinese*	*Japanese*	*Korean*	*Vietnamese*	*Indonesian*	*Arabic*

I. Linguistic Features

Semantic and Lexical Classes of Nouns

Enumerative		**0.54****	**0.44**	**0.51**	**0.78***	**0.80**	**0.46**	**0.37****
	Range	2.78	1.61	1.79	3.48	4.00	1.60	2.40
Adv./retroact.		**0.40**	**0.41**	**0.38**	**0.42**	**0.51**	**0.26**	**0.48**
	Range	2.22	1.59	3.10	0.96	2.78	1.78	1.54
Illocution		**0.00**	**0.00***	**0.00***	**0.52**	**0.51**	**0.00***	**0.27**
	Range	3.70	1.40	3.00	3.68	2.17	1.39	2.86
Resultative		**0.00**	**0.00**	**0.00**	**0.00**	**0.00***	**0.22***	**0.00***
	Range	0.68	2.80	0.56	0.66	1.00	1.78	1.03
Language activity		**0.57**	**0.19***	**0.42**	**0.00****	**0.25***	**0.00***	**0.00****
	Range	7.41	2.10	1.79	1.75	5.16	1.47	1.16
Interpretive		**0.31**	**3.70****	**3.24****	**0.43**	**1.33****	**1.97****	**1.87****
	Range	2.16	6.79	8.54	5.56	4.65	8.93	9.52
Vague		**2.26**	**3.68***	**4.80****	**4.17****	**1.48***	**3.57****	**2.96**
	Range	7.73	9.03	9.61	11.50	5.65	8.02	12.92

Personal Pronouns

First person		**2.60**	**2.38**	**7.44****	**3.11**	**3.97**	**4.51***	**1.52***
	Range	15.41	13.60	20.59	13.13	15.04	18.21	6.39
Second person		**0.00**	**2.27****	**1.05****	**0.00**	**0.00**	**0.00**	**0.69***
	Range	2.05	18.25	18.63	9.40	5.42	6.32	8.48
Third person		**4.14**	**5.00**	**3.03**	**3.50**	**3.90**	**3.67**	**3.17**
	Range	13.40	15.91	16.67	12.20	13.33	16.80	12.80

Slot Fillers

It-subject		**0.31**	**0.51***	**0.51**	**0.00***	**0.26**	**0.00***	**0.00***
	Range	2.55	1.59	2.50	0.91	1.59	1.00	0.96
There-subject		**0.35**	**0.00**	**0.00**	**0.26**	**0.25**	**0.26**	**0.26**
	Range	1.53	1.42	1.71	1.57	1.44	3.55	1.36

Indirect Pronouns

Universal		**0.00**	**0.35***	**0.00**	**0.71****	**0.27**	**0.30***	**0.39***
	Range	1.04	4.81	5.50	2.86	0.89	1.79	5.77
Assertive		**0.77**	**0.98***	**1.05***	**0.85**	**0.81**	**1.10***	**0.54**
	Range	2.10	7.14	6.67	3.95	2.63	3.19	1.66
Nominalization		**4.62**	**4.13**	**3.83**	**2.63***	**2.69***	**2.20****	**2.42***
	Range	11.53	7.30	8.61	12.66	8.42	6.21	6.26
Gerunds		**1.85**	**1.58**	**1.04***	**1.05****	**0.80****	**1.51***	**1.⌣8***
	Range	6.94	3.84	5.56	4.00	4.17	5.33	4.63

(Continued)

TABLE 12.3
(Continued)

		NS	Chinese	Japanese	Korean	Vietnamese	Indonesian	Arabic
					L1			

Verb Tenses

		NS	Chinese	Japanese	Korean	Vietnamese	Indonesian	Arabic
Past		**1.81**	**2.10***	**3.57****	**3.45**	**1.78**	**2.78***	**0.49***
	Range	10.13	16.35	11.26	11.82	5.83	9.98	5.47
Present		**9.77**	**8.89**	**10.50**	**8.47**	**8.08***	**9.23**	**8.97**
	Range	14.18	10.38	9.14	23.96	7.96	17.03	8.60
Future		**0.82**	**0.69**	**0.44**	**0.44***	**0.26***	**1.03**	**0.42**
	Range	5.68	3.18	5.21	2.22	2.56	4.46	2.77

Verb Aspects

Progressive		**0.51**	**0.00****	**0.00***	**0.00****	**0.00****	**0.25***	**0.25***
	Range	2.26	1.96	1.79	0.87	2.08	2.66	1.36
Perfect		**0.36**	**0.00****	**0.00***	**0.00***	**0.26**	**0.00***	**0.00**
	Range	2.68	1.01	1.18	1.07	1.75	0.88	1.18

Semantic and Lexical Classes of Verbs

Public		**0.30**	**0.44**	**0.59****	**1.00****	**0.60***	**0.67****	**0.77***
	Range	2.04	4.44	4.17	6.06	1.92	2.59	2.40
Private		**1.92**	**4.26****	**4.98****	**3.04****	**3.17***	**5.02****	**3.64****
	Range	5.04	7.98	7.56	8.44	8.42	7.89	7.58
Suasive		**0.28**	**0.74****	**0.50**	**0.00**	**0.80****	**0.67****	**1.03****
	Range	1.70	2.11	1.74	1.39	3.36	2.12	2.70
Log./sem. relat.		**0.79**	**0.77**	**0.55**	**0.37****	**0.82**	**0.96**	**0.78**
	Range	2.84	4.30	3.65	1.97	2.27	4.63	2.77
Tentative		**0.64**	**0.79**	**1.77****	**2.50****	**0.35***	**1.52****	**0.77***
	Range	3.41	3.92	5.50	8.55	3.35	5.37	2.13
Seem/appear		**0.00**	**0.00**	**0.00**	**0.00**	**0.00**	**0.00**	**0.00**
	Range	0.51	0.51	0.42	0.56	0.49	0.32	0.30

Modal Verbs

Possibility		**1.13**	**1.54***	**2.00****	**1.33**	**0.74**	**0.88**	**0.88**
	Range	3.57	4.44	5.08	4.00	4.40	3.57	2.34
Necessity		**0.54**	**0.96***	**1.30****	**1.42****	**0.51**	**0.77***	**0.69**
	Range	2.26	5.56	5.41	6.00	2.00	5.00	2.96
Predictive		**0.38**	**0.00**	**0.00***	**0.00***	**0.00***	**0.00**	**0.34**
	Range	2.58	2.68	2.56	2.50	1.19	2.07	2.69
Passive		**1.81**	**0.74****	**0.98****	**0.89****	**0.44****	**0.44****	**0.30****
	Range	4.90	2.27	3.13	2.37	3.10	2.14	3.37
Be-main		**1.50**	**3.59****	**4.88****	**3.74****	**3.37****	**4.38****	**3.10****
	Range	5.15	4.75	7.84	8.86	5.56	6.40	4.21
Infinitives		**5.79**	**6.29**	**5.88**	**1.85****	**2.38****	**5.25**	**2.73****
	Range	9.96	8.80	10.51	6.50	6.15	7.05	3.73

(Continued)

TABLE 12.3
(Continued)

		L1						
		NS	Chinese	Japanese	Korean	Vietnamese	Indonesian	Arabic
Participles								
Present		**0.63**	**0.22***	**0.00***	**0.23***	**0.52**	**0.00****	**0.21***
	Range	2.92	1.82	1.77	1.82	1.98	1.23	1.26
Past		**0.79**	**0.00****	**0.38***	**0.00***	**0.33****	**0.28****	**0.26****
	Range	3.80	1.23	4.53	2.88	2.13	1.36	1.18
Adjectives								
Attributive		**6.12**	**4.06****	**4.00****	**2.36****	**4.00***	**3.45****	**2.05****
	Range	10.95	11.44	7.06	10.61	7.22	9.79	7.08
Predicative		**1.74**	**3.02****	**3.79****	**3.39****	**3.79****	**2.96****	**2.44***
	Range	4.10	7.34	10.12	8.08	10.42	8.00	12.56
Semantic and Lexical Classes of Adverbs								
Time		**0.93**	**0.95**	**0.91**	**1.30**	**1.25**	**1.15**	**1.66***
	Range	4.59	4.20	3.92	2.94	2.66	2.70	3.85
Frequency		**0.32**	**0.00***	**0.00***	**0.00***	**0.00***	**0.00***	**0.00**
	Range	1.87	0.93	0.92	1.30	1.15	1.78	1.25
Place		**2.43**	**1.95**	**1.73**	**1.07****	**2.66**	**1.58**	**1.06***
	Range	4.07	5.56	5.23	4.04	5.72	4.32	3.10
Amplifiers		**1.79**	**3.12****	**3.74****	**3.33***	**1.59**	**3.17****	**2.82***
	Range	5.07	6.88	12.09	7.19	3.01	5.94	12.76
Downtoners		**0.81**	**0.93**	**0.56**	**0.44***	**0.48***	**0.92***	**0.83**
	Range	3.80	2.38	2.78	2.34	1.68	2.96	1.72
Other		**0.00**	**1.01****	**0.40***	**0.75****	**1.03****	**0.60****	**2.05****
	Range	1.52	2.10	2.27	2.78	2.92	3.70	3.96
Noun and Adjective Clauses								
Noun		**1.46**	**1.40**	**2.28***	**1.33**	**1.49**	**1.82***	**1.56**
	Range	5.11	4.29	6.67	8.75	2.84	3.70	2.93
Full adjective		**1.42**	**1.30**	**1.55**	**0.90***	**1.19***	**1.85**	**1.56**
	Range	4.52	3.49	5.41	4.44	4.09	4.17	3.17
Reduced adjective		**0.00**	**0.00**	**0.00**	**0.00**	**0.00**	**0.00***	**0.00**
	Range	2.94	1.75	1.93	2.69	0.77	0.49	1.43
Adverb Clauses								
Full: Cause		**0.33**	**0.38**	**0.56***	**0.56**	**0.54**	**0.83***	**0.30**
	Range	2.72	1.85	2.50	1.52	1.19	2.67	1.72
Concession		**0.00**	**0.00**	**0.00**	**0.00**	**0.00**	**0.00**	**0.00**
	Range	0.68	0.91	1.06	1.68	0.48	0.60	0.54
Condition		**0.33**	**0.95***	**1.06****	**0.56***	**0.26**	**0.49***	**0.29**
	Range	2.27	1.92	3.92	1.68	1.49	2.37	1.95

(Continued)

TABLE 12.3
(Continued)

		L1						
		NS	Chinese	Japanese	Korean	Vietnamese	Indonesian	Arabic
Purpose		**0.00**	**0.00**	**0.00**	**0.00***	**0.00***	**0.00**	**0.00***
	Range	1.15	0.79	0.98	0.51	0.49	1.19	0.39
Other		**0.30**	**0.88***	**0.28**	**0.50***	**0.51**	**0.64****	**0.49***
	Range	1.88	3.50	1.67	1.90	2.08	2.53	1.92
Reduced adverb clause		**0.52**	**0.45**	**0.00****	**0.00***	**0.25***	**0.00****	**0.00****
	Range	2.08	2.38	0.83	1.36	0.89	0.62	0.96

II. RHETORICAL FEATURES

Coordinating and Logical Conjunctions/Prepositions

		NS	Chinese	Japanese	Korean	Vietnamese	Indonesian	Arabic
Phrase-level		**3.47**	**4.24***	**3.83**	**3.78**	**3.87**	**3.21**	**4.05***
	Range	6.16	16.93	9.42	8.48	7.15	5.92	14.29
Sentence-level		**0.61**	**1.88****	**2.54****	**1.72****	**1.12***	**1.67****	**1.03***
	Range	2.61	3.56	7.62	6.61	3.45	3.32	3.33
Log./sem. conjunctions		**1.23**	**1.21**	**1.27**	**0.48****	**0.95**	**1.18**	**0.92***
	Range	3.80	4.29	4.65	2.22	2.92	2.43	1.81
Exemplification		**0.00**	**0.49****	**0.50****	**0.35****	**0.37****	**0.44****	**0.59****
	Range	0.58	2.42	1.56	1.67	1.33	1.58	3.81

Hedges

		NS	Chinese	Japanese	Korean	Vietnamese	Indonesian	Arabic
Epistemic		**0.51**	**0.53**	**0.42**	**0.26***	**0.38**	**0.62**	**0.24***
	Range	3.40	2.38	2.70	1.43	2.23	2.31	1.76
Lexical		**1.30**	**0.70****	**0.56****	**2.73***	**0.77****	**0.00****	**0.18****
	Range	4.63	2.73	3.53	12.32	2.08	1.33	1.56
Possibility		**0.00**	**0.00**	**0.00***	**0.00***	**0.00**	**0.00**	**0.00**
	Range	1.36	1.89	0.57	0.66	0.71	0.70	0.59
Quality		**0.20**	**0.49***	**0.00**	**0.00***	**0.00**	**0.27**	**0.19**
	Range	1.85	2.02	1.29	1.17	0.83	2.07	1.54
Performative		**0.00**	**0.00**	**0.00**	**0.00**	**0.00**	**0.00**	**0.00**
	Range	3.70	0.23	0.51	0.66	0.38	0.40	0.00
Rhetorical Questions		**0.00**	**0.00**	**0.19***	**0.00**	**0.00**	**0.00**	**0.00**
	Range	2.04	1.82	2.44	2.63	0.77	1.15	1.08
Demonstrative		**0.52**	**1.11****	**0.89***	**1.33****	**1.09***	**1.25***	**1.72****
	Range	2.78	3.13	2.56	6.25	6.03	3.85	2.88
Emphatics		**1.42**	**3.33****	**4.53****	**2.33***	**2.82****	**3.33****	**3.31****
	Range	4.08	5.47	9.29	8.64	4.73	7.27	6.65
Presupp. Markers		**0.00**	**0.00**	**0.00**	**0.00**	**0.00**	**0.00**	**0.00**
	Range	0.61	2.10	0.76	0.48	0.48	0.32	0.53
Fixed Strings		**4.44**	**1.16****	**1.28****	**1.01****	**1.01****	**1.00****	**0.95****
	Range	17.86	3.16	4.58	2.02	3.46	2.37	3.38

Note. All comparisons are relative to NSs.
*one-tailed $p \leq 0.05$. **two-tailed $p \leq 0.05$.

but first-person plural pronouns are seen as a device for establishing unity and building rapport between the writer and the reader. Most important, however, in ESL/EFL training in Japan and Indonesia, writing instruction often focuses on narrating personal stories and events in diary-like writing exercises to promote writing fluency (I. Taylor, 1995). For example, *I had this similar problem when I was deciding my major in [the] sophomore year. I wanted to major in fine arts, but I was too concerned about job possibilities after I finish my school. I ended up studying business but I never liked it. Therefore, my grades were not very pleasant. Also, I didn't learn very much because I wasn't interested in business* (Japanese).

On the other hand, the NS and NNS frequency rates for third-person pronouns in Major essays did not exhibit significant differences, as they did in the pooled data (chaps. 6–10).

It Slot Filler.   In the pooled data for all essays, NNS writers in all groups used the *it*-cleft structure consistently less frequently than NSs. On the other hand, in the Major essays of Chinese, the slot filler *it* was used with a significantly higher median rate than in NS text. For example, *It would be better to know a little concept rather than to know nothing about the operation of the companies for a boss* (Chinese). As was noted in chapter 6, in the Confucian rhetorical tradition, depersonalization of text projects an authoritative stance in discourse, and third-person pronouns are used to impart an elevated style. It should be noted that in Major essays, Chinese speakers actually employed fewer first-person and more third-person pronouns than NSs did, although their rates did not differ significantly.

Frequency and Place Adverbs.   Frequency adverbs did not show significant differences in their rates of use in NS and NNS data for all essays combined. However, in Major essays (Table 12.3), NNSs in all groups (medians 0.00), except Arabic speakers, employed these features significantly more rarely than NSs. On the other hand, in NS texts written toward the Major prompt, the median rate for place adverbs was twice that in the pooled data (chap. 8), when NSs discussed where they plan to study and look for jobs after choosing their majors. For example, *I do not plan to work in an office for the rest of my life; Say, you work in this big company that pays you a lot of money and you can make a nice living; or I see myself in a hospital helping those who really need help* (NSs).

Reduced Adjective Clauses.   Neither NSs nor NNSs employed many reduced adjective clauses in their Major essays (medians 0.00), and hence, the differences in the NS and NNS median rates for this feature were not significant overall.

Condition Clauses.   Although in the pooled data (chap. 9), the NS and NNS rates for conditional clauses were significantly different because most

L2 writers did not use them nearly as often as NSs did. In the NNS texts on the Major prompt, conditional clauses were found significantly more frequently in Chinese, Japanese, Korean, and Indonesian speaker essays than in those of NSs. Essentially, in most cases, L2 writers hedged their bets when writing about choices of a major based on one's interests or the demands of the employment market because they were keenly aware of the pitfall in either option. For example, *If you study in history major and if the market need people* who study in business of computer field, you won't be able to get a job. *If we can find a job in the future* that is not in our field, we will not have a good salary. . . . *If one student graduates in finance major and the other graduates in accounting major*, the one who graduates in accounting major will get high salary (Indonesian).

 Logical/Semantic Conjunctions. Logical/semantic conjunctions have diverse text-cohesive functions, such as causative, dismissive, or additive *(because of, besides, despite, except, in contrast, instead, in this way, too)*. They are somewhat more lexically complex than, for instance, phrase-coordinating conjunctions. As has been mentioned, the Major prompt presented students with a dual and somewhat ambiguous context, in which both NSs and NNSs hedged their considerations in choices of majors. In NS, Chinese, and Japanese speaker Major essays, the rate of logical/semantic conjunction uses was twice that in the pooled data (chap. 10), and the rates of all other groups of writers were higher, as well (with the exception of Korean speaker texts). For example, *If you have no interest in the field, you cannot get what you want, even money, in it. In contrast, the bad majors will not be bad if you are good enough in that field. Besides that, I believe a person with a true great interest in a field will get success* (Chinese) or *If I choose a major which I am not interested in, my future may not be happy, and instead, I'll be sad all the time. People's lives can be in a disaster because of their jobs* (Japanese).

 An important conclusion is that the types of prompts administered in essay writing for various academic purposes have an important outcome for the types of text that students produce. For instance, prompts, such as Manner, Opinions, and Major, that draw on students' personal experiences, beliefs, and opinions are most likely to lead to personal narrative, or belief/opinion essays. Specifically, when writing about an appropriate classroom Manner a vast majority of students stated that in their opinion, entertaining classes are far better than formal and serious classes. Similarly, most writers expressed a belief that children should be allowed to form their own opinions and that choosing majors based on one's personal interests provides more advantages than being concerned about future employment options.

 Expressing these opinions and beliefs required the students to invest little thought because their choices of positions in Manner, Opinions, and Major prompts were based on the obvious: Being entertained in class, having the freedom of making decisions, and having fun while studying is unquestion-ably preferable to not having fun or having to live with restrictions. Manner, Opinions, and Major topics elicited opinions and expressions of belief that could be supported almost exclusively by means of students' personal expe-riences and required little beyond recounts of personal narratives and exam-ples in lieu of argumentation.

It is interesting to note that these three prompts were particularly popu-lar with teachers who selected them precisely because students could relate to the topics and could produce large amounts of text when writing the placement tests. Teachers' expectations of the prompts were unquestion-ably correct: The average length of most NNS essays exceeded that of NSs, and clearly, students had little trouble producing text. However, as Bereiter and Scardamalia (1985) pointed out, knowledge telling that requires stu-dents to simply write down their thoughts is distinct from advanced think-ing and writing tasks entailed in knowledge transforming. According to the authors, knowledge telling in producing essays is accessible to most NS chil-dren in elementary school due to many similarities between conversational discourse and written text that results in simply writing down what they already know.

13

The Differences That the
Prompts Make

Chapters 6–10, Part II, examined the variations in feature use in student essays written toward a particular prompt relative to the data for all prompts combined. It seems rather clear that the essays written on different prompts exhibit a substantial amount of variability in the employment of textual features. This chapter compares the median frequency rates of feature occurrences in the essays on particular prompts written by the speakers of the same language, to determine, for example, whether NS essays on the Parents prompt involved different frequency rates of certain features compared to those written by NSs on Grades, Wealth, Manner, Opinions, and Major prompts.

If essays by speakers of Chinese, Japanese, Korean, Vietnamese, Indonesian, and Arabic exhibit distinct differences across various prompts, it may be that particular topics for elicitation of writing induce prevalent or reduced uses of specific language features. That is, a comparison of textual features in essays on the different prompts can identify the features that are prone to topic variability.

Statistical comparisons of median frequency rates employed in essays are relatively easy to obtain, and the comparison data is extensive, that is, 685,440 data points consisting of median and range values. If speakers of seven languages write essays on six different prompts, multiple comparisons of the 68 median feature rates are necessary to present a complete picture. The importance of the features in student essays, however, ranges greatly from the present tense and infinitives, which were found in practically every essay, to rhetorical questions and presupposition markers that were used only in some student texts.

To determine the importance of features in student texts, the rank order of the median frequency rates is identified and presented in Appendix A (see chaps. 6–10 for a detailed overview). In this chapter, the discussion of feature variability in the essays of speakers of the same language focuses on those characteristics of text that are most common in all essays combined. To focus on data most relevant to the purposes of this book, a decision was made to present medians and ranges for the top 30 features (slightly fewer than half) in Appendix B. The 30 most common features include, in declining order:

- (1) The present tense.
- (2) Infinitives.
- (3) Third-person pronouns.
- (4) Attributive adjectives.
- (5) Fixed strings.
- (6) Phrase-level coordinators.
- (7) Copula *be* as the main verb.
- (8) Private verbs.
- (9) First-person pronouns.
- (10) Nominalizations.
- (11) Amplifiers.
- (12) Predicative adjectives.
- (13) The past tense.
- (14) Gerunds.
- (15) Noun clauses.
- (16) Place adverbs.
- (17) Vague nouns.
- (18) Emphatics.
- (19) The passive voice.
- (20) Adjective clauses.
- (21) Advance/retroactive nouns.
- (22) Possibility modals.
- (23) Present participles.
- (24) Demonstrative pronouns.
- (25) Past participles.
- (26.5) Time adverbs.

- (26.5) Lexical hedges.
- (28) Sentence transitions.
- (29) Necessity modals.
- (30) Logical/semantic conjunctions and prepositions.

However, even the reduced data in Appendix B, consist of over 150,000 median values alone, and for this reason, the discussion that follows highlights only the most important differences in their uses in essays written by each group of speakers, based on their L1s. This chapter focuses on the top 10 most common text features, identified in NS texts for all essays combined. The Mann–Whitney U test employed for the comparative analysis of text features in essays written by various groups of speakers (see chap. 5) was also used in the comparisons of text features in the compositions written by speakers of the same language across the six topics, Parents, Grades, Wealth, Manner, Opinions, and Major. The order and the discussion of the feature data follow the pattern adopted in earlier chapters throughout the book, beginning with pronouns and nominalizations and then moving to the verb phrase, adjectives, conjunctions, and fixed strings.

To present important differences or similarities in feature uses across the texts written to the six prompts, as well as to avoid redundancy, the illustrative graphs focus on one feature at a time and highlight significant divergences between median rates in comparisons across the prompts. The organization of comparisons in the graphs follows the rows marked by essay labels from Parents to Opinions. For example, for NS texts, the comparisons of median rates of features in Parents and Wealth essays show that Wealth texts elicited significantly fewer first-person pronouns than the Parents prose (Parents median 2.00 and Wealth median 1.19*). In this case, on the graph, this important divergence is marked by a minus sign (–) in the cell corresponding to the intersection of the Parents row and the Wealth column. On the other hand, the Manner prompt (median 3.87*) elicited significantly higher median rates than the Wealth topic (median 1.19) (see Appendix B). This difference is denoted by a plus sign (+) in the cell at the intersection of the Wealth row and the Manner column. If no significant differences are found in the feature use in essays on two prompts, then no graphic denotation is made in intersecting cells, and it is left blank.

For example, in the graph that follows, in Wealth essays, the median rates for a particular feature were significantly lower than those in Parents texts (the minus [–] sign at the intersection of the Parents row and the Wealth column). No significant differences are noted between the first-person pronoun median rates in Parents texts versus Grades, Manner, Opinions, and Major texts.

Prompts	Grades	Wealth	Manner	Opinions	Major
Parents		−			

On the other hand, the Manner and Major texts for this feature contained significantly higher rates than the Wealth essays did: plus (+) signs at the intersection of the Wealth row and the Manner column, as well as at the intersection of Wealth row and the Major column.

Prompts	Grades	Wealth	Manner	Opinions	Major
Wealth			+		+

ESSAYS OF NATIVE SPEAKERS

The discussion of the 10 most common features begins with first-person pronouns and follows to fixed strings. The data for the most common features of NS text demonstrate that, compared to the essays on the Parents prompt, the uses of first-person pronouns were largely similar across all topics, with the exception of Wealth essays, which elicited significantly fewer of them than Parents or Grades prompts. In addition, the essays about the choices of Major contained markedly more of these pronouns than Wealth or Opinions texts.

The median rates for third-person pronouns were significantly greater in Opinions essays than in compositions on any other topic, with the exception of Major (see Table 13.1). However, important divergences in NS essays across topics become readily apparent in the comparisons of median rates for nominalizations. Clearly, Manner, Opinions, and Major prompts consistently elicited more abstract and generic nouns marked by such suffixes as *–ion, -ness,* and *–ity* than Parents, Grades, or Wealth topics. It is important to keep in mind, however, the wording of the Major prompt included four nominalizations, one of which was repeated (*employment, possibilities, options,* and *position*). On the other hand, the essays written on the Manners prompt dealt exclusively with academic and abstract concepts, such as *encouragement* (the verb form *encourage* is included in the prompt), *education, examination, explanation, requirement, presentation, discussion, improvement, development,* all of which represent common items in an academic context.

The median rates for the uses of the present tense are significantly higher in Major texts, compared to those about Parents, Wealth, and Opinions (Table 13.1). Grades and Wealth essays contain more present-tense occurrences than essays on the Parents prompt. Parents and Wealth texts elicited

TABLE 13.1
Cross-Prompt Comparisons of Top 10 Features in NSs' Texts

First-Person Pronouns

Prompts	Grades	Wealth	Manner	Opinions	Major
Parents		−			
Grades		−			
Wealth			+		+
Manner					
Opinions					+

Third-Person Pronouns

	Grades	Wealth	Manner	Opinions	Major
Parents			−	+	
Grades		+		+	+
Wealth			−	+	
Manner				+	+
Opinions					−

Nominalization

	Grades	Wealth	Manner	Opinions	Major
Parents			+	+	+
Grades			+	+	+
Wealth			+	+	+
Manner					+
Opinions					+

Present Tense

	Grades	Wealth	Manner	Opinions	Major
Parents	+	+			+
Grades			−		
Wealth			−		+
Manner					
Opinions					+

Private Verbs

	Grades	Wealth	Manner	Opinions	Major
Parents	+		+	+	+
Grades		−			−
Wealth			+	+	+
Manner					−
Opinions					

(Continued)

TABLE 13.1
(Continued)

Be-*copula as Main Verb*

	Grades	Wealth	Manner	Opinions	Major
Parents			+	+	
Grades			+	+	
Wealth			+	+	
Manner					−
Opinions					−

Infinitives

	Grades	Wealth	Manner	Opinions	Major
Parents	+	+	+	+	+
Grades		−		+	
Wealth				+	+
Manner				+	
Opinions					−

Attributive Adjectives

	Grades	Wealth	Manner	Opinions	Major
Parents	+	+	+	+	+
Grades		+	+	+	+
Wealth			+	+	+
Manner					−
Opinions					+

Phrase-Level Conjunctions

	Grades	Wealth	Manner	Opinions	Major
Parents	+	+	+	+	+
Grades		+	+	+	+
Wealth				+	
Manner				+	
Opinions					−

Fixed Strings

	Grades	Wealth	Manner	Opinions	Major
Parents	+	+	+	+	+
Grades		+	+	+	+
Wealth			+	+	+
Manner				−	−
Opinions					−

lower rates of private verbs, compared to all other prompts. Because private verbs usually refer to emotive or mental activities *(think, feel, believe, understand)*, they are more common in expressive rather than academic texts.

A prevalence of the copula verb *be* in the function of the main clausal verb also tends to mark text for lexical and structural simplicity. The preponderance of *be* in NS essays on the Manner and Opinion prompts, compared to all other prompts, seems rather striking. One implication of the significantly greater median rates of private and *be*-verbs is that the essays on these two prompts contained a relatively large number of lexically and syntactically simple constructions.

The usage of infinitives also seems to be promoted by some prompts more than others. For instance, the Opinions prompt clearly contributes to higher median rates of infinitives than all other topics, except the choice of Major. A similar clear-cut pattern of feature usage is apparent in the median rates of attributive adjectives across the six prompts. Manner and Opinion prompts led to the writers' greatest employment of these features, followed by the Major topic. It is interesting to note that the wording of Parents and Grades prompts included no attributive adjectives, whereas the Wealth topic relied on two *(wealthiest and famous)*. On the other hand, the lexis of the Manner and Major prompts hinged on four and three descriptive adjectives, respectively. The context of the Opinions compositions expectably leads to the usage of numerous relatively simple attributive adjectives, such as *young, little, big, old (-er), good, bad, patient, intelligent, smart, wise, stupid, dangerous, terrible, innocent (children), mature.*

The Opinion prompt seems to elicit the highest median rates of phrase-level conjunctions, such as *and, but, yet, either, or, both,* followed by the Manner and Major topics, respectively. Again, the compositions about Parents appear to contain the lowest numbers of phrase-level conjunctions, followed by the Grades and Wealth essays, respectively. Specifically, Parents, Grade, and Wealth topics appear to be more similar to one another than any of these to Manner, Opinions, and Major prompts, which seem to elicit text features significantly different from the other three (Table 13.1).

This observation, based on the feature usage in NS essays, is further supported by the median frequencies of fixed strings across the six topics. Parents, Grades, and Wealth prompts elicited texts with lower median frequencies of idiomatic expressions and, possibly clichés, compared to those written to discuss Manner, Opinion, and Major prompts. Of the latter three, Manner essays induced the greatest frequencies of fixed string usage.

To sum up, in NS essays, the various prompts led to divergent uses of the most common features and affected practically all aspects of text construction, including pronoun, tense, and fixed expressions. Furthermore, even the prompts that were developed according to the goal of eliciting argumentation/position essays (on the one hand, there is *xxx,* and on the other, there is *yyy;* choose either *xxx* or *yyy* and explain your reasons) give rise to the usage of different linguistic and rhetorical features of text. Furthermore, despite superficial similarities in the prompt construction, various topics and the lexical content of prompts can induce certain essay types. For instance, among the six prompts administered in NS placement and diagnostic tests, two rather distinct patterns are readily apparent: Parents, Grades, and Wealth essays are more similar to one another than to any among the Manner, Opinions, or Major texts, which also lead to higher frequencies of particular features than others. Further discussion of this point follows in the conclusion of this chapter.

ESSAYS OF CHINESE SPEAKERS

The comparisons of median rates for the top 10 features (see Appendix A) in the essays of Chinese speakers is presented in Table 13.2. The use of first-person pronouns in the essays of Chinese speakers was similar across all topics, with the exception of Grades and Wealth texts, in which their median frequency rates were significantly higher.

The comparisons of third-person pronouns in the essays of Chinese speakers show that Opinion compositions include greater frequencies of third-person pronouns than Grades, Wealth, and Manner prose did. On the other hand, the essays on the Major prompt clearly contained significantly higher median rates of nominalizations than those written on any other topic. In compositions on all prompts, except Opinions, the median frequency rates of present-tense markers are similar. However, the essays on the topic of whether parents should allow children to form their own Opinions contained higher rates of past-time narratives, and hence reduced occurrences of the present tense, compared to Parents, Grades, or Wealth text.

The median frequencies of private verbs were significantly greater in Major essays than in those about Parents, Wealth, or Opinions, and the usage of *be*-copula predominates in Manner, Opinions, and Major prose. Parents and Grades prompts elicited the lowest rates of infinitives, with Opinions exhibiting the highest rates, followed by Manner and Major writing tasks, respectively. The Manner topic, with four attributive adjectives in the wording of the prompt, clearly leads to the greatest median rates of these features, compared to any of the other five topics. On the other hand, Parents texts of Chinese speakers contained the lowest rates of descriptive adjectives.

Phrase-level conjunctions were used at similar median rates in Parents, Grades, and Wealth essays, whereas the Manner, Opinions, and Major texts included higher frequencies of these cohesive features. Opinion essays of

TABLE 13.2
Cross-Prompt Comparisons of Top 10 Features in Chinese Speaker' Texts

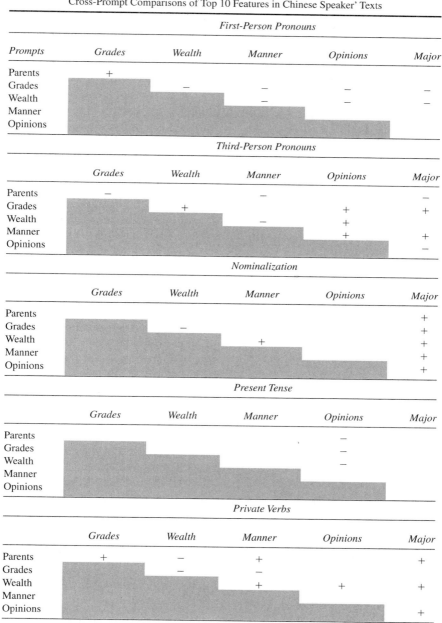

First-Person Pronouns

Prompts	Grades	Wealth	Manner	Opinions	Major
Parents	+				
Grades		−	−	−	−
Wealth			−	−	−
Manner					
Opinions					

Third-Person Pronouns

Prompts	Grades	Wealth	Manner	Opinions	Major
Parents	−		−		−
Grades		+		+	+
Wealth			−	+	
Manner				+	+
Opinions					−

Nominalization

Prompts	Grades	Wealth	Manner	Opinions	Major
Parents					+
Grades		−			+
Wealth			+		+
Manner					+
Opinions					+

Present Tense

Prompts	Grades	Wealth	Manner	Opinions	Major
Parents				−	
Grades				−	
Wealth				−	
Manner					
Opinions					

Private Verbs

Prompts	Grades	Wealth	Manner	Opinions	Major
Parents	+	−	+		+
Grades		−	−		
Wealth			+	+	+
Manner					
Opinions					+

(Continued)

TABLE 13.2
(Continued)

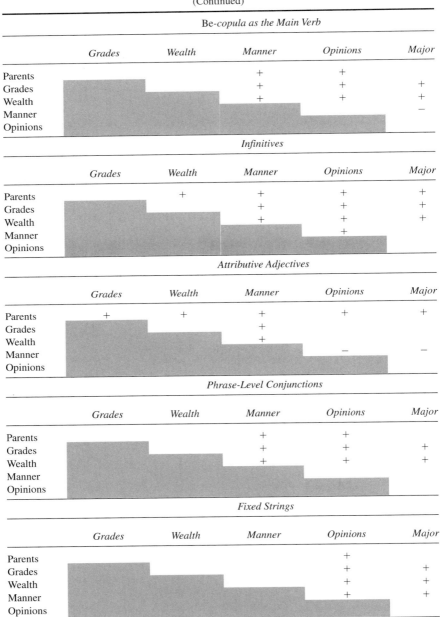

Be-*copula as the Main Verb*

	Grades	Wealth	Manner	Opinions	Major
Parents			+	+	
Grades			+	+	+
Wealth			+	+	+
Manner					−
Opinions					

Infinitives

	Grades	Wealth	Manner	Opinions	Major
Parents		+	+	+	+
Grades			+	+	+
Wealth			+	+	+
Manner				+	
Opinions					

Attributive Adjectives

	Grades	Wealth	Manner	Opinions	Major
Parents	+	+	+	+	+
Grades			+		
Wealth			+		
Manner				−	−
Opinions					

Phrase-Level Conjunctions

	Grades	Wealth	Manner	Opinions	Major
Parents			+	+	
Grades			+	+	+
Wealth			+	+	+
Manner					
Opinions					

Fixed Strings

	Grades	Wealth	Manner	Opinions	Major
Parents				+	
Grades				+	+
Wealth				+	+
Manner				+	+
Opinions					

Chinese speakers exhibited the greatest use of fixed expressions, followed by the Major texts. In general, Chinese speaker texts showed clear-cut patterns in feature uses in essays on Parents, Grades, and Wealth, and Manner, Opinions, and Major prompts.

ESSAYS OF JAPANESE SPEAKERS

The information in Table 13.3 demonstrates that in the texts of Japanese speakers, Major, Opinions and Manner prompts elicited most of the 10 features at significantly higher rates than the Parents, Grades, and Wealth prompts. Such features as first- and third-person pronouns are more common in essays on the former three prompts than in the texts on the three latter topics.

The median frequency rates of nominalizations and private verbs are indisputably higher in Major texts than those written to any other prompt. The usage of the present tense, which is often expected in generalizations and statements of belief, was significantly more frequent in Parents, Opinions, and Major essays compared to that employed in Manner, Grades, and Wealth prose, respectively. In addition, as in the essays of Chinese speakers, *be*-copula, infinitives, and fixed strings are most frequently employed in Manner, Opinions, and Major texts than in those on Parents, Grades, and Wealth. Manner, Opinions, Major, and Wealth compositions contained significantly higher rates of adjectival descriptors than either Parents or Grades texts, in which the median rates of adjectives were not markedly distinct.

In general terms, various topics did not make a great deal of difference in the rates of phrase-level conjunctions in compositions of Japanese speakers. The only exception may be the Major writing task, which induced a preponderance of these cohesive devices.

ESSAYS OF KOREAN SPEAKERS

Table 13.4 presents the information of cross-prompt comparisons in Korean speaker essays. In the texts of Korean speakers, the Parents, Grades, Opinions, and Major, respectively, prompts elicited higher rates of first-person pronoun uses than Wealth or Major. In addition, however, the Parents topic was also conducive to the greatest median rates of third-person pronouns, followed by Opinions, Wealth, Major, and Manner, respectively. As in texts of Chinese and Japanese speakers, the Major prompt elicited the highest rates of nominalizations, as well.

TABLE 13.3

Cross-Prompt Comparisons of Top 10 Features in Japanese Speakers' Texts

First-Person Pronoun

Prompts	Grades	Wealth	Manner	Opinions	Major
Parents	+	−	+		+
Grades		−			
Wealth			+	+	+
Manner					+
Opinions					+

Third-Person Pronouns

	Grades	Wealth	Manner	Opinions	Major
Parents	−	−	−	+	−
Grades		+		+	+
Wealth			−	+	
Manner				+	+
Opinions					−

Nominalization

	Grades	Wealth	Manner	Opinions	Major
Parents					+
Grades		−			+
Wealth			+	+	+
Manner					+
Opinions					+

Present Tense

	Grades	Wealth	Manner	Opinions	Major
Parents	−	−	−		
Grades		+		+	+
Wealth				+	+
Manner				+	+
Opinions					

Private Verbs

	Grades	Wealth	Manner	Opinions	Major
Parents	+	−	+	+	+
Grades		−			+
Wealth			+	+	+
Manner					+
Opinions					+

(Continued)

TABLE 13.3
(Continued)

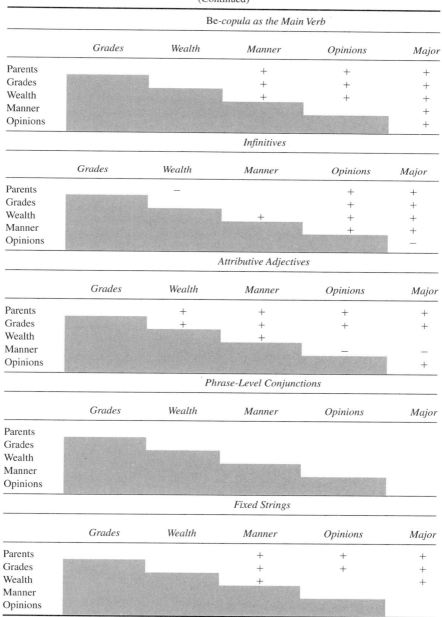

Be-*copula as the Main Verb*

	Grades	Wealth	Manner	Opinions	Major
Parents			+	+	+
Grades			+	+	+
Wealth			+	+	+
Manner					+
Opinions					+

Infinitives

	Grades	Wealth	Manner	Opinions	Major
Parents		−		+	+
Grades				+	+
Wealth			+	+	+
Manner				+	+
Opinions					−

Attributive Adjectives

	Grades	Wealth	Manner	Opinions	Major
Parents		+	+	+	+
Grades		+	+	+	+
Wealth			+		
Manner				−	−
Opinions					+

Phrase-Level Conjunctions

	Grades	Wealth	Manner	Opinions	Major
Parents					
Grades					
Wealth					
Manner					
Opinions					

Fixed Strings

	Grades	Wealth	Manner	Opinions	Major
Parents			+	+	+
Grades			+	+	+
Wealth			+		+
Manner					
Opinions					

TABLE 13.4
Cross-Prompt Comparisons of Ten Top Features in Korean Speakers' Texts

First-Person Pronouns

	Grades	Wealth	Manner	Opinions	Major
Parents		−	−		
Grades		−	−		
Wealth				+	+
Manner				+	+
Opinions					

Third-Person Pronouns

	Grades	Wealth	Manner	Opinions	Major
Parents	−	−	−	−	−
Grades		+		+	+
Wealth			−		−
Manner				+	+
Opinions					−

Nominalization

	Grades	Wealth	Manner	Opinions	Major
Parents		−			+
Grades		−			+
Wealth			+	+	+
Manner					+
Opinions					+

The Present Tense

	Grades	Wealth	Manner	Opinions	Major
Parents	−		−	−	−
Grades		+	−		
Wealth			−		
Manner				+	+
Opinions					

Private Verbs

	Grades	Wealth	Manner	Opinions	Major
Parents	+	−	+		+
Grades		−		−	
Wealth			+	+	+
Manner				−	
Opinions					+

(Continued)

TABLE 13.4
(Continued)

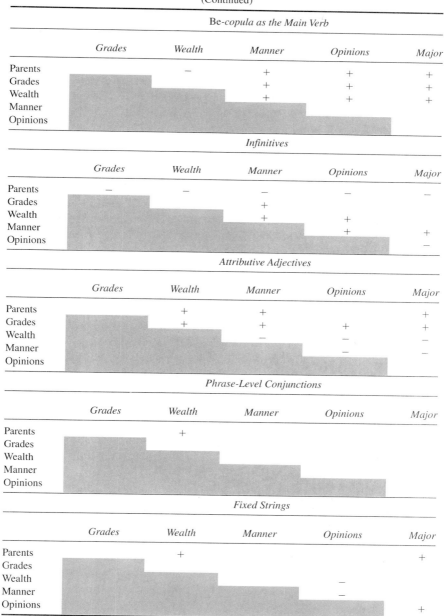

Be-*copula as the Main Verb*

	Grades	Wealth	Manner	Opinions	Major
Parents		−	+	+	+
Grades			+	+	+
Wealth			+	+	+
Manner					
Opinions					

Infinitives

	Grades	Wealth	Manner	Opinions	Major
Parents	−	−	−	−	−
Grades			+		
Wealth			+	+	
Manner				+	
Opinions					+
					−

Attributive Adjectives

	Grades	Wealth	Manner	Opinions	Major
Parents		+	+		+
Grades		+	+	+	+
Wealth			−	−	−
Manner				−	−
Opinions					

Phrase-Level Conjunctions

	Grades	Wealth	Manner	Opinions	Major
Parents		+			
Grades					
Wealth					
Manner					
Opinions					

Fixed Strings

	Grades	Wealth	Manner	Opinions	Major
Parents		+			+
Grades					
Wealth					
Manner				−	
Opinions				−	+

In essays of Korean speakers, the Parents prompt also led to the highest frequencies of present-tense and infinitives usage, whereas the Manner compositions included the lowest rates of present-tense constructions. The usage of infinitives in Korean speakers' text appears to be markedly different from that in the compositions of NSs, Chinese, or Japanese, examined earlier. Whereas in the essays of NSs, Chinese, and Japanese speakers on the Parents prompts frequencies of the infinitive usage are lower than in essays on most other prompts, the Parents prompt induced the highest median rates of infinitives in Korean speaker texts.

Private verbs, usually associated with emotive explanations of personal views and texts dealing with self-expression, are most common in Major texts, which directly require writers to elaborate on their personal views and considerations in choosing their academic programs.

There is little doubt that Manner, Opinions, and Major writing tasks induce high rates of *be*-copula constructions in the essays of many NSs and NNSs alike. Thus, the finding that these three topics have the same effect on the text production of Korean speakers is not surprising.

However, the rate of attributive adjectives in Korean speaker texts follows the distribution patterns identified earlier in NS, Chinese, and Japanese prose; that is, high rates of these descriptors are found in Major, Opinions, and Manner compositions and comparatively lower frequencies in Wealth, Parents, and Grades essays, respectively.

As in the texts of Japanese speakers, in the texts of Korean speakers, the various prompts made little difference on the rates of phrase-level conjunctions. Furthermore, the uses of fixed strings in Korean composition do not seem to vary greatly across prompts. Opinions essays included fewer of them than Wealth or Manner prompts, and the Major texts more than Parents or Opinions.

ESSAYS OF VIETNAMESE SPEAKERS

Table 13.5 lists significant differences between median rates of features in essays of Vietnamese speakers. In general terms, across the six writing tasks, the essays of Vietnamese speakers displayed patterns of feature use that are both similar to and different from those identified earlier in the essays of NS, Chinese, Japanese, and Korean speakers. For example, as in NS prose, the frequencies of first-person pronouns in Parents texts are similar to those across the other five prompts. Also, as in NS and Chinese speakers' Grades compositions, the rates of these pronouns in the writing of Vietnamese speakers are greater in Wealth, Manner, Opinion, and Major texts.

However, in the essays of NS, Chinese, and Japanese speakers, the Opinions prompt induced consistently higher rates of third-person pronouns

TABLE 13.5
Cross-Prompt Comparisons of Top 10 Features in Vietnamese Speakers' Texts

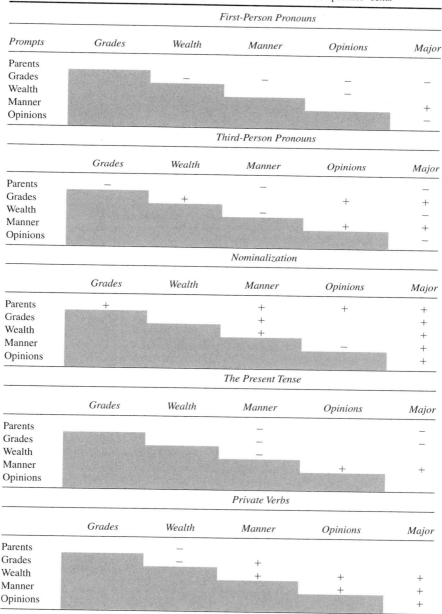

First-Person Pronouns

Prompts	Grades	Wealth	Manner	Opinions	Major
Parents					
Grades		−	−	−	−
Wealth				−	
Manner					+
Opinions					−

Third-Person Pronouns

Prompts	Grades	Wealth	Manner	Opinions	Major
Parents	−		−		−
Grades		+		+	+
Wealth			−		−
Manner				+	+
Opinions					−

Nominalization

Prompts	Grades	Wealth	Manner	Opinions	Major
Parents	+		+	+	+
Grades			+		+
Wealth			+		+
Manner				−	+
Opinions					+

The Present Tense

Prompts	Grades	Wealth	Manner	Opinions	Major
Parents			−		−
Grades			−		−
Wealth			−		
Manner				+	+
Opinions					

Private Verbs

Prompts	Grades	Wealth	Manner	Opinions	Major
Parents		−			
Grades		−	+		
Wealth			+	+	+
Manner				+	+
Opinions					+

(Continued)

TABLE 13.5
(Continued)

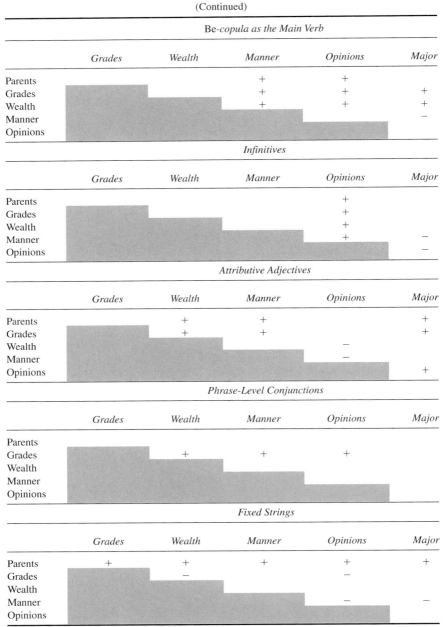

Be-*copula as the Main Verb*

	Grades	Wealth	Manner	Opinions	Major
Parents			+	+	
Grades			+	+	+
Wealth			+	+	+
Manner					−
Opinions					

Infinitives

	Grades	Wealth	Manner	Opinions	Major
Parents				+	
Grades				+	
Wealth				+	
Manner				+	−
Opinions					−

Attributive Adjectives

	Grades	Wealth	Manner	Opinions	Major
Parents		+	+		+
Grades		+	+		+
Wealth				−	
Manner				−	
Opinions					+

Phrase-Level Conjunctions

	Grades	Wealth	Manner	Opinions	Major
Parents					
Grades		+	+	+	
Wealth					
Manner					
Opinions					

Fixed Strings

	Grades	Wealth	Manner	Opinions	Major
Parents	+	+	+	+	+
Grades		−		−	
Wealth					
Manner				−	−
Opinions					

than other topics. The usage of third-person pronouns in the compositions of Vietnamese speakers does not show a proximate trend. Parents texts elicited the highest usage rates of these pronouns, followed by Opinions, Wealth, and Major, respectively.

Major and Manner writing tasks determined the preponderance of nominalizations and attributive adjectives in student texts in all language groups, including the Vietnamese. Similar to the pattern of present-tense occurrences in Korean speakers' text, the Parents prompt elicited the highest rate of generalizations and statements of belief. Patterns of private verb uses in the essays of Vietnamese speakers are similar only to those in the compositions of Chinese speakers. Manner, Opinions, and Major essays of Vietnamese speakers contained also high rates of constructions with copula *be,* and the Opinions prompt induced particularly high frequencies of infinitive uses. Unlike the Major essays of NSs, Chinese, or Japanese, the Vietnamese speaker prose on the Major prompt does not display a preponderance of infinitive structures.

Phrase conjunction uses do not appear to be particularly prompt-dependent in the essays of Vietnamese speakers, nor were they in those of NSs, Chinese, Japanese, or Korean speakers. However, breaking with the pattern for the fixed string usage that predominates in Manner, Opinions, and Major compositions of NS, Chinese, and Japanese speakers, the Grades compositions of the Vietnamese speakers contained the highest rates of fixed expressions. On the other hand, as with NS and Japanese speaker Parents texts, Parents essays of Vietnamese included their lowest occurrences.

ESSAYS OF INDONESIAN SPEAKERS

Information on cross-prompt comparisons of features median rates in essays of Indonesian speakers is illustrated in Table 13.6. Unlike the texts examined earlier, compositions of Indonesian speakers displayed the highest rates of first-person pronouns in response to the Manner and Major prompts, whereas Opinions and Wealth induced the lowest rates of these features. The depersonalization of context by means of reduced first-person pronoun usage in Parents essays of Indonesian speakers is further reflected in the highest rates of third-person pronouns on this topic.

The greatest frequencies of nominalizations and private verbs are found in Major essays, followed by Grades and Manner. Departing from the patterns of the present-tense uses in generalizations and statements of belief in NS, Chinese, and Japanese speakers' compositions, the essays of Indonesian speakers do not exhibit marked differences in the frequencies of present-tense constructions across the six prompts. However, the lives of the rich

TABLE 13.6

Cross-Prompt Comparisons of Top 10 Features in Indonesian Speakers' Texts

First-Person Pronouns

Prompts	Grades	Wealth	Manner	Opinions	Major
Parents		−	+	−	+
Grades		−	+	−	+
Wealth			+		+
Manner				−	
Opinions					+

Third-Person Pronouns

	Grades	Wealth	Manner	Opinions	Major
Parents	−		−		
Grades		+		+	+
Wealth			−	+	
Manner				+	+
Opinions					−

Nominalization

	Grades	Wealth	Manner	Opinions	Major
Parents					+
Grades		−		−	
Wealth			+		+
Manner				−	+
Opinions					+

The Present Tense

	Grades	Wealth	Manner	Opinions	Major
Parents				−	
Grades				−	
Wealth					
Manner					
Opinions					

Private Verbs

	Grades	Wealth	Manner	Opinions	Major
Parents	+	−	+	+	+
Grades		−			+
Wealth			+	+	+
Manner				−	+
Opinions					+

(Continued)

TABLE 13.6
(Continued)

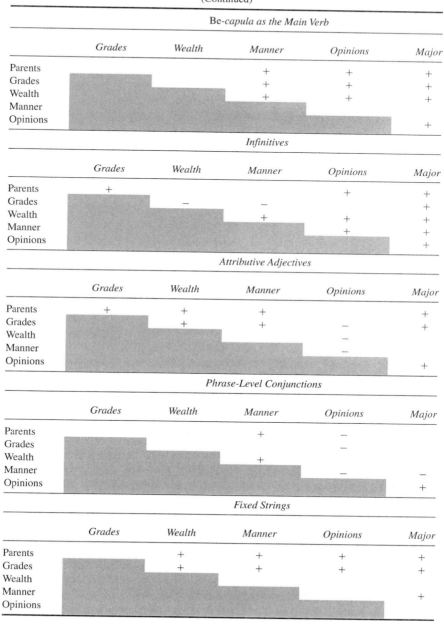

Be-*capula as the Main Verb*

	Grades	Wealth	Manner	Opinions	Major
Parents			+	+	+
Grades			+	+	+
Wealth			+	+	+
Manner					
Opinions					+

Infinitives

	Grades	Wealth	Manner	Opinions	Major
Parents	+			+	+
Grades		−	−		+
Wealth			+	+	+
Manner				+	+
Opinions					+

Attributive Adjectives

	Grades	Wealth	Manner	Opinions	Major
Parents	+	+	+		+
Grades		+	+	−	+
Wealth				−	
Manner				−	
Opinions					+

Phrase-Level Conjunctions

	Grades	Wealth	Manner	Opinions	Major
Parents			+	−	
Grades				−	
Wealth			+		
Manner				−	−
Opinions					+

Fixed Strings

	Grades	Wealth	Manner	Opinions	Major
Parents		+	+	+	+
Grades		+	+	+	+
Wealth					
Manner					+
Opinions					

and famous described in Wealth compositions of Indonesian speakers gave rise to the highest rates of attributive adjectival constructions. Nonetheless, Major and Manner prompts also created similar contexts with frequent uses of attributive adjectives, as they did in the texts of other language groups.

The Manner topic in Indonesian speakers' essays induced the highest rates of phrase conjunctions. Overall, however, the rates of conjunction use in texts of most speakers in all language groups do not seem to be prompt-dependent. Counter to the fixed string trends identified in the texts earlier in this chapter, the Indonesian speaker essays about Wealthy singers and movie stars contained the highest rates of idiomatic expressions. On the other hand, Major and Opinions texts of Indonesian speakers incorporate higher frequencies of these features than either Parents or Grades texts.

ESSAYS OF ARABIC SPEAKERS

As the data in Table 13.7 demonstrate, the essays of Arabic speakers exhibited somewhat different patterns of feature uses than those found in texts for speakers of other languages. For instance, the usage of first-person pronouns seemed largely uniform across all topics, with the exception of Grades and Opinions when compared to the rates of pronoun use in Parents texts.

On the other hand, third-person pronouns are used in different patterns across various topics. Unlike Parents essays of Chinese, Japanese, and Korean speakers, for instance, which did not contain high frequencies of these features, third-person pronouns predominated in Parents texts, followed by Wealth, Grades, Opinions, and Major. In addition, nominalizations appear very frequently in not only the Major texts but also Grades essays, where they are employed at similar rates.

The frequency rates of the present-tense constructions did not vary substantially across all texts written by speakers of Arabic, and Wealth essays elicited the greatest frequencies of these structures, compared to other prompts. Another distinction in the patterns of feature use in the prose of Arabic speakers is in the employment of private verbs, which are found in greatest frequencies in Major and lowest in Parents texts. This pronounced dependence of the private verb use on the prompt is not found in the texts of other NNSs mentioned earlier.

Although in the compositions of NS, Chinese, Japanese, Korean, and Vietnamese speakers the structures with *be*-copula were concentrated predominantly in Manner, Opinions, and Major texts, in the essays of Arabic speakers, their highest frequencies were identified in the Manner, Wealth, and Grades prose. The lowest rates of *be*-constructions were found in Major essays. Overall, however, copula *be* seemed to be similarly common in essays across the prompts. The rates of infinitives in Manner, Opinion, and Major

TABLE 13.7
Cross-Prompt Comparisons of Top 10 Features in Arabic Speakers' Texts

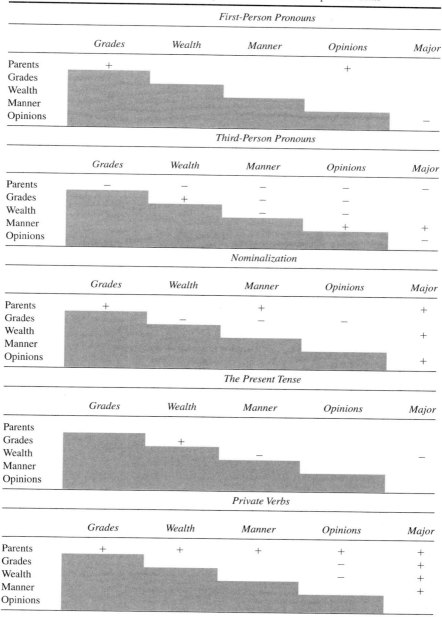

First-Person Pronouns

	Grades	Wealth	Manner	Opinions	Major
Parents	+			+	
Grades					
Wealth					
Manner					
Opinions					−

Third-Person Pronouns

	Grades	Wealth	Manner	Opinions	Major
Parents	−	−	−	−	−
Grades		+	−	−	
Wealth			−	−	
Manner				+	+
Opinions					−

Nominalization

	Grades	Wealth	Manner	Opinions	Major
Parents	+		+		+
Grades		−	−	−	
Wealth					+
Manner					
Opinions					+

The Present Tense

	Grades	Wealth	Manner	Opinions	Major
Parents					
Grades		+			
Wealth			−		−
Manner					
Opinions					

Private Verbs

	Grades	Wealth	Manner	Opinions	Major
Parents	+	+	+	+	+
Grades					+
Wealth				−	+
Manner				−	+
Opinions					+

(Continued)

TABLE 13.7
(Continued)

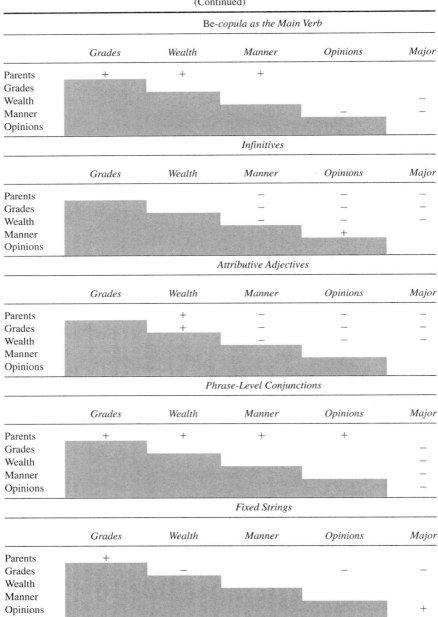

Be-*copula as the Main Verb*

	Grades	Wealth	Manner	Opinions	Major
Parents	+	+	+		
Grades					
Wealth					−
Manner				−	−
Opinions					

Infinitives

	Grades	Wealth	Manner	Opinions	Major
Parents			−	−	−
Grades			−	−	−
Wealth			−	−	−
Manner				+	
Opinions					

Attributive Adjectives

	Grades	Wealth	Manner	Opinions	Major
Parents		+	−	−	−
Grades		+	−	−	−
Wealth			−	−	−
Manner					
Opinions					

Phrase-Level Conjunctions

	Grades	Wealth	Manner	Opinions	Major
Parents	+	+	+	+	
Grades					−
Wealth					−
Manner					−
Opinions					−

Fixed Strings

	Grades	Wealth	Manner	Opinions	Major
Parents	+				
Grades		−		−	−
Wealth					
Manner					
Opinions					+

texts also seemed to be distinct from those in Parents, Grades, and Wealth essays, as has been the noted in earlier examination of text features in compositions of speakers of other language.

Unlike the rates of attributive adjectives and conjunctions in the essays of speakers of other languages, in texts of Arabic speakers, the greatest frequencies of attributive adjectives and phrase-level conjunctions are employed in addressing the Wealth prompt. Furthermore, in distinction from the essays examined earlier in this chapter, in Arabic speaker essays, there were only a few notable differences in the median rates of the fixed string usage. The Grades essays contained the highest rates of these expressions, with the lowest found in responses to the Opinions prompt.

In general terms, despite their superficial similarity of construction, prompts for writing tasks and placement tests may have different effects on the text that NSs and NNSs alike produce in response. One of the most important considerations in syntactic and lexical prompt contents is that many of the lexis and syntactic constructions in the wording of the prompt are repeated directly or with modifications in the student texts. Thus, there is little doubt that to a great extent, the quality of the text in student writing is determined by the grammar and vocabulary in the prompt itself.

However, it is important to keep in mind that speakers of different languages socialized in different cultures with diverse discourse and rhetorical traditions may construct texts with identifiably distinct patterns of feature usage.

The summary of the chapter's findings:

- The Major prompt elicited most personal narratives and statements of personal belief, marked by the highest frequencies of first-person pronouns and private verbs.
- Also, this prompt, the wording of which contained four nominalizations, led to the greatest frequencies of these constructions in texts of all language groups.
- For speakers of all seven languages, the texts on the Opinion prompt contained the highest rates of infinitives.
- In the texts of NSs, as well as Korean and Vietnamese speakers, the Manner prompt led to the lowest rates of the present-tense uses. The Opinion prompt had a similar effect on the texts of Chinese speakers.
- Manner, Opinions, and Major prompts elicited the highest rates of *be*-copula as a main clause verb in essays of speakers of six languages, except Arabic.
- Manner, Opinions, and Major prompts also induced the greatest frequencies of phrase-level conjunctions in the texts of NSs and Chinese

speakers, whereas Manner and Major prompts elicited the highest rates in essays of Indonesian speakers. By and large, various prompts had no effect on the median rates of conjunctions in Japanese, Vietnamese, or Korean speaker texts.

- These three prompts also led to the highest rates of fixed strings in the NS, Chinese, Japanese, and Indonesian speakers. However, prompts seem to have little influence in the fixed string usage in the essays of Vietnamese, Korean, and Arabic speakers.

The thematic and contextual content of the prompt also influences the quality of the text that emerges in student responses. The prompts intended to elicit argumentation/exposition essays are usually constructed by means of summarizing two (or more) opposing positions on an issue, and writers are expected to support one of these by means of argumentation or information derived from their personal experiences. However, it is important to keep in mind that the more appeal one of the positions has to the students who write the response essays, that is, the easier the choice between the two positions is to make, the simpler the syntactic constructions become in student texts. For example, the Parents, Grades, and Wealth prompts may require student writers to actually consider both aspects of the topic. Although while taking a placement test clearly may not be the best time to ponder issues in any degree of depth, Parents, Grades, and Wealth prompts generated relatively diverse range of responses. For instance, the Parents and Grades prompts touch on the quandary familiar to most parents and teachers but not necessarily children and students. The Wealth prompt may speak of the sentiments of working adults who toil in their offices for years and little pay rather than young people at the beginning of their careers.

On the other hand, the contexts of Manner, Opinions, and Major prompts, constructed superficially similarly to those dealing with Parents, Grades, and Wealth, resulted in large numbers of responses with relatively simple contexts and linguistic and lexical constructions. A vast majority of students found it obvious that enjoyable and entertaining classes are preferable to formal and serious classroom Manner, that children should be allowed to form their own Opinions, and that Majors should be chosen based on one's personal interests rather than future employment opportunities. One of the outcomes of the ease with which writers made their choices of positions and arguments to support them is that they invested little effort and thought in their texts. They simply wrote down what they thought on many previous occasions when sitting in formal classes, being lectured by their parents, or filling out university application forms. In this sense, responses to the Manner, Opinion, and Major prompts do not require writers to do any work beyond simply stating what they already know.

Thus, counter to the existing popular wisdom that university students can best write on topics that are close to their personal experiences, the degree of exposure and/or a way of thinking about a particular issue may influence the quality of the resulting text. In fact, the greater writers' familiarity and experience with a topic is and the easier it is to write about, the simpler the text can be. In the case of placement essays, however, simplicity is not always a virtue.

IV

Conclusion

Although the analyses and discussions of data in this book are interesting in and of themselves, they can also be useful in developing curricula and materials for teaching the most important syntactic and linguistic features employed in essay texts. For this purpose, chapter 14 presents applications of the study findings to identifying priorities in L2 language pedagogy and curriculum specifically geared toward academic writing. Based on the analysis of features uses in chapters 6–10, Part II, the pooled data in NNS texts were ranked relative to those in NS essays. The divergences of NS and NNS ranks of features can serve as general guides to focused instruction in L2 grammar and vocabulary. Chapter 14 is structured to examine the order of priorities in teaching, beginning with the features in greatest need of attention.

Chapter 15 follows with a brief note on strategic implications for L2 writing instruction. The importance of attention and noticing in L2 learning is emphasized, together with possible outcomes of the study for classroom teaching and material design. Most important, the Epilogue touches on issues in teacher training and preparation for helping university-bound learners attain academic writing skills. If the goal of L2 teaching is to prepare students for the tasks they need to perform in the academy, it is incumbent on teachers to help learners acquire the tools for academic survival.

14

Determining Priorities in Teaching and Curriculum

The data discussed in chapters 6–10, Part II, are based on analysis of the pooled frequency rates and ranges of the feature usage in all NS and NNS essays (i.e., 1,457 essays written to six prompts to comprise the total of 434,768 words). The chapters in Part II discussed large amounts of data, and in those chapters, the features are presented in the order of their priority in sentence construction, for example, beginning with nouns and noun phrase elements, followed by the verb phrase, as well as adjectives, adverbs, and clauses. It is also important, however, to identify the priorities of the features based on their prevalence in the texts for practical applications, such as teaching, curriculum development, and/or materials design.

To this end, the pooled data of median frequency rates for all features across NNS student groups were ranked in order of their prevalence in the essays relative to that in NS texts.[1] It is possible to think of these rankings in terms of rankings of universities published annually in various media and school guides. Specifically, the median rates of features in NS essays

---

[1] An ongoing debate continues whether NS uses of text features should determine the target for NNS writers. This issue is identified explicitly in the term ''the target language'' in which learners set out to attain proficiency that, by definition, NSs of any variety of English already have (B. Kachru, 1992). In the case of NS student essay texts, because NSs already have native proficiency in English, they can be taught to improve their writing skills with far greater ease than L2 learners, who first need to learn the language to be able to write in it.

were ranked from the most frequently used features to the least frequently used, and then those of each L1 group of NNS were ranked independently. The lower the number, the more frequently the feature showed up in the essays. As the last step, the rank of that particular feature in each group of NNSs was identified according to the corresponding rank of a particular feature in NS text. For example, in NS essays infinitives were the 2nd most frequently used feature; however, they were the 3rd most prevalent feature in Chinese and 11th in Korean texts. The tied ranks are resolved according to the classical statistical procedure: The mean of the tied ranks is assigned to each of the ties. For example, if two features had identical median frequency rates and both share the 16th place, their assigned ranks are 16.5 each, and the following rank would be 18. If three features share the 20th place, then they are all assigned rank 21, and the following rank would be 23.

The 10 highest median frequency rates are presented in Table 14.1 together with their corresponding NNS median rates. In both NS and NNS essays written to the test prompts, the uses of the present tense clearly have the highest medians, as is inevitable in tasks that require writers to make nonspecific observations and comments. The same can be said about the uses of infinitives, third-person pronouns, and attributive adjectives.

The rest of this chapter discusses clusters of relevant and related ranked features to specifically identify curricular goals that can be addressed in a coherent form in L2 language development and instruction. Subsequent sections in this chapter include other excerpted rows from the complete list of rankings relative to the order of frequency in NS essays, which is included in Appendix A.

TABLE 14.1
10 Highest NS and Corresponding NNS Median Frequency Rates, by Rank

Features	NS	CH	JP	KR	VT	IN	AR
Present tense	1	1	1	1	1	1	1
Infinitives	2	3	2	11	6	5	4
Third-person pronouns	3	2	3	2	2	2	3
Attributive adjectives	4	5	7	9	7.5	8	6
Fixed strings	5	27	20	24	18	28	23
Phrase-level coordinators	6	4	5	3	3	4	2
Be as a main verb	7	6	6	4	5	3	5
Private verbs	8	8	10	10	10	6	11
First-person pronouns	9	13	4	7	4	9.5	13
Nominalization	10	15	15.5	16.5	15	15	12

TOP-TIER PRIORITIES

Clearly, the present tense represents the most frequently used feature in the essays of all student groups. However, with the exception of the tied ranks for infrequently used features (see Appendix A for further information), most similarities end where they begin at the frequency rates for the present tense.

The most glaring disparity in NS and NNS ranks of feature frequencies undoubtedly falls on the uses of fixed strings (Table 14.2). Although idiomatic expressions occupy a prominent fifth place in NS texts, they are far less common in the text of all NNS, with their ranks largely between 20 and 28. Clearly, the conclusion that can be drawn from this difference in feature uses is that NNSs need to learn more contextualized and advanced academic vocabulary, as well as idioms and collocations to develop a substantial lexical arsenal to improve their writing in English.

Similarly, vague nouns *(people, world, life, kid, society)* need to be replaced by those with greater semantic and lexical content. The employment of too few nominalizations and gerunds can be addressed in instruction devoted to increasing the NNS range of accessible vocabulary and idiomatic expressions. Vague nouns are a characteristic of conversational and informal register, whereas nominalizations and gerunds are far more common in formal academic discourse. Keeping in mind that the majority of NNS writers whose essays were included in the analysis were holders of U.S. associates degrees or graduate students, it seems evident that mere exposure to academic texts, such as those found in textbooks or other readings, does not lead to NNSs' learning the range of lexis and the collocational uses of vocabulary that they need to produce appropriate text and discourse in their writing.

Other evidence that supports a high degree of need for teaching idiomatic vocabulary use comes from disparate ranks for various lexical classes of nouns (Table 14.3), such as interpretive *(cause, idea, knowledge, opinion, success)*, enumerative *(advantage, disadvantage, fact, period, plan, problem, reason, type)*, and language activity nouns *(contrast, example, language, proof, sentence, story, talk)*, all of which are lexically uncomplicated and are

TABLE 14.2
Rank Order of Median Frequency Rates of Fixed Strings and Some Other Nouns

Features	NS	CH	JP	KR	VT	IN	AR
Fixed strings	5	27	20	24	18	28	23
Nominalization	10	15	15.5	16.5	15	15	12
Gerunds	14.5	22	23	23	19.5	19	16
Vague nouns	17	12	13	6	12	12	10

TABLE 14.3
Rank Order of Median Frequency for Common Nouns and Expecting Verbs

Features	NS	CH	JP	KR	VT	IN	AR
Interpretive nouns	38.5	28	24	22	26.5	29	21.5
Enumerative nouns	43	40	41.5	35	35	41	37
Language activity nouns	59	47	41.5	47	37	40	43.5
Resultative nouns	59	50	58.5	57.5	48	49	59.5
Expecting/tentative verbs	34	29	21	16.5	29	20	30

overused in NNS essays, relative to NS essays. Similarly, the simple resultative nouns *(result, end, outcome)* were also used very frequently in NNS texts, compared to those of NSs. The data also demonstrate that NNSs may have a limited lexical range of verbs, for example, tentative/expecting verbs *(attempt, expect, like, plan, try, want).*

The uses of first-person pronouns as a characteristic of personal narratives in Japanese, Korean, and Vietnamese texts, as well recounts of past-time events and experiences reflected in the high NNS employment of the past tense represents an important venue in L2 essays (Table 14.4). Nonetheless, research has shown that these are not always appropriate in formal academic texts, which largely require displays of knowledge and argumentation. As has been noted, giving examples to illustrate and clarify one's views and position is strongly encouraged in writing instruction, but in NNS essays, examples are employed far more often than in NS texts (NS rank 51 and NNS between 34.5 and 38.5). In many cases, NNSs overuse exemplification to a point where example giving and recounts of past-time events represent the main content of their academic text (see a detailed discussion in chap. 10).

In addition, if NNSs are to be enabled to produce appropriate academic texts and develop their arguments, second-person pronouns that mark direct appeals to the reader should be replaced by expressing ideas with content and argumentation. Furthermore, in NNS essays, public verbs *(admit, agree, argue, explain, promise, repeat, say, speak, state, tell, write)* are more

TABLE 14.4
Rank Order of Median Frequency of Personal Narrative Features

Features	NS	CH	JP	KR	VT	IN	AR
First-person pronouns	9	13	4	7	4	9.5	13
Past tense	13	10	9	5	7.5	9.5	33
Exemplification	51	42.5	38.5	41	35	34.5	39
Second-person pronouns	59	23.5	37	26	32.5	59	40
Public verbs	45.5	19	25	25	19.5	22.5	19

popular than in those of NSs. The frequency of public verb use marks narration of conversations and direct reporting of one's opinions, which is also characteristic of telling one's views without arguing for a particular position. To accomplish the goal of expanding students' language base, vocabulary and collocations, and discourse conventions, NNS academically bound students need to be taught not only what textual devices are considered to be less appropriate but also how ideational content and persuasive discourse are constructed in Anglo-American discourse.

Another feature of language use that appears to be in urgent need of attention deals with the issues of text cohesion. In NS essays, advance and retroactive nouns (Table 14.5) that have the main function of establishing cohesion between text ideas and flow are ranked far higher in NS than in NNS essays. NNSs seem to rely more on phrase-level coordinators, sentence transitions, and demonstrative pronouns to provide cohesion. Although it is evident that NNSs need to be taught to employ fewer of these features, a more important objective can be to provide students a greater range of syntactic and lexical means of developing cohesion in their text.

Although this finding may hold few surprises for experienced ESL teachers and curriculum developers, it implies a certain degree of urgency. It may not be possible for NNS students to write good L2 essays without a substantial increase in their vocabulary range and collocational fluency even after they have achieved advanced levels of L2 proficiency to enroll as juniors and graduate students in U.S. universities. As has been mentioned, a majority of NSs who wrote the essays were brand-new first-year students.

Many language features discussed in this analysis that have been identified as underused in NNS essays, compared to those of NS students, largely deal with issues of familiarity with and access to syntactic and lexical features associated with academic and formal written discourse and register. Similarly, the linguistic features that predominate in NNS essays in many cases reflect those that are characteristic of conversational and spoken English, as well as those transferred from L1 to L2 discourse and text paradigms. Syntactic and lexical features appropriate in formal written register are rarely addressed in L2 writing instruction because in the teaching of the writing process (Zamel, 1982, 1983) and "communicative writing" to

TABLE 14.5
Rank Order of Median Frequency of Cohesive Features

Features	NS	CH	JP	KR	VT	IN	AR
Advanced/retroactive nouns	21	42.5	41.5	38.5	49	42.5	32
Phrase-level coordinators	6	4	5	3	3	4	2
Sentence transitions	28	17	15.5	14	17	16.5	17.5
Demonstrative pronouns	24	20	26	18	21.5	22.5	14.5

NNSs, a greater value is placed on expressing "personal feeling, experience, or reactions" (Reid, 1993, pp. 30–31) than on the norms and features of academic discourse and its attendant range of lexical and syntactic variety. On the other hand, it is evident that however immature the writing of NS first-year students and however conversational their writing style, their familiarity with and access to the conventions of academic written text and syntactic and lexical range far exceeds that of NNSs with greater academic exposure and training.

SECOND-TIER PRIORITIES

In addition to the essential work on vocabulary, collocations, and the fundamental conventions of academic discourse, the range of syntactic structures in NNS essays also requires expansion and advancement (Table 14.6).

Attributive and predicative adjectives have divergent syntactic functions. Attributive adjectives are the most common type of noun and noun phrase modifiers that provide description, add definition to abstract nouns, and develop cohesion in text. On the other hand, predictive adjectives serve as part of clause predicates following *be* or other linking verbs. Predicative adjectives are usually found in syntactically simple structures, for example, *students are responsible*. Because in academic texts, the primary function of adjectives is to provide descriptions and express attitudes, NS essays tended toward attributive adjectives (rank #4) that were not as common in NNS prose (ranks from 6 to 9). In English, the syntactic devices for developing descriptions are numerous, and it is apparent that they may need to occupy a relatively high priority in L2 writing instruction. The divergent textual functions of adjectives can be relatively easily addressed in teaching to encourage descriptive development without an imbalance in adjective uses in text.

The copula *be*, as an attendant feature of predicative adjectives, is often considered to be devoid of ideational content. The simplistic syntactic structures manifested in the NNSs' high rates of *be* as the main verb (as well

TABLE 14.6
Rank Order of Median Frequency of Prevalent Syntactic Features

Features	NS	CH	JP	KR	VT	IN	AR
Attributive adjectives	4	5	7	9	7.5	8	6
Predicative adjectives	12	7	8	8	9	7	7
Be as a main verb	7	6	6	4	5	3	5
Infinitives	2	3	2	11	6	5	4
Passive voice	19	33	28	33	39	39	31

as other linking verbs, such as *become*) were not as prevalent in NS texts as in NNS prose. Combined with instruction on the functions of predicative adjectives, L2 learners can be taught that the use of *be* provides little lexical advantage in academic texts and, worse still, frequent uses of *be* as the main verb impart a sense of expressive paucity and comparative simplicity. This is not to say that *be* verbs can and should be avoided, but in NNS text, their frequency can certainly be reduced.

Although infinitives are the second most prevalent features in NS prose, it appears that most L2 students need additional work to deal with the textual functions of infinitives. In most ESL grammar textbooks, infinitives (as well as gerunds) are often listed as obscure lexical items that follow certain verbs (e.g., *decide, hope,* and *promise* are followed by infinitives and *enjoy, go,* and *avoid* are followed by gerunds). However, the role of infinitives in constructions of purpose, reduced noun clauses, or information reporting is rarely addressed in any depth.

The uses and functions of the passive voice in academic text are numerous, despite the fact that the passive voice is discouraged in composition writing. In NS text, passive constructions were common, but in accordance with the negative view of passive uses, NNS texts did not contain as many of these structures (ranks between 28 and 39). It is important to note that much research on academic text carried out in the domain of corpus analysis points to high frequencies of passive voice constructions in such diverse disciplines as engineering, sociology, natural sciences, psychology, and education. Thus, for academically bound NNSs, instruction on how and when the passive voice is employed in context and discourse is highly desirable.

To express the power of their conviction and create persuasive essays, NNSs rely on emphatics, amplifiers, and universal pronouns (*every-* and *no-* words) (Table 14.7). However, overstatements and exaggerations are not considered to be an appropriate means of creating persuasive text in academic discourse in English, and L2 students need to be taught that amplification is not considered to be appropriate in academic texts in English and that the writer's conviction is conveyed by means of detailed descriptions and thorough argumentation.

TABLE 14.7
Rank Order of Median Frequency of Overstatements and Impersonal Structures

Features	NS	CH	JP	KR	VT	IN	AR
Emphatics	18	11	12	13	11	14	9
Amplifiers	11	9	11	12	13	11	8
Universal pronouns	41	30	30.5	27	28	38	25.5
It-subject (cleft)	31.5	49	46	57.5	46	51	43.5

Impersonal constructions with *it*-cleft are syntactically complex, and their uses in English academic text are often conventionalized. The uses of this structure mark the text for a relatively formal register that is considered to be appropriate in university essays. The NS median frequency rank for *it*-cleft was substantially higher than those of NNSs, which ranged between 43.5 and 57.5. Because the text function of *it*-cleft is to project the writer's distance, impartiality, objectivity, and hedging in academic text, the syntactic complexities and the textual functions of the impersonal *it* structures may be one option for replacing the overused emphatics, amplifiers, and universal pronouns. A need for focused instruction on the importance of hedging and other distancing constructions is evident in the NNS data (see also hedging in the next section).

THIRD-TIER PRIORITIES

In conjunction with focusing on the syntactic and lexical features of text, expanding the learners repertoire of structures also needs to include verbal aspects, participles, the importance of hedging in academic prose, and adverb clauses (Table 14.8).

Although the teaching of verb tenses usually takes place together with progressive and perfect aspects, the data demonstrate that this approach may not need to be exclusive. Though many NNSs employ the past tense to recount personal experiences and stories, the disparities between NS and NNS uses of aspects appear to be greater still. The NS ranks for the progressive and the perfect aspects were far higher than those of NNSs. Generally, test essays are considered to be relatively static and require writers to produce texts based on their general thoughts and observations relevant to a particular theme. For this reason, the uses of progressive and perfect aspects in such texts are usually not expected to be prevalent and are more characteristic of spoken than written discourse. On the other hand, judging from NNS ranks for these features, neither progressive nor perfect aspect was hardly ever found in L2 text.

TABLE 14.8
Rank Order of Median Frequency of Verbal Features

Features	NS	CH	JP	KR	VT	IN	AR
Past tense	13	10	9	5	7.5	9.5	33
Progressive aspect	45.5	60	58.5	57.5	59.5	59	59.5
Present participles	23	38	41.5	43	42	48	59.5
Reduced adverb clauses	48	60	58.5	57.5	59.5	59	59.5

In the assessment of L2 writing, participles have been noted as markers of advanced language proficiency, and indeed, in NS texts they appear to be relatively common. Although in ESL textbooks and instruction participles are often presented as a part of reduced adverb and adjective clauses, in NS texts, participles were used with varied functions, such as adjectives. Notably, in NS prose, reduced adverb clauses ranked 48 and reduced adjective clauses 59 (tied for last place with several other features). The present and past participles in NS texts are used primarily in the function of adjectives (e.g., *bored students, entertaining class, concerned parents*). In fact, it is not the reduced adverb or adjective clauses that are in need of attention and teaching, but the adjectival uses of participles that need to become a more prominent component in L2 teaching curricula to expand NNSs' vocabulary and collocational range.

The uses of hedging represent an important facet of academic writing in English. Yet, their ranks in NNS text did not seem to match those in NS text (Table 14.9). For example, NSs employed more lexical and epistemic hedges *(actually, about, likely, potentially, probably)* but fewer frequency adverbs *(occasionally, sometimes, usually)*. Even though most lexical and epistemic hedges in NS essays were simple, frequency adverbs are far more prevalent in informal speech. Thus, it stands to reason that NNSs' accessible repertoire of hedges was restricted to those found in conversational discourse. Similarly, the predictive modal *(would)* that often serves as a syntactic hedge was far less popular in NNS than in NS texts. On the other hand, assertive pronouns *(some-* and *any-*words) with their vague and indeterminant meanings were used with greater proportional frequency in NNS essays than in those of NSs. The teaching of the meanings and discourse functions of hedging devices can take place in tandem with instruction on overstatements and exaggerations, although avoiding overstatements clearly has a higher priority.

In NNS prose, the ranks for complex sentences with various types of dependent clauses, such as adverb clauses of cause and condition, also present a mixed picture (Table 14.10). Whereas NNS essays rank high in uses of cause clauses, the ranks of conditional clauses seems to be relatively

TABLE 14.9
Rank Order of Median Frequency of Hedging Devices

Features	NS	CH	JP	KR	VT	IN	AR
Lexical hedges	26.5	37	35.5	32	38	44.5	46.5
Epistemic hedges	31.5	41	34	34	45	37	59.5
Frequency adverbs	59	52	58.5	57.5	50	50	51
Predictive modals	43	60	58.5	57.5	59.5	59	49.5
Assertive pronouns	36.5	26	30.5	30.5	31	26	28.5

TABLE 14.10
Rank Order of Median Frequency of Some Subordinate Clauses and Questions

Features	NS	CH	JP	KR	VT	IN	AR
Cause clauses	49	44	35.5	40	43.5	36	41
Condition clauses	35	36	38.5	38.5	47	42.5	46.5
Adjective clauses	20	23.5	22	30.5	26.5	18	17.5
Rhetorical questions	59	52	50	57.5	59.5	59	49.5

low, compared to those in NS texts. There is little doubt that, in academic discourse, elucidations of causal relationships between actions and events represents the meat and potatoes of argumentative writing. Test essays written to argumentation/exposition prompts are likely to promote frequent uses of causal explanations, but, as the NS rank implies, they do not necessarily have to be constructed as cause subordinate clauses. Clearly, NNSs need to expand their accessible means of describing causes and outcomes of events (note also a high rate of resultative nouns in NNS texts). In addition, condition clauses that mark more sophisticated lines of reasoning in argumentation/exposition discourse were not frequently employed in NNS texts. It is evident that NNS written argumentation and text development skills require an expansion of accessible ranges of complex sentence constructions.

Adjective clause uses are similarly somewhat unbalanced. Whereas essays of Korean, Vietnamese, and Chinese speakers contained too many, Indonesian and Arabic essays employed too few of them, compared to those in NS texts. Among complex sentences, adjective clauses are probably one of the simplest to use, nonetheless, they entail a certain amount of syntactic and lexical fluency. Their textual functions of providing expanded descriptions can be taught in conjunction with those of attributive and predicative adjectives.

On the other hand, the usage of rhetorical questions in NNSs essays also needs to be addressed, despite (or because of) the fact that they are often seen to be an acceptable means of establishing the rapport and direct interaction between the writer and the reader in non-Anglo-American rhetorical traditions. In all likelihood, NNSs transferred their preference for rhetorical questions in formal text as appropriate means of establishing writer–reader interaction and indirect persuasion from L1 to L2 discourse. However, the NS rank of 59 for rhetorical questions was the last in median frequencies, tied with median rates of other features rarely used. Therefore, it seems evident that even immature writers among NSs are aware of the fact that rhetorical questions are considered to be overly conversational and casual in formal text.

In composition instruction, however, because many conventions of formal writing have been rejected as restrictive, rhetorical questions are often described as journalistic, exploratory, or introductory attention getters. Although this approach to teaching the rare and specialized uses of rhetorical questions to NSs does not necessarily lead to their increased frequencies of use, in teaching L2 writing, instruction about the acceptability of direct questions in text may simply fit into learners' views on appropriate discourse paradigms and text features. L2 writing instruction needs to note that frequent uses of rhetorical questions in formal discourse, be it spoken or written, will clash with the expectations that most Anglo-American Academic readers have of discourse, usually to the disadvantage of the writer who uses rhetorical questions.

In sum, the ranks of frequently employed features of NS and NNS text can certainly help to determine priorities in curriculum development and instruction. It appears to be rather obvious that NNSs' language work needs to include a concerted effort to build their vocabulary, collocational, and syntactic range of accessible structures. It also seems to be obvious that it would be practically impossible to write a good essay without the necessary text-construction tools, even if NNSs' discourse and organizational skills are fully developed. In fact, judging from the disparate ranks of features in NS and NNS essays, the teaching of L2 lexical and syntactic features of text may not and should not be separated from the teaching of discourse organizational skills.

However, it is also obvious that merely providing L2 learners exposure to English discourse and text does not lead to a thorough learning of Anglo-American rhetorical conventions. In order to succeed in the Anglo-American academic environment, NNSs need to learn the text and discourse conventions of the Anglo-American academy. Furthermore, recent developments of new technology, means of communication, and business globalization across political, ethnic, and discourse boundaries continue to increase students' needs for proficiency in English. It seems rather clear that the economic hegemony of English is likely to be sustained for the foreseeable future. As an outcome, learning Anglo-American text and discourse conventions can allow NNS students not only to make choices but also to have opportunities, which, without the necessary language skills, they simply may not have (Walker, 1993).

One of the more interesting publications on the learning of L2 textual and rhetorical paradigms was not written by an applied linguist who analyzes discourse, but a teacher of L2 writing at a large U.S. university (Fox, 1994). She described persistent difficulties, strife, and unhappiness that many NNS students experience in the Anglo-American academy. The author emphasized that the dilemma has two possible solutions: Either the university has to change or the students have to. It may be, however, that neither is possible to the extent that would make ''the problem" disappear. An ability to construct intelligible text in a second or foreign language, however, represents one of the necessary characteristics of L2 proficiency and advanced literacy. Furthermore, in any language, educated adults are usually expected to display levels of L2 skills commensurate with their training and professional knowledge. The purpose of teaching L2 vocabulary, grammar, and text and discourse construction is to allow university students and graduates opportunities and respect commensurate with their academic standing.

15

Epilogue

The findings of this study clearly show that despite their many years of instruction in English, L2 students are not well prepared for their studies in the academy in the English medium of instruction, and most produce written discourse not too distant from that found in the texts of elementary school students (Bereiter & Scardamalia, 1985). The results of this study demonstrate that first-year NS students with only high school training in writing and composition have access to far greater ranges of syntactic structures, vocabulary, and collocations than even trained and highly advanced NNSs, most of whom are holders of U.S. academic degrees. Merely exposing NNS students to written academic text and engaging them in the writing process to encourage their self-expression do not lead to learners' being able to attain levels of English proficiency that approximates near-native even after several years of study. It is clear that even NNSs who have received years of L2 training need to substantially expand their accessible linguistic and lexical repertoire before they begin to approach those demonstrated in the placement essays of first-year NS students.

Specifically, academic essays of advanced NNS students at the junior- and graduate-level academic standing in U.S. universities tend to rely on personal narratives, examples without elaboration, and statements of belief to explain their positions in argumentation/exposition texts. In practically all cases, compared to NS essays, NNS texts employ too many vague and

interpretive nouns, private and expecting verbs, and *be*-copular and predicative adjectives as clause predicate constructions, all of which are more
typical of informal and spoken than written academic register (Biber,
1988). Furthermore, because in most cases NNS writing exhibits a weak lexical arsenal, many L2 writers resort to emphatics and amplifiers to convey
their views and convictions instead of explication and developed argumentation. In addition, L2 text further demonstrates a lack of cohesive features
beyond the prominent use of simple phrase-level conjunctions or cause
clauses. Overall, in their writing, NNSs employ a great number of lexical
and syntactic features of text that may not be particularly appropriate in
constructing academic texts. On the other hand, various advanced syntactic constructions that are commonly associated with academic texts seem to
be largely missing from NNS essays, for example, the passive voice, reduced
adverb and adjective clauses, *it*-cleft, predictive modal *would*, and stock
idiomatic expressions.

IMPLICATIONS FOR TEACHER TRAINING
AND THE TRAINING OF TRAINERS

In general terms, two types of reactions to the formal and rigid discourse
conventions in the academy have been adopted in preparatory programs
for both ESL/EAP teachers and students. The critical discourse analysis
and critical pedagogy movements propose to change the ways and discourse conventions of the academy. On the other hand, communicative
and process-based methodologies choose to overlook the fact that academic discourse conventions and expectations of learners' L2 proficiencies
have remained relatively constant in the past half a century, despite the
calls for their change. In the end, however, it is NNS students who bear the
brunt of the political trends in L2 and teacher training. In their desire to
benefit students and provide them with entertaining language work, teachers and teacher trainers alike in actuality seem to contribute to the very
socio-academic inequality that they are trying to make disappear.

Since the "revolution" that took place in the teaching of ESL and L2
writing in the late 1970s and 1980s, the teaching of formal academic written discourse and the attendant features of text has taken a backseat to
communicative teaching and naturalistic learning. One outcome of these
intuitively appealing approaches to attaining L2 proficiency is that teacher-
training programs have begun to focus on various aspects of classroom
teaching that have little to do with the teachers' knowledge of the subject
matter that they are employed to teach, that is, linguistic features of text, be
it spoken or written. Today, it would be difficult to find newly graduated

teachers who can, for example, make the learning of grammar productive for students and teach students to become aware and learn to notice. To be sure, every teacher can correct errors in student papers. However, usually, teaching involves far more than correcting and grading papers. As most administrators of academic ESL programs know from experience, it may be very hard to find an ESL instructor who can, for example, identify the subject in a sentence with several prepositional phrases and explain the benefits of subject and verb agreement.

The naturalistic approach to L2 teaching has spilled over into naturalistic methodologies for training teachers. It seems obscure to claim that advanced L2 skills need to be taught to students, if they are not actually taught to teachers. Enjoyable and relaxing language classes and teacher-training courses are unquestionably easier than having to study anything that requires serious studying, be it mathematics, chemistry, accounting, or the linguistic system of the English language.

As any advanced and proficient learner knows, high-level L2 skills are attained by means of hard work. Similarly, for teachers, achieving an advanced level of professional knowledge of language also takes a lot of work and persistence. For NNS students to move closer toward the language proficiency necessary in the academy, teachers who teach them need to obtain training in the linguistic systems of English (and possibly, in those of their students' L1s). Within the trickle-down knowledge flow of teaching, teacher trainers need to provide teachers the knowledge base on which they can build, if ultimately NNS students are to obtain the L2 skills that they demonstrably do not have to do well in their studies. To be sure, most NSs of English do not learn the conventions of advanced academic discourse naturalistically, and most go through many years of education in their first language to learn to produce formal written discourse. It is not obvious why according to communicative and process-centered methodologies for teaching, NNS students are expected to accomplish greater feats in a second language than most NS students aspire to in their first.

However, teachers cannot teach what they themselves do not know. If teachers work with academically bound students, the needs of both teachers and students should be addressed in teacher-training programs to prepare teachers to deal with the advanced syntactic and lexical structures expected in academic writing. To meet this goal, the training of teachers of English as a second language needs to provide a greater focus on language—beyond conversational discourse. In the end, teacher trainers and teachers may need to be reminded that the academic skills they themselves require in teaching and learning are not far removed from those of their NNS students.

LEARNING ADVANCED ACADEMIC SKILLS

The model of the writing process developed by Bereiter and Scardamalia (1985) explains that personal and past-time narratives, as well as statements of belief represent the simplest and most immediately accessible type of text that even basic writers can produce with ease. Knowledge-telling essays require writers merely to write down what they already know without accumulating and transforming their knowledge into a carefully thought out and organized discourse. In addition, Bereiter and Scardamalia emphasized that knowledge transforming entails advanced text-generating skills that require writers to analyze and integrate content, consider the expectations of the audience and the conventions of the academic genre, as well as employ the necessary language features and rhetorical structures within the frameworks of a particular genre. Knowledge telling and knowledge transforming represent different cognitive processes of producing text and discourse. The cognitive and mental processes needed to transform knowledge are far more advanced than those involved in knowledge telling and consequently require developed language skills.

Keeping in mind that knowledge transforming also takes place during reading, it is not clear whether NNS students in this study possess the language skills (e.g., syntactic and lexical) to process text in ways that can lead to writing essays beyond recounts of personal experiences and generalized statements of belief. The findings of this study point to the fact that exposing NNS students to academic text and discourse for many years does not seem to lead to nativelike uses of syntactic and lexical features of written text and, by outcome, cognitively advanced information processing. Thus, if syntactic and lexical features of L2 are not learned naturally even in the case of educated adults and if they are not taught by means of thorough and explicit instruction, it is actually not clear how NNS students can in fact attain the advanced L2 proficiency requisite for their success in the academy.

Investigations into the discourse and sentence-level features of academic writing in the disciplines carried out in the 1980s and 1990s have been very fruitful, and much useful data have been uncovered to benefit ESL teaching, curricula, and materials. Other studies have provided insights into the expectations of the faculty in the academy and the specific characteristics of the various types of academic genre in writing. Although ESL researchers and curriculum designers have learned a great deal about the language needs of academically bound NNSs, their findings have had a minimal influence on teaching L2 writing because the prevalent ESL pedagogy addresses preparation for English composition courses and process-centered writing practically to the exclusion of all other.

It seems striking that the reactions of faculty to the shortfalls in ESL writing, such as a lack of rhetorical organization, discourse coherence, and grammatical accuracy, have remained from the time when they were first investigated in the late 1970s. In standardized and institutional testing, the discourse and linguistic features that often indicate good quality of writing do not appear to have changed, either. What has changed, however, is the methodology for teaching ESL writing and composition. On the other hand, these changes seem to have made little difference in the NNSs' learning gains or improvements in their writing skills, evaluated outside ESL teaching. In fact, NNS university students become excellent knowledge tellers but not necessarily good writers (or learners of discourse and text construction) because they lack the fundamental language tools to enable them to continue learning.

Although there is little doubt that pedagogy based on communicative activities or the writing process is more enjoyable and creative than teaching students to construct rhetorically organized essays or attending to the issues of grammatical accuracy, the evaluative criteria of student writing outside English composition courses do not include communicative games or the writing process. As is the case with all students in educational institutions, learners who seek to advance their L2 skills enroll in academic ESL programs hoping to achieve their objectives because evaluation in the larger academic environment remains focused on the end product (see Horowitz, 1986; Johns, 1997; Santos, 1984; and other publications cited earlier in chap. 2).

ATTENTION, AWARENESS, AND NOTICING

The data presented in this book imply that NNS students who wrote the essays examined have been exposed to the characteristics of formal academic discourse. Their texts contain introductions that often copy portions of the prompt, as well as clearly marked divisions of text, such as *my first reason . . . , my second reason . . . , the third reason . . . ,* and *in conclusion. . . .* However, it is also apparent that despite their exposure to academic texts in the course of their study, NNS students have not been able to identify or did not care to employ other, less superficial characteristics of formal written text. That the wording of the prompt has great influence on the type of lexical and syntactic structures that find their way into L2 essay text is not a particularly novel finding. However, the reason for the effect of the linguistic features of the prompt on student text seems to be relatively easy to identify: Not only do NNS writers have a limited repertoire of lexis and syntax, but they have not attended to the essential features of academic discourse and text because they may simply not be aware of them. If L2 learners are not aware of the fact that somewhat rigid conventions govern how academic discourse and text are constructed, they may further be unaware of the fact that they were expected to learn them.

Recent research in applied linguistics has begun to underscore the importance of awareness and noticing that are key to L2. Citing substantial findings from psychology and cognitive science, Schmidt (1995) explained that in general, the value of noticing, attention, and awareness has not received much prominence in L2 research, despite the fact that cognitive scientists have long known that these mental processes are of crucial importance. He further explained that, for example, in learning academic writing a high degree of awareness of discourse structure can lead to learners' understanding how formal written discourse is constructed. Schmidt emphasized that an effective and productive learning environment must take advantage of all aspects of language learning, including developing explicit skills and implicit opportunities to maximize learning. However, in his view, awareness alone is not sufficient for learning: Knowing how something works does not enable one to actually perform the task. The teaching of ESL and its methodologies can benefit from research findings on how L2 is learned and what explicit instruction can contribute to improve the quality of student skills in grammar, vocabulary, and text production.

A key to successful learning also lies in practicing, a point that was examined in detail by Ellis (1985, 1994, 1997). Ellis, for instance, distinguished between communicative and formal language uses that can be approached and taught differently, depending on learning needs. The results of this study clearly demonstrate that NNS students have had substantial exposure to spoken and informal uses of language in communicative situations but demonstrably lack the lexical, syntactic, and text-construction skills essential in formal academic writing.

As has been mentioned, many, if not most, L2 essays examined in this study employ high rates of grammatical and vocabulary structures that are typically associated with informal speech rather than written discourse. It is also important to note that, evidently, NNS students in all language groups included in this study have received ample communicative training and have achieved high degrees of communicative fluency. Specifically, NNS students in all groups, except Japanese and Korean speakers, produced essays as long or longer than NS students did. In fact, Indonesian and Vietnamese speakers wrote essays, the average length of which substantially exceeded that of NS texts. However, fluency and communicative skills in writing seem to have little to do with the NNSs' ability to construct text according to the conventions and norms commonly expected in the formal written genre.

IMPLICATIONS IN THE CLASSROOM

It seems baffling that in many ESL and EAP programs, students are taught L2 skills without regard to the tasks that students are expected to and will need to perform once they complete their L2 training and move on to continue their academic careers (Leki & Carson, 1997). Both ESL and teacher-training programs seem to be particularly devoid of accountability to their students and to those who are faced with the shortfalls in NNS students' academic skills. The findings of the research presented in this book point to the need for substantial changes in L2 grammar, vocabulary/reading, and writing curricula in EAPs and other ESL programs that train students prior to their arrival in universities.

The most common approach to grammar teaching relies on presentations of particular structures or grammar points followed by exercises or tasks that concentrate on them, one or two constructions at a time. Usually, the grammar textbook adopted in a course determines the curriculum, as teachers follow the material layout developed by the textbook's author. The most common way of practicing grammar structures involves fill-in-the-blank single-sentence tasks, and by the time learners reach the intermediate level of proficiency, they are well versed in blank filling. However, as most teachers know from experience, filling blanks in sentences or choosing the correct option in multiple-choice exercises does little to improve the quality of L2 text in essays and compositions. One of the most important reasons for the shortfall of L2 grammar instruction is that, in many cases, learners see little connection between grammar exercises and text production. In fact, my students have often told me that not only have they studied "all the grammar" before but also that they truly believe that they have learned everything they need to know to write a good essay.

Although there is little doubt that advanced students have studied "all the grammar" before they arrive in mainstream university classes, studying does not necessarily translate into grammar learning or acquisition (Ellis, 1994, 1997). Furthermore, the fact that a particular grammar structure is studied in a grammar book and that the necessary blanks are filled in does not mean that textual functions of structures are similarly addressed and practiced. That is, the traditional curriculum of grammar textbooks does little to address the structures that learners have to learn to notice and produce when working with academic text. The textual functions of grammar structures rarely represent the focus of grammar exercises. The fact that a particular construction is very common and another is hardly ever encountered is also not a part of traditional grammar teaching. In many grammar textbooks, subject and verb agreement, which is as common as the uses of the present tense, is given the same prominence as adverb clause reduction, which even the NSs in this study rarely used. The prevalence and function of structures in text needs to drive grammar curriculum and instruction if learners are to benefit from grammar teaching.

The teaching of vocabulary is usually closely associated with reading text excerpts selected by either the textbook author or the classroom teacher. As with the teaching of grammar, the vocabulary encountered in the text is then practiced based on various types of exercises and tasks, the importance of fill-in-the-blank activities not to be underestimated. Most teachers hope that with exposure to and experience with academic texts in students' subsequent coursework, learners' vocabulary ranges would increase and become more diverse. However, according to the findings of this study, learners' vocabulary and lexical arsenal do not expand through exposure to academic texts but rather in the course of daily communication.

According to Arnaud and Savignon (1997), a vocabulary range of only 3,000 words is necessary for understanding 95% of an average text, and an average NS university student has a vocabulary range of 17,000 word families (approximately 116,000 words). Much research carried out since the 1970s has shown that intensive and extensive vocabulary study is imperative for NNS students in the U.S. academy. Yet, the prevalent methodology for L2 teaching continues to rely on exposure to text and communication as the primary means of increasing learners' lexicons. Thus, a contradiction emerges between the methodological approaches and their idealistic expectations of learners' progress and the realistic outcomes of learners' lexical gains. Such contradictions between teachers' hopes and tangible results play out to the disadvantage of students who are caught between what and how they are taught and what they need to learn and how to use it. If the goal of communicative L2 teaching is to develop learners' fluency and ability to produce essay-length amounts of text, these goals have clearly been accomplished. On the other hand, if the purpose of instruction is to provide learners the skills that they cannot attain on their own in the course of daily communication in an English-speaking environment, this target has been missed.

As with the teaching and learning of grammar, vocabulary instruction and learning requires considerable effort and persistence. The prevalence of vocabulary in academic texts and the functionality of lexis need to underlie consistent and thorough L2 instruction. There is little doubt that for learners who wish to attain English proficiency sufficient for their daily lives and informal interactions (the level of L2 skills that my students call "grocery store English"), instruction in advanced academic lexis may not be necessary. On the other hand, if students' goals are to enter U.S. universities where a far greater range of vocabulary is not only expected but essential, expanding L2 lexicon requires a great deal of work from both students and teachers. Persistent, focused, and systematic vocabulary teaching and learning are a great deal more complex and laborious than entertaining activities to promote fluency.

In my job, each year (and I have been teaching ESL for 20 years), I encounter hundreds of NNS university students who often have trouble constructing complete sentences after many years of studying English in English-speaking countries. Most of these students are bright and diligent, as can be ascertained by their slow and steady progress through the rungs of the academy. These learners are usually 2 years away from graduating with their university degrees, and one question has really troubled me for a long time: If these people haven't learned to construct a sentence and make sure that each clause has a verb by the time they arrive in my office, how certain can I be that they will eventually learn to write a coherent memo or a reasonably grammatical e-mail? Unless students are rigorously taught the language fundamentals, many of which are identified in this book, the quality of their learning has little chance for improvement. Furthermore, they will be hindered in their future academic or professional progress, regardless of how much fun they have in the ESL classroom. If teachers can give their students the highest quality language learning tools, it seems imperative that they do so. The research findings in this book seek to help teachers and teacher trainers to focus on the most relevant features of L2 text in curriculum and instruction.

Appendix A

Rank Order of Median Frequency Rates of Linguistic Features in NS and NNS Texts

Features	NS	CH	JP	KR	VT	IN	AR
Present tense	1	1	1	1	1	1	1
Infinitives	2	3	2	11	6	5	4
Third-person pronouns	3	2	3	2	2	2	3
Attributive adjectives	4	5	7	9	7.5	8	6
Fixed strings	5	27	20	24	18	28	23
Phrase-level coordinators	6	4	5	3	3	4	2
Be as a main verb	7	6	6	4	5	3	5
Private verbs	8	8	10	10	10	6	11
First-person pronouns	9	13	4	7	4	9.5	13
Nominalization	10	15	15.5	16.5	15	15	12
Amplifiers	11	9	11	12	13	11	8
Predicative adjectives	12	7	8	8	9	7	7
Past tense	13	10	9	5	7.5	9.5	33
Gerunds	14.5	22	23	23	19.5	19	16
Noun clauses	14.5	14	14	15	16	13	14.5
Place adverbs	16	16	17	21	14	16.5	20
Vague nouns	17	12	13	6	12	12	10
Emphatics	18	11	12	13	11	14	9
Passive voice	19	33	28	33	39	39	31
Adjective clauses	20	23.5	22	30.5	26.5	18	17.5
Advance/retroactive nouns	21	42.5	41.5	38.5	49	42.5	32
Possibility modals	22	21	18	20	23	21	24

(Continued)

(Continued)

Features	NS	CH	JP	KR	VT	IN	AR
Present participles	23	38	41.5	43	42	48	59.5
Demonstrative pronouns	24	20	26	18	21.5	22.5	14.5
Past participles	25	45	47	45	51.5	46	48
Time adverbs	26.5	25	27	28	25	27	28.5
Lexical hedges	26.5	37	35.5	32	38	44.5	46.5
Sentence transitions	28	17	15.5	14	17	16.5	17.5
Necessity modals	29	18	19	19	21.5	24.5	27
Logical semantic conj./prep.	30	35	30.5	37	30	30	25.5
It-subject (cleft)	31.5	49	46	57.5	46	51	43.5
Epistemic hedges	31.5	41	34	34	45	37	59.5
Adverb clause (other)	33	31	33	36	32.5	31	42
Expecting/tentative verbs	34	29	21	16.5	29	20	30
Condition clauses	35	36	38.5	38.5	47	42.5	46.5
Assertive pronouns	36.5	26	30.5	30.5	31	26	28.5
Other adverbs	36.5	34	30.5	29	24	24.5	21.5
Downtoners	38.5	46	44.5	46	43.5	33	35
Interpretive nouns	38.5	28	24	22	26.5	29	21.5
Logical/sem. relat. verbs	40	39	44.5	44	35	34.5	38
Universal pronouns	41	30	30.5	27	28	38	25.5
Future tense	43	32	49	42	41	32	35
Predictive modals	43	60	58.5	57.5	59.5	59	49.5
Enumerative nouns	43	40	41.5	35	35	41	37
Progressive aspect	45.5	60	58.5	57.5	59.5	59	59.5
Public verbs	45.5	19	25	25	19.5	22.5	19
Perfect aspect	47	60	58.5	57.5	51.5	59	59.5
Reduced adverb clauses	48	60	58.5	57.5	59.5	59	59.5
Cause clauses	49	44	35.5	40	43.5	36	41
Suasive verbs	50	48	48	57.5	40	44.5	35
Exemplification	51	42.5	38.5	41	35	34.5	39
Second-person pronouns	59	23.5	37	26	32.5	59	40
There-subject	59	60	58.5	48	59.5	59	45
Reduced adjective clauses	59	60	58.5	57.5	59.5	59	59.5
Concession clauses	59	60	58.5	57.5	59.5	59	59.5
Purpose clauses	59	60	58.5	57.5	59.5	59	59.5
Frequency adverbs	59	52	58.5	57.5	50	50	51
Possibility hedges	59	60	58.5	57.5	59.5	59	59.5
Quality hedges	59	52	58.5	57.5	59.5	47	52
Performative hedges	59	60	58.5	57.5	59.5	59	59.5
Seem/appear	59	60	58.5	57.5	59.5	59	59.5
Illocutionary nouns	59	60	58.5	57.5	59.5	59	59.5
Resultative nouns	59	50	58.5	57.5	48	49	59.5
Language activity nouns	59	47	41.5	47	37	40	43.5
Rhetorical questions	59	52	50	57.5	59.5	59	49.5
Presupposition markers	59	60	58.5	57.5	59.5	59	59.5

Appendix B

Comparisons of Frequency Rates for Features in Student Texts by L1 Group

This appendix presents comparisons of median and range values for the features used across texts written to various prompts by speakers of the same language, that is, NSs, Chinese, Japanese, Korean, Vietnamese, Indonesian, and Arabic. Because the comparison data are extensive, only the top 30 features are presented, as determined by the rank order for NS features uses, contained in Appendix A. The data for the top 10 features are discussed in detail in chapter 11.

TABLE B1-1
Medians and Ranges for Top 30 Features in NS Essays, Compared to Parents Texts

L1	NSPARENTS		NSGRADES		NSWEALTH		NSMANNER		NSOPINIONS		NSMAJOR	
	Median	Range	Median	Range	Median	Range	Median	Range	Median	Range	Median	Range
Semantic and Lexical Classes of Nouns												
adv./retroact.	1.80	7.95	1.89	6.80	1.92	4.51	0.82*	3.41	0.50*	4.81	0.40**	2.22
vague	0.87	3.11	0.52	3.54	1.00	6.43	1.94**	6.25	1.60*	5.00	2.26**	7.73
Personal Pronouns												
first person	2.00	14.35	3.57	11.17	1.19*	5.00	3.87	9.69	0.97	9.64	2.60	15.41
third person	4.09	7.93	2.87	9.52	4.13	10.29	2.78*	7.50	5.77**	16.80	4.14	13.40
Nominalization	0.98	4.76	1.10	6.92	1.12	3.17	2.50**	7.60	2.20**	7.46	4.62**	11.53
Gerunds	0.83	2.27	1.79**	5.24	0.95	3.13	2.08**	4.71	1.50**	4.46	1.85**	6.94
Verb Tenses												
past	0.93	10.95	1.25	9.57	0.53	4.48	2.38*	11.88	2.20**	9.62	1.81*	10.13
present	8.26	13.08	10.62*	13.88	10.23*	8.66	8.48	13.15	8.47	31.63	9.77**	14.18
Semantic and Lexical Classes of Verbs												
private	1.07	4.09	2.86**	7.80	1.06	3.85	2.94**	10.42	2.56**	8.33	1.92*	5.04
Modal Verbs												
possibility	1.03	4.29	0.83	4.40	0.78	3.83	1.07	4.35	1.02	5.00	1.13	3.57
necessity	0.43	2.17	0.47	2.20	0.57	3.76	0.46	2.94	1.42**	4.81	0.54	2.26
Passive	0.75	3.03	0.96	3.85	1.03*	3.65	1.16*	4.12	1.50*	10.58	1.81**	4.90
be-main	2.01	5.13	1.89	4.17	1.86	4.51	3.33**	5.56	2.50**	10.71	1.50	5.15
Infinitives	2.36	6.37	6.14**	9.65	5.07**	8.09	5.36**	6.30	7.33**	22.07	5.79**	9.96

(Continued)

TABLE B1-1
(Continued)

LI	NSPARENTS		NSGRADES		NSWEALTH		NSMANNER		NSOPINIONS		NSMAJOR	
	Median	Range	Median	Range	Median	Range	Median	Range	Median	Range	Median	Range
Participles												
present	0.00	1.93	2.67**	6.15	1.73**	3.72	1.85**	4.76	0.50**	2.03	0.63**	2.92
past	0.43	5.71	1.82**	4.44	1.72**	5.26	0.77**	3.33	0.44	5.00	0.79*	3.80
Adjectives												
attributive	1.42	4.92	2.63**	6.73	3.76**	7.98	8.50**	11.57	5.13**	8.99	6.12**	10.95
predicative	1.49	3.61	1.33	4.64	1.14	3.92	2.17*	7.04	1.50	8.06	1.74	4.10
Semantic and Lexical Classes of Adverbs												
time	0.90	3.78	0.37*	2.08	0.68	3.65	0.50*	2.22	0.88	5.00	0.93	4.59
place	1.23	3.91	0.95	2.86	0.75	2.50	2.07*	4.31	1.89*	4.76	2.43**	4.07
amplifiers	1.40	4.76	1.60	4.35	1.71*	4.98	1.93*	3.52	1.52	7.50	1.79*	5.07
Noun and Adjective Clauses												
noun	0.90	3.91	2.30**	5.19	1.38*	6.94	1.25	5.41	2.02**	8.33	1.46*	5.11
full adjective	0.43	1.44	1.01*	2.93	1.52**	2.90	1.43**	3.37	0.81*	2.88	1.42**	4.52
Coordinating and Logical Conjunctions/Prepositions												
phrase-level	2.00	5.52	3.07*	4.76	4.17**	5.44	4.08***	6.00	4.50**	8.55	3.47**	6.16
sentence-level	0.83	2.27	0.38*	3.08	0.36***	2.26	0.93	2.35	0.66	4.81	0.61	2.61
log/sem conjunctions	0.00	1.68	0.00	0.99	0.38***	2.35	1.10***	2.63	1.11**	3.85	1.23**	3.80
Hedges												
lexical	0.48	2.63	0.29*	1.48	0.43	1.70	1.93**	5.99	0.83*	7.58	1.30**	4.63
Demonstrative	0.95	2.94	1.19*	4.15	1.68*	3.25	0.93	2.68	0.68	4.46	0.52*	2.78
Emphatics	0.98	4.26	0.71*	2.38	0.77	4.33	1.32	3.54	1.71*	5.77	1.42	4.08
Fixed Strings	1.49	7.14	2.29*	5.65	2.68**	5.80	5.50**	12.65	5.30**	20.19	4.44**	17.86

*1-tailed $p \leq 0.05$. **2-tailed $p \leq 0.05$.

TABLE B1-2
Medians and Ranges for Top 30 Features in NS Essays, Compared to Grades Texts

L1	NSGRADES Median	Range	NSWEALTH Median	Range	NSMANNER Median	Range	NSOPINIONS Median	Range	NSMAJOR Median	Range
Semantic and Lexical Classes of Nouns										
adv./retroact.	**1.89**	6.80	**1.92**	4.51	**0.82***	3.41	**0.50***	4.81	**0.40****	2.22
vague	**0.52**	3.54	**1.00***	6.43	**1.94****	6.25	**1.60****	5.00	**2.26****	7.73
Personal Pronouns										
first person	**3.57**	11.17	**1.19****	5.00	**3.87**	9.69	**0.97**	9.64	**2.60**	15.41
third person	**2.87**	9.52	**4.13***	10.29	**2.78**	7.50	**5.77****	16.80	**4.14***	13.40
Nominalization	**1.10**	6.92	**1.12**	3.17	**2.50****	7.60	**2.20****	7.46	**4.62****	11.53
Gerunds	**1.79**	5.24	**0.95***	3.13	**2.08**	4.71	**1.50**	4.46	**1.85**	6.94
Verb Tenses										
past	**1.25**	9.57	**0.53***	4.48	**2.38***	11.88	**2.20****	9.62	**1.81***	10.13
present	**10.62**	13.88	**10.23**	8.66	**8.48***	13.15	**8.47**	31.63	**9.77**	14.18
Semantic and Lexical Classes of Verbs										
private	**2.86**	7.80	**1.06****	3.85	**2.94**	10.42	**2.56**	8.33	**1.92***	5.04
Modal Verbs										
possibility	**0.83**	4.40	**0.78**	3.83	**1.07**	4.35	**1.02***	5.00	**1.13***	3.57
necessity	**0.47**	2.20	**0.57**	3.76	**0.46**	2.94	**1.42****	4.81	**0.54**	2.26
Passive	**0.96**	3.85	**1.03**	3.65	**1.16***	4.12	**1.50***	10.58	**1.81****	4.90
be-main	**1.89**	4.17	**1.86**	4.51	**3.33****	5.56	**2.50****	10.71	**1.50**	5.15
Infinitives	**6.14**	9.65	**5.07***	8.09	**5.36**	6.30	**7.33****	22.07	**5.79**	9.96

(Continued)

TABLE B1-2
(Continued)

L1	NSGRADES		NSWEALTH		NSMANNER		NSOPINIONS		NSMAJOR	
	Median	Range	Median	Range	Median	Range	Median	Range	Median	Range
Participles										
present	**2.67**	6.15	**1.73***	3.72	**1.85**	4.76	**0.50****	2.03	**0.63****	2.92
past	**1.82**	4.44	**1.72**	5.26	**0.77***	3.33	**0.44***	5.00	**0.79***	3.80
Adjectives										
attributive	**2.63**	6.73	**3.76****	7.98	**8.50****	11.57	**5.13****	8.99	**6.12****	10.95
predicative	**1.33**	4.64	**1.14**	3.92	**2.17***	7.04	**1.50***	8.06	**1.74**	4.10
Semantic and Lexical Classes of Adverbs										
time	**0.37**	2.08	**0.68**	3.65	**0.50**	2.22	**0.88****	5.00	**0.93***	4.59
place	**0.95**	2.86	**0.75**	2.50	**2.07****	4.31	**1.89****	4.76	**2.43****	4.07
amplifiers	**1.60**	4.35	**1.71**	4.98	**1.93***	3.52	**1.52***	7.50	**1.79***	5.07
Noun and Adjective Clauses										
noun	**2.30**	5.19	**1.38****	6.94	**1.25***	5.41	**2.02**	8.33	**1.46***	5.11
full adjective	**1.01**	2.93	**1.52***	2.90	**1.43***	3.37	**0.81**	2.88	**1.42***	4.52
Coordinating and Logical Conjunctions/Prepositions										
phrase-level	**3.07**	4.76	**4.17****	5.44	**4.08****	6.00	**4.50****	8.55	**3.47****	6.16
sentence-level	**0.38**	3.08	**0.36**	2.26	**0.93***	2.35	**0.66****	4.81	**0.61**	2.61
log/sem conjunctions	**0.00**	0.99	**0.38***	2.35	**1.10****	2.63	**1.11****	3.85	**1.23****	3.80
Hedges										
lexical	**0.29**	1.48	**0.43**	1.70	**1.93****	5.99	**0.83****	7.58	**1.30****	4.63
Demonstrative	**1.19**	4.15	**1.68**	3.25	**0.93**	2.68	**0.68**	4.46	**0.52****	2.78
Emphatics	**0.71**	2.38	**0.77**	4.33	**1.32****	3.54	**1.71****	5.77	**1.42****	4.08
Fixed Strings	**2.29**	5.65	**2.68***	5.80	**5.50****	12.65	**5.30****	20.19	**4.44****	17.86

*1-tailed $p \leq 0.05$. **2-tailed $p \leq 0.05$.

TABLE B1-3

Medians and Ranges for Top 30 Features in NS Essays, Compared to Wealth Texts

L1	NSWEALTH		NSMANNER		NSOPINIONS		NSMAJOR	
	Median	Range	Median	Range	Median	Range	Median	Range
Semantic and Lexical Classes of Nouns								
adv./retroact.	1.92	4.51	0.82*	3.41	0.50*	4.81	0.40**	2.22
vague	1.00	6.43	1.94**	6.25	1.60*	5.00	2.26**	7.73
Personal Pronouns								
first person	1.19	5.00	3.87*	9.69	0.97	9.64	2.60*	15.41
third person	4.13	10.29	2.78*	7.50	5.77**	16.80	4.14	13.40
Nominalization	1.12	3.17	2.50**	7.60	2.20**	7.46	4.62**	11.53
Gerunds	0.95	3.13	2.08**	4.71	1.50**	4.46	1.85**	6.94
Verb Tenses								
past	0.53	4.48	2.38**	11.88	2.20**	9.62	1.81**	10.13
present	10.23	8.66	8.48*	13.15	8.47	31.63	9.77	14.18
Semantic and Lexical Classes of Verbs								
private	1.06	3.85	2.94**	10.42	2.56**	8.33	1.92**	5.04
Modal Verbs								
possibility	0.78	3.83	1.07	4.35	1.02*	5.00	1.13*	3.57
necessity	0.57	3.76	0.46	2.94	1.42**	4.81	0.54	2.26
Passive	1.03	3.65	1.16*	4.12	1.50*	10.58	1.81**	4.90
***be*-main**	1.86	4.51	3.33**	5.56	2.50**	10.71	1.50	5.15
Infinitives	5.07	8.09	5.36	6.30	7.33*	22.07	5.79*	9.96

(Continued)

L1	NSWEALTH		NSMANNER		NSOPINIONS		NSMAJOR	
	Median	Range	Median	Range	Median	Range	Median	Range
Participles								
present	1.73	3.72	1.85	4.76	0.50*	2.03	0.63**	2.92
past	1.72	5.26	0.77*	3.33	0.44*	5.00	0.79**	3.80
Adjectives								
attributive	3.76	7.98	8.50**	11.57	5.13**	8.99	6.12**	10.95
predicative	1.14	3.92	2.17**	7.04	1.50*	8.06	1.74**	4.10
Semantic and Lexical Classes of Adverbs								
time	0.68	3.65	0.50	2.22	0.88*	5.00	0.93	4.59
place	0.75	2.50	2.07**	4.31	1.89**	4.76	2.43**	4.07
amplifiers	1.71	4.98	1.93	3.52	1.52	7.50	1.79	5.07
Noun and Adjective Clauses								
noun	1.38	6.94	1.25	5.41	2.02*	8.33	1.46	5.11
full adjective	1.52	2.90	1.43	3.37	0.81	2.88	1.42	4.52
Coordinating and Logical Conjunctions/Prepositions								
phrase-level	4.17	5.44	4.08	6.00	4.50**	8.55	3.47	6.16
sentence-level	0.36	2.26	0.93**	2.35	0.66***	4.81	0.61*	2.61
log/sem conjunctions	0.38	2.35	1.10**	2.63	1.11**	3.85	1.23**	3.80
Hedges								
lexical	0.43	1.70	1.93**	5.99	0.83**	7.58	1.30**	4.63
Demonstrative	1.68	3.25	0.93	2.68	0.68	4.46	0.52**	2.78
Emphatics	0.77	4.33	1.32*	3.54	1.71**	5.77	1.42**	4.08
Fixed Strings	2.68	5.80	5.50**	12.65	5.30**	20.19	4.44**	17.86

*1-tailed $p \leq 0.05$. **2-tailed $p \leq 0.05$.

TABLE B1-4
Medians and Ranges for Top 30 Features in NS Essays, Compared to Manner Texts

L1	NSMANNER		NSOPINIONS		NSMAJOR	
	Median	Range	Median	Range	Median	Range
Semantic and Lexical Classes of Nouns						
adv./retroact.	**0.82**	3.41	**0.50**	4.81	**0.40***	2.22
vague	**1.94**	6.25	**1.60**	5.00	**2.26***	7.73
Personal Pronouns						
first person	**3.87**	9.69	**0.97**	9.64	**2.60**	15.41
third person	**2.78**	7.50	**5.77****	16.80	**4.14****	13.40
Nominalization	**2.50**	7.60	**2.20**	7.46	**4.62****	11.53
Gerunds	**2.08**	4.71	**1.50**	4.46	**1.85**	6.94
Verb Tenses						
past	**2.38**	11.88	**2.20**	9.62	**1.81**	10.13
present	**8.48**	13.15	**8.47**	31.63	**9.77***	14.18
Semantic and Lexical Classes of Verbs						
private	**2.94**	10.42	**2.56**	8.33	**1.92***	5.04
Modal Verbs						
possibility	**1.07**	4.35	**1.02**	5.00	**1.13**	3.57
necessity	**0.46**	2.94	**1.42****	4.81	**0.54**	2.26
Passive	**1.16**	4.12	**1.50**	10.58	**1.81***	4.90
be-main	**3.33**	5.56	**2.50**	10.71	**1.50****	5.15
Infinitives	**5.36**	6.30	**7.33****	22.07	**5.79**	9.96

(Continued)

L1	NSMANNER		NSOPINIONS		NSMAJOR	
	Median	Range	Median	Range	Median	Range
Participles						
present	**1.85**	4.76	**0.50****	2.03	**0.63****	2.92
past	**0.77**	3.33	**0.44**	5.00	**0.79**	3.80
Adjectives						
attributive	**8.50**	11.57	**5.13***	8.99	**6.12***	10.95
predicative	**2.17**	7.04	**1.50**	8.06	**1.74***	4.10
Semantic and Lexical Classes of Adverbs						
time	**0.50**	2.22	**0.88***	5.00	**0.93***	4.59
place	**2.07**	4.31	**1.89**	4.76	**2.43**	4.07
amplifiers	**1.93**	3.52	**1.52**	7.50	**1.79**	5.07
Noun and Adjective Clauses						
noun	**1.25**	5.41	**2.02****	8.33	**1.46**	5.11
full adjective	**1.43**	3.37	**0.81**	2.88	**1.42**	4.52
Coordinating and Logical Conjunctions/Prepositions						
phrase-level	**4.08**	6.00	**4.50***	8.55	**3.47**	6.16
sentence-level	**0.93**	2.35	**0.66**	4.81	**0.61**	2.61
log/sem conjunctions	**1.10**	2.63	**1.11***	3.85	**1.23**	3.80
Hedges						
lexical	**1.93**	5.99	**0.83***	7.58	**1.30***	4.63
Demonstrative	**0.93**	2.68	**0.68**	4.46	**0.52***	2.78
Emphatics	**1.32**	3.54	**1.71****	5.77	**1.42**	4.08
Fixed Strings	**5.50**	12.65	**5.30***	20.19	**4.44***	17.86

*1-tailed $p \leq 0.05$. **2-tailed $p \leq 0.05$.

TABLE B1-5
Medians and Ranges for Top 30 Features in NS Essays, Compared to Opinions Texts

L1	NSOPINIONS		NSMAJOR	
	Median	*Range*	*Median*	*Range*
Semantic and Lexical Classes of Nouns				
adv./retroact.	**0.50**	4.81	**0.40***	2.22
vague	**1.60**	5.00	**2.26****	7.73
Personal Pronouns				
first person	**0.97**	9.64	**2.60***	15.41
third person	**5.77**	16.80	**4.14***	13.40
Nominalization	**2.20**	7.46	**4.62****	11.53
Gerunds	**1.50**	4.46	**1.85***	6.94
Verb Tenses				
past	**2.20**	9.62	**1.81**	10.13
present	**8.47**	31.63	**9.77***	14.18
Semantic and Lexical Classes of Verbs				
private	**2.56**	8.33	**1.92**	5.04
Modal Verbs				
possibility	**1.02**	5.00	**1.13**	3.57
necessity	**1.42**	4.81	**0.54****	2.26
Passive	**1.50**	10.58	**1.81***	4.90
***be*-main**	**2.50**	10.71	**1.50****	5.15
Infinitives	**7.33**	22.07	**5.79***	9.96

(Continued)

TABLE B1-5
(Continued)

L1	NSOPINIONS		NSMAJOR	
	Median	*Range*	*Median*	*Range*
Participles				
present	**0.50**	2.03	**0.63**	2.92
past	**0.44**	5.00	**0.79***	3.80
Adjectives				
attributive	**5.13**	8.99	**6.12***	10.95
predicative	**1.50**	8.06	**1.74**	4.10
Semantic and Lexical Classes of Adverbs				
time	**0.88**	5.00	**0.93**	4.59
place	**1.89**	4.76	**2.43***	4.07
amplifiers	**1.52**	7.50	**1.79***	5.07
Noun and Adjective Clauses				
noun	**2.02**	8.33	**1.46**	5.11
full adjective	**0.81**	2.88	**1.42****	4.52
Coordinating and Logical Conjunctions/Prepositions				
phrase-level	**4.50**	8.55	**3.47***	6.16
sentence-level	**0.66**	4.81	**0.61**	2.61
log/sem conjunctions	**1.11**	3.85	**1.23**	3.80
Hedges				
lexical	**0.83**	7.58	**1.30**	4.63
Demonstrative	**0.68**	4.46	**0.52**	2.78
Emphatics	**1.71**	5.77	**1.42**	4.08
Fixed Strings	**5.30**	20.19	**4.44***	17.86

*1-tailed $p \leq 0.05$. **2-tailed $p \leq 0.05$.

TABLE B2-1
Medians and Ranges for Top 30 Features in Chinese Speakers Essays, Compared to Parents Texts

L1	CHPARENTS		CHGRADES		CHWEALTH		CHMANNER		CHOPINIONS		CHMAJOR	
	Median	*Range*	*Median*	*Range*	*Median*	*Range*	*Median*	*Range*	*Median*	*Range*	*Median*	*Range*
Semantic and Lexical Classes of Nouns												
adv./retroact.	**0.00**	1.43	**1.07****	4.36	**0.71***	4.29	**0.65***	3.21	**0.40**	2.39	**0.41**	1.59
vague	**2.27**	9.72	**2.33**	10.83	**2.50**	13.19	**2.78****	6.62	**2.76***	7.47	**3.68****	9.03
Personal Pronouns												
first person	**2.19**	17.65	**4.58***	13.33	**1.58**	4.76	**3.72**	9.05	**2.02**	17.04	**2.38**	13.60
third person	**7.03**	22.20	**3.03****	10.00	**6.76**	9.70	**2.60****	11.15	**8.00**	10.25	**5.00***	15.91
Nominalization	**1.62**	4.55	**2.02**	9.17	**1.28**	4.79	**1.67**	6.19	**1.01**	5.17	**4.13****	7.30
Gerunds	**0.63**	2.65	**2.12****	5.83	**0.71**	3.72	**1.35*****	4.83	**1.28***	3.83	**1.58*****	3.84
Verb Tenses												
past	**2.94**	7.27	**3.92***	9.50	**0.45****	4.56	**2.86**	10.13	**3.50***	13.56	**2.10**	16.35
present	**10.00**	12.31	**9.87**	10.55	**11.15**	10.89	**9.63**	10.73	**9.30***	8.98	**8.89**	10.38
Semantic and Lexical Classes of Verbs												
private	**2.69**	8.47	**4.25***	8.09	**1.52****	3.21	**3.80***	7.27	**3.16**	5.56	**4.26***	7.98
Modal Verbs												
possibility	**1.40**	3.79	**0.91***	4.17	**0.83***	3.21	**1.52**	7.14	**1.05**	4.37	**1.54**	4.44
necessity	**1.85**	7.62	**1.18****	5.00	**0.79****	3.72	**1.11****	5.09	**2.02**	4.81	**0.96****	5.56
Passive	**1.39**	6.25	**0.36****	2.06	**0.43****	1.79	**0.83**	2.28	**0.73***	4.02	**0.74***	2.27
be-main	**3.03**	11.64	**2.94**	9.42	**2.50**	5.87	**4.55****	6.54	**4.17***	8.89	**3.59**	4.75
Infinitives	**3.00**	8.77	**4.04**	11.50	**3.58***	6.62	**5.00****	8.13	**7.41****	9.67	**6.29****	8.80

(Continued)

TABLE B2-1
(Continued)

L1	CHPARENTS		CHGRADES		CHWEALTH		CHMANNER		CHOPINIONS		CHMAJOR	
	Median	Range	Median	Range	Median	Range	Median	Range	Median	Range	Median	Range
Participles												
present	0.50	4.81	0.50	4.58	1.07	3.54	1.35*	4.17	0.00**	1.15	0.22*	1.82
past	0.36	4.17	0.74	2.30	0.79	2.83	0.30	2.02	0.00*	1.33	0.00*	1.23
Adjectives												
attributive	2.14	6.09	3.27*	12.42	4.78**	7.43	7.05**	10.50	4.29**	8.68	4.06**	11.44
predicative	2.73	8.05	3.12	10.83	2.78	7.69	4.29*	4.36	3.04	6.10	3.02	7.34
Semantic and Lexical Classes of Adverbs												
time	1.00	4.36	1.06	6.54	0.64	2.63	0.98	3.35	1.01	3.33	0.95	4.20
place	1.35	4.38	1.43	3.92	1.20	5.26	2.22**	5.68	1.28	4.76	1.95*	5.56
amplifiers	2.60	8.40	3.52	9.45	2.05*	5.40	3.56*	6.64	3.70	4.91	3.12	6.88
Noun and Adjective Clauses												
noun	1.46	4.64	2.61**	4.99	1.42	4.33	1.95*	5.60	2.43**	4.72	1.40	4.29
full adjective	1.20	4.00	0.67*	2.30	1.04*	2.63	1.85	7.14	0.63**	2.14	1.30	3.49
Coordinating and Logical Conjunctions/Prepositions												
phrase-level	3.81	8.95	3.53	10.04	3.57	6.37	5.14*	7.52	5.31*	13.10	4.24	16.93
sentence-level	1.90	4.05	1.14**	4.17	1.09**	2.69	1.74	5.56	1.25**	2.50	1.88	3.56
log/sem conjunctions	0.38	3.17	0.95**	5.19	0.22	1.39	1.07*	2.88	0.76*	2.22	1.21**	4.29
Hedges												
lexical	1.40	5.63	0.41**	2.00	1.09	6.38	0.39**	1.79	0.54**	1.85	0.70**	2.73
Demonstrative	0.79	4.00	1.10	8.44	1.26*	3.40	1.78*	5.32	1.48*	4.63	1.11	3.13
Emphatics	2.32	7.50	1.90	6.57	1.30*	6.85	3.41*	4.06	3.85**	6.80	3.33**	5.47
Fixed Strings	0.94	4.23	0.79	3.81	1.05	4.76	0.78	2.38	1.25*	3.68	1.16	3.16

*1-tailed $p \leq 0.05$. **2-tailed $p \leq 0.05$.

281

TABLE B2-2

Medians and Ranges for Top 30 Features in Chinese Speaker Essays, Compared to Grades Texts

L1	CHGRADES		CHWEALTH		CHMANNER		CHOPINIONS		CHMAJOR	
	Median	*Range*	*Median*	*Range*	*Median*	*Range*	*Median*	*Range*	*Median*	*Range*
Semantic and Lexical Classes of Nouns										
adv./retroact.	**1.07**	4.36	**0.71**	4.29	**0.65***	3.21	**0.40****	2.39	**0.41****	1.59
vague	**2.33**	10.83	**2.50**	13.19	**2.78**	6.62	**2.76**	7.47	**3.68***	9.03
Personal Pronouns										
first person	**4.58**	13.33	**1.58****	4.76	**3.72***	9.05	**2.02***	17.04	**2.38***	13.60
third person	**3.03**	10.00	**6.76****	9.70	**2.60**	11.15	**8.00****	10.25	**5.00***	15.91
Nominalization	**202**	9.17	**1.28***	4.79	**1.67**	6.19	**1.01***	5.17	**4.613****	7.30
Gerunds	**2.12**	5.83	**0.71****	3.72	**1.35***	4.83	**1.28****	3.83	**1.58**	3.84
Verb Tenses										
past	**3.92**	9.50	**0.45****	4.56	**2.86***	10.13	**3.50****	13.56	**2.10***	16.35
present	**9.87**	10.55	**11.15**	10.89	**9.63**	10.73	**9.30***	8.98	**8.89**	10.38
Semantic and Lexical Classes of Verbs										
private	**4.25**	8.09	**1.52****	3.21	**3.80**	7.27	**3.16***	5.56	**4.26**	7.98
Modal Verbs										
possibility	**091**	4.17	**0.83**	3.21	**1.52***	7.14	**1.05**	4.37	**1.54***	4.44
necessity	**1.18**	5.00	**0.79***	3.72	**1.11**	5.09	**2.02***	4.81	**0.96**	5.56
Passive	**0.36**	2.06	**0.43**	1.79	**0.83***	2.28	**0.73***	4.02	**0.74***	2.27
be-main	**2.94**	9.42	**2.50**	5.87	**4.55****	6.54	**4.17***	8.89	**3.59***	4.75
Infinitives	**4.04**	11.50	**3.58**	6.62	**5.00***	8.13	**7.41****	9.67	**6.29****	8.80

(Continued)

TABLE B2-2
(Continued)

L1	CHGRADES Median	Range	CHWEALTH Median	Range	CHMANNER Median	Range	CHOPINIONS Median	Range	CHMAJOR Median	Range
Participles										
present	0.50	4.58	1.07	3.54	1.35	4.17	0.00**	1.15	0.22*	1.82
past	0.74	2.30	0.79	2.83	0.30*	2.02	0.00**	1.33	0.00*	1.23
Adjectives										
attributive	3.27	12.42	4.78	7.43	7.05**	10.50	4.29	8.68	4.06	11.44
predicative	3.13	10.83	2.78*	7.69	4.29	4.36	3.04	6.10	3.02	7.34
Semantic and Lexical Classes of Adverbs										
time	1.06	6.54	0.64*	2.63	0.98	3.35	1.01	3.33	0.95	4.20
place	1.43	3.92	1.20	5.26	2.22*	5.68	1.28	4.76	1.95*	5.56
amplifiers	3.52	9.45	2.05**	5.40	3.56	6.64	3.70	4.91	3.12	6.88
Noun and Adjective Clauses										
noun	2.61	4.99	142**	4.33	1.95*	5.60	2.43	4.72	1.40*	4.29
full adjective	0.67	2.30	1.04	2.63	1.85**	7.14	0.63	2.14	1.30*	3.49
Coordinating and Logical Conjunctions/Prepositions										
phrase-level	3.53	10.04	3.57	6.37	5.14**	7.52	5.31**	13.10	4.24*	16.93
sentence-level	1.14	4.17	1.09	2.69	1.74*	5.56	1.25	2.50	1.88*	3.56
log/sem conjunctions	0.95	5.19	0.22**	1.39	1.07	2.88	0.76	2.22	1.21	4.29
Hedges										
lexical	0.41	2.00	1.09*	6.38	0.39**	1.79	0.54	1.85	0.70	2.73
Demonstrative	1.10	8.44	1.26	3.40	1.78	5.32	1.48	4.63	1.11*	3.13
Emphatics	1.90	6.57	1.30	6.85	3.41**	4.06	3.85**	6.80	3.33**	5.47
Fixed Strings	0.79	3.81	1.05	4.76	0.78	2.38	1.25*	3.68	1.16*	3.16

*1-tailed $p \leq 0.05$. **2-tailed $p \leq 0.05$.

TABLE B2-3
Medians and Ranges for Top 30 Features in Chinese Speaker Essays, Compared to Wealth Texts

L1	CHWEALTH		CHMANNER		CHOPINIONS		CHMAJOR	
	Median	*Range*	*Median*	*Range*	*Median*	*Range*	*Median*	*Range*
Semantic and Lexical Classes of Nouns								
adv./retroact.	**0.71**	4.29	**0.65**	3.21	**0.40***	2.39	**0.41**	1.59
vague	**2.50**	13.19	**2.78****	6.62	**2.76***	7.47	**3.68****	9.03
Personal Pronouns								
first person	**1.58**	4.76	**3.72****	9.05	**2.02***	17.04	**2.38***	13.60
third person	**6.76**	9.70	**2.60***	11.15	**8.00****	10.25	**5.00**	15.91
Nominalization	**1.28**	4.79	**1.67***	6.19	**1.01**	5.17	**4.13****	7.30
Gerunds	**0.71**	3.72	**1.35****	4.83	**1.28***	3.83	**1.58****	3.84
Verb Tenses								
past	**0.45**	4.56	**2.86****	10.13	**3.50*****	13.56	**2.10****	16.35
present	**11.15**	10.89	**9.63**	10.73	**9.30***	8.98	**8.89**	10.38
Semantic and Lexical Classes of Verbs								
private	**1.52**	3.21	**3.80****	7.27	**3.16****	5.56	**4.26****	7.98
Modal Verbs								
possibility	**0.83**	3.21	**1.52****	7.14	**1.05***	4.37	**1.54*****	4.44
necessity	**0.79**	3.72	**1.11***	5.09	**2.02****	4.81	**0.96***	5.56
Passive	**0.43**	1.79	**0.83****	2.28	**0.73***	4.02	**0.74***	2.27
be-main	**2.50**	5.87	**4.55****	6.54	**4.17****	8.89	**3.59****	4.75
Infinitives	**3.58**	6.62	**5.00****	8.13	**7.41****	9.67	**6.29****	8.80

(Continued)

TABLE B2-3
(Continued)

L1	CHWEALTH		CHMANNER		CHOPINIONS		CHMAJOR	
	Median	*Range*	*Median*	*Range*	*Median*	*Range*	*Median*	*Range*
Participles								
present	1.07	3.54	1.35*	4.17	0.00**	1.15	0.22*	1.82
past	0.79	2.83	0.30*	2.02	0.00**	1.33	0.00**	1.23
Adjectives								
attributive	4.78	7.43	7.05**	10.50	4.29	8.68	4.06	11.44
predicative	2.78	7.69	4.29**	4.36	3.04*	6.10	3.02*	7.34
Semantic and Lexical Classes of Adverbs								
time	0.64	2.63	0.98*	3.35	1.01*	3.33	0.95**	4.20
place	1.20	5.26	2.22**	5.68	1.28	4.76	1.95*	5.56
amplifiers	2.05	5.40	3.56**	6.64	3.70**	4.91	3.12**	6.88
Noun and Adjective Clauses								
noun	1.42	4.33	1.95**	5.60	2.43**	4.72	1.40*	4.29
full adjective	1.04	2.63	1.85**	7.14	0.63	2.14	1.30*	3.49
Coordinating and Logical Conjunctions/Prepositions								
phrase-level	3.57	6.37	5.14**	7.52	5.31**	13.10	4.24**	16.93
sentence-level	1.09	2.69	1.74**	5.56	1.25*	2.50	1.88**	3.56
log/sem conjunctions	0.22	1.39	1.07**	2.88	0.76**	2.22	1.21**	4.29
Hedges								
lexical	1.09	6.38	0.39*	1.79	0.54*	1.85	0.70	2.73
Demonstrative	1.26	3.40	1.78*	5.32	1.48	4.63	1.11	3.13
Emphatics	1.30	6.85	3.41**	4.06	3.85**	6.80	3.33**	5.47
Fixed Strings	1.05	4.76	0.78	2.38	1.25*	3.68	1.16*	3.16

*1-tailed $p \leq 0.05$. **2-tailed $p \leq 0.05$.

TABLE B2-4

Medians and Ranges for Top 30 Features in Chinese Speaker Essays, Compared to Manner Texts

L1	CHMANNER		CHOPINIONS		CHMAJOR	
	Median	*Range*	*Median*	*Range*	*Median*	*Range*
Semantic and Lexical Classes of Nouns						
adv./retroact.	**0.65**	3.21	**0.40***	2.39	**0.41***	1.59
vague	**2.78**	6.62	**2.76**	7.47	**3.68***	9.03
Personal Pronouns						
first person	**3.72**	9.05	**2.02**	17.04	**2.38**	13.60
third person	**2.60**	11.15	**8.00****	10.25	**5.00****	15.91
Nominalization	**1.67**	6.19	**1.01**	5.17	**4.13****	7.30
Gerunds	**1.35**	4.83	**1.28**	3.83	**1.58**	3.84
Verb Tenses						
past	**2.86**	10.13	**3.50***	13.56	**2.10**	16.35
present	**9.63**	10.73	**9.30**	8.98	**8.89**	10.38
Semantic and Lexical Classes of Verbs						
private	**3.80**	7.27	**3.16**	5.56	**4.26**	7.98
Modal Verbs						
possibility	**1.52**	7.14	**1.05***	4.37	**1.54**	4.44
necessity	**1.11**	5.09	**2.02***	4.81	**0.96**	5.56
Passive	**0.83**	2.28	**0.73**	4.02	**0.74**	2.27
be-main	**4.55**	6.54	**4.17**	8.89	**3.59***	4.75
Infinitives	**5.00**	8.13	**7.41***	9.67	**6.29**	8.80

(Continued)

TABLE B2-4
(Continued)

L1	CHMANNER		CHOPINIONS		CHMAJOR	
	Median	Range	Median	Range	Median	Range
Participles						
present	1.35	4.17	0.00**	1.15	0.22**	1.82
past	0.30	2.02	0.00	1.33	0.00	1.23
Adjectives						
attributive	7.05	10.50	4.29**	8.68	4.06**	11.44
predicative	4.29	4.36	3.04*	6.10	3.02*	7.34
Semantic and Lexical Classes of Adverbs						
time	0.98	3.35	1.01	3.33	0.95	4.20
place	2.22	5.68	1.28**	4.76	1.95	5.56
amplifiers	3.56	6.64	3.70	4.91	3.12	6.88
Noun and Adjective Clauses						
noun	1.95	5.60	2.43*	4.72	1.40*	4.29
full adjective	1.85	7.14	0.63***	2.14	1.30*	3.49
Coordinating and Logical Conjunctions/Prepositions						
phrase-level	5.14	7.52	5.31	13.10	4.24	16.93
sentence-level	1.74	5.56	1.25*	2.50	1.88	3.56
log/sem conjunctions	1.07	2.88	0.76	2.22	1.21	4.29
Hedges						
lexical	0.39	1.79	0.54	1.85	0.70*	2.73
Demonstrative	1.78	5.32	1.48	4.63	1.11*	3.13
Emphatics	3.41	4.06	3.85*	6.80	3.33	5.47
Fixed Strings	0.78	2.38	1.25**	3.68	1.16*	3.16

*1-tailed $p \leq 0.05$. **2-tailed $p \leq 0.05$.

TABLE B2-5

Medians and Ranges for Top 30 Features in Chinese Speaker Essays, Compared to Opinions Texts

L1	CHOPINIONS		CHMAJOR	
	Median	Range	Median	Range
Semantic and Lexical Classes of Nouns				
adv./retroact.	0.40	2.39	0.41	1.59
vague	2.76	7.47	3.68*	9.03
Personal Pronouns				
first person	2.02	17.04	2.38	13.60
third person	8.00	10.25	5.00*	15.91
Nominalization	1.01	5.17	4.13**	7.30
Gerunds	1.28	3.83	1.58*	3.84
Verb Tenses				
past	3.50	13.56	2.10	16.35
present	9.30	8.98	8.89	10.38
Semantic and Lexical Classes of Verbs				
private	3.16	5.56	4.26*	7.98
Modal Verbs				
possibility	1.05	4.37	1.54*	4.44
necessity	2.02	4.81	0.96*	5.56
Passive	0.73	4.02	0.74	2.27
be-main	4.17	8.89	3.59	4.75
Infinitives	7.41	9.67	6.29	8.80

(Continued)

TABLE B2-5
(Continued)

L1	CHOPINIONS		CHMAJOR	
	Median	*Range*	*Median*	*Range*
Participles				
present	**0.00**	1.15	**0.22***	1.82
past	**0.00**	1.33	**0.00**	1.23
Adjectives				
attributive	**4.29**	8.68	**4.06**	11.44
predicative	**3.04**	6.10	**3.02**	7.34
Semantic and Lexical Classes of Adverbs				
time	**1.01**	3.33	**0.95**	4.20
place	**1.28**	4.76	**1.95***	5.56
amplifiers	**3.70**	4.91	**3.12**	6.88
Noun and Adjective Clauses				
noun	**2.43**	4.72	**1.40***	4.29
full adjective	**0.63**	2.14	**1.30****	3.49
Coordinating and Logical Conjunctions/Prepositions				
phrase-level	**5.31**	13.10	**4.24**	16.93
sentence-level	**1.25**	2.50	**1.88****	3.56
log/sem conjunctions	**0.76**	2.22	**1.21***	4.29
Hedges				
lexical	**0.54**	1.85	**0.70***	2.73
Demonstrative	**1.48**	4.63	**1.11**	3.13
Emphatics	**3.85**	6.80	**3.33**	5.47
Fixed Strings	**1.25**	3.68	**1.16**	3.16

*1-tailed $p \leq 0.05$. **2-tailed $p \leq 0.05$.

TABLE B3-1

Medians and Ranges for Top 30 Features in Japanese Speaker Essays, Compared to Parents Texts

L1	JPPARENTS		JPGRADES		JPWEALTH		JPMANNER		JPOPINIONS		JPMAJOR	
	Median	Range	Median	Range	Median	Range	Median	Range	Median	Range	Median	Range
Semantic and Lexical Classes of Nouns												
adv./retroact.	0.43	3.48	0.32	1.59	1.42*	7.41	0.73	2.27	0.37	1.42	0.38	3.10
vague	2.20	9.17	1.62	7.64	2.36	7.81	1.06*	5.08	2.96*	11.97	4.80**	9.61
Personal Pronouns												
first person	3.21	14.10	4.76*	15.63	0.93**	13.49	5.14*	16.06	2.65	11.74	7.44**	20.59
third person	7.59	12.13	2.47**	6.25	6.36*	12.24	1.56**	6.18	8.25*	17.56	3.03*	16.67
Nominalization	1.61	5.83	1.43	6.25	1.32	5.00	1.56	5.71	1.48	4.13	3.83**	8.61
Gerunds	0.72	2.88	1.65*	4.86	0.50	4.09	1.11*	4.76	0.63*	5.43	1.04*	5.56
Verb Tenses												
past	1.74	6.92	3.70*	12.48	1.30	7.29	4.85**	9.92	3.04*	8.05	3.57**	11.26
present	12.30	14.91	8.54*	14.84	10.00*	11.62	9.09*	13.52	10.05	9.00	10.50	9.14
Semantic and Lexical Classes of Verbs												
private	3.03	6.30	3.83*	8.33	0.41**	6.12	3.65*	7.21	3.29*	5.77	4.98**	7.56
Modal Verbs												
possibility	1.65	5.26	0.85*	3.64	1.00*	2.92	1.06	3.65	1.32	3.17	2.00*	5.08
necessity	1.45	5.80	1.17	4.94	0.36**	2.50	0.78	4.38	1.92**	4.76	1.30	5.41
Passive	2.14	6.35	0.55**	2.38	0.43**	2.48	0.57**	3.00	1.32	3.13	0.98	3.13
be-main	3.23	9.02	2.67	6.83	3.17	5.67	4.86**	8.29	3.23*	11.02	4.88**	7.84
Infinitives	5.02	7.42	4.55	11.90	4.41*	9.36	4.86	13.85	7.39**	10.89	5.88**	10.51

(Continued)

L1	JPPARENTS		JPGRADES		JPWEALTH		JPMANNER		JPOPINIONS		JPMAJOR	
	Median	Range	Median	Range	Median	Range	Median	Range	Median	Range	Median	Range
Participles												
present	1.06	2.88	0.00*	2.30	0.93	5.26	1.04*	4.00	0.00*	1.14	0.00*	1.77
past	0.60	2.88	0.00*	0.91	1.01	3.01	0.40	2.65	0.00*	1.33	0.38	4.53
Adjectives												
attributive	2.69	4.42	1.74	6.77	4.55**	7.36	6.29**	12.01	2.84*	6.26	4.00**	7.06
predicative	3.23	9.79	2.08*	7.21	1.95*	10.91	3.99*	11.39	3.86*	10.55	3.79*	10.12
Semantic and Lexical Classes of Adverbs												
time	1.30	2.36	0.81	3.85	1.04	2.85	0.57*	3.03	0.57	2.71	0.91	3.92
place	1.60	3.46	1.63	4.83	1.30	5.45	2.27*	6.25	0.96	3.76	1.73*	5.23
amplifiers	3.08	7.50	2.30	7.01	1.79*	4.27	2.86	11.98	4.05*	8.45	3.74*	12.09
Noun and Adjective Clauses												
noun	2.69	4.62	2.08	6.25	1.72**	3.68	1.56*	3.50	1.52	4.65	2.28	6.67
full adjective	0.96	3.41	0.62	2.19	1.14	2.26	0.83	3.65	0.89	3.93	1.55**	5.41
Coordinating and Logical Conjunctions/Prepositions												
phrase-level	3.29	8.88	3.69	7.86	3.90	6.88	4.00*	6.06	2.82	6.55	3.83*	9.42
sentence-level	1.59	3.47	1.92*	3.85	1.07*	4.23	2.08*	5.87	2.12**	5.34	2.54**	7.62
log/sem conjunctions	0.38	2.17	0.62*	1.75	0.36	4.35	1.11**	3.65	0.56*	3.57	1.27**	4.65
Hedges												
lexical	0.53	1.92	0.30	1.44	0.87	2.26	0.77*	2.92	0.38	1.42	0.56	3.53
Demonstrative	0.43	1.56	0.40*	2.60	1.05**	5.80	1.62**	8.37	0.83**	4.33	0.89**	2.56
Emphatics	2.65	7.14	1.49*	4.09	0.93**	2.60	0.00**	3.41	3.83**	12.50	4.53**	9.29
Fixed Strings	0.80	4.76	0.96	2.73	1.25	8.70	1.60**	3.32	1.14*	3.95	1.28**	4.58

*1-tailed $p \leq 0.05$. **2-tailed $p \leq 0.05$.

TABLE B3-2
Medians and Ranges for Top 30 Features in Japanese Speaker Essays, Compared to Grades Texts

L1	JPGRADES		JPWEALTH		JPMANNER		JPOPINIONS		JPMAJOR	
	Median	*Range*	*Median*	*Range*	*Median*	*Range*	*Median*	*Range*	*Median*	*Range*
Semantic and Lexical Classes of Nouns										
adv./retroact.	**0.32**	1.59	**1.42****	7.41	**0.73***	2.27	**0.37**	1.42	**0.38**	3.10
vague	**1.62**	7.64	**2.36**	7.81	**1.06***	5.08	**2.96***	11.97	**4.80****	9.61
Personal Pronouns										
first person	**4.76**	15.63	**0.93****	13.49	**5.14**	16.06	**2.65**	11.74	**7.44***	20.59
third person	**2.47**	6.25	**6.36*****	12.24	**1.56**	6.18	**8.25****	17.56	**3.03***	16.67
Nominalization	**1.43**	6.25	**1.32***	5.00	**1.56**	5.71	**1.48**	4.13	**3.83*****	8.61
Gerunds	**1.65**	4.86	**0.50***	4.09	**1.11**	4.76	**0.63**	5.43	**1.04**	5.56
Verb Tenses										
past	**3.70**	12.48	**1.30***	7.29	**4.85**	9.92	**3.04**	8.05	**3.57**	11.26
present	**8.54**	14.84	**10.00***	11.62	**9.09**	13.52	**10.05***	9.00	**10.50****	9.14
Semantic and Lexical Classes of Verbs										
private	**3.83**	8.33	**0.41****	6.12	**3.65**	7.21	**3.29**	5.77	**4.98***	7.56
Modal Verbs										
possibility	**0.85**	3.64	**1.00**	2.92	**1.06**	3.65	**1.32***	3.17	**2.00****	5.08
necessity	**1.17**	4.94	**0.36***	2.50	**0.78**	4.38	**1.92****	4.76	**1.30***	5.41
Passive	**0.55**	2.38	**0.43**	2.48	**0.57**	3.00	**0.90****	3.13	**0.98****	3.13
be-main	**2.67**	6.83	**3.17**	5.67	**4.86****	8.29	**3.23***	11.02	**4.88*****	7.84
Infinitives	**4.55**	11.90	**4.41**	9.36	**4.86**	13.85	**7.39****	10.89	**5.88****	10.51

(Continued)

TABLE B3-2
(Continued)

L1	JPGRADES Median	JPGRADES Range	JPWEALTH Median	JPWEALTH Range	JPMANNER Median	JPMANNER Range	JPOPINIONS Median	JPOPINIONS Range	JPMAJOR Median	JPMAJOR Range
Participles										
present	**0.00**	2.30	**0.93***	5.26	**1.04****	4.00	**0.00**	1.14	**0.00**	1.77
past	**0.00**	0.91	**1.01****	3.01	**0.40***	2.65	**0.00**	1.33	**0.38***	4.53
Adjectives										
attributive	**1.74**	6.77	**4.55****	7.36	**6.29****	12.01	**2.84****	6.26	**4.00****	7.06
predicative	**2.08**	7.21	**1.95**	10.91	**3.99****	11.39	**3.86****	10.55	**3.79****	10.12
Semantic and Lexical Classes of Adverbs										
time	**0.81**	3.85	**1.04**	2.85	**0.57***	3.03	**0.57**	2.71	**0.91***	3.92
place	**1.63**	4.83	**1.30**	5.45	**2.27***	6.25	**0.96**	3.76	**1.73***	5.23
amplifiers	**2.30**	7.01	**1.79**	4.27	**2.86**	11.98	**4.05****	8.45	**3.74****	12.09
Noun and Adjective Clauses										
noun	**2.08**	6.25	**1.72***	3.68	**1.56***	3.50	**1.52**	4.65	**2.28**	6.67
full adjective	**0.63**	2.19	**1.14**	2.26	**0.83**	3.65	**0.89**	3.93	**1.55****	5.41
Coordinating and Logical Conjunctions/Prepositions										
phrase-level	**3.69**	7.86	**3.90**	6.88	**4.00**	6.06	**2.82**	6.55	**3.83***	9.42
sentence-level	**1.92**	3.85	**1.07****	4.23	**2.08**	5.87	**2.12**	5.34	**2.54***	7.62
log/sem conjunctions	**0.62**	1.75	**0.36***	4.35	**1.11**	3.65	**0.56**	3.57	**1.27****	4.65
Hedges										
lexical	**0.30**	1.44	**0.87***	2.26	**0.77***	2.92	**0.38**	1.42	**0.56***	3.53
Demonstrative	**0.40**	2.60	**1.05***	5.80	**1.62****	8.37	**0.83***	4.33	**0.89***	2.56
Emphatics	**1.49**	4.09	**0.93***	2.60	**0.00****	3.41	**3.83****	12.50	**4.53****	9.29
Fixed Strings	**0.96**	2.73	**1.25**	8.70	**1.60***	3.32	**1.14***	3.95	**1.28***	4.58

*1-tailed $p \leq 0.05$. **2-tailed $p \leq 0.05$.

293

TABLE B3-3

Medians and Ranges for Top 30 Features in Japanese Speaker Essays, Compared to Wealth Texts

L1	JPWEALTH		JPMANNER		JPOPINIONS		JPMAJOR	
	Median	Range	Median	Range	Median	Range	Median	Range
Semantic and Lexical Classes of Nouns								
adv./retroact.	1.42	7.41	0.73	2.27	0.37*	1.42	0.38	3.10
vague	2.36	7.81	1.06*	5.08	2.96*	11.97	4.80**	9.61
Personal Pronouns								
first person	0.93	13.49	5.14**	16.06	2.65**	11.74	7.44***	20.59
third person	6.36	12.24	1.56***	6.18	8.25**	17.56	3.03	16.67
Nominalization	1.32	5.00	1.56*	5.71	1.48*	4.13	3.83**	8.61
Gerunds	0.50	4.09	1.11*	4.76	0.63*	5.43	1.04**	5.56
Verb Tenses								
past	1.30	7.29	4.85**	9.92	3.04**	8.05	3.57***	11.26
present	10.00	11.62	9.09	13.52	10.05*	9.00	10.50*	9.14
Semantic and Lexical Classes of Verbs								
private	0.41	6.12	3.65**	7.21	3.29**	5.77	4.98**	7.56
Modal Verbs								
possibility	1.00	2.92	1.06	3.65	1.32*	3.17	2.00**	5.08
necessity	0.36	2.50	0.78*	4.38	1.92**	4.76	1.30**	5.41
Passive	0.43	2.48	0.57*	3.00	0.90*	3.13	0.98**	3.13
be-main	3.17	5.67	4.86**	8.29	3.23*	11.02	4.88***	7.84
Infinitives	4.41	9.36	4.86*	13.85	7.39**	10.89	5.88***	10.51

(Continued)

TABLE B3-3
(Continued)

L1	JPWEALTH		JPMANNER		JPOPINIONS		JPMAJOR	
	Median	Range	Median	Range	Median	Range	Median	Range
Participles								
present	0.93	5.26	1.04	4.00	0.00**	1.14	0.00*	1.77
past	1.01	3.01	0.40	2.65	0.00**	1.33	0.38	4.53
Adjectives								
attributive	4.55	7.36	6.29**	12.01	2.84	6.26	4.00	7.06
predicative	1.95	10.91	3.99**	11.39	3.86**	10.55	3.79**	10.12
Semantic and Lexical Classes of Adverbs								
time	1.04	2.85	0.57	3.03	0.57	2.71	0.91*	3.92
place	1.30	5.45	2.27**	6.25	0.96	3.76	1.73**	5.23
amplifiers	1.79	4.27	2.86**	11.98	4.05**	8.45	3.74**	12.09
Noun and Adjective Clauses								
noun	1.72	3.68	1.56	3.50	1.52*	4.65	2.28**	6.67
full adjective	1.14	2.26	0.83	3.65	0.89	3.93	1.55**	5.41
Coordinating and Logical Conjunctions/Prepositions								
phrase-level	3.90	6.88	4.00	6.06	2.82	6.55	3.83*	9.42
sentence-level	1.07	4.23	2.08**	5.87	2.12**	5.34	2.54**	7.62
log/sem conjunctions	0.36	4.35	1.11**	3.65	0.56*	3.57	1.27**	4.65
Hedges								
lexical	0.87	2.26	0.77	2.92	0.38	1.42	0.56	3.53
Demonstrative	1.05	5.80	1.62*	8.37	0.83	4.33	0.89	2.56
Emphatics	0.93	2.60	0.00**	3.41	3.83**	12.50	4.53**	9.29
Fixed Strings	1.25	8.70	1.60*	3.32	1.14	3.95	1.28*	4.58

*1-tailed $p \leq 0.05$. **2tailed $p \leq 0.05$.

TABLE B3-4

Medians and Ranges for Top 30 Features in Japanese Speaker Essays, Compared to Manner Texts

L1	JPMANNER		JPOPINIONS		JPMAJOR	
	Median	*Range*	*Median*	*Range*	*Median*	*Range*
Semantic and Lexical Classes of Nouns						
adv./retroact.	**0.73**	2.27	**0.37***	1.42	**0.38**	3.10
vague	**1.06**	5.08	**2.96****	11.97	**4.80****	9.61
Personal Pronouns						
first person	**5.14**	16.06	**2.65**	11.74	**7.44***	20.59
third person	**1.56**	6.18	**8.25****	17.56	**3.03****	16.67
Nominalization	**1.56**	5.71	**1.48**	4.13	**3.83****	8.61
Gerunds	**1.11**	4.76	**0.63**	5.43	**1.04**	5.56
Verb Tenses						
past	**4.85**	9.92	**3.04***	8.05	**3.57**	11.26
present	**9.09**	13.52	**10.05***	9.00	**10.50***	9.14
Semantic and Lexical Classes of Verbs						
private	**3.65**	7.21	**3.29**	5.77	**4.98****	7.56
Modal Verbs						
possibility	**1.06**	3.65	**1.32***	3.17	**2.00****	5.08
necessity	**0.78**	4.38	**1.92****	4.76	**1.30***	5.41
Passive	**0.57**	3.00	**0.90***	3.13	**0.98***	3.13
be-main	**4.86**	8.29	**3.23**	11.02	**4.88***	7.84
Infinitives	**4.86**	13.85	**7.39****	10.89	**5.88***	10.51

(Continued)

TABLE B3-4
(Continued)

L1	JPMANNER		JPOPINIONS		JPMAJOR	
	Median	*Range*	*Median*	*Range*	*Median*	*Range*
Participles						
present	**1.04**	4.00	**0.00****	1.14	**0.00****	1.77
past	**0.40**	2.65	**0.00***	1.33	0.38	4.53
Adjectives						
attributive	**6.29**	12.01	**2.84****	6.26	**4.00***	7.06
predicative	**3.99**	11.39	3.86	10.55	3.79	10.12
Semantic and Lexical Classes of Adverbs						
time	**0.57**	3.03	**0.57***	2.71	**0.91****	3.92
place	**2.27**	6.25	**0.96***	3.76	1.73	5.23
amplifiers	**2.86**	11.98	**4.05***	8.45	**3.74****	12.09
Noun and Adjective Clauses						
noun	**1.56**	3.50	**1.52***	4.65	**2.28****	6.67
full adjective	**0.83**	3.65	0.89	3.93	**1.55****	5.41
Coordinating and Logical Conjunctions/Prepositions						
phrase-level	**4.00**	6.06	2.82	6.55	3.83	9.42
sentence-level	**2.08**	5.87	2.12	5.34	**2.54***	7.62
log/sem conjunctions	**1.11**	3.65	0.56	3.57	**1.27***	4.65
Hedges						
lexical	**0.77**	2.92	**0.38***	1.42	0.56	3.53
Demonstrative	**1.62**	8.37	**0.83***	4.33	**0.89***	2.56
Emphatics	**0.00**	3.41	**3.83****	12.50	**4.53****	9.29
Fixed Strings	**1.60**	3.32	1.14	3.95	1.28	4.58

*1-tailed $p \leq 0.05$. **2-tailed $p \leq 0.05$.

TABLE B3-5
Medians and Ranges for Top 30 Features in Japanese Speaker Essays, Compared to Opinions Texts

L1	JPOPINIONS		JPMAJOR	
	Median	*Range*	*Median*	*Range*
Semantic and Lexical Classes of Nouns				
adv./retroact.	**0.37**	1.42	**0.38**	3.10
vague	**2.96**	11.97	**04.80****	9.61
Personal Pronouns				
first person	**2.65**	11.74	**7.44****	20.59
third person	**8.25**	17.56	**3.03****	16.67
Nominalization	**1.48**	4.13	**3.83****	8.61
Gerunds	**0.63**	5.43	**1.04**	5.56
Verb Tenses				
past	**3.04**	8.05	**3.57***	11.26
present	**10.05**	9.00	**10.50**	9.14
Semantic and Lexical Classes of Verbs				
private	**3.29**	5.77	**4.98****	7.56
Modal Verbs				
possibility	**1.32**	3.17	**2.00****	5.08
necessity	**1.92**	4.76	**1.30****	5.41
Passive	**0.90**	3.13	**0.98**	3.13
be-main	**3.23**	11.02	**4.88****	7.84
Infinitives	**7.39**	10.89	**5.88***	10.51

(Continued)

TABLE B3-5
(Continued)

LI	JPOPINIONS		JPMAJOR	
	Median	Range	Median	Range
Participles				
present	0.00	1.14	0.00	1.77
past	0.00	1.33	0.38*	4.53
Adjectives				
attributive	2.84	6.26	4.00*	7.06
predicative	3.86	10.55	3.79	10.12
Semantic and Lexical Classes of Adverbs				
time	0.57	2.71	0.91*	3.92
place	0.96	3.76	1.73*	5.23
amplifiers	4.05	8.45	3.74	12.09
Noun and Adjective Clauses				
noun	1.52	4.65	2.28*	6.67
full adjective	0.89	3.93	1.55*	5.41
Coordinating and Logical Conjunctions/Prepositions				
phrase-level	2.82	6.55	3.83*	9.42
sentence-level	2.12	5.34	2.54*	7.62
log/sem conjunctions	0.56	3.57	1.27**	4.65
Hedges				
lexical	0.38	1.42	0.56*	3.53
Demonstrative	0.83	4.33	0.89	2.56
Emphatics	3.83	12.50	4.53	9.29
Fixed Strings	1.14	3.95	1.28	4.58

* 1-tailed $p \leq 0.05$. **2-tailed $p \leq 0.05$.

TABLE B4-1

Medians and Ranges for Top 30 Features in Korean Speaker Essays, Compared to Parents Texts

L1	KRPARENTS		KRGRADES		KRWEALTH		KRMANNER		KROPINIONS		KRMAJOR	
	Median	Range	Median	Range	Median	Range	Median	Range	Median	Range	Median	Range
Semantic and Lexical Classes of Nouns												
adv./retroact.	**0.42**	3.70	**0.55**	3.25	**1.23***	3.33	**0.47**	5.28	**0.35**	2.31	**0.42**	0.96
vague	**2.94**	8.82	**3.38**	8.73	**1.67***	4.68	**3.49**	13.29	**4.29***	7.84	**4.17***	11.50
Personal Pronouns												
first person	**5.23**	9.57	**3.33**	12.96	**1.17****	9.03	**0.69****	11.82	**03.49**	13.15	**3.11**	13.13
third person	**9.32**	15.58	**2.92****	8.90	**6.49***	9.02	**2.19****	5.22	**7.26***	11.40	**03.50****	12.20
Nominalization	**1.76**	5.82	**1.63**	6.43	**0.63****	6.43	**1.01**	13.33	**1.71**	13.33	**2.63***	12.66
Gerunds	**1.00**	4.02	**1.39**	5.52	**0.53***	1.73	**0.83**	3.24	**1.25**	8.23	**1.05**	4.00
Verb Tenses												
past	**0.85**	7.64	**5.80****	9.55	**1.01**	7.22	**5.08****	8.67	**4.73****	10.92	**3.45***	11.82
present	**11.96**	16.63	**8.77***	10.06	**11.69**	10.93	**6.99****	12.34	**9.14***	11.50	**8.47***	23.96
Semantic and Lexical Classes of Verbs												
private	**2.50**	8.20	**4.44***	9.57	**1.36***	5.70	**4.17***	9.01	**2.74**	7.75	**3.04***	8.44
Modal Verbs												
possibility	**1.50**	3.78	**1.39**	4.39	**1.02***	2.66	**1.69**	4.07	**1.28***	3.45	**1.33**	4.00
necessity	**1.16**	4.76	**1.37**	6.43	**0.58***	5.56	**1.01**	5.00	**02.96****	8.35	**1.42**	6.00
Passive	**1.00**	3.81	**0.34***	3.26	**0.00****	2.22	**1.18**	2.78	**0.68***	1.54	**0.89**	2.37
be-main	**3.43**	8.24	**3.12**	5.93	**2.92***	5.13	**4.47***	10.56	**4.95***	12.82	**3.74***	8.86
Infinitives	**4.73**	10.46	**2.78****	5.16	**2.38****	2.78	**3.72***	11.67	**2.99****	8.05	**01.85****	6.50

(Continued)

TABLE B4-1
(Continued)

L1	KRPARENTS		KRGRADES		KRWEALTH		KRMANNER		KROPINIONS		KRMAJOR	
	Median	Range	Median	Range	Median	Range	Median	Range	Median	Range	Median	Range
Participles												
present	1.10	3.81	0.00**	2.17	0.56*	2.27	0.42*	1.69	0.00***	0.71	0.23*	1.82
past	0.71	3.00	0.27*	1.07	0.68	2.22	0.00*	1.75	0.00***	5.64	0.00	2.88
Adjectives												
attributive	2.27	7.14	1.72	6.06	7.20**	11.61	3.85**	13.07	2.18	6.60	2.36*	10.61
predicative	3.30	5.90	2.02	6.21	3.19	10.28	3.85*	20.09	2.81	6.96	3.39	8.08
Semantic and Lexical Classes of Adverbs												
time	0.50	4.86	1.36*	4.76	0.89	2.88	0.68	2.93	0.70	2.00	1.30*	2.94
place	1.19	4.76	1.10	5.45	1.62*	7.02	1.92*	6.10	0.94	4.29	1.07	4.04
amplifiers	3.09	11.06	2.64	7.35	1.27**	4.93	2.82	9.65	2.65	5.26	3.33	7.19
Noun and Adjective Clauses												
noun	1.78	5.27	2.17	4.42	1.30	2.26	1.25*	7.08	2.30	4.72	1.33	8.75
full adjective	0.86	2.69	0.46*	2.38	0.69	3.06	1.40*	4.39	0.85	2.30	0.90	4.44
Coordinating and Logical Conjunctions/Prepositions												
phrase-level	3.50	10.00	4.29	9.66	4.67*	11.03	4.20	9.79	4.10	12.23	3.78	8.48
sentence-level	2.03	4.86	1.72	5.08	1.52	2.81	2.10	8.85	1.51	3.13	1.72	6.61
log/sem conjunctions	0.33	2.14	0.46*	1.77	0.00*	1.25	0.96**	2.00	1.09**	1.50	0.48*	2.22
Hedges												
lexical	0.37	2.21	0.00*	1.01	1.48**	3.19	1.05**	4.17	0.32	1.45	2.73**	12.32
Demonstrative	1.47	7.33	0.94	3.33	1.30	3.25	2.00*	10.00	1.42	5.56	1.33	6.25
Emphatics	2.67	6.43	1.32	5.88	0.00**	1.89	2.37	9.38	3.71*	9.86	2.33	8.64
Fixed Strings	0.73	3.81	0.79	3.33	1.52*	2.27	1.40	4.55	0.69	1.81	1.01*	2.02

*1-tailed $p \leq 0.05$. **2-tailed $p \leq 0.05$.

301

TABLE B4-2

Medians and Ranges for Top 30 Features in Korean Speaker Essays, Compared to Grades Texts

L1	KRGRADES		KRWEALTH		KRMANNER		KROPINIONS		KRMAJOR	
	Median	*Range*	*Median*	*Range*	*Median*	*Range*	*Median*	*Range*	*Median*	*Range*
Semantic and Lexical Classes of Nouns										
adv./retroact.	**0.55**	3.25	**1.23***	3.33	**0.47**	5.28	**0.35**	2.31	**0.42***	0.96
vague	**3.38**	8.73	**1.67***	4.68	**3.49**	13.29	**4.29**	7.84	**4.17***	11.50
Personal Pronouns										
first person	**3.33**	12.96	**1.17***	9.03	**0.69***	11.82	**3.49**	13.15	**3.11**	13.13
third person	**2.92**	8.90	**6.49****	9.02	**2.19**	5.22	**7.26****	11.40	**3.50***	12.20
Nominalization	**1.63**	6.43	**0.63***	6.43	**1.01**	13.33	**1.71**	13.33	**2.63***	12.66
Gerunds	**1.39**	5.52	**0.53***	1.73	**0.83**	3.24	**1.25**	8.23	**1.05**	4.00
Verb Tenses										
past	**5.80**	9.55	**1.01****	7.22	**5.08**	8.67	**4.73***	10.92	**3.45***	11.82
present	**8.77**	10.06	**11.69***	10.93	**6.99****	12.34	**9.14**	11.50	**8.47**	23.96
Semantic and Lexical Classes of Verbs										
private	**4.44**	9.57	**1.36****	5.70	**4.17**	9.01	**2.74***	7.75	**3.04**	8.44
Modal Verbs										
possibility	**1.39**	4.39	**1.02**	2.66	**1.69**	4.07	**1.28**	3.45	**1.33**	4.00
necessity	**1.37**	6.43	**0.58****	5.56	**1.01**	5.00	**2.96****	8.35	**1.42**	6.00
Passive	**0.34**	3.26	**0.00***	2.22	**1.18****	2.78	**0.68**	1.54	**0.89****	2.37
be-main	**3.13**	5.93	**2.92**	5.13	**4.47***	10.56	**4.95****	12.82	**3.74***	8.86
Infinitives	**2.78**	5.16	**2.38**	2.78	**3.72***	11.67	**2.99**	8.05	**1.85***	6.50

(Continued)

TABLE B4-2
(Continued)

LI	KRGRADES		KRWEALTH		KRMANNER		KROPINIONS		KRMAJOR	
	Median	*Range*	*Median*	*Range*	*Median*	*Range*	*Median*	*Range*	*Median*	*Range*
Participles										
present	**0.00**	2.17	**0.56***	2.27	**0.42**	1.69	**0.00***	0.71	**0.23**	1.82
past	**0.27**	1.07	**0.68***	2.22	**0.00**	1.75	**0.00***	5.64	**0.00**	2.88
Adjectives										
attributive	**1.72**	6.06	**7.20****	11.61	**3.85****	13.07	**2.18***	6.60	**2.36***	10.61
predicative	**2.02**	6.21	**3.19**	10.28	**3.85***	20.09	**2.81***	6.96	**3.39***	8.08
Semantic and Lexical Classes of Adverbs										
time	**1.36**	4.76	**0.89***	2.88	**0.68***	2.93	**0.70***	2.00	**1.30**	2.94
place	**1.10**	5.45	**1.62**	7.02	**1.92***	6.10	**0.94***	4.29	**1.07**	4.04
amplifiers	**2.64**	7.35	**1.27****	4.93	**2.82**	9.65	**2.65**	5.26	**3.33**	7.19
Noun and Adjective Clauses										
noun	**2.17**	4.42	**1.30***	2.26	**1.25***	7.08	**2.30**	4.72	**1.33**	8.75
full adjective	**0.46**	2.38	**0.69**	3.06	**1.40****	4.39	**0.85**	2.30	**0.90***	4.44
Coordinating and Logical Conjunctions/Prepositions										
phrase-level	**4.29**	9.66	**4.67**	11.03	**4.20**	9.79	**4.10**	12.23	**3.78**	8.48
sentence-level	**1.72**	5.08	**1.52***	2.81	**2.10**	8.85	**1.51**	3.13	**1.72**	6.61
log/sem conjunctions	**0.46**	1.77	**0.00***	1.25	**0.96***	2.00	**1.09****	1.50	**0.48**	2.22
Hedges										
lexical	**0.00**	1.01	**1.48****	3.19	**1.05****	4.17	**0.32***	1.45	**2.73****	12.32
Demonstrative	**0.94**	3.33	**1.30**	3.25	**2.00***	10.00	**1.42***	5.56	**1.33***	6.25
Emphatics	**1.32**	5.88	**0.00****	1.89	**2.37***	9.38	**3.71****	9.86	**2.33***	8.64
Fixed Strings	**0.79**	3.33	**1.52**	2.27	**1.40**	4.55	**0.69**	1.81	**1.01**	2.02

*1-tailed $p \le 0.05$. **2-tailed $p \le 0.05$.

303

TABLE B4-3

Medians and Ranges for Top 30 Features in Korean Speaker Essays, Compared to Wealth Texts

L1	KRWEALTH		KRMANNER		KROPINIONS		KRMAJOR	
	Median	Range	Median	Range	Median	Range	Median	Range
Semantic and Lexical Classes of Nouns								
adv./retroact.	1.23	3.33	0.47	5.28	0.35*	2.31	0.42**	0.96
vague	1.67	4.68	3.49**	13.29	4.29**	7.84	4.17**	11.50
Personal Pronouns								
first person	1.17	9.03	0.69	11.82	3.49*	13.15	3.11*	13.13
third person	6.49	9.02	2.19**	5.22	7.26	11.40	3.50*	12.20
Nominalization	0.63	6.43	1.01*	13.33	1.71*	13.33	2.63**	12.66
Gerunds	0.53	1.73	0.83*	3.24	1.25**	8.23	1.05**	4.00
Verb Tenses								
past	1.01	7.22	5.08***	8.67	4.73**	10.92	3.45*	11.82
present	11.69	10.93	6.99***	12.34	9.14	11.50	8.47	23.96
Semantic and Lexical Classes of Verbs								
private	1.36	5.70	4.17**	9.01	2.74*	7.75	3.04**	8.44
Modal Verbs								
possibility	1.02	2.66	1.69*	4.07	1.28	3.45	1.33*	4.00
necessity	0.58	5.56	1.01**	5.00	2.96**	8.35	1.42**	6.00
Passive	0.00	2.22	1.18**	2.78	0.68**	1.54	0.89**	2.37
be-main	2.92	5.13	4.47**	10.56	4.95**	12.82	3.74**	8.86
Infinitives	2.38	2.78	3.72**	11.67	2.99*	8.05	1.85	6.50

(Continued)

TABLE B4-3
(Continued)

L1	KRWEALTH		KRMANNER		KROPINIONS		KRMAJOR	
	Median	Range	Median	Range	Median	Range	Median	Range
Participles								
present	**0.56**	2.27	**0.42**	1.69	**0.00****	0.71	**0.23***	1.82
past	**0.68**	2.22	**0.00***	1.75	**0.00***	5.64	**0.00**	2.88
Adjectives								
attributive	**7.20**	11.61	**3.85****	13.07	**2.18****	6.60	**2.36****	10.61
predicative	**3.19**	10.28	**3.85***	20.09	**2.81**	6.96	**3.39**	8.08
Semantic and Lexical Classes of Adverbs								
time	**0.89**	2.88	**0.68**	2.93	**0.70**	2.00	**1.30***	2.94
place	**1.62**	7.02	**1.92**	6.10	**0.94***	4.29	**1.07**	4.04
amplifiers	**1.27**	4.93	**2.82****	9.65	**2.65****	5.26	**3.33****	7.19
Noun and Adjective Clauses								
noun	**1.30**	2.26	**1.25**	7.08	**2.30****	4.72	**1.33**	8.75
full adjective	**0.69**	3.06	**1.40****	4.39	**0.85**	2.30	**0.90***	4.44
Coordinating and Logical Conjunctions/Prepositions								
phrase-level	**4.67**	11.03	**4.20**	9.79	**4.10**	12.23	**3.78**	8.48
sentence-level	**1.52**	2.81	**2.10***	8.85	**1.51**	3.13	**1.72***	6.61
log/sem conjunctions	**0.00**	1.25	**0.96****	2.00	**1.09****	1.50	**0.48****	2.22
Hedges								
lexical	**1.48**	3.19	**1.05**	4.17	**0.32****	1.45	**2.73****	12.32
Demonstrative	**1.30**	3.25	**2.00***	10.00	**1.42**	5.56	**1.33***	6.25
Emphatics	**0.00**	1.89	**2.37****	9.38	**3.71****	9.86	**2.33****	8.64
Fixed Strings	**1.52**	2.27	**1.40**	4.55	**0.69****	1.81	**1.01**	2.02

*1-tailed $p \leq 0.05$. **2-tailed $p \leq 0.05$.

TABLE B4-4

Medians and Ranges for Top 30 Features in Korean Speaker Essays, Compared to Manner Texts

L1	KRMANNER		KROPINIONS		KRMAJOR	
	Median	*Range*	*Median*	*Range*	*Median*	*Range*
Semantic and Lexical Classes of Nouns						
adv./retroact.	**0.47**	5.28	**0.35**	2.31	**0.42**	0.96
vague	**3.49**	13.29	**4.29**	7.84	**4.17***	11.50
Personal Pronouns						
first person	**0.69**	11.82	**3.49***	13.15	**3.11***	13.13
third person	**2.19**	5.22	**7.26****	11.40	**3.50***	12.20
Nominalization	**1.01**	13.33	**1.71**	13.33	**2.63***	12.66
Gerunds	**0.83**	3.24	**1.25**	8.23	**1.05**	4.00
Verb Tenses						
past	**5.08**	8.67	**4.73**	10.92	**3.45***	11.82
present	**6.99**	12.34	**9.14***	11.50	**8.47***	23.96
Semantic and Lexical Classes of Verbs						
private	**4.17**	9.01	**2.74***	7.75	**3.04**	8.44
Modal Verbs						
possibility	**1.69**	4.07	**1.28***	3.45	**1.33**	4.00
necessity	**1.01**	5.00	**2.96****	8.35	**1.42***	6.00
Passive	**1.18**	2.78	**0.68***	1.54	**0.89**	2.37
be-main	**4.47**	10.56	**4.95**	12.82	**3.74**	8.86
Infinitives	**3.72**	11.67	**2.99***	8.05	**1.85****	6.50

(Continued)

TABLE B4-4
(Continued)

L1	KRMANNER		KROPINIONS		KRMAJOR	
	Median	Range	Median	Range	Median	Range
Participles						
present	**0.42**	1.69	**0.00****	0.71	**0.23**	1.82
past	**0.00**	1.75	**0.00**	5.64	**0.00**	2.88
Adjectives						
attributive	**3.85**	13.07	**2.18***	6.60	**2.36***	10.61
predicative	**3.85**	20.09	**2.81***	6.96	**3.39**	8.08
Semantic and Lexical Classes of Adverbs						
time	**0.68**	2.93	**0.70**	2.00	**1.30***	2.94
place	**1.92**	6.10	**0.94***	4.29	**1.07**	4.04
amplifiers	**2.82**	9.65	**2.65**	5.26	**3.33**	7.19
Noun and Adjective Clauses						
noun	**1.25**	7.08	**2.30****	4.72	**1.33**	8.75
full adjective	**1.40**	4.39	**0.85***	2.30	**0.90**	4.44
Coordinating and Logical Conjunctions/Prepositions						
phrase-level	**4.20**	9.79	**4.10**	12.23	**3.78**	8.48
sentence-level	**2.10**	8.85	**1.51***	3.13	**1.72**	6.61
log/sem conjunctions	**0.96**	2.00	**1.09**	1.50	**0.48***	2.22
Hedges						
lexical	**1.05**	4.17	**0.32****	1.45	**2.73****	12.32
Demonstrative	**2.00**	10.00	**1.42**	5.56	**1.33**	6.25
Emphatics	**2.37**	9.38	**3.71***	9.86	**2.33**	8.64
Fixed Strings	**1.40**	4.55	**0.69***	1.81	**1.01**	2.02

*1-tailed $p \leq 0.05$. **2-tailed $p \leq 0.05$.

TABLE B4-5
Medians and Ranges for Top 30 Features in Korean Speaker Essays, Compared to Opinions Texts

L1	KROPINIONS		KRMAJOR	
	Median	Range	Median	Range
Semantic and Lexical Classes of Nouns				
adv./retroact.	**0.35**	2.31	**0.42**	0.96
vague	**4.29**	7.84	**4.17**	11.50
Personal Pronouns				
first person	**3.49**	13.15	**3.11**	13.13
third person	**7.26**	11.40	**3.50***	12.20
Nominalization	**1.71**	13.33	**2.63****	12.66
Gerunds	**1.25**	8.23	**1.05**	4.00
Verb Tenses				
past	**4.73**	10.92	**3.45**	11.82
present	**9.14**	11.50	**8.47**	23.96
Semantic and Lexical Classes of Verbs				
private	**2.74**	7.75	**3.04***	8.44
Modal Verbs				
possibility	**1.28**	3.45	**1.33**	4.00
necessity	**2.96**	8.35	**1.42***	6.00
Passive	**0.68**	1.54	**0.89***	2.37
be-main	**4.95**	12.82	**3.74**	8.86
Infinitives	**2.99**	8.05	**1.85***	6.50

(Continued)

308

TABLE B4-5
(Continued)

L1	KROPINIONS		KRMAJOR	
	Median	*Range*	*Median*	*Range*
Participles				
present	**0.00**	0.71	**0.23***	1.82
past	**0.00**	5.64	**0.00***	2.88
Adjectives				
attributive	**2.18**	6.60	**2.36**	10.61
predicative	**2.81**	6.96	**3.39**	8.08
Semantic and Lexical Classes of Adverbs				
time	**0.70**	2.00	**1.30***	2.94
place	**0.94**	4.29	**1.07***	4.04
amplifiers	**2.65**	5.26	**3.33***	7.19
Noun and Adjective Clauses				
noun	**2.30**	4.72	**1.33**	8.75
full adjective	**0.85**	2.30	**0.90***	4.44
Coordinating and Logical Conjunctions/Prepositions				
phrase-level	**4.10**	12.23	**3.78**	8.48
sentence-level	**1.51**	3.13	**1.72**	6.61
log/sem conjunctions	**1.09**	1.50	**0.48***	2.22
Hedges				
lexical	**0.32**	1.45	**2.73****	12.32
Demonstrative	**1.42**	5.56	**1.33**	6.25
Emphatics	**3.71**	9.86	**2.33**	8.64
Fixed Strings	**0.69**	1.81	**1.01***	2.02

*1-tailed $p \leq 0.05$. **2-tailed $p \leq 0.05$.

TABLE B5-1

Medians and Ranges for Top 30 Features in Vietnamese Speaker Essays, Compared to Parents Texts

L1	VTPARENTS		VTGRADES		VTWEALTH		VTMANNER		VTOPINIONS		VTMAJOR	
	Median	Range	Median	Range	Median	Range	Median	Range	Median	Range	Median	Range
Semantic and Lexical Classes of Nouns												
adv./retroact.	0.00	5.00	0.19	2.16	0.20	3.72	0.43	2.22	0.00	0.87	0.51	2.78
vague	2.58	5.34	1.67*	6.42	2.21	7.34	3.17	7.94	1.88*	4.40	1.48*	5.65
Personal Pronouns												
first person	2.38	21.40	6.23**	11.44	3.60	16.77	2.00	8.93	1.47	10.19	3.97	15.04
third person	8.08	12.18	2.56**	9.36	7.17	13.21	2.10**	4.48	7.86	17.90	3.90**	13.33
Nominalization	0.96	3.62	1.61*	5.42	1.27	4.79	1.82**	2.54	1.26*	2.86	2.69**	8.42
Gerunds	0.74	3.03	1.48*	3.33	0.76	1.96	1.39*	2.09	0.65	3.03	0.80	4.17
Verb Tenses												
past	3.56	10.71	3.67	7.21	5.24*	12.43	2.78	7.68	0.99**	9.00	1.78*	5.83
present	11.60	10.27	10.00	13.51	9.52	10.47	7.74**	9.46	9.29*	5.82	8.08**	7.96
Semantic and Lexical Classes of Verbs												
private	2.86	7.10	2.56	5.87	1.18**	2.93	2.72	3.19	2.96	6.02	3.17	8.42
Modal Verbs												
possibility	1.07	4.61	0.87	4.14	0.68*	5.71	0.56*	2.33	1.52*	3.13	0.74*	4.40
necessity	0.78	2.72	1.19	4.43	0.74	4.29	0.60	2.56	1.90**	2.71	0.51*	2.00
Passive	0.52	5.00	0.51	2.96	0.59	1.94	0.40*	1.11	0.50	1.50	0.44	3.10
be-main	2.75	6.55	2.92	4.02	2.30	5.01	5.36**	10.79	3.72*	6.22	3.37	5.56
Infinitives	2.67	11.11	2.86	7.13	3.35	4.61	3.19	3.62	4.29**	5.48	2.38	6.15

(Continued)

TABLE B5-1
(Continued)

LI	VTPARENTS Median	Range	VTGRADES Median	Range	VTWEALTH Median	Range	VTMANNER Median	Range	VTOPINIONS Median	Range	VTMAJOR Median	Range
Participles												
present	**0.30**	2.86	**0.49**	2.27	**0.59**	4.94	**1.39****	4.44	**0.00***	0.76	**0.52**	1.98
past	**0.00**	4.17	**0.00***	1.07	**0.00**	1.90	**0.27**	1.33	**0.26**	1.00	**0.33**	2.13
Adjectives												
attributive	**2.17**	7.14	**2.02**	5.60	**3.82****	14.64	**3.67***	3.60	**1.48**	4.41	**4.00****	7.22
predicative	**2.36**	9.85	**1.56***	6.34	**2.74**	8.49	**3.60****	10.94	**2.78**	4.29	**3.79***	10.42
Semantic and Lexical Classes of Adverbs												
time	**0.97**	3.24	**0.97**	4.00	**0.49**	2.42	**0.56***	1.79	**0.94**	2.55	**1.25**	2.66
place	**1.35**	5.09	**2.00***	5.45	**2.21**	4.35	**2.08***	4.22	**1.39**	2.68	**2.66****	5.72
amplifiers	**2.88**	8.16	**2.73**	6.07	**2.05***	5.76	**2.38**	6.18	**1.99**	4.35	**1.59***	3.01
Noun and Adjective Clauses												
noun	**1.97**	4.09	**2.24**	4.38	**1.08***	5.88	**0.89****	2.39	**2.27**	3.77	**1.49***	2.84
full adjective	**0.68**	2.73	**1.01**	1.95	**0.74**	3.68	**0.67**	2.61	**0.48**	2.87	**1.19***	4.09
Coordinating and Logical Conjunctions/Prepositions												
phrase-level	**4.00**	11.15	**3.43**	12.67	**4.50**	12.22	**4.34**	9.40	**4.55**	5.23	**3.87**	7.15
sentence-level	**1.47**	2.82	**1.28**	4.55	**0.90***	3.92	**1.28**	2.75	**1.73**	3.89	**1.12**	3.45
log/sem conjunctions	**0.48**	2.22	**0.42**	1.10	**0.30***	1.96	**1.28****	1.71	**0.76***	2.21	**0.95***	2.92
Hedges												
lexical	**0.34**	2.65	**0.49**	1.63	**1.50****	5.24	**0.40**	2.22	**0.25**	1.28	**0.77**	2.08
Demonstrative	**0.45**	3.66	**0.63**	1.97	**1.08***	3.68	**1.80****	4.57	**0.77***	2.46	**1.09***	6.03
Emphatics	**2.02**	6.25	**2.33**	4.88	**1.76**	6.85	**3.53***	6.09	**2.95**	3.84	**2.82**	4.73
Fixed Strings	**1.01**	2.66	**1.61****	4.74	**1.32***	3.42	**1.20***	5.61	**1.01***	3.24	**1.01***	3.46

*1-tailed $p \leq 0.05$. **2-tailed $p \leq 0.05$.

311

TABLE B5-2
Medians and Ranges for Top 30 Features in Vietnamese Speaker Essays, Compared to Grades Texts

L1	VTGRADES		VTWEALTH		VTMANNER		VTOPINIONS		VTMAJOR	
	Median	Range	Median	Range	Median	Range	Median	Range	Median	Range
Semantic and Lexical Classes of Nouns										
adv./retroact.	**0.19**	2.16	**0.20***	3.72	**0.43**	2.22	**0.00**	0.87	**0.51**	2.78
vague	**1.67**	6.42	**2.21**	7.34	**3.17***	7.94	**1.88**	4.40	**1.48**	5.65
Personal Pronouns										
first person	**6.23**	11.44	**3.60***	16.77	**2.00****	8.93	**1.47****	10.19	**3.97***	15.04
third person	**2.56**	9.36	**7.17****	13.21	**2.10**	4.48	**7.86****	17.90	**3.90***	13.33
Nominalization	**1.61**	5.42	**1.27**	4.79	**1.82***	2.54	**1.26**	2.86	**2.69****	8.42
Gerunds	**1.48**	3.33	**0.76****	1.96	**1.39**	2.09	**0.65***	3.03	**0.80***	4.17
Verb Tenses										
past	**3.67**	7.21	**5.24**	12.43	**2.78**	7.68	**0.99****	9.00	**1.78***	5.83
present	**10.00**	13.51	**9.52**	10.47	**7.74***	9.46	**9.29**	5.82	**8.08***	7.96
Semantic and Lexical Classes of Verbs										
private	**2.56**	5.87	**1.18****	2.93	**2.72***	3.19	**2.96**	6.02	**3.17**	8.42
Modal Verbs										
possibility	**0.87**	4.14	**0.68**	5.71	**0.56**	2.33	**1.52***	3.13	**0.74**	4.40
necessity	**1.19**	4.43	**0.74**	4.29	**0.60**	2.56	**1.90***	2.71	**0.51***	2.00
Passive	**0.51**	2.96	**0.59**	1.94	**0.40**	1.11	**0.50**	1.50	**0.44**	3.10
be-main	**2.92**	4.02	**2.30**	5.01	**5.36****	10.79	**3.72****	6.22	**3.37***	5.56
Infinitives	**2.86**	7.13	**3.35**	4.61	**3.19**	3.62	**4.29***	5.48	**2.38**	6.15

(Continued)

TABLE B5-2
(Continued)

L1	VTGRADES		VTWEALTH		VTMANNER		VTOPINIONS		VTMAJOR	
	Median	*Range*	*Median*	*Range*	*Median*	*Range*	*Median*	*Range*	*Median*	*Range*
Participles										
present	**0.49**	2.27	**0.59**	4.94	**1.39****	4.44	**0.00****	0.76	**0.52**	1.98
past	**0.00**	1.07	**0.00**	1.90	**0.27***	1.33	**0.26***	1.00	**0.33***	2.13
Adjectives										
attributive	**2.02**	5.60	**3.82****	14.64	**3.67***	3.60	**1.48**	4.41	**4.00****	7.22
predicative	**1.56**	6.34	**2.74**	8.49	**3.60****	10.94	**2.78***	4.29	**3.79***	10.42
Semantic and Lexical Classes of Adverbs										
time	**0.97**	4.00	**0.49**	2.42	**0.56***	1.79	**0.94**	2.55	**1.25***	2.66
place	**2.00**	5.45	**2.21**	4.35	**2.08**	4.22	**1.39***	2.68	**2.66***	5.72
amplifiers	**2.73**	6.07	**2.05***	5.76	**2.38**	6.18	**1.99***	4.35	**1.59***	3.01
Noun and Adjective Clauses										
noun	**2.24**	4.38	**1.08***	5.88	**0.89****	2.39	**2.27**	3.77	**1.49***	2.84
full adjective	**1.01**	1.95	**0.74**	3.68	**0.67**	2.61	**0.48***	2.87	**1.19**	4.09
Coordinating and Logical Conjunctions/Prepositions										
phrase-level	**3.43**	12.67	**4.50***	12.22	**4.34***	9.40	**4.55***	5.23	**3.87**	7.15
sentence-level	**1.28**	4.55	**0.90***	3.92	**1.28**	2.75	**1.73**	3.89	**1.12**	3.45
log/sem conjunctions	**0.42**	1.10	**0.30**	1.96	**1.28****	1.71	**0.76****	2.21	**0.95****	2.92
Hedges										
lexical	**0.49**	1.63	**1.50****	5.24	**0.40**	2.22	**0.25**	1.28	**0.77**	2.08
Demonstrative	**0.63**	1.97	**1.08***	3.68	**1.80****	4.57	**0.77***	2.46	**1.09****	6.03
Emphatics	**2.33**	4.88	**1.76**	6.85	**3.53***	6.09	**2.95***	3.84	**2.82***	4.73
Fixed Strings	**1.61**	4.74	**1.32***	3.42	**1.20**	5.61	**1.01***	3.24	**1.01**	3.46

*1-tailed $p \leq 0.05$. **2-tailed $p \leq 0.05$.

313

TABLE B5-3
Medians and Ranges for Top 30 Features in Vietnamese Speaker Essays, Compared to Wealth Texts

L1	VTWEALTH		VTMANNER		VTOPINIONS		VTMAJOR	
	Median	Range	Median	Range	Median	Range	Median	Range
Semantic and Lexical Classes of Nouns								
adv./retroact.	0.20	3.72	0.43	2.22	0.00*	0.87	0.51	2.78
vague	2.21	7.34	3.17*	7.94	1.88	4.40	1.48	5.65
Personal Pronouns								
first person	3.60	16.77	2.00*	8.93	1.47*	10.19	3.97	15.04
third person	7.17	13.21	2.10**	4.48	7.86	17.90	3.90*	13.33
Nominalization	1.27	4.79	1.82*	2.54	1.26	2.86	2.69**	8.42
Gerunds	0.76	1.96	1.39**	2.09	0.65	3.03	0.80*	4.17
Verb Tenses								
past	5.24	12.43	2.78*	7.68	0.99**	9.00	1.78*	5.83
present	9.52	10.47	7.74**	9.46	9.29	5.82	8.08	7.96
Semantic and Lexical Classes of Verbs								
private	1.18	2.93	2.72**	3.19	2.96**	6.02	3.17**	8.42
Modal Verbs								
possibility	0.68	5.71	0.56	2.33	1.52**	3.13	0.74	4.40
necessity	0.74	4.29	0.60	2.56	1.90*	2.71	0.51	2.00
Passive	0.59	1.94	0.40*	1.11	0.50*	1.50	0.44	3.10
be-main	2.30	5.01	5.36**	10.79	3.72**	6.22	3.37*	5.56
Infinitives	3.35	4.61	3.19	3.62	4.29*	5.48	2.38	6.15

(Continued)

TABLE B5-3
(Continued)

LI	VTWEALTH		VTMANNER		VTOPINIONS		VTMAJOR	
	Median	Range	Median	Range	Median	Range	Median	Range
Participles								
present	0.59	4.94	1.39*	4.44	0.00*	0.76	0.52	1.98
past	0.00	1.90	0.27	1.33	0.26	1.00	0.33	2.13
Adjectives								
attributive	3.82	14.64	3.67	3.60	1.48**	4.41	4.00	7.22
predicative	2.74	8.49	3.60**	10.94	2.78	4.29	3.79*	10.42
Semantic and Lexical Classes of Adverbs								
time	0.49	2.42	0.56	1.79	0.94	2.55	1.25**	2.66
place	2.21	4.35	2.08	4.22	1.39	2.68	2.66*	5.72
amplifiers	2.05	5.76	2.38*	6.18	1.99	4.35	1.59	3.01
Noun and Adjective Clauses								
noun	1.08	5.88	0.89	2.39	2.27*	3.77	1.49*	2.84
full adjective	0.74	3.68	0.67	2.61	0.48	2.87	1.19*	4.09
Coordinating and Logical Conjunctions/Prepositions								
phrase-level	4.50	12.22	4.34	9.40	4.55	5.23	3.87	7.15
sentence-level	0.90	3.92	1.28*	2.75	1.73*	3.89	1.12*	3.45
log/sem conjunctions	0.30	1.96	1.28**	1.71	0.76**	2.21	0.95**	2.92
Hedges								
lexical	1.50	5.24	0.40*	2.22	0.25**	1.28	0.77*	2.08
Demonstrative	1.08	3.68	1.80*	4.57	0.77*	2.46	1.09	6.03
Emphatics	1.76	6.85	3.53**	6.09	2.95*	3.84	2.82**	4.73
Fixed Strings	1.32	3.42	1.20	5.61	1.01	3.24	1.01	3.46

*1-tailed $p \leq 0.05$. **2-tailed $p \leq 0.05$.

TABLE B5-4
Medians and Ranges for Top 30 Features in Vietnamese Speaker Essays, Compared to Manner Texts

L1	VTMANNER		VTOPINIONS		VTMAJOR	
	Median	Range	Median	Range	Median	Range
Semantic and Lexical Classes of Nouns						
adv./retroact.	**0.43**	2.22	**0.00***	0.87	**0.51**	2.78
vague	**3.17**	7.94	**1.88***	4.40	**1.48***	5.65
Personal Pronouns						
first person	**2.00**	8.93	**1.47**	10.19	**3.97***	15.04
third person	**2.10**	4.48	**7.86****	17.90	**3.90***	13.33
Nominalization	**1.82**	2.54	**1.26***	2.86	**2.69***	8.42
Gerunds	**1.39**	2.09	**0.65****	3.03	**0.80***	4.17
Verb Tenses						
past	**2.78**	7.68	**00.99***	9.00	**1.78**	5.83
present	**7.74**	9.46	**9.29****	5.82	**8.08***	7.96
Semantic and Lexical Classes of Verbs						
private	**2.72**	3.19	**2.96***	6.02	**3.17***	8.42
Modal Verbs						
possibility	**0.56**	2.33	**1.52****	3.13	**0.74**	4.40
necessity	**0.60**	2.56	**1.90****	2.71	**0.51***	2.00
Passive	**0.40**	1.11	**0.50**	1.50	**0.44**	3.10
be-main	**5.36**	10.79	**3.72***	6.22	**3.37***	5.56
Infinitives	**3.19**	3.62	**4.29****	5.48	**2.38***	6.15

(Continued)

TABLE B5-4
(Continued)

LI	VTMANNER		VTOPINIONS		VTMAJOR	
	Median	*Range*	*Median*	*Range*	*Median*	*Range*
Participles						
present	**1.39**	4.44	**0.00****	0.76	**0.52***	1.98
past	0.27	1.33	0.26	1.00	0.33	2.13
Adjectives						
attributive	**3.67**	3.60	**1.48****	4.41	**4.00**	7.22
predicative	**3.60**	10.94	**2.78***	4.29	**3.79**	10.42
Semantic and Lexical Classes of Adverbs						
time	0.56	1.79	0.94	2.55	**1.25****	2.66
place	2.08	4.22	1.39	2.68	**2.66***	5.72
amplifiers	2.38	6.18	**1.99***	4.35	**1.59****	3.01
Noun and Adjective Clauses						
noun	**0.89**	2.39	**2.27****	3.77	**1.49***	2.84
full adjective	0.67	2.61	0.48	2.87	1.19	4.09
Coordinating and Logical Conjunctions/Prepositions						
phrase-level	4.34	9.40	4.55	5.23	**3.87**	7.15
sentence-level	1.28	2.75	1.73	3.89	**1.12**	3.45
log/sem conjunctions	1.28	1.71	**0.76****	2.21	**0.95**	2.92
Hedges						
lexical	0.40	2.22	0.25	1.28	0.77	2.08
Demonstrative	1.80	4.57	**0.77****	2.46	**1.09***	6.03
Emphatics	3.53	6.09	2.95	3.84	2.82	4.73
Fixed Strings	1.20	5.61	**1.01***	3.24	**1.01***	3.46

*1-tailed $p \leq 0.05$. **2-tailed $p \leq 0.05$.

TABLE B5-5

Medians and Ranges for Top 30 Features in Vietnamese Speaker Essays, Compared to Opinions Texts

L1	VTOPINIONS		VTMAJOR	
	Median	*Range*	*Median*	*Range*
Semantic and Lexical Classes of Nouns				
adv./retroact.	0.00	0.87	0.51*	2.78
vague	1.88	4.40	1.48	5.65
Personal Pronouns				
first person	1.47	10.19	3.97*	15.04
third person	7.86	17.90	3.90**	13.33
Nominalization	1.26	2.86	2.69**	8.42
Gerunds	0.65	3.03	0.80*	4.17
Verb Tenses				
past	0.99	9.00	1.78*	5.83
present	9.29	5.82	8.08	7.96
Semantic and Lexical Classes of Verbs				
private	2.96	6.02	3.17*	8.42
Modal Verbs				
possibility	1.52	3.13	0.74*	4.40
necessity	1.90	2.71	0.51**	2.00
Passive	0.50	1.50	0.44	3.10
be-main	3.72	6.22	3.37	5.56
Infinitives	4.29	5.48	2.38*	6.15

(Continued)

TABLE B5-5
(Continued)

L1	VTOPINIONS		VTMAJOR	
	Median	*Range*	*Median*	*Range*
Participles				
present	**0.00**	0.76	**0.52****	1.98
past	**0.26**	1.00	**0.33***	2.13
Adjectives				
attributive	**1.48**	4.41	**4.00****	7.22
predicative	**2.78**	4.29	**3.79***	10.42
Semantic and Lexical Classes of Adverbs				
time	**0.94**	2.55	**1.25***	2.66
place	**1.39**	2.68	**2.66****	5.72
amplifiers	**1.99**	4.35	**1.59**	3.01
Noun and Adjective Clauses				
noun	**2.27**	3.77	**1.49***	2.84
full adjective	**0.48**	2.87	**1.19***	4.09
Coordinating and Logical Conjunctions/Prepositions				
phrase-level	**4.55**	5.23	**3.87**	7.15
sentence-level	**1.73**	3.89	**1.12**	3.45
log/sem conjunctions	**0.76**	2.21	**0.95**	2.92
Hedges				
lexical	**0.25**	1.28	**0.77**	2.08
Demonstrative	**0.77**	2.46	**1.09***	6.03
Emphatics	**2.95**	3.84	**2.82**	4.73
Fixed Strings	**1.01**	3.24	**1.01**	3.46

*1-tailed $p \leq 0.05$. **2-tailed $p \leq 0.05$.

TABLE B6-1

Medians and Ranges for Top 30 Features in Indonesian Speaker Essays, Compared to Parents Texts

L1	INDPARENTS		INDGRADES		INDWEALTH		INDMANNER		INDOPINIONS		INDMAJOR	
	Median	*Range*	*Median*	*Range*	*Median*	*Range*	*Median*	*Range*	*Median*	*Range*	*Median*	*Range*
Semantic and Lexical Classes of Nouns												
adv./retroact.	**0.57**	8.18	**0.74**	5.12	**0.00****	0.94	**0.28***	2.22	**0.43***	2.80	**0.26***	1.78
vague	**2.22**	5.42	**1.45**	5.14	**1.67***	5.42	**1.45***	5.86	**2.08**	6.41	**3.57****	8.02
Personal Pronouns												
first person	**2.29**	14.24	**3.55**	13.33	**1.09***	9.60	**5.45****	14.47	**0.71***	9.09	**4.51***	18.21
third person	**7.84**	12.45	**3.02****	10.30	**6.36**	9.69	**2.01****	8.84	**8.08**	14.09	**3.67**	16.80
Nominalization	**1.37**	6.25	**1.89**	6.67	**0.91**	2.78	**1.52**	7.37	**0.94**	5.65	**2.20***	6.21
Gerunds	**1.22**	2.78	**1.47**	4.32	**0.59***	1.99	**0.88**	2.75	**1.00**	4.80	**1.51***	5.33
Verb Tenses												
past	**0.98**	8.79	**3.44****	9.09	**1.96**	7.43	**3.48****	11.11	**0.00***	6.46	**2.78****	9.98
present	**10.42**	20.04	**11.23**	12.27	**9.24**	10.35	**9.72**	12.36	**9.29***	8.47	**9.23**	17.03
Semantic and Lexical Classes of Verbs												
private	**2.27**	7.27	**3.85****	9.03	**0.99****	2.93	**4.13****	11.11	**3.36****	11.51	**5.02****	7.89
Modal Verbs												
possibility	**1.36**	3.27	**1.14***	4.04	**0.78***	5.71	**1.03**	4.21	**0.96***	2.38	**0.88**	3.57
necessity	**0.88**	2.16	**1.03**	3.33	**0.59**	3.53	**0.51***	3.00	**1.49***	2.70	**0.77**	5.00
Passive	**1.46**	6.25	**0.30****	1.28	**0.57****	3.24	**0.29****	2.90	**0.32***	2.88	**0.44****	2.14
be-main	**2.94**	7.90	**2.95**	6.14	**2.67**	5.24	**4.13****	8.77	**3.64****	7.24	**4.38****	6.40
Infinitives	**2.38**	6.70	**3.68****	11.26	**2.10**	4.82	**2.75**	3.65	**3.64***	8.64	**5.25****	7.05

(Continued)

TABLE B6-1
(Continued)

L1	INDPARENTS Median	Range	INDGRADES Median	Range	INDWEALTH Median	Range	INDMANNER Median	Range	INDOPINIONS Median	Range	INDMAJOR Median	Range
Participles												
present	**0.61**	4.69	**1.27**	5.68	**0.00****	3.90	**0.61**	3.94	**0.00****	0.89	**0.00***	1.23
past	**1.30**	7.19	**0.89**	3.03	**0.00****	0.91	**0.00****	1.16	**0.00****	0.52	**0.28***	1.36
Adjectives												
attributive	**1.79**	8.85	**2.17***	9.77	**5.79****	14.64	**3.33****	9.18	**1.77**	5.02	**3.45****	9.79
predicative	**2.90**	4.42	**2.35**	6.47	**2.00***	8.60	**3.99****	11.52	**3.76***	8.00	**2.96****	8.00
Semantic and Lexical Classes of Adverbs												
time	**0.85**	2.60	**0.81**	3.01	**0.83**	3.39	**0.38**	3.44	**0.64**	3.30	**1.15***	2.70
place	**1.33**	5.91	**1.05**	3.86	**1.25**	3.61	**2.55****	4.96	**0.89**	3.20	**1.58***	4.32
amplifiers	**2.38**	9.38	**2.70**	7.27	**1.71***	4.35	**2.86***	6.01	**2.52**	6.85	**3.17****	5.94
Noun and Adjective Clauses												
noun	**1.41**	4.58	**2.70****	4.57	**1.24**	5.88	**1.75**	5.00	**2.81****	5.78	**1.82***	3.70
full adjective	**0.98**	2.78	**1.41***	4.67	**0.61**	3.68	**1.13**	2.94	**0.74**	3.13	**1.85****	4.17
Coordinating and Logical Conjunctions/Prepositions												
phrase-level	**3.69**	6.99	**3.90**	9.59	**3.64**	5.34	**4.01***	4.40	**2.88***	3.02	**3.21**	5.92
sentence-level	**1.52**	2.30	**1.11***	3.59	**0.98***	3.27	**1.36**	2.82	**1.60**	4.95	**1.67***	3.32
log/sem conjunctions	**0.25**	1.48	**0.77****	3.41	**0.39**	2.29	**1.03****	2.81	**0.84****	2.14	**1.18****	2.43
Hedges												
lexical	**0.40**	1.74	**0.25**	1.23	**1.33****	5.24	**0.35**	2.68	**0.00****	0.85	**0.00**	1.33
Demonstrative	**0.49**	1.62	**0.76**	2.70	**1.30*****	5.14	**0.91****	3.45	**0.67**	1.82	**1.25****	3.85
Emphatics	**2.27**	5.91	**1.03****	2.77	**0.84****	4.01	**1.39***	4.48	**2.60**	5.30	**3.33****	7.27
Fixed Strings	**0.40**	1.78	**0.35**	2.23	**1.20****	3.85	**0.69***	1.70	**0.96***	2.38	**1.00****	2.37

*1-tailed $p \leq 0.05$. **2-tailed $p \leq 0.05$.

TABLE B6-2

Medians and Ranges for Top 30 Features in Indonesian Speaker Essays, Compared to Grades Texts

L1	INDGRADES		INDWEALTH		INDMANNER		INDOPINIONS		INDMAJOR	
	Median	Range	Median	Range	Median	Range	Median	Range	Median	Range
Semantic and Lexical Classes of Nouns										
adv./retroact.	0.74	5.12	0.00**	0.94	0.28*	2.22	0.43*	2.80	0.26*	1.78
vague	1.45	5.14	1.67	5.42	1.45	5.86	2.08*	6.41	3.57**	8.02
Personal Pronouns										
first person	3.55	13.33	1.09**	9.60	5.45*	14.47	0.71**	9.09	4.51*	18.21
third person	3.02	10.30	6.36**	9.69	2.01	8.84	8.08**	14.09	3.67*	16.80
Nominalization	1.89	6.67	0.91*	2.78	1.52	7.37	0.94*	5.65	2.20	6.21
Gerunds	1.47	4.32	0.59*	1.99	0.88	2.75	1.00	4.80	1.51*	5.33
Verb Tenses										
past	3.44	9.09	1.96*	7.43	3.48	11.11	0.00**	6.46	2.78	9.98
present	11.23	12.27	9.24	10.35	9.72	12.36	9.29*	8.47	9.23	17.03
Semantic and Lexical Classes of Verbs										
private	3.85	9.03	0.99**	2.93	4.13	11.11	3.36	11.51	5.02*	7.89
Modal Verbs										
possibility	1.14	4.04	0.78*	5.71	1.03	4.21	0.96	2.38	0.88	3.57
necessity	1.03	3.33	0.59*	3.53	0.51*	3.00	1.49*	2.70	0.77	5.00
Passive	0.30	1.28	0.57	3.24	0.29	2.90	0.32	2.88	0.44	2.14
be-main	2.95	6.14	2.67	5.24	4.13**	8.77	3.64*	7.24	4.38**	6.40
Infinitives	3.68	11.26	2.10**	4.82	2.75**	3.65	3.64	8.64	5.25**	7.05

(Continued)

TABLE B6-2
(Continued)

L1	INDGRADES Median	Range	INDWEALTH Median	Range	INDMANNER Median	Range	INDOPINIONS Median	Range	INDMAJOR Median	Range
Participles										
present	1.27	5.68	0.00**	3.90	0.61	3.94	0.00**	0.89	0.00**	1.23
past	0.89	3.03	0.00**	0.91	0.00**	1.16	0.00**	0.52	0.28**	1.36
Adjectives										
attributive	2.17	9.77	5.79**	14.64	3.33*	9.18	1.77*	5.02	3.45**	9.79
predicative	2.35	6.47	2.00*	8.60	3.99*	11.52	3.76**	8.00	2.96*	8.00
Semantic and Lexical Classes of Adverbs										
time	0.81	3.01	0.83	3.39	0.38*	3.44	0.64	3.30	1.15*	2.70
place	1.05	3.86	1.25	3.61	2.55**	4.96	0.89	3.20	1.58**	4.32
amplifiers	2.70	7.27	1.71*	4.35	2.86*	6.01	2.52	6.85	3.17*	5.94
Noun and Adjective Clauses										
noun	2.70	4.57	1.24*	5.88	1.75*	5.00	2.81	5.78	1.82	3.70
full adjective	1.41	4.67	0.61*	3.68	1.13	2.94	0.74**	3.13	1.85*	4.17
Coordinating and Logical Conjunctions/Prepositions										
phrase-level	3.90	9.59	3.64	5.34	4.01	4.40	2.88*	3.02	3.21	5.92
sentence-level	1.11	3.59	0.98	3.27	1.36	2.82	1.60*	4.95	1.67**	3.32
log/sem conjunctions	0.77	3.41	0.39*	2.29	1.03	2.81	0.84	2.14	1.18*	2.43
Hedges										
lexical	0.25	1.23	1.33**	5.24	0.35	2.68	0.00*	0.85	0.00	1.33
Demonstrative	0.76	2.70	1.30*	5.14	0.91*	3.45	0.67	1.82	1.25*	3.85
Emphatics	1.03	2.77	0.84	4.01	1.39*	4.48	2.60**	5.30	3.33**	7.27
Fixed Strings	0.35	2.23	1.20**	3.85	0.69*	1.70	0.96*	2.38	1.00**	2.37

*1-tailed $p \leq 0.05$. **2-tailed $p \leq 0.05$.

TABLE B6-3

Medians and Ranges for Top 30 Features in Indonesian Speaker Essays, Compared to Wealth Texts

L1	INDWEALTH		INDMANNER		INDOPINIONS		INDMAJOR	
	Median	*Range*	*Median*	*Range*	*Median*	*Range*	*Median*	*Range*
Semantic and Lexical Classes of Nouns								
adv./retroact.	**0.00**	0.94	**0.28****	2.22	**0.43****	2.80	**0.26****	1.78
vague	**1.67**	5.42	**1.45**	5.86	**2.08*****	6.41	**3.57*****	8.02
Personal Pronouns								
first person	**1.09**	9.60	**5.45****	14.47	**0.71**	9.09	**4.51****	18.21
third person	**6.36**	9.69	**2.01***	8.84	**8.08*****	14.09	**3.67**	16.80
Nominalization	**0.91**	2.78	**1.52***	7.37	**0.94**	5.65	**2.20*****	6.21
Gerunds	**0.59**	1.99	**0.88*****	2.75	**1.00***	4.80	**1.51****	5.33
Verb Tenses								
past	**1.96**	7.43	**3.48*****	11.11	**0.00***	6.46	**2.78***	9.98
present	**9.24**	10.35	**9.72**	12.36	**9.29**	8.47	**9.23**	17.03
Semantic and Lexical Classes of Verbs								
private	**0.99**	2.93	**4.13****	11.11	**3.36****	11.51	**5.02****	7.89
Modal Verbs								
possibility	**0.78**	5.71	**1.03***	4.21	**0.96***	2.38	**0.88***	3.57
necessity	**0.59**	3.53	**0.51**	3.00	**1.49*****	2.70	**0.77****	5.00
Passive	**0.57**	3.24	**0.29**	2.90	**0.32**	2.88	**0.44**	2.14
be-main	**2.67**	5.24	**4.13*****	8.77	**3.64*****	7.24	**4.38*****	6.40
Infinitives	**2.10**	4.82	**2.75***	3.65	**3.64*****	8.64	**5.25****	7.05

(Continued)

L1	INDWEALTH		INDMANNER		INDOPINIONS		INDMAJOR	
	Median	Range	Median	Range	Median	Range	Median	Range
Participles								
present	**0.00**	3.90	**0.61****	3.94	**0.00**	0.89	**0.00**	1.23
past	**0.00**	0.91	**0.00**	1.16	**0.00**	0.52	**0.28***	1.36
Adjectives								
attributive	**5.79**	14.64	**3.33**	9.18	**1.77****	5.02	**3.45**	9.79
predicative	**2.00**	8.60	**3.99****	11.52	**3.76****	8.00	**2.96****	8.00
Semantic and Lexical Classes of Adverbs								
time	**0.83**	3.39	**0.38**	3.44	**0.64**	3.30	**1.15****	2.70
place	**1.25**	3.61	**2.55****	4.96	**0.89**	3.20	**1.58***	4.32
amplifiers	**1.71**	4.35	**2.86****	6.01	**2.52****	6.85	**3.17****	5.94
Noun and Adjective Clauses								
noun	**1.24**	5.88	**1.75***	5.00	**2.81****	5.78	**1.82****	3.70
full adjective	**0.61**	3.68	**1.13****	2.94	**0.74**	3.13	**1.85****	4.17
Coordinating and Logical Conjunctions/Prepositions								
phrase-level	**3.64**	5.34	**4.01****	4.40	**2.88**	3.02	**3.21**	5.92
sentence-level	**0.98**	3.27	**1.36***	2.82	**1.60***	4.95	**1.67****	3.32
log/sem conjunctions	**0.39**	2.29	**1.03****	2.81	**0.84****	2.14	**1.18****	2.43
Hedges								
lexical	1.33	5.24	**0.35***	2.68	**0.00****	0.85	**0.00****	1.33
Demonstrative	1.30	5.14	**0.91**	3.45	**0.67***	1.82	**1.25**	3.85
Emphatics	0.84	4.01	**1.39****	4.48	**2.60****	5.30	**3.33****	7.27
Fixed Strings	1.2?	3.85	**0.69**	1.70	**0.96**	2.38	**1.00**	2.37

*1-tailed $p \leq 0.05$. **2-tailed $p \leq 0.05$.

TABLE B6-4

Medians and Ranges for Top 30 Features in Indonesian Speaker Essays, Compared to Manner Texts

L1	INDMANNER		INDOPINIONS		INDMAJOR	
	Median	Range	Median	Range	Median	Range
Semantic and Lexical Classes of Nouns						
adv./retroact.	**0.28**	2.22	**0.43**	2.80	**0.26**	1.78
vague	**1.45**	5.86	**2.08***	6.41	**3.57****	8.02
Personal Pronouns						
first person	**5.45**	14.47	**0.71****	9.09	**4.51**	18.21
third person	**2.01**	8.84	**8.08****	14.09	**3.67****	16.80
Nominalization	**1.52**	7.37	**0.94***	5.65	**2.20***	6.21
Gerunds	**0.88**	2.75	**1.00**	4.80	**1.51***	5.33
Verb Tenses						
past	**3.48**	11.11	**0.00****	6.46	**2.78**	9.98
present	**9.72**	12.36	**9.29**	8.47	**9.23**	17.03
Semantic and Lexical Classes of Verbs						
private	**4.13**	11.11	**3.36***	11.51	**5.02***	7.89
Modal Verbs						
possibility	**1.03**	4.21	**0.96**	2.38	**0.88**	3.57
necessity	**0.51**	3.00	**1.49****	2.70	**0.77***	5.00
Passive	**0.29**	2.90	**0.32**	2.88	**0.44**	2.14
be-main	**4.13**	8.77	**3.64**	7.24	**4.38**	6.40
Infinitives	**2.75**	3.65	**3.64****	8.64	**5.25****	7.05

(Continued)

TABLE B6-4
(Continued)

L1	INDMANNER		INDOPINIONS		INDMAJOR	
	Median	*Range*	*Median*	*Range*	*Median*	*Range*
Participles						
present	**0.61**	3.94	**0.00****	0.89	**0.00****	1.23
past	**0.00**	1.16	**0.00**	0.52	**0.28***	1.36
Adjectives						
attributive	**3.33**	9.18	**1.77****	5.02	**3.45**	9.79
predicative	**3.99**	11.52	**3.76**	8.00	**2.96***	8.00
Semantic and Lexical Classes of Adverbs						
time	**0.38**	3.44	**0.64**	3.30	**1.15****	2.70
place	**2.55**	4.96	**0.89****	3.20	**1.58***	4.32
amplifiers	**2.86**	6.01	**2.52**	6.85	**3.17**	5.94
Noun and Adjective Clauses						
noun	**1.75**	5.00	**2.81****	5.78	**1.82**	3.70
full adjective	**1.13**	2.94	**0.74***	3.13	**1.85****	4.17
Coordinating and Logical Conjunctions/Prepositions						
phrase-level	**4.01**	4.40	**2.88****	3.02	**3.21***	5.92
sentence-level	**1.36**	2.82	**1.60***	4.95	**1.67***	3.32
log/sem conjunctions	**1.03**	2.81	**0.84**	2.14	**1.18***	2.43
Hedges						
lexical	**0.35**	2.68	**0.00***	0.85	**0.00**	1.33
Demonstrative	**0.91**	3.45	**0.67***	1.82	**1.25**	3.85
Emphatics	**1.39**	4.48	**2.60***	5.30	**3.33****	7.27
Fixed Strings	**0.69**	1.70	**0.96**	2.38	**1.00***	2.37

*1-tailed $p \leq 0.05$. **2-tailed $p \leq 0.05$.

TABLE B6-5

Medians and Ranges for Top 30 Features in Indonesian Speaker Essays, Compared to Opinions Texts

L1	INDOPINIONS		INDMAJOR	
	Median	Range	Median	Range
Semantic and Lexical Classes of Nouns				
adv./retroact.	0.43	2.80	0.26	1.78
vague	2.08	6.41	3.57**	8.02
Personal Pronouns				
first person	0.71	9.09	4.51**	18.21
third person	8.08	14.09	3.67*	16.80
Nominalization	0.94	5.65	2.20**	6.21
Gerunds	1.00	4.80	1.51*	5.33
Verb Tenses				
past	0.00	6.46	2.78**	9.98
present	9.29	8.47	9.23	17.03
Semantic and Lexical Classes of Verbs				
private	3.36	11.51	5.02**	7.89
Modal Verbs				
possibility	0.96	2.38	0.88	3.57
necessity	1.49	2.70	0.77	5.00
Passive	0.32	2.88	0.44	2.14
be-main	3.64	7.24	4.38*	6.40
Infinitives	3.64	8.64	5.25**	7.05

(Continued)

TABLE B6-5
(Continued)

L1	INDOPINIONS		INDMAJOR	
	Median	*Range*	*Median*	*Range*
Participles				
present	**0.00**	0.89	**0.00**	1.23
past	**0.00**	0.52	**0.28****	1.36
Adjectives				
attributive	**1.77**	5.02	**3.45****	9.79
predicative	**3.76**	8.00	**2.96**	8.00
Semantic and Lexical Classes of Adverbs				
time	**0.64**	3.30	**1.15****	2.70
place	**0.89**	3.20	**1.58*****	4.32
amplifiers	**2.52**	6.85	**3.17***	5.94
Noun and Adjective Clauses				
noun	**2.81**	5.78	**1.82***	3.70
full adjective	**0.74**	3.13	**1.85*****	4.17
Coordinating and Logical Conjunctions/Prepositions				
phrase-level	**2.88**	3.02	**3.21***	5.92
sentence-level	**1.60**	4.95	**1.67***	3.32
log/sem conjunctions	**0.84**	2.14	**1.18***	2.43
Hedges				
lexical	**0.00**	0.85	**0.00**	1.33
Demonstrative	**0.67**	1.82	**1.25***	3.85
Emphatics	**2.60**	5.30	**3.33****	7.27
Fixed Strings	**0.96**	2.38	**1.00**	2.37

*1-tailed $p \leq 0.05$. **2-tailed $p \leq 0.05$.

TABLE B7-1
Medians and Ranges for Top 30 Features in Arabic Speaker Essays, Compared to Parents Texts

LI	ARPARENTS		ARGRADES		ARWEALTH		ARMANNER		AROPINIONS		ARMAJOR	
	Median	Range	Median	Range	Median	Range	Median	Range	Median	Range	Median	Range
Semantic and Lexical Classes of Nouns												
adv./retroact.	0.25	1.52	0.61*	8.59	0.00*	1.52	0.78*	2.86	0.72*	1.56	0.48	1.54
vague	3.13	5.53	3.51*	7.41	5.00**	12.85	0.79*	6.07	1.68***	3.20	2.96	12.92
Personal Pronouns												
first person	1.04	14.67	1.42*	10.00	2.07	7.50	1.72	5.42	2.27*	5.62	1.52	6.39
third person	8.93	13.14	4.76***	10.64	5.39**	13.62	2.08**	12.10	4.55***	11.81	3.17**	12.80
Nominalization	1.81	3.38	2.50**	6.61	1.78	5.56	2.10*	6.29	1.74	4.76	2.42**	6.26
Gerunds	1.84	6.25	3.78*	9.70	1.08*	4.97	1.70	4.55	0.93*	4.69	1.38*	4.63
Verb Tenses												
past	0.92	5.30	1.33	5.77	1.10	7.41	0.00*	4.29	0.00**	3.41	0.49	5.47
present	9.39	14.18	8.64	10.56	10.00	17.32	8.61	12.11	9.23	8.64	8.97	8.60
Semantic and Lexical Classes of Verbs												
private	0.65	2.41	2.86**	9.47	2.42**	9.24	2.99**	5.44	1.43**	5.38	3.64**	7.58
Modal Verbs												
possibility	1.09	4.22	1.28	3.83	0.68	4.50	1.80*	4.04	0.95	3.69	0.88	2.34
necessity	0.53	3.00	0.44	2.88	1.20	5.12	0.55	2.86	1.47*	5.00	0.69	2.96
Passive	0.52	3.19	0.59	2.33	0.38	3.17	1.03	2.50	0.71	1.77	0.30	3.37
be-main	3.23	4.64	3.87*	8.73	4.19*	10.20	4.53*	8.35	3.46	5.73	3.10	4.21
Infinitives	5.98	7.44	5.71	10.46	5.62	10.55	2.40**	7.31	3.03**	8.29	2.73**	3.73

(Continued)

TABLE B7-1
(Continued)

L1	ARPARENTS		ARGRADES		ARWEALTH		ARMANNER		AROPINIONS		ARMAJOR	
	Median	Range	Median	Range	Median	Range	Median	Range	Median	Range	Median	Range
Participles												
present	**0.00**	3.23	**0.00**	1.28	**0.00**	0.84	**0.43**	1.79	**0.00**	1.04	**0.21**	1.26
past	**0.53**	2.69	**0.00***	2.48	**0.00***	0.93	**0.31***	1.56	**0.23***	1.04	**0.26****	1.18
Adjectives												
attributive	**3.79**	9.39	**5.29**	12.79	**6.44****	12.14	**2.72***	6.62	**2.42****	4.51	**2.05****	7.08
predicative	**3.01**	5.05	**3.17**	5.66	**3.23**	10.94	**3.85***	8.03	**2.86**	3.76	**2.44**	12.56
Semantic and Lexical Classes of Adverbs												
time	**0.52**	2.59	**0.71**	3.49	**0.79**	3.75	**0.62**	1.74	**0.85***	2.61	**1.66****	3.85
place	**0.40**	4.02	**1.06***	4.69	**1.35***	6.05	**1.58****	4.34	**1.26***	4.47	**1.06***	3.10
amplifiers	**4.29**	6.60	**2.92***	7.18	**3.12**	13.89	**3.06**	6.67	**2.78**	8.30	**2.82***	12.76
Noun and Adjective Clauses												
noun	**2.38**	5.32	**2.00**	4.82	**2.07**	5.56	**1.52**	3.89	**2.17**	4.41	**1.56***	2.93
full adjective	**1.77**	7.74	**0.77***	3.33	**1.80**	4.17	**1.81**	5.36	**1.24**	5.28	**1.56**	3.17
Coordinating and Logical Conjunctions/Prepositions												
phrase-level	**4.23**	12.33	**5.72***	7.14	**6.28***	9.51	**4.91***	12.36	**5.97***	12.78	**4.05**	14.29
sentence-level	**3.54**	4.89	**1.59****	4.06	**1.45****	6.64	**1.04****	2.22	**1.05*****	3.08	**1.03****	3.33
log/sem conjunctions	**0.00**	1.09	**0.00***	2.80	**0.62***	2.82	**1.28****	3.13	**1.20****	2.25	**0.92****	1.81
Hedges												
lexical	**0.38**	2.13	**0.66**	3.37	**0.89***	5.25	**0.26**	1.11	**0.00**	1.01	**0.18**	1.56
Demonstrative	**2.11**	4.82	**2.40**	13.66	**2.88***	9.26	**1.89**	6.62	**1.44***	4.57	**1.72***	2.88
Emphatics	**5.00**	10.34	**4.76**	12.76	**4.38**	10.51	**2.56***	6.89	**2.10****	5.59	**3.31***	6.65
Fixed Strings	**0.82**	4.26	**1.44***	4.28	**1.10**	4.20	**1.56**	3.06	**0.76**	2.00	**0.95**	3.38

*1-tailed $p \leq 0.05$. **2-tailed $p \leq 0.05$.

TABLE B7-2

Medians and Ranges for Top 30 Features in Arabic Speaker Essays, Compared to Grades Texts

L1	ARGRADES		ARWEALTH		ARMANNER		AROPINIONS		ARMAJOR	
	Median	Range	Median	Range	Median	Range	Median	Range	Median	Range
Semantic and Lexical Classes of Nouns										
adv./retroact.	**0.61**	8.59	**0.00****	1.52	**0.78**	2.86	**0.72**	1.56	**0.48**	1.54
vague	**3.51**	7.41	**5.00***	12.85	**0.79****	6.07	**1.68****	3.20	**2.96**	12.92
Personal Pronouns										
first person	**1.42**	10.00	**2.07**	7.50	**1.72**	5.42	**2.27**	5.62	**1.52**	6.39
third person	**4.76**	10.64	**5.39***	13.62	**2.08***	12.10	**4.55***	11.81	**3.17**	12.80
Nominalization	**2.50**	6.61	**1.78***	5.56	**2.10***	6.29	**1.74***	4.76	**2.42**	6.26
Gerunds	**3.78**	9.70	**1.08****	4.97	**1.70****	4.55	**0.93****	4.69	**1.38****	4.63
Verb Tenses										
past	**1.33**	5.77	**1.10**	7.41	**0.00***	4.29	**0.00***	3.41	**0.49**	5.47
present	**8.64**	10.56	**10.00***	17.32	**8.61**	12.11	**9.23**	8.64	**8.97**	8.60
Semantic and Lexical Classes of Verbs										
private	**2.86**	9.47	**2.42**	9.24	**2.99**	5.44	**1.43***	5.38	**3.64***	7.58
Modal Verbs										
possibility	**1.28**	3.83	**0.68***	4.50	**1.80**	4.04	**0.95**	3.69	**0.88***	2.34
necessity	**0.44**	2.88	**1.20***	5.12	**0.55**	2.86	**1.47****	5.00	**0.69***	2.96
Passive	**0.59**	2.33	**0.38**	3.17	**1.03**	2.50	**0.71**	1.77	**0.30**	3.37
***be*-main**	**3.87**	8.73	**4.19**	10.20	**4.53**	8.35	**3.46**	5.73	**3.10**	4.21
Infinitives	**5.71**	10.46	**5.62**	10.55	**2.40****	7.31	**3.03****	8.29	**2.73****	3.73

(Continued)

TABLE B7-2
(Continued)

L1	ARGRADES		ARWEALTH		ARMANNER		AROPINIONS		ARMAJOR	
	Median	Range	Median	Range	Median	Range	Median	Range	Median	Range
Participles										
present	0.00	1.28	0.00	0.84	0.43*	1.79	0.00	1.04	0.21	1.26
past	0.00	2.48	0.00	0.93	0.31	1.56	0.23	1.04	0.26	1.18
Adjectives										
attributive	5.29	12.79	6.44*	12.14	2.72**	6.62	2.42**	4.51	2.05**	7.08
predicative	3.17	5.66	3.23	10.94	3.85	8.03	2.86	3.76	2.44*	12.56
Semantic and Lexical Classes of Adverbs										
time	0.71	3.49	0.79	3.75	0.62	1.74	0.85	2.61	1.66*	3.85
place	1.06	4.69	1.35	6.05	1.58*	4.34	1.26	4.47	1.06	3.10
amplifiers	2.92	7.18	3.12	13.89	3.06	6.67	2.78	8.30	2.82	12.76
Noun and Adjective Clauses										
noun	2.00	4.82	2.07	5.56	1.52*	3.89	2.17	4.41	1.56*	2.93
full adjective	0.77	3.33	1.80*	4.17	1.81**	5.36	1.24	5.28	1.56*	3.17
Coordinating and Logical Conjunctions/Prepositions										
phrase-level	5.72	7.14	6.28	9.51	4.91	12.36	5.97	12.78	4.05*	14.29
sentence-level	1.59	4.06	1.45	6.64	1.04*	2.22	1.05*	3.08	1.03**	3.33
log/sem conjunctions	0.00	2.80	0.62	2.82	1.28*	3.13	1.20**	2.25	0.92*	1.81
Hedges										
lexical	0.66	3.37	0.89	5.25	0.26*	1.11	0.00*	1.01	0.18*	1.56
Demonstrative	2.40	13.66	2.88	9.26	1.89	6.62	1.44**	4.57	1.72**	2.88
Emphatics	4.76	12.76	4.38	10.51	2.56*	6.89	2.10**	5.59	3.31	6.65
Fixed Strings	1.44	4.28	1.10*	4.20	1.56	3.06	0.76**	2.00	0.95*	3.38

*1-tailed $p \leq 0.05$. **2-tailed $p \leq 0.05$.

TABLE B7-3

Medians and Ranges for Top 30 Features in Arabic Speaker Essays, Compared to Wealth Texts

L1	ARWEALTH		ARMANNER		ARDOPINIONS		ARMAJOR	
	Median	Range	Median	Range	Median	Range	Median	Range
Semantic and Lexical Classes of Nouns								
adv./retroact.	0.00	1.52	0.78**	2.86	0.72**	1.56	0.48*	1.54
vague	5.00	12.85	0.79**	6.07	1.68**	3.20	2.96*	12.92
Personal Pronouns								
first person	2.07	7.50	1.72	5.42	2.27	5.62	1.52	6.39
third person	5.39	13.62	2.08*	12.10	4.55	11.81	3.17*	12.80
Nominalization	1.78	5.56	2.10	6.29	1.74	4.76	2.42*	6.26
Gerunds	1.08	4.97	1.70	4.55	0.93	4.69	1.38	4.63
Verb Tenses								
past	1.10	7.41	0.00*	4.29	0.00**	3.41	0.49	5.47
present	10.00	17.32	8.61*	12.11	9.23	8.64	8.97*	8.60
Semantic and Lexical Classes of Verbs								
private	2.42	9.24	2.99	5.44	1.43*	5.38	3.64*	7.58
Modal Verbs								
possibility	0.68	4.50	1.80*	4.04	0.95	3.69	0.88	2.34
necessity	1.20	5.12	0.55	2.86	1.47	5.00	0.69	2.96
Passive	0.38	3.17	1.03*	2.50	0.71	1.77	0.30	3.37
be-main	4.19	10.20	4.53	8.35	3.46	5.73	3.10*	4.21
Infinitives	5.63	10.55	2.40*	7.31	3.03*	8.29	2.73*	3.73

(Continued)

TABLE B7-3
(Continued)

L1	ARWEALTH		ARMANNER		ARDOPINIONS		ARMAJOR	
	Median	Range	Median	Range	Median	Range	Median	Range
Participles								
present	**0.00**	0.84	**0.43***	1.79	**0.00**	1.04	**0.21**	1.26
past	**0.00**	0.93	**0.31**	1.56	**0.23**	1.04	**0.26**	1.18
Adjectives								
attributive	**6.44**	12.14	**2.72***	6.62	**2.42***	4.51	**2.05***	7.08
predicative	**3.23**	10.94	**3.85**	8.03	**2.86**	3.76	**2.44***	12.56
Semantic and Lexical Classes of Adverbs								
time	**0.79**	3.75	**0.62**	1.74	**0.85**	2.61	**1.66***	3.85
place	**1.35**	6.05	**1.58**	4.34	**1.26**	4.47	**1.06**	3.10
amplifiers	**3.13**	13.89	**3.06**	6.67	**2.78**	8.30	**2.82**	12.76
Noun and Adjective Clauses								
noun	**2.07**	5.56	**1.52**	3.89	**2.17**	4.41	**1.56**	2.93
full adjective	**1.80**	4.17	**1.81***	5.36	**1.24**	5.28	**1.56**	3.17
Coordinating and Logical Conjunctions/Prepositions								
phrase-level	**6.28**	9.51	**4.91**	12.36	**5.97**	12.78	**4.05***	14.29
sentence-level	**1.45**	6.64	**1.04**	2.22	**1.05**	3.08	**1.03***	3.33
log/sem conjunctions	**0.62**	2.82	**1.28***	3.13	**1.20***	2.25	**0.92***	1.81
Hedges								
lexical	**0.89**	5.25	**0.26***	1.11	**0.00****	1.01	**0.18****	1.56
Demonstrative	**2.88**	9.26	**1.89**	6.62	**1.44***	4.57	**1.72****	2.88
Emphatics	**4.38**	10.51	**2.56***	6.89	**2.10****	5.59	**3.31***	6.65
Fixed Strings	**1.10**	4.20	**1.56**	3.06	**0.76**	2.00	**0.95**	3.38

*1-tailed $p \leq 0.05$. **2-tailed $p \leq 0.05$.

TABLE B7-4

Medians and Ranges for Top 30 Features in Arabic Speaker Essays, Compared to Manner Texts

L1	ARMANNER		AROPINIONS		ARDMAJOR	
	Median	*Range*	*Median*	*Range*	*Median*	*Range*
Semantic and Lexical Classes of Nouns						
adv./retroact.	**0.78**	2.86	**0.72**	1.56	**0.48***	1.54
vague	**0.79**	6.07	**1.68**	3.20	**2.96****	12.92
Personal Pronouns						
first person	**1.72**	5.42	**2.27***	5.62	**1.52**	6.39
third person	**2.08**	12.10	**4.55****	11.81	**3.17***	12.80
Nominalization	**2.10**	6.29	**1.74**	4.76	**2.42**	6.26
Gerunds	**1.70**	4.55	**0.93**	4.69	**1.38**	4.63
Verb Tenses						
past	**0.00**	4.29	**0.00**	3.41	**0.49**	5.47
present	**8.61**	12.11	**9.23**	8.64	**8.97**	8.60
Semantic and Lexical Classes of Verbs						
private	**2.99**	5.44	**1.43***	5.38	**3.64***	7.58
Modal Verbs						
possibility	**1.80**	4.04	**0.95***	3.69	**0.88****	2.34
necessity	**0.55**	2.86	**1.47***	5.00	**0.69**	2.96
Passive	**1.03**	2.50	**0.71***	1.77	**0.30***	3.37
***be*-main**	**4.53**	8.35	**3.46***	5.73	**3.10***	4.21
Infinitives	**2.40**	7.31	**3.03***	8.29	**2.73**	3.73

(Continued)

TABLE B7-4
(Continued)

L1	ARMANNER		AROPINIONS		ARDMAJOR	
	Median	*Range*	*Median*	*Range*	*Median*	*Range*
Participles						
present	**0.43**	1.79	**0.00****	1.04	**0.21***	1.26
past	**0.31**	1.56	**0.23**	1.04	**0.26**	1.18
Adjectives						
attributive	**2.72**	6.62	**2.42**	4.51	**2.05**	7.08
predicative	**3.85**	8.03	**2.86***	3.76	**2.44***	12.56
Semantic and Lexical Classes of Adverbs						
time	**0.62**	1.74	**0.85***	2.61	**1.66****	3.85
place	**1.58**	4.34	**1.26**	4.47	**1.06***	3.10
amplifiers	**3.06**	6.67	**2.78**	8.30	**2.82**	12.76
Noun and Adjective Clauses						
noun	**1.52**	3.89	**2.17***	4.41	**1.56**	2.93
full adjective	**1.81**	5.36	**1.24***	5.28	**1.56***	3.17
Coordinating and Logical Conjunctions/Prepositions						
phrase-level	**4.91**	12.36	**5.97**	12.78	**4.05***	14.29
sentence-level	**1.04**	2.22	**1.05**	3.08	**1.03**	3.33
log/sem conjunctions	**1.28**	3.13	**1.20**	2.25	**0.92**	1.81
Hedges						
lexical	**0.26**	1.11	**0.00**	1.01	**0.18**	1.56
Demonstrative	**1.89**	6.62	**1.44***	4.57	**1.72***	2.88
Emphatics	**2.56**	6.89	**2.10**	5.59	**3.31***	6.65
Fixed Strings	**1.56**	3.06	**0.76***	2.00	**0.95**	3.38

*1-tailed $p \leq 0.05$. **2-tailed $p \leq 0.05$.

TABLE B7-5

Medians and Ranges for Top 30 Features in Arabic Speaker Essays, Compared to Opinions Texts

L1	AROPINIONS		ARMAJOR	
	Median	Range	Median	Range
Semantic and Lexical Classes of Nouns				
adv./retroact.	0.72	1.56	0.48*	1.54
vague	1.68	3.20	2.96**	12.92
Personal Pronouns				
first person	2.27	5.62	1.52*	6.39
third person	4.55	11.81	3.17*	12.80
Nominalization	1.74	4.76	2.42*	6.26
Gerunds	0.93	4.69	1.38	4.63
Verb Tenses				
past	0.00	3.41	0.49*	5.47
present	9.23	8.64	8.97	8.60
Semantic and Lexical Classes of Verbs				
private	1.43	5.38	3.64**	7.58
Modal Verbs				
possibility	0.95	3.69	0.88	2.34
necessity	1.47	5.00	0.69*	2.96
Passive	0.71	1.77	0.30	3.37
be-main	3.46	5.73	3.10	4.21
Infinitives	3.03	8.29	2.73	3.73

(Continued)

TABLE B7-5
(Continued)

LI	AROPINIONS		ARMAJOR	
	Median	*Range*	*Median*	*Range*
Participles				
present	**0.00**	1.04	**0.21***	1.26
past	**0.23**	1.04	**0.26**	1.18
Adjectives				
attributive	**2.42**	4.51	**2.05**	7.08
predicative	**2.86**	3.76	**2.44**	12.56
Semantic and Lexical Classes of Adverbs				
time	**0.85**	2.61	**1.66****	3.85
place	**1.26**	4.47	**1.06**	3.10
amplifiers	**2.78**	8.30	**2.82**	12.76
Noun and Adjective Clauses				
noun	**2.17**	4.41	**1.56***	2.93
full adjective	**1.24**	5.28	**1.56***	3.17
Coordinating and Logical Conjunctions/Prepositions				
phrase-level	**5.97**	12.78	**4.05***	14.29
sentence-level	**1.05**	3.08	**1.03**	3.33
log/sem conjunctions	**1.20**	2.25	**0.92***	1.81
Hedges				
lexical	**0.00**	1.01	**0.18**	1.56
Demonstrative	**1.44**	4.57	**1.72**	2.88
Emphatics	**2.10**	5.59	**3.31***	6.65
Fixed Strings	**0.76**	2.00	**0.95***	3.38

*1-tailed $p \leq 0.05$. **2-tailed $p \leq 0.05$.

Glossary

The glossary supplies only brief definitions of important terms used in this book and other texts on applied linguistics, discourse analysis, text linguistics, and contrastive rhetoric, as well as syntax and lexis. In general, most of these terms are common in professional literature and L2 research. Whenever possible, examples are also provided:

adjective: The function of adjectives is to describe nouns: *tall, beautiful*. Adjectives can have **comparative** *(taller, more beautiful)* and **superlative** *(tallest, most beautiful)* forms.

adjective clause: A clause that has the same grammatical function as an attributive adjective: *The boy who plays in the sandbox is my neighbor's son.*

adverb: A word that modifies a verb, an adjective, or an entire clause: *Occasionally, we go to the ocean, Dogs run fast/quickly, Cats can meow particularly loudly.*

adverb clause: A clause that has the same grammatical function as an adverb: *The tree swayed while the storm was raging.*

anaphora: Text cohesion based on presupposition of information referred to previously (but not necessarily in the preceding sentence): *Bob and Peter live in New York and hope to move soon. They hate the prices there.*

aspect: A grammatical means of marking (the verb for) progression, completion, or repetition: *I was singing (be+*verb*+ing)* (the past time and the progressive aspect), *He has read the book(have/has + read)* (the present time and the perfect aspect to mark completion), or *I eat at the cafeteria (eat)* (the present time and unmarked aspect to denote repetition).

attributive adjectives: Adjectives that usually describe the noun directly as a part of a noun phrase: *a tall woman, a beautiful house.*

auxiliary verb: A verb that contains grammatical information in questions or negative clauses: *Does Mary live here? Squirrels didn't eat the berries.*

clause: A syntactic unit that contains at least a subject and a predicate: *John left.*

clause theme/rheme: Clauses express propositions, and in clauses grammatical relationships correspond to thematic (meaning) relationships. In general terms, the clause topic (noun, noun phrase, or noun clause) is the theme, and the remainder is the rheme, which often contains new information about the topic. In English, the theme as the main element of meaning in clauses is usually (but not always) placed in the front of the proposition: *The students* (theme) *study very hard* (rheme). Theme creating is considered to be a universal phenomenon because it occurs in all languages, and theme fronting is also very common. However, different languages front clause themes in different ways.

cohesion: Relations of meaning that exist within the text and that define it as text. A text is cohesive when its elements can be interpreted and understood in connection to one another.

complement: A word, phrase, or clause required to make a structure grammatical: *He decided to go, She said he was an engineer.*

complex sentence: A sentence that contains a main clause and at least one subordinate clause: *His father didn't want him to marry her + because she had no money.*

compound phrase/sentence: A phrase/sentence that contains two or more equal grammatical phrases/clauses joined by a coordinating conjunction: *We ate the pie, but we were still hungry.*

conjunction: A word that joins words, phrases, and/or clauses: *John and Mary, but not Peter.*

coordinating conjunction: A conjunction that joins syntactically equal elements, such as nouns, verbs, phrases or clauses: *Students study, and teachers teach.*

deictic: In discourse and pragmatics, the context of utterance/text/writing determines the expressions and linguistic means according to which it is produced; for example, a text that tells about past-time events requires the past tense, and formal contexts of writing require different types of lexis than informal discourse. In all languages, utterances and discourse are always deictic (indexal) in regard to their time, place, and the participant role of the speaker/writer and the audience; for example, formal discourse would not be appropriate in a letter to a friend or conversational register may not be the best idea in a petition to the dean.

deixis: A particular type of reference that always depends on the time and/or the place of an utterance/narrative/discourse (e.g., the tense, pronouns, and adverbs of place), as well as the speaker/writer and the audience of the utterance/narrative.

demonstrative pronoun: A pronoun, such as *this, that, these,* and *those.*

derivation: A grammatical structure (a word or a phrase) that is obtained from another structure by means of lexical or syntactic changes: *happy-happiness, do-undo, John ate the apple-The apple was eaten by John.*

discourse focus: A word, phrase, or clause that presents the new and most important information in a grammatical unit: *Jane is a dentist, It is 5 o'clock, I'll never understand why he said this.*

discourse marker: A linguistic or lexical form that indicates a point in the flow of discourse: *To begin,* marks a starting point of an idea, or *For example,* marks a start of an example that follows.

ellipsis: An omission of a part of a phrase or clause: *John loves his mother more than his wife,* for example, *more than he loves his wife* or *more than his wife loves his mother.*

epistemic: A meaning (or use) of modal verbs to refer to the truthfulness or falsity of a proposition, as well as possibility: *Can he come tomorrow?* (true or false, yes or no) or *If John is not at the office, he must be sick today.*

evidential: A word or phrase that expresses an element of doubt due to insufficient substantiation, used to avoid challenge: *Peter might help you with this job.*

existential subject: The subject *there* in clauses where only one noun or noun phrase participant is known to exist; *there* is empty of semantic and lexical content: *When there is smoke, there is fire.*

gerund: A word that has many properties of a noun, but is derived from a verb by means of adding *-ing: Reading is important in education.*

grammatical/syntactic cohesion: The connectivity of text and relations of meaning in text established by means of syntactic elements (e.g., pronouns, articles, and verb tenses): *The company was located in California before it moved to Washington.*

ideational: Pertaining to ideas and content in text and discourse.

indefinite pronoun: A class of pronouns that includes words such as *anything, anyone, someone, nothing.*

lexical: Pertaining to word, root, prefix and suffix meaning.

lexical cohesion: The connectivity of text and relations of text meanings established through the meanings of words in text: *Bob works very hard. The young man deserves much praise.*

lexical cohesive link: A cohesive link is a sequence in which a pronoun refers to the nouns that immediately precede it (but may necessitate skipping a few words in between): *John and Mary are happy together, but they have occasional disagreements, particularly when they can't decide how to advise their children.*

lexical substitution: Lexical replacement of words with similar (contextual) meanings used in text to establish cohesion between ideas/propositions and to avoid repetition: *I need to buy a book. The volume is expensive, but it is the best text I've ever used.*

lexicon: Words, word roots, prefixes, and suffixes of a language.

marker: An overt linguistic or lexical form that indicates a presence of a grammatical or semantic feature: *sings,* in which *-s* is a marker of the simple present tense and third-person singular.

modal verb: A verb that expresses, among other, meanings of obligation, necessity, or possibility: *can, could, may, should, must.*

noun clause: A clause that has the same function in a sentence as a noun (usually, as a subject or an object): *What became of her is a big mystery* or *He reported that he saw a deer.*

particle: In English, words such as *up, down, off* in phrases: *turn up, look down (on), fall off.* In other languages, particles are very common and have many grammatical functions.

partitive: A quantifier or qualifier of count or mass nouns, such as a *crowd of people, a number of books, a drop of water. I'd like another piece of candy. Siamese are the best kind of house cats.*

pragmatics: The study of various aspects of broad contexts and participant roles (e.g., the speaker/writer and the listener/reader) that affect how utterance, text, and discourse are produced and understood.

predicative adjective: An adjective that is a part of the predicate used after a linking verb or copula *be: He became/grew old. Actors are wealthy.*

proposition: A semantic and grammatical unit that consists of a predicate and an object (a noun, phrase, or clause) required by the grammatical properties of the predicate: *John + mentioned + that he would be late for dinner.*

quantifier: A word that denotes count or mass quantity: *one, two, three, many, some, a lot, few.*

reference: A semantic and pragmatic relation between the linguistic name (or the linguistic expression) for something in discourse and the object, entity, or person in the real world, for which this name/expression stands: *Yesterday* in English refers to the day-long time period determined by the convention to start at midnight that immediately precedes the current day-long time period similarly determined by a convention.

reference markers: In practically all languages, there are words in text or discourse that do not have meaning of their own but are understood in context because they refer to something else; for example, *John is 26, and he is in college,* where *he* refers to *John.* In this case, the pronoun *he* is a reference marker. In general terms, in language, there are two types of references, textual and situational, where textual references are made in text, and situational references are made to identifiable objects and things; for example, *John* represents a situational reference to a man who is 26 and whose name is John (in this case, the name *John* is also a reference marker that points to a particular person).

rhetorical question: A question used in written text to achieve a rhetorical effect rather than obtain information.

scale: A gradient quality of lexical or pragmatic meanings of expressions: *immediately-soon-some time, satisfactory-good-excellent-superior,* or *might-may-need to-have to-must.*

semantics: The study of meanings of various words, forms, and construction in language.

subordinator/subordinating conjunction: A conjunction that joins a subordinate clause to the main clause, such as *that, what, when, who, why, because,* or *although:He tells everyone <u>what</u> they want to hear* or *It's hard to tell <u>why</u> she did this.*

tag question: An inverse question construction attached to the end of sentence in which positive structures become negative and negative become positive, and nouns are converted to pronouns: *John is always late, <u>isn't he</u>?* or *Bob doesn't like cream pie, <u>does he</u>?*

tense: In most cases, a grammatical means of marking (the verb for) time reference either relative to the time of speaking or some other time or event; for example, present and past.

truth-value: A semantic and pragmatic concept that distinguishes between whether a proposition is true or is believed to be true. Generally, the truth-value of the proposition does not change, but if new information emerges that requires the revision of the proposition, its propositional status may change. The concept of truth-value is particularly important in written discourse when authors assert something that they believe to be true or in discussions of cultural beliefs accepted in some societies but not in others; for example, the truth-value of the proposition *the earth is flat* was very high at one time, but its value has diminished substantially.

References

Aarts, J. (1991). Intuition-based and observation-based grammars. In K. Aijmer & B. Altenberg (Eds.), *English corpus linguistics* (pp. 44–62). New York: Longman.

Ahn, B.-K. (1995). The teaching of writing in Korea [Special Issue, R. B. Kaplan, Ed.] *Journal of Asian Pacific Communication, 1 & 2*, 67–76.

Aoki, H. (1986). Evidentials in Japanese. In W. Chafe & J. Nichols (Eds.), *Evidentiality: The linguistic coding of epistemology* (pp. 223–238). Norwood, NJ: Ablex.

Arnaud, P., & Savignon, S. (1997). Rare words, complex lexical units and the advanced learner. In J. Coady & T. Huckin (Eds.), *Second language vocabulary acquisition* (pp. 157–173). Cambridge: Cambridge University Press.

Atkinson, D. (1991). Discourse analysis and written discourse conventions. *Annual Review of Applied Linguistics, 11*, 57–76.

Aziz, Y. (1988). Theme-rheme organization and paragraph structure in standard Arabic. *Word, 39*(2), 117–128.

Bar-Lev, Z. (1986). Discourse theory and "contrastive rhetoric." *Discourse Processes, 9*(2), 235–246.

Baynham, M. (1995). *Literacy practices.* London: Longman.

Benesch, S. (1996). Needs analysis and curriculum development in EAP: An example of a critical approach. *TESOL Quarterly, 30*(3), 723–738.

Bereiter, C., & Scardamalia, M. (1985). Cognitive coping strategies and the problem of "inert knowledge." In S. Chipman, J. Segal, & R. Glaser (Eds.), *Thinking and learning skills: Research and open questions* (vol. 2, pp. 65–80). Hillsdale, NJ: Lawrence Erlbaum Associates.

Bereiter, C., & Scardamalia, M. (1987). *The psychology of written composition.* Hillsdale, NJ: Lawrence Erlbaum Associates.

Bereiter, C., & Scardamalia, M. (1989). Intentional learning as a goal of instruction. In L. Resnick (Ed.), *Knowing, learning, and instruction* (pp. 361–391). Hillsdale, NJ: Lawrence Erlbaum Associates.

Berkenkotter, C., & Huckin, T. (1995). *Genre knowledge in disciplinary communities.* Hillsdale, NJ: Lawrence Erlbaum Associates.

Bhatia, V. (1992). Pragmatics of the use of nominals in academic and professional genres. In L. Bouton & Y. Kachru (Eds.), *Pragmatics and language learning* (Vol. 3, pp. 217–230). Urbana-Champaign: University of Illinois.

Bhatia, V. (1993). *Analysing genre: Language use in professional settings.* London: Longman.

Biber, D. (1988). *Variation across speech and writing.* Cambridge: Cambridge University Press.

Biber, D. (1995). *Dimensions of register variation.* Cambridge: Cambridge University Press.

Biber, D., Conrad, S., & Reppen, R. (1998). *Corpus linguistics.* Cambridge: Cambridge University Press.

Biber, D., & Finegan, E. (1991). On the exploitation of computerized corpora in variation studies. In K. Aijmer & B. Altenberg (Eds.), *English corpus linguistics* (pp. 204–220). London: Longman.

Biber, D., Johansson, S., Leech, G., Conrad, S., & Finnegan, E. (1999). *Longman grammar of spoken and written English.* Harlow, Essex: Pearson.

Bickner, R., & Peyasantiwong, P. (1988). Cultural variation in reflective writing. In A. Purves (Ed.), *Writing across languages and cultures: Issues in contrastive rhetoric* (pp. 160–175). Newbury Park, CA: Sage.

Biq, Y.-O. (1990). Question words as hedges in Chinese. In L. Bouton & Y. Kachru (Eds.), *Pragmatics and language learning,* (Vol. 1, pp. 141–158). Urbana-Champaign: University of Illinois.

Bloor, M. (1996). Academic writing in computer science: A comparison of genres. In E. Ventola and A. Mauranen (Eds.), *Academic writing,* pp. 59–88. Amsterdam: John Benjamins.

Brinton, D., Snow, M., & Wesche, M. (1989). *Content-based second language instruction.* New York: Newbury House.

Brown, P., & Levinson, S. (1987). *Politeness.* Cambridge: Cambridge University Press.

Carlson, S. (1988). Cultural differences in writing and reasoning skills. In A. Purves (Ed.), *Writing across languages and cultures: Issues in contrastive rhetoric* (pp. 109–137). Newbury Park, CA: Sage.

Carson, J. (1993). Reading for writing: Cognitive perspectives. In J. Carson & I. Leki (Eds.), *Reading in the composition classroom* (pp. 85–104). Boston: Heinle & Heinle.

Carson, J., & Leki, I. (Eds.). (1993) *Reading in the composition classroom.* Boston: Heinle & Heinle.

Chafe, W. (1970). *Meaning and the structure of language.* Chicago: University of Chicago Press.

Chafe, W. (1985). Linguistic differences produced by differences between speaking and writing. In D. R. Olson, N. Torrance, & A. Hildyard (Eds.), *Literature, language, and learning: The nature and consequences of reading and writing* (pp. 105–123). Cambridge: Cambridge University Press.

Chafe, W. (1986). Evidentiality in English conversation and academic writing. In W. Chafe & J. Nichols (Eds.), *Evidentiality: The linguistic coding of epistemology* (pp. 261–272). Norwood, NJ: Ablex.

Chafe, W. (1994). *Discourse, consciousness, and time.* Chicago: University of Chicago Press.

Chang, Y.-Y., & Swales, J. (1999). Informal elements in English academic writing: Threats or opportunities for advanced non-native speakers. In C. Candlin & K. Hyland (Eds.), *Writing texts, processes and practices* (pp. 145–167). London: Longman.

Channel, J. (1994). *Vague language.* Oxford, Oxford University Press.

Cherry, R. (1988). Politeness in written persuasion. *Journal of Pragmatics,* 12(2), 63–81.

Chung, C. H. (1988). The language situation of Vietnamese Americans. In S. L. McKay & S.-L. Wong (Eds.), *Language diversity: Problem or resource?* (pp. 276–292). Boston: Heinle & Heinle.

Coates, J. (1983). *The semantics of the modal auxiliaries.* Beckenham, Kent, UK: Croom Helm.

Collins, P. (1991). The modals of obligation and necessity in Australian English. In K. Aijmer & B. Altenberg (Eds.), *English corpus linguistics* (pp. 145–165). New York: Longman.

Connor, U. (1996). *Contrastive rhetoric.* Cambridge: Cambridge University Press.

Connor, U., & Carrell, P. (1993). The interpretation of tasks by writers and readers in holistically rated direct assessment of writing. In J. Carson & I. Leki (Eds.), *Reading in the composition classroom* (pp. 141–160). Boston: Heinle & Heinle.

Connor, U., & Kaplan, R. B. (Eds.). (1987). *Writing across languages: Analysis of L2 text.* Reading, MA: Addison-Wesley.

Connor, U., & Lauer, J. (1988). Cross-cultural variation in persuasive student writing. In A. Purves (Ed.), *Writing across languages and cultures: Issues in contrastive rhetoric* (pp. 138–159). Newbury Park, CA: Sage.

Coulthard, M. (1985). *An introduction to discourse analysis* (2nd ed). London: Longman. (Original work published 1977).

Coulthard, M. (1992). *Advances in spoken discourse analysis.* New York: Routledge.

Coulthard, M. (1994). *Advances in written text analysis.* New York: Routledge.

Cribb, R., & Brown, C. (1995). *Modern history of Indonesia.* Harlow, UK: Longman.

Croft, W. (1998). The structure of events and the structure of language. In M. Tomasello (Ed.), *The new psychology of language* (pp. 67–92). Mahwah, NJ: Lawrence Erlbaum Associates.

Davidson, F. (1991). Statistical support for training in ESL composition rating. In L. Hamp-Lyons (Ed.), *Assessing second language writing* (pp. 155–165). Norwood, NJ: Ablex.

de Beaugrande, R. (1997). *New foundations for a science of text and discourse.* Norwood, NJ: Ablex.

de Beaugrande, R., & Dressler, W. (1981). *Introduction to text linguistics.* London: Longman. (Original work published 1972).

Deitrich, R., Klein, W., & Noyau, C. (1995). *The acquisition of temporality in a second language.* Amsterdam: John Benjamins.

Dixon, R. M. W. (1995). Complement clauses and complementation strategies. In F. R. Palmer (Ed.), *Grammar and meaning* (pp. 175–220). Cambridge: Cambridge University Press.

Dudley-Evans, T. & St. John, M. J. (1998). *Developments in English for specific purposes.* Cambridge: Cambridge University Press.

Duffley, P. J. (1992). *The English infinitive.* London: Longman.

Educational Testing Service. (2000). *TOEFL 2000–2001, Information bulletin for computer-based testing.* Princeton, NJ: Author.

Ellis, R. (1985). *Understanding second language acquisition.* Oxford, Oxford University Press.

Ellis, R. (1994). *The study of second language acquisition.* Oxford, Oxford University Press.

Ellis, R. (1997). *SLA research and language teaching.* Oxford, Oxford University Press.

Fairclough, N. (1989). *Language and power.* London: Longman.

Fairclough, N. (1995). *Critical discourse analysis.* London: Longman.

Fakhri, A. (1995). Topical structure in Arabic-English interlanguage. *Pragmatics and Language Learning, 6,* 155–169.

Fathman, A., & Whalley, E. (1990). Teacher response to student writing: Focus on form versus content. In B. Kroll (Ed.), *Second language writing* (pp. 178–190). Cambridge: Cambridge University Press.

Ferris, D., & Hedgcock, J. (1998). *Teaching ESL composition.* Mahwah, NJ: Lawrence Erlbaum Associates.

Flowerdew, J. (1995). *Academic listening.* Cambridge: Cambridge University Press.

Ford, C. (1993). *Grammar in interaction.* Cambridge: Cambridge University Press.

Fox, H. (1994). *Listening to the world: Cultural issues in academic writing.* Urbana, IL: NCTE.

Francis, G. (1994). Labelling discourse: An aspect of nominal-group cohesion. In M. Coulthard (Ed.), *Advances in written text analysis* (pp. 83–101). New York: Routledge.

Friedlander, A. (1990). Composing in English: Effects of a first language on writing in English as a second language. In B. Kroll (Ed.), *Second language writing* (pp. 109–125). Cambridge: Cambridge University Press.

Fu, G. S., & Poon, E. Y. W. (1995). The teaching of writing in Hong Kong: Quality assured or inferior product [Special issue, R. B. Kaplan, Ed.]. *Journal of Asian Pacific Communication, 1 & 2*, 45–54..

Gee, J. (1990). *Social linguistics and literacies*. Bristol, PA: Falmer Press.

Gee, J. (1994). Orality and literacy: From *The savage mind* to *Ways with words*. In J. Maybin (Ed.), *Language and literacy in social practice* (pp. 168–192). Clevedon, UK: Multilingual Matters.

Grabe, W., & Kaplan, R. B. (1987). Writing in a second language: Contrastive rhetoric. In D. Johnson & D. Roen (Eds.), *Richness in writing* (pp. 263–283). New York: Longman.

Grabe, W., & Kaplan, R. B. (1989). Writing in a second language: Contrastive rhetoric. In D. Johnson & D. Roen (Eds.), *Richness in writing* (pp. 263–283). New York: Longman.

Grabe, W., & Kaplan, R. B. (1996). *Theory and practice of writing*. London: Longman.

Greenbaum, S., & Quirk, R. (1990). *A student's grammar of the English language*. London: Longman.

Guiora, A. (1983). The dialectic of language acquisition. *Language Learning, 33*(1), 3–12.

Hacker, D. (1994). *The Bedford handbook for writers* (4th ed.). Boston: Bedford.

Hairston, M. (1982). The winds of change: Thomas Kuhn and the revolution in the teaching of writing. *College Composition and Communication, 33*(1), 76–88.

Halliday, M. A. K. (1978). *Language as a social semiotic*. London: Edward Arnold.

Halliday, M. A. K. (1994). The construction of knowledge and value in the grammar of scientific discourse, with reference to Charles Darwin's *The Origin of Species*. In M. Coulthard (Ed.), *Advances in written text analysis* (pp. 136–156). New York: Routledge.

Halliday, M. A. K., & Hasan, R. (1976). *Cohesion in English*. London: Longman.

Hamp-Lyons, L. (1990). Second language writing: Assessment issues. In B. Kroll (Ed.), *Second language writing* (pp. 69–86). Cambridge: Cambridge University Press.

Hamp-Lyons, L. (1991). Scoring procedures for ESL contexts. In L. Hamp-Lyons (Ed.), *Assessing second language writing* (pp. 241–277). Norwood, NJ: Ablex.

Hermeren, L. (1978). On modality in English. *Lund Studies in English, 53*. Lund, Sweden: Gleerup.

Herrington, A., & Moran, C. (Eds.). (1992). *Writing, teaching, and learning in the disciplines*. New York: MLA.

Heycock, C., & Lee, Y.-S. (1990). Subjects and predication in Korean and Japanese. In H. Hoji (Ed.), *Japanese and Korean linguistics* (pp. 239–254). Stanford, CA: CSLI/Stanford University Press.

Hinds, J. (1975). Korean discourse types. In H. Sohn (Ed.), *Korean language* (pp. 81–90). Honolulu: University of Hawaii Press.

Hinds, J. (1976). *Aspects of Japanese discourse structure*. Tokyo: Kaitakusha.

Hinds, J. (1983). Contrastive rhetoric. *Text, 3*(2), 183–195.

Hinds, J. (1984). Retention of information using a Japanese style of presentation. *Studies in Language, 8*(1), 45–69.

Hinds, J. (1987). Reader versus writer responsibility: A new typology. In U. Connor & R. B. Kaplan (Eds.). *Writing across languages: Analysis of L2 text* (pp. 141–152). Reading, MA: Addison-Wesley.

Hinds, J. (1990). Inductive, deductive, quasi-inductive: Expository writing in Japanese, Korean, Chinese, and Thai. In U. Connor & A. Johns (Eds.), *Coherence in writing* (pp. 87–110). Alexandria, VA: TESOL.

Hinkel, E. (1992). L2 tense and time reference. *TESOL Quarterly, 26*(3), 556–572.

Hinkel, E. (1994). Native and nonnative speakers' pragmatic interpretation of English text. *TESOL Quarterly, 28*(2), 353–376.

Hinkel, E. (1995a, April). *Projecting credibility in academic writing: L1 and L2 discourse paradigms*. Paper presented at the Ninth International Conference on Pragmatics & Language Learning, University of Illinois, Urbana.

Hinkel, E. (1995b). The use of modal verbs as a reflection of cultural values. *TESOL Quarterly, 29*(3), 325–343.

Hinkel, E. (1995c, March). *What is your point? Indirectness in L2 writing*. Paper presented at the meeting of TESOL, Long Beach, CA.

Hinkel, E. (1996, March). *Audience and the writer's stance in L2 writing*. Paper presented at the meeting of TESOL, Chicago.

Hinkel, E. (1997a). Indirectness in L1 and L2 academic writing. *Journal of Pragmatics, 27*(3), 360–386.

Hinkel, E. (1997b). The past tense and temporal verb meanings in a contextual frame. *TESOL Quarterly, 31*(2), 289–314.

Hinkel, E. (1999a). Introduction: Culture in research and second language pedagogy. In E. Hinkel (Ed.), *Culture in second language teaching and learning* (pp. 1–7). Cambridge: Cambridge University Press.

Hinkel, E. (1999b). Objectivity and credibility in L1 and L2 academic writing. In E. Hinkel (Ed.), *Culture in second language teaching and learning* (pp. 90–108). Cambridge: Cambridge University Press.

Hinkel, E. (in press). Why English passive is difficult to teach (and learn). In E. Hinkel & S. Fotos (Eds.), *New perspectives on grammar teaching*. Mahwah, NJ: Lawrence Erlbaum Associates.

Hoey, M. (1991). *Patterns of lexis in text*. Oxford, England: Oxford University Press.

Holmes, J. (1984). Hedging your bets and sitting on the fence: Some evidence for hedges as support structures. *Te Reo, 27*(1), 47–62.

Horowitz, D. (1986). What professors actually require: Academic tasks for the ESL classroom. *TESOL Quarterly, 20*(4), 445–462.

Hoshi, H. (1993). The role of Pro in Ni passive in Japanese. In P. Clancy (Ed.), *Japanese and Korean linguistics* (pp. 355–374). Stanford, CA: CSLI/Standford University Press.

Hoye, L. (1997). *Adverbs and modality in English*. London: Longman.

Huebler, A. (1983). *Understatements and hedges in English*. Amsterdam: John Benjamins.

Hunston, S., & Francis, G. (2000). *Pattern grammar*. Amsterdam: John Benjanims.

Hwang, S. J. J. (1987). *Discourse features of Korean narration*. Arlington: The Summer Institute of Linguistics and The University of Texas.

Hyland, K. (1998). *Hedging in scientific research articles*. Amsterdam: John Benjamins.

Hyland, K. (1999). Disciplinary discourses: Writer stance in research articles. In C. Candlin & K. Hyland (Eds.), *Writing texts, processes and practices* (pp. 99–120). London: Longman.

Indrasuta, C. (1988). Narrative styles in the writing of Thai and American students. In A. Purves (Ed.), *Writing across languages and cultures: Issues in contrastive rhetoric* (pp. 206–227). Newbury Park, CA: Sage.

Iwasaki, S. (1993). Functional transfer in the history of Japanese language. In P. Clancy (Ed.), *Japanese and Korean linguistics* (pp. 20–32). Stanford, CA: CSLI/Standford University Press.

Jacobs, R. (1995). *English syntax: A grammar for English language professionals*. Oxford, Oxford University Press.

James, C. (1998). *Errors in language learning and use*. London: Longman.

Johns, A. (1981). Necessary English: A faculty survey. *TESOL Quarterly, 15*(1), 51–57.

Johns, A. (1990a). Coherence as a cultural phenomenon: Employing ethnographic principles in the academic milieu. In U. Connor & A. Johns (Eds.), *Coherence in writing* (pp. 211–225). Alexandria, VA: TESOL.

Johns, A. (1990b). L1 composition theories: Implications for developing theories for L2 composition. In B. Kroll (Ed.), *Second language writing* (pp. 24–36). Cambridge: Cambridge University Press.

Johns, A. (1991). Faculty assessment of ESL student literacy skills: Implications for writing assessment. In L. Hamp-Lyons (Ed.), *Assessing second language writing* (pp. 167–180). Norwood, NJ: Ablex.

Johns, A. (1997). *Text, role, and context: Developing academic literacies.* Cambridge: Cambridge University Press.

Johnson, D. (1989). Politeness strategies in L2 written discourse. *Journal of Intensive English Studies, 3,* 71–91.

Johnson, D. (1995, March). *Constructing social groups in discourse.* Paper presented at the Ninth Annual International Conference on Pragmatics and Language Learning, Urbana-Champaign, IL.

Johnstone, B. (1989). Linguistic strategies and cultural styles for persuasive discourse. In S. Ting-Toomey & F. Korzenny (Eds.), *Language, communication, and culture* (pp. 139–157). Newbury Park, CA: Sage.

Jordan, R. (1997). *English for academic purposes.* Cambridge: Cambridge University Press.

Kachru, B. (1992). *The other tongue: English across cultures* (2nd ed.). Urbana: University of Illinois Press.

Kachru, Y. (1999). Culture, context, and writing. In E. Hinkel (Ed.), *Culture in second language teaching and learning* (pp. 75–89). Cambridge: Cambridge University Press.

Kaplan, R. B. (1966). Cultural thought patterns in intercultural education. *Language Learning, 16*(1), 1–20.

Kaplan, R. B. (1983). Contrastive rhetorics: Some implications for the writing process. In A. Freedman, I. Pringle, & J. Yalden (Eds.), *Learning to write: First language/second language* (pp. 139–161). London: Longman.

Kaplan, R. B. (1987). Cultural thought patterns revisited. In U. Connor & R. B. Kaplan (Eds.), *Writing across languages: Analysis of L2 text* (pp. 9–22). Reading, MA: Addison-Wesley.

Kaplan, R. B. (1988). Contrastive rhetoric and second language learning: Notes toward a theory of contrastive rhetoric. In A. Purves (Ed.), *Writing across languages and cultures: Issues in contrastive rhetoric* (pp. 275–303). Newbury Park, CA: Sage.

Kaplan, R. B. (2000). Contrastive rhetoric and discourse analysis: Who writes what to whom? When? In what circumstances? In S. Sarangi & M. Coulthard (Eds.), *Discourse and social life* (pp. 82–102). Harlow, Longman.

Kay, P. (1997). *Words and the grammar of context.* Stanford, CA: CSLI.

Kaye, A. (1987). Arabic. In B. Comrie (Ed.), *The world's major languages* (pp. 664–685). Oxford, England: Oxford University Press.

Kennedy, G. (1991). *Between* and *through*: The company they keep and the functions they serve. In K. Aijmer & B. Altenberg (Eds.), *English corpus linguistics* (pp. 95–110). New York: Longman.

Kim, N.-L. (1987). Korean. In B. Comrie (Ed.), *The world's major languages* (pp. 881–898). Oxford, Oxford University Press.

Kincaid, L. (1987). (Ed.), *Communication theory: Eastern and Western perspectives.* San Diego, CA: Academic Press.

Kitahara, H. (1993). Inalienable possession constructions in Korean: Scrambling, the Proper Binding condition, and case percolation. In P. Clancy (Ed.), *Japanese and Korean linguistics* (pp. 394–408). Stanford, CA: CSLI/Stanford University Press.

Kjellmer, G. (1991). A mint of phrases. In K. Aijmer & B. Altenberg (Eds.), *English corpus linguistics* (pp. 111–127). New York: Longman.

Kohn, J. (1992). Literacy strategies for Chinese university learners. In F. Dubin & N. Kuhlman (Eds.), *Cross-cultural literacy* (pp. 113–126). New York: Pearson.

Krapels, A. (1990). An overview of second language writing process research. In B. Kroll (Ed.), *Second language writing* (pp. 27–56). Cambridge: Cambridge University Press.

Kroll, B. (1979). A survey of writing needs of foreign and American college freshmen. *English Language Teaching Journal, 33*(2), 219–227.

Kroll, B. (1990a). *Second language writing.* Cambridge: Cambridge University Press.

Kroll, B. (1990b). What does time buy? ESL student performance on home versus class compositions. In B. Kroll (Ed.), *Second language writing* (pp. 140–154). Cambridge: Cambridge University Press.

Lee, C., & Scarcella, R. (1992). Building upon Korean writing practices. In F. Dubin & N. Kuhlman (Eds.), *Cross-cultural literacy* (pp. 143–161). New York: Pearson.

Lee, J.-H. (1993). Postverbal adverbs and verb movement in Korean. In P. Clancy (Ed.), *Japanese and Korean linguistics* (pp. 429–446). Stanford, CA: CSLI/Standford University Press.

Lee, S.-H. (1987). The teachings of Yi Yulgok: Communication from a Neo-Confucian perspective. In L. Kincaid (Ed.), *Communication theory: Eastern and Western perspectives* (pp. 101–114). San Diego: Academic Press.

Leech, G. (1983). *Principles of pragmatics.* London: Longman.

Leeds, B. (1996). *Writing in a second language.* New York: Longman.

Leki, I. (1990). Coaching from the margins: Issues in written response. In B. Kroll (Ed.), *Second language writing* (pp. 57–68). Cambridge: Cambridge University Press.

Leki, I. (1993). Reciprocal themes in ESL reading and writing. In J. Carson & I. Leki (Eds.), *Reading in the composition classroom* (pp. 9–32). Boston: Heinle & Heinle.

Leki, I. (1995). Coping strategies of ESL students. *TESOL Quarterly, 29*(2), 235–260.

Leki, I. (1999). *Academic writing. Techniques and tasks* (3rd ed.). New York: Cambridge University Press.

Leki, I., & Carson, J. (1997). "Completely Different Worlds": EAP and the writing experiences of ESL students in university courses. *TESOL Quarterly, 31*(1), 39–70.

Levinson, S. (1983). *Pragmatics.* Cambridge: Cambridge University Press.

Li, C. N., & Thompson, S. (1981). *Mandarin Chinese.* Berkeley: University of California Press.

Li, C. N., & Thompson, S. (1987). Chinese. In B. Comrie (Ed.), *The world's major languages* (pp. 811–833). Oxford, England: Oxford University Press.

Lunsford, A., & Connors, R. (1997). *The every day writer.* New York: St. Martin's Press.

Master, P. (1991). Active verbs with inanimate subjects in scientific prose. *English for Specific Purposes, 10*(1), 15–33.

Matalene, C. (1985). Contrastive rhetoric: An American writing teacher in China. *College English, 47*(4), 789–807.

Matthiessen, C. (1996). Tense in English seen through systemic-functional theory. In M. Berry, C. Butler, R. Fawcett, & G. Hwang (Eds.), *Meaning and form: Systemic functional interpretations* (pp. 431–498). Norwood, NJ: Ablex.

Maynard, S. (1993). *Discourse modality: Subjectivity, emotion and voice in the Japanese language.* Amsterdam: John Benjamins.

Maynard, S. (1997). *Japanese communication.* Honolulu: University of Hawaii Press.

McCarthy, M. (1991). *Discourse analysis for language teachers.* Cambridge: Cambridge University Press.

McCarthy, M. (1994). It, this, and that. In M. Coulthard (Ed.), *Advances in written text analysis* (pp. 266–275). New York: Routledge.

McCarthy, M., & Carter, R. (1994). *Language as discourse.* London: Longman.

McGloin, N. (1984). Some politeness strategies in Japanese. In S. Miyagawa & C. Kitagawa (Eds.), *Studies in Japanese language use* (pp. 127–146). Carbondale, IL: Linguistic Research.

MELAB technical manual. (1994). Ann Arbor: University of Michigan.

Meyer, C. (1991). A corpus-based study of apposition in English. In K. Aijmer & B. Altenberg (Eds.), *English corpus linguistics* (pp. 166–181). New York: Longman.

Milton, J. (1999). Lexical thickets and electronic gateways: Making text accessible by novice writers. In C. Candlin & K. Hyland (Eds.), *Writing texts, processes and practices* (pp. 221–243). London: Longman.

Mohan, B., & Lo, W. A.-Y. (1985). Academic writing and Chinese students: Transfer and developmental factors. *TESOL Quarterly, 19*(3), 515–534.

Moon, R. (1994). The analysis of fixed expressions in text. In M. Coulthard (Ed.), *Advances in written text analysis* (pp. 117–135). New York: Routledge.

Moon, R. (1998). *Fixed expressions and idioms in English.* Oxford England: Oxford University Press.

Myers, G. (1989). The pragmatics of politeness in scientific articles. *Applied Linguistics, 10*(1), 1–35.

Myers, G. (1996). Strategic vagueness in academic writing. In E. Ventola & A. Mauranen (Eds.), *Academic writing* (pp. 1–18). Amsterdam: John Benjamins.

Myers, G. (1999). Interaction in writing: Principles and problems. In C. Candlin & K. Hyland (Eds.), *Writing texts, processes and practices* (pp. 40–61). London: Longman.

Namba, T. (1995). The teaching of writing in Japan [Special issue, R. B. Kaplan, Ed.], *Journal of Asian Pacific Communication, 1 & 2,* 55–66.

Nguyen, D.-H. (1987). Vietnamese. In B. Comrie (Ed.), *The world's major languages* (pp. 777–796). Oxford, Oxford University Press.

Norman, J. (1990). *Chinese.* Cambridge: Cambridge University Press.

Nydell, M. (1997). *Understanding Arabs* (2nd ed.). Yarmouth, ME: Intercultural Press.

Ohta, A. S. (1991). Evidentiality and politeness in Japanese. *Issues in Applied Linguistics, 2*(2), 183–210.

Oliver, R. (1971). *Communication and culture in ancient India and China.* Syracuse, NY: Syracuse University Press.

Olson, D. (1994). *The world on paper.* Cambridge: Cambridge University Press.

Open Doors. (1997/1998). New York: Institute of International Education.

Ostler, S. (1980). A survey of needs of advanced ESL. *TESOL Quarterly, 14*(4), 489–502.

Ostler, S. (1987). English in parallels: A comparison of English and Arabic prose. In U. Connor & R. Kaplan (Eds.), *Writing across languages: Analysis of L2 text* (pp. 169–185). Reading, MA: Addison-Wesley.

Owen, C. (1993). Corpus-based grammar and the Heineken effect: Lexico-grammatical description for language learners. *Applied Linguistics, 14*(2), 167–187.

Pagano, A. (1994). Negatives in written text. In M. Coulthard (Ed.), *Advances in written text analysis* (pp. 250–265). New York: Routledge.

Pakir, A., & Ling, L. E. (1995). The teaching of writing in Singapore [Special issue, R. B. Kaplan, Ed.]. *Journal of Asian Pacific Communication, 1 & 2,* 103–116.

Palmer, F. R. (1990). *Modality and the English modals* (2nd ed.). London: Longman.

Palmer, F. R. (1994). *Grammatical roles and relations.* Cambridge: Cambridge University Press.

Park, M.-R. (1990). Conflict avoidance in social interaction. In H. Hoji (Ed.), *Japanese and Korean linguistics* (pp. 111–128). Stanford, CA: CSLI/Standford University Press.

Park, Y.-M. (1988). Academic and ethnic background as factors affecting writing performance. In A. Purves (Ed.), *Writing across languages and cultures: Issues in contrastive rhetoric* (pp. 261–273). Beverly Hills, CA: Sage.

Partington, A. (1998). *Patterns and meanings.* Amsterdam: John Benjamins.

Pennycook, A. (1994). *English as an international language.* London: Longman.

Phillipson, R. (1991). Some items on the hidden agenda of second/foreign language acquisition. In R. Phillipson, E. Kellerman, L. Selinker, M. Sharwood Smith, & M. Swain (Eds.), *Foreign/second language pedagogy research* (pp. 38–51). Clevedon, UK: Multilingual Matters.

Poole, D. (1991). Discourse analysis in enthnographic research. *Annual Review of Applied Linguistics, 11,* 42–56.

Poynton, C. (1996). Amplification as a prosody: Attitudinal modification in the nominal group. In M. Berry, C. Butler, R. Fawcett, & G. Hwang (Eds.), *Meaning and form: Systemic functional interpretations* (pp. 212–227). Norwood, NJ: Ablex.

Prentice, D. J. (1987). Malay (Indonesian and Malaysian). In B. Comrie (Ed.), *The world's major languages* (pp. 913–935). Oxford, Oxford University Press.

Prior, P. (1998). *Writing/disciplinarity: A sociohistoric account of literate activity in the academy.* Mahwah, NJ: Lawrence Erlbaum Associates.

Purves, A. (1988). *Writing across languages and cultures: Issues in contrastive rhetoric.* Newbury Park, CA: Sage.

Quirk, R., Greenbaum, S., Leech, G., & Svartvik, J. (1985). *A comprehensive grammar of the English language.* New York: Longman.

Raimes, A. (1983). *Techniques in teaching writing.* Oxford, England: Oxford University Press.

Raimes, A. (1992). *Exploring though writing* (2nd ed.). New York: St. Martin's Press.

Reid, J. (1990). Responding to different topic types: A quantitative analysis from a contrastive rhetoric perspective. In B. Kroll (Ed.), *Second language writing* (pp. 191–210). Cambridge, England: Cambridge University Press.

Reid, J. (1993). *Teaching ESL writing.* Englewood Cliffs, NJ: Prentice-Hall.

Reid, J. (2000a). *The process of composition* (3rd ed.). New York: Longman.

Reid, J. (2000b). *The process of paragraph writing* (3rd ed.). New York: Longman.

Renouf, A., & Sinclair, J. (1991). Collocational frameworks in English. In K. Aijmer & B. Altenberg (Eds.), *English corpus linguistics* (pp. 128–143). New York: Longman.

Riddle, E. (1986). Meaning and discourse function of the past tense in English. *TESOL Quarterly, 20*(2), 267–286.

Sa'adeddin, M. A. (1989). Text development and Arabic-English negative interference. *Applied Linguistics, 10*(1), pp. 36–51.

Santos, T. (1984). Error gravity: A study of faculty opinion of ESL errors. *TESOL Quarterly, 18*(1), 69–90.

Scarcella, R. (1984). How writers orient their readers to expository essays: A comparative study of native and non-native English writers. *TESOL Quarterly, 18*(4), 671–688.

Scarcella, R. (1994). *Power through the written word.* Boston: Heinle & Heinle.

Scarcella, R., & Lee, C. (1989). Different paths to writing proficiency in a second language? A preliminary investigation of ESL writers of short-term and long-term residence in the United States. In M. Eisenstein (Ed.), *The dynamic interlanguage* (pp. 137–153). New York: Plenum.

Scardamalia, M., & Bereiter, C. (1987). Literate expertise. In K. A. Erickson & J. Smith (Eds.), *Toward a general theory of expertise* (pp. 172–194). Cambridge: Cambridge University Press.

Schiffrin, D. (1981). Tense variation in narrative. *Language, 57,* 45–62.

Schiffrin, D. (1987). *Discourse markers.* Cambridge: Cambridge University Press.

Schiffrin, D. (1994). *Approaches to discourse.* Oxford, Blackwell.

Schmidt, R. (1995). Consciousness and foreign language learning; A tutorial on the role of attention and awareness in learning. In R. Schmidt (Ed.), *Attention & awareness in foreign language learning* (pp. 9–64). Honolulu: University of Hawaii Press.

Schumann, J. (1977). Second language acquisition: The pidginization hypothesis. *Language Learning, 26*(3), 391–408.

Scollon, R. (1991). Eight legs and one elbow: Stance and structure in Chinese English compositions. In *Proceedings of the Second North American Conference on Adult and Adolescent Literacy.* Multiculturalism and citizenship Canada: International Reading Association.

Scollon, R. (1993a). Cumulative ambiguity: Conjunctions in Chinese–English intercultural communication. In *Working Papers of the Department of English* (Vol. 5, pp. 55–73). Hong Kong: City Polytechnic of Hong Kong.

Scollon, R. (1993b). *Maxims of stance* (Research Rep. No. 26). Hong Kong: City Polytechnic of Hong Kong.

Scollon, R. (1994). As a matter of fact: The changing ideology of authorship and responsibility in discourse. *World Englishes, 13*(1), 33–46.

Scollon, R., & Scollon, S. (1981). *Narrative, literacy and face in interethnic communication.* Norwood, NJ: Ablex.

Scollon, R., & Scollon, S. W. (1991). Topic confusion in English–Asian discourse. *World Englishes, 10*(2), 113–125.

Scollon, R., & Scollon, S. W. (2001). *Intercultural communication.* (3rd ed.) Oxford, UK: Blackwell.

Sharwood Smith, M., & Rutherford, W. (1988). *Grammar and second language teaching.* New York: Newbury House.

Shibatani, M. (1987). Japanese. In B. Comrie (Ed.), *The world's major languages* (pp. 855–880). Oxford, Oxford University Press.

Shibatani, M. (1990). *The languages of Japan.* Cambridge: Cambridge University Press.

Silva, T, Leki, I., & Carson, J. (1997). Broadening the perspective of mainstream composition studies. *Written Communication, 14*(3), 398–428.

Sinclair, J. (1990). *Corpus, concordance, collocation.* Oxford, Oxford University Press.

Skutnabb-Kangas, T. (1991). Bicultural competence and strategies for negotiating ethnic identity. In R. Phillipson, E. Kellerman, L. Selinker, M. Sharwood Smith & M. Swain (Eds.), *Foreign/second language pedagogy research* (pp. 307–332). Clevedon, UK: Multilingual Matters.

Smoke, T. (1999). *A writer's workbook* (3rd ed.). New York: Cambridge University Press.

Sneddon, J. (1996). *Indonesian: A comprehensive grammar.* New York: Routledge.

Sohn, S.-O. (1995). *Tense and aspect in Korean.* Honolulu: University of Hawaii Press.

Soter, A. (1988). The second language learner and cultural transfer in narration. In A. Purves (Ed.), *Writing across languages and cultures: Issues in contrastive rhetoric* (pp. 177–205). Newbury Park, CA: Sage.

Sternglass, M. (1997). *Time to know them: A longitudinal study of writing and learning at the college level.* Mahwah, NJ: Lawrence Erlbaum Associates.

Strevens, P. (1987). Cultural barriers to language learning. In L. Smith (Ed.), *Discourse across cultures,* pp. 169–179. New York: Prentice Hall.

Stubbs, M. (1996). *Text and corpus analysis.* Oxford, Blackwell.

Swales, J. (1990a). *Genre analysis.* Cambridge: Cambridge University Press.

Swales, J. (1990b). Nonnative speaker graduate engineering students and their introductions: Global coherence and local management. In U. Connor & A. Johns (Eds.), *Coherence in writing* (pp. 189–207). Alexandria, VA: TESOL.

Swales, J., & Feak, C. (1994). *Academic writing for graduate students.* Ann Arbor: University of Michigan Press.

Tadros, A. (1994). Predictive categories in expository text. In M. Coulthard (Ed.), *Advances in written text analysis* (pp. 69–82). New York: Routledge.

Taylor, G., & Chen, T. (1991). Linguistic, cultural, and subcultural issues in contrastive discourse analysis: Anglo-American and Chinese scientific texts. *Applied Linguistics, 12*(3), 319–336.

Taylor, I. (1995). *Writing and literacy in Chinese, Korean, and Japanese.* Amsterdam: John Benjamins.

Tickoo, A. (1992). Seeking a pedagogically useful understanding of given-new: An analysis of native speaker errors in written discourse. In L. Bouton & Y. Kachru (Eds.), *Pragmatics and language learning* (Vol. 3, pp. 130–143. Urbana-Champaign: University of Illinois.

Tse, J. K.-P. (1995). The teaching of writing in Taiwan [Special issue, R. B. Kaplan, Ed.]. *Journal of Asian Pacific Communication, 1 & 2,* 117–124.

Tsujimura, A. (1987). Some characteristics of the Japanese way of communication. In D. L. Kincaid (Ed.), *Communication theory: Eastern and Western perspectives* (pp. 115–126). San Diego: Academic Press.

van Dijk, T. (Ed.). (1985). *Handbook of discourse analysis* (4 vols.). London: Academic Press.

van Dijk, T. (Ed.). (1997). Discourse as structure and process (2 vols.). London: Sage.

Vann, R., Lorenz, F., & Meyer, D. (1991). Error gravity: Response to errors in the written discourse of nonnative speakers of English. In L. Hamp-Lyons (Ed.), *Assessing second language writing* (pp. 181–196). Norwood, NJ: Ablex.

Vann, R., Meyer, D., & Lorenz, F. (1984). Error gravity: A study of faculty opinion of ESL errors. *TESOL Quarterly, 18*(3), 427–440.

Varley, P. (2000). *Japanese culture* (4th ed.). Honolulu: University of Hawaii Press.

Vaughan, C. (1991). Holistic assessment: What goes on in the raters' minds? In L. Hamp-Lyons (Ed.), *Assessing second language writing* (pp. 111–126). Norwood, NJ: Ablex.

Ventola, E., & Mauranen, A. (1996). *Academic writing*. Amsterdam: John Benjamins.

Walker, R. (1993). Language shift in Europe and Irian Jaya, Indonesia: Toward the heart of the matter. *AILA Review, 10,* 71–87.

Watanabe, S. (1993). A note on so-called "donkey sentences" in Japanese: A preliminary study. In P. Clancy (Ed.), *Japanese and Korean linguistics* (pp. 299–315). Stanford, CA: CSLI/Standford University Press.

Weese, K., Fox, S., & Greene, S. (Eds.). (1999). *Teaching academic literacy*. Mahwah, NJ: Lawrence Erlbaum Associates.

Wildavsky, B. (2000, April 24). Crossed signals. *U.S. News & World Report*, p. 12.

Wong, H. (1990). The use of rhetorical questions in written argumentative discourse. In L. Bouton & Y. Kachru (Eds.), *Pragmatics and language learning* (Vol. 1, pp. 187–208). Urbana-Champaign: University of Illinois.

World book almanac. (1998). Chicago: World Book.

Yum, J.-O. (1987). Korean philosophy and communication. In D. L. Kincaid (Ed.), *Communication theory: Eastern and Western perspectives* (pp. 71–86). San Diego: Academic Press.

Zamel, V. (1982). Writing: The process of discovering meaning. *TESOL Quarterly, 16*(1), 195–210.

Zamel, V. (1983). The composing processes of advanced ESL students: Six case studies. *TESOL Quarterly, 17*(1), 165–187.

Zamel, V., & Spack, R. (1998). *Negotiating academic literacies*. Mahwah, NJ: Lawrence Erlbaum Associates.

Zhu, Y. (1996). Modality and modulation in Chinese. In M. Berry, C. Butler, R. Fawcett, & G. Hwang (Eds.), *Meaning and form: Systemic functional interpretations* (pp. 183–209). Norwood, NJ: Ablex.

Author Index

Subject Index